**INTERNET**
**Concepts,**
**Second Ed** ~~061 3 00~~

DATE DUE

D0825976

Internetworking is one of the fastest growing markets in the field of computer communications. However, the interconnection of LANs and WANs tends to cause significant technological and administrative difficulties. This updated version provides valuable guidance, enabling the reader to avoid the pitfalls and achieve successful connection.
**1998  0 471 97514 1**

---

**THE MULTIPLEXER REFERENCE MANUAL**

Designed to provide the reader with a detailed insight into the operation, utilization and networking of six distinct types of multiplexers, this book will appeal to practising electrical, electronic and communications engineers, students in electronics, network analysts and designers.
**1993  0 471 93484 4**

---

**PRACTICAL NETWORK DESIGN TECHNIQUES**

Many network design problems are addressed and solved in this informative volume. Gil Held confronts a range of issues including  through-put problems, line facilities, economic trade-offs and multiplexers. Readers are also shown how to determine the numbers of ports, dial-in lines and channels to install on communications equipment in order to provide a defined level of service.
**1991  0 471 93007 5  (Book)**
**      0 471 92942 5  (Disk)**
**      0 471 92938 7  (Set)**

---

**NETWORK MANAGEMENT**
**Techniques, Tools and Systems**

Techniques,tools and systems form the basis of network management. Exploring and evaluating these three key areas, this book shows the reader how to operate an effective network.
**1992  0 471 92781 3**

*Please refer to the back of the book for further details*

# INTERNETWORKING LANs AND WANs

**Second Edition**

R

# INTERNETWORKING LANs AND WANs
## CONCEPTS, TECHNIQUES AND METHODS

**Second Edition**

**Gilbert Held**

*4-Degree Consulting*
*Macon, Georgia, USA*

**JOHN WILEY & SONS**

CHICHESTER · NEW YORK · WEINHEIM · BRISBANE · SINGAPORE · TORONTO

Riverside Community College
Library
MAY '99
4800 Magnolia Avenue
Riverside, CA 92506

TK 5105.7 .H439 1998

Held, Gilbert, 1943-

Internetworking LANs and
WANs

Copyright © 1993, 1998 by John Wiley & Sons Ltd,
Baffins Lane, Chichester,
ex PO19 1UD, England

01243 779777
al (+44) 1243 779777
e enquiries): cs-books@wiley.co.uk

iley.co.uk or http://www.wiley.com

k may be reproduced, stored in a retrieval system, or transmitted,
by any means, electronic, mechanical, photocopying, recording, scanning or otherwise,
except under the terms of the Copyright, Designs and Patents Act 1988 or under the terms of a licence
issued by the Copyright Licensing Agency, 90 Tottenham Court Road, London, W1P 9HE, UK without the
permission in writing of the Publisher.

Neither the authors nor John Wiley & Sons accept any responsibility or liability for loss or damage
occasioned to any person or property through using the material, instructions, methods or ideas contained
herein, or acting or refraining from acting as a result of such use. The author and Publisher expressly
disclaim all implied warranties, including merchantability of fitness for any particular purpose.

Designations used by companies to distinguish their products are often claimed as trademarks. In all
instances where John Wiley & Sons is aware of a claim, the product names appear in initial capital or all
capital letters. Readers, however, should contact the appropriate companies for more complete
information regarding trademarks and registration.

*Other Wiley Editorial Offices*

John Wiley & Sons, Inc., 605 Third Avenue,
New York, NY 10158-0012, USA

Wiley-VCH Verlag GmbH,
Pappelallee 3, D-69469 Weinheim, Germany

Jacaranda Wiley Ltd, 33 Park Road, Milton,
Queensland 4064, Australia

John Wiley & Sons (Asia) Pte Ltd, 2 Clementi Loop #02-01,
Jin Xing Distripark, Singapore 129809

John Wiley & Sons (Canada) Ltd, 22 Worcester Road,
Rexdale, Ontario M9W 1L1, Canada

***Library of Congress Cataloging-in-Publication Data***
Held, Gilbert, 1943–
    Internetworking LANs and WANs : concepts, techniques, and methods
/ Gilbert Held. — 2nd ed.
      p.   cm.
    Includes index.
      ISBN 0-471-97514-1 (pbk. : alk. paper)
    1. Local area networks (Computer networks)   2. Wide area networks
(Computer networks)   3. Internetworking (Telecommunication)
I. Title
TK5105.7.H439   1998
004.67—dc21                                                97-41702
                                                             CIP

***British Library Cataloguing in Publication Data***
A catalogue record for this book is available from the British Library

ISBN 0 471 97514 1

Typeset in $10\frac{1}{2}$ /$12\frac{1}{2}$ pt Bookman by Dobbie Typesetting Ltd, Tavistock, Devon
Printed and bound in Great Britain by Bookcraft (Bath) Ltd
This book is printed on acid-free paper responsibly manufactured from sustainable forestry,
in which at least two trees are planted for each one used for paper production.

# CONTENTS

**Preface**    **xix**

**Acknowledgements**    **xxi**

**1**    **Network Concepts**    **1**

1.1    Wide Area Networks    1

1.1.1    Computer-communications evolution    1

Remote batch transmission    2
IBM 3270 Information Display System    3
Communications controller    4
Control units    4

1.1.2    Modern mainframe access    5

1.1.3    Network construction    7

1.1.4    Network characteristics    10

1.2    Local Area Networks    10

1.2.1    Comparison to WANs    11

Geographic area    11
Data transmission and error rates    12
Ownership    13
Regulation    13
Data routing and topology    14
Type of information carried    14

1.2.2    Utilization benefits    15

1.3    Standards Organizations and the OSI Reference
Model    16

1.3.1    International standards organizations    17

ITU-T    18
ISO    18
The ISO Reference Model    19
Layered architecture    20

1.3.2    IEEE    26

802 Committees    26
Data link subdivision    28
Physical layer subdivision    29

1.3.3   ATM Forum   29

## 2    Local Area Networks   31

2.1    Technological Characteristics   31

2.1.1   Topology   32
    Loop   32
    Bus   33
    Ring   33
    Star   34
    Tree   34
    Mixed topologies   35
    Comparison of topologies   35

2.1.2   Signaling methods   36
    Broadband versus baseband   36
     Broadband signaling   37
     Baseband signaling   38

2.1.3   High speed encoding techniques   39
    MLT-3   40
    Bit transformation   41
    4B5B   42
    Other coding techniques   43

2.1.4   Transmission medium   43
    Twisted-pair wire   44
    Coaxial cable   45
     Hardware interface   46
     Broadband coaxial cable   47
    Fiber optic cable   49

2.1.5   Cabling standards   50
    Backbone cabling   50
    Horizontal cabling   50
    UTP categories   51

2.1.6   Access method   52
    Listeners and talkers   53
    Carrier-Sense Multiple Access with Collision Detection (CSMA/CD)   53
    Carrier-Sense Multiple Access with Collision Avoidance (CSMA/CA)   55
    Token passing   56
    Switch-based, connection-oriented   56

2.2    Popular Types of LANs   58

2.2.1   Ethernet   59
    Ethernet frame   60
    Types of Ethernet   62
     Coaxial versus twisted-pair   64

2.2.2   Fast Ethernet   65
    Frame format   66
     Start of stream delimiter   67
     End of stream delimiter   67
    100BASE-T overview   67

Physical layer     68
100BASE-T4     69
100BASE-TX     71
  4B5B coding     72
100BASE-FX     72

2.2.3   Token passing     72

Bus operation     72
Ring operation     74
  Data flow     75
  Network access, token and frame formats     75
  Data flow example     81

2.2.4   FDDI     82

Advantages     82
Hardware components     83
  Dual Attached Station     84
  Single Attached Station     84
Encoding and signaling     85
Frame formats     86
  FDDI token     88
  FDDI frame     88
Bandwidth allocation     89
  Classes of traffic     89
  Timers     90
  Synchronous transmission     91
  Asynchronous transmission     91
  Transmission example     92
Status     93

2.2.5   Logical link control frame format     94

Types and classes of service     95
  Type 1     96
  Type 2     96
  Type 3     97
  Classes of Service     97
Other Ethernet frame types     97
  Ethernet-802.3     97
  Ethernet-SNAP     98
  Frame determination     99

2.3     ATM     100

2.3.1   Rationale     100

The ATM cell     100
Scalability     101
Transparency     101
Traffic classification     102

2.3.2   The ATM protocol stack     103

ATM Adaptation Layer     104
The ATM Layer     104
Physical Layer     105

2.3.3   ATM operation     106

Components     106
  ATM network interface cards     106
  LAN switch     106

ATM router    107
ATM switches    107
ATM service processor    108
2.3.4    Network interfaces    108
User-to-network interface    109
Network-to-node interface    109
2.3.5    The ATM cell header    109
Generic flow control field    109
Virtual path identifier field    110
Virtual channel identifier field    111
Payload type identifier field    112
Cell loss priority field    112
Header error check field    112
2.3.6    ATM connections and cell switching    113
Connections    113
Cell switching    113
Types of switch    114
Using connection identifiers    114
General operation    116


**3    Local Area Networking    117**

3.1    Hardware Components    118
3.1.1    Repeaters    118
Types    118
Utilization    119
Repeater rules    121
3.1.2    Bridges    121
Operation    121
Flooding    123
Filtering and forwarding    125
Types    125
Transparent bridge    125
Translating bridge    126
Features    127
Filtering and forwarding    127
Selective forwarding    128
Multiple port support    129
Local and wide area interface support    129
Transparent operation    130
Frame translation    130
Frame encapsulation    131
Fabrication    131
Routing method    132
3.1.3    Routers    132
Network address utilization    134
Table operation    135
Advantages of use    135
Multiple path transmission and routing control    136
Flow control    136
Frame fragmentation    137

3.1.4   Brouters   137
        Operation   137
        Utilization   138
3.1.5   Gateway   139
        Definition   140
        Operation   141
3.1.6   File servers   142
        Types of server   142
        Location considerations   144
3.1.7   Wire hubs   145
        Advantages   145
        Intelligent hubs   145
3.1.8   LAN switches   146
        Conventional hub bottlenecks   147
          Ethernet hub operations   147
          Token-Ring hub operation   149
          Bottleneck creation   149
        Switching operations   150
          Basic components   151
          Key advantages of use   152
          Delay times   153
        Switching techniques   154
          Cross-point switching   154
          Store-and-forward   155
          Hybrid   157
          Port-based switching   158
          Segment-based switching   159
        Using LAN switches   161
          Network redistribution   161
          Server segmentation   162
          Backbone operation   164
          Handling speed incompatibilities   165
          Backpressure   165
          Server software module   166
          ATM considerations   166

3.2     Software Requirements   169

3.2.1   DOS   170

3.2.2   Network operating system   172
        Services   173
        Looking at NetWare   173
          Architecture   174
        Looking at Windows NT   175
        Multiple protocol support   176
3.2.3   Application software   189

4       Constructing Local Area Networks   191

4.1     10BASE-T Ethernet   191
4.1.1   Wire hub   192
        Interconnecting hubs   194

4.1.2   Network access   195

4.1.3   Attachment Unit Interface   195

4.1.4   Using fiber optic technology   197
        Optical transceiver   198

4.1.5   Fiber hubs   198

4.1.6   Fiber adapter   198
        Distance limits   199

4.1.7   Coax adapter   200

4.1.8   Expanding a 10BASE-T network   201
        Segmentation options   202
        Bridge segmentation   203

4.2     100BASE-T Fast Ethernet   205

4.2.1   Repeater rules   205

4.2.2   Segmentation methods   206

4.2.3   Backbone operation   206

4.2.4   Switch segmentation   208

4.3     IBM Token-Ring Networks   209

4.3.1   Multistation access unit   209

4.3.2   IBM Cabling System   211
        Cable types   211
            Type 1    212
            Type 2    212
            Type 3    212
            Type 5    213
            Type 6    213
            Type 7    213
            Type 8    213
            Type 9    214
        Connectors   214
        Cable distance   214

4.3.3   Network adapters   215

4.3.4   Device and wiring constraints   217
        Ring size   217
        Adjusted ring length   217

4.3.5   Token-Ring repeaters   219

4.3.6   Bridge   220

4.3.7   Controlled Access Unit   221

4.3.8   Network processor   222

4.3.9   Connectivity overview   224
        Gateways   226
            SDLC adapter connectivity   227
            3278/9 adapter connectivity   227

4.3.10  The Interconnect Controller   228

4.3.11  Token-Ring switching   229

Backbone ring performance     230
Creating a collapsed backbone     231
Token-Ring switch operations     232
The dedicated Token-Ring standard     232
Recent developments     233

**5      Wide Area Networks and Network Facilities      235**

5.1      Circuit Switched Networks     235

5.1.1     Types of facility     237
Analog     237
Modem utilization     238
DSL     239
Operation     241
Discrete multitone modulation     242
Carrierless amplitude/phase modulation     242
Digital     243
DSU utilization     243
ISDN     245
Basic Rate Interface     245
Primary Rate Interface     247
Utilization     248

5.2      Leased Line Networks     249

5.2.1     Frequency division multiplexing     249
ITU-T FDM recommendations     250
Analog leased lines     251
Modem utilization     251

5.2.2     Time division multiplexing     253

5.2.3     T-carrier evolution     253
Channel banks     254
Digital transmission facilities     255
T3     256

5.3      Packet Switching Networks     259

5.3.1     Multiplexing versus packet switching     259

5.3.2     Packet network construction     259

5.3.3     Packet network recommendations     260

5.3.4     The PDN and value-added networks     261

5.3.5     Packet network architecture     262
Datagram packet networks     262
Virtual circuit packet networks     263

5.3.6     Packet formation     264
X.25     264
Packet format and content     265
Call establishment     266
Flow control     267

5.3.7     Advantages of X.25 packet networks     269

5.3.8     Internetwork utilization     269

5.3.9     Remote access     270

5.3.10 Technological advances    271
     Packet network delay problems    271
     Fast packet switching    272
     Frame relay    273
     Comparison to X.25    273
     Utilization    275
     Operation    276
     The CIR    277
     Voice over frame relay    280

## 6    Network Layer Operations    283

6.1    NetWare IPX/SPX and related protocols    284

6.1.1   IPX    284
     Checksum field    284
     Length field    285
     Transport Control field    286
     Packet Type field    286
     Destination Network field    286
     Destination Node field    287
     Destination Socket field    287
     Source Network field    288
     Source Node and Source Socket fields    288
     IPX data field composition    288

6.1.2   SPX    289
     Connection Control field    289
     Datastream Type field    290
     Source and Destination Connection ID fields    291
     Sequence Number field    292
     Acknowledgment Number field    292
     Allocation Number field    292

6.1.3   SAP and RIP    292
     SAP operation    292
     SAP fields    293
     RIP operation    294
     Performance issues    294

6.1.4   NCP    294
     Request/Response Type fields    295
     Sequence Number field    295
     Connection Number fields    296
     Task Number field    296
     Function and Completion Code fields    296
     Packet bursting    296

6.2    TCP/IP    297

6.2.1   Protocol development    297

6.2.2   The TCP/IP structure    298

6.2.3   Datagrams versus virtual circuits    300

6.2.4   ICMP and ARP    304

6.2.5   TCP    304
     Source and Destination Port fields    305

Sequence fields    305
Control field flags    306
Window field    306
Checksum field    307
Urgent Pointer field    307
TCP transmission sequence example    307

6.2.6    UDP    310

Source and Destination Port fields    310
Length fields    310

6.2.7    IP    311

IP header format    311
Version field    311
Header Length and Total Length fields    311
Type of Service field    312
Identification and Fragment Offset fields    312
Time To Live field    314
Flags field    314
Protocol field    314
Source and Destination Address fields    314
IP addressing    315
Class A    315
Class B    315
Class C    316
Host restrictions    316
Subnetting    317
Subnet masks    317
Domain Name Service    319
Name server    320

6.2.8    TCP/IP configuration    321

6.2.9    Operating multiple stacks    325

## 7    Bridging Methods    327

7.1    Bridging Methods    327

7.1.1    Transparent bridging    327

Port/address table construction    328
Advantages    329
Disadvantages    329
Spanning tree protocol    330
Operation    331
Physical versus active topology    331
Spanning tree algorithm    332
Constructing the spanning tree    336
Bridge Protocol Data Unit    337
Protocol dependency    338

7.1.2    Source routing    339

Operation    341
Advantages    342
Disadvantages    342

7.1.3    Source routing transport bridges    343

Operation    344
Advantages    344

7.2     Network Utilization     344
7.2.1   Serial and sequential bridging     344
7.2.2   Parallel bridging     345

7.3     Performance Issues     347
7.3.1   Traffic flow     347
7.3.2   Network types     348
7.3.3   Type of bridge     348
7.3.4   Estimating network traffic     348
        Internet traffic     350
        Network types     350
        Bridge type     351
7.3.5   Bridge operational considerations     351
        Ethernet traffic     352
        Token-Ring traffic     354

**8      Routers     361**

8.1     Router Operation     361
        IP support overview     362
8.1.1   Networking capability     364

8.2     Communications and Routing Protocols     366
        Routing protocols     366
8.2.1   Handling non-portable protocols     366
8.2.2   Communications protocols     367
8.2.3   Protocol-dependent routers     367
        NetWare IPX example     368
        Addressing differences     369
        Other problems     369
8.2.4   Protocol-independent router     371
        Advantages     371
        Supporting SNA traffic     372
          Methods to consider     373
8.2.5   Routing protocols     373
        Vector distance protocol     374
          Examples     375
        Link state protocol     380
          SPF algorithms     381
          Operation example     381

8.3     Performance Considerations     382

**9      Gateway Functions, Methods and
        Applications     385**

9.1     SNA and APPN Architecture     386
9.1.1   SNA concepts     387
        The SSCP     387

The PU      388
The LU      388

9.1.2   SNA network structure      389
        Types of PUs      390
        Multiple domains      391
        SNA layers      393
        SNA developments      395

9.1.3   SNA sessions      395
        LU-to-LU sessions      396
        Addressing      396

9.1.4   Advanced peer-to-peer networking      398
        APPC concepts      399
        APPN architecture      400
          LEN nodes      400
          End nodes      401
          Network nodes      401
        Operation      401
        Route selection      403

9.2     The 3270 Information Display System      405

9.2.1   Data flow      406

9.2.2   3270 protocols      407

9.2.3   Types of control unit      407

9.2.4   Terminal displays      408

9.2.5   3270 keyboard functions      410
        Emulation considerations      411

9.3     SNA and APPN Gateway Options      412

9.3.1   Ethernet connectivity      412

9.3.2   Alternative gateway methods      414
        SDLC connectivity      414
        X.25 connectivity      416
        The TIC connection      418
        3278/9 coaxial connection      419

9.3.3   Using the 3172 Interconnect Controller      420
        Software considerations      421
        TN3270 operations      424

9.4     Data Link Switching      425

9.4.1   Overview      426

9.4.2   Operation      427

9.5     Communications Servers      428

9.5.1   MPTN      429

9.5.2   Other gateways      430

10      Network Security      433

10.1    Routers      433

10.1.1  Access lists     434
    Configuring an access list     435
    Extended access lists     437
    Additional extensions     438
10.1.2  Router access     439
10.1.3  Threats not handled     440

10.2  Firewall     440
10.2.1  Placement     441
10.2.2  Features     442
    Proxy services     442
      Using classes     443
    Address translation     444
    Stateful inspection     445
    Alerts     446
    Authentication     447
      Static passwords     447
      Token-based passwords     448
      One-time passwords     448
      Packet filtering     450
10.2.3  The gap to consider     452

## 11  vLANs and Virtual Networking     453

11.1  vLANs     453
11.1.1  Port-grouping vLANs     453
    Operation     454
    Port versus segment switching     454
    Advantages     454
    Disadvantages     454
    Supporting inter-vLAN communications     455
11.1.2  MAC-based switching     456
    Operational example     457
    Advantages     458
      Flexibility     459
      Bandwidth and expandability     459
    Disadvantages     460
      MAC address lists     460
      Interswitch communications     460
      Router restrictions     461
11.1.3  Layer-3 based vLANs     464
    Subnet-based vLANs     464
      Advantages     465
      Disadvantages     466
    Protocol-based vLANs     466
      Advantages     467
      Disadvantages     468
11.1.4  Rule-based vLANs     469
    Capabilities     469
    Multicast support     469
    Advantages     470
    Disadvantages     471

11.1.5 Comparing vLAN creation features    471
Connectivity beyond the workgroup    471
Ease of station assignment    471
Flexibility    472
Improved workgroup bandwidth    472
Multicast support    472
Multiple vLANs per port    472
Security    473
vLAN spanning    474

11.2    Virtual Networking    474
11.2.1 Rationale    475
Reliability    475
Economics    476
11.2.2 Applications    477
Voice and fax    478
Micom's V/IP    478
11.2.3 Remote server Access    479
PPTP    480
Utilization    480
L2F    481
L2TP    481
11.2.4 Local virtual networking    482
Inter-vLAN, intra-switch communications    482
Creative communications    482
Using a router    483
Inter-vLAN, inter-switch communications    486
Creative communications    486
Using a router    486
Single vLAN per swtich    487
Multiple vLANs per switch    487
Backbone switching    487
ATM considerations    488
11.2.5 Using the Internet    489
Security considerations    490
Encryption    490
Authentication    491
11.2.6 Testing considerations    492

12    Performance Issues    495

12.1    Interactive Sessions    495
12.1.1 Text display    496
Considering multiple transfer requests    497
12.1.2 Graphics display    498

12.2    File Transfers    500
12.2.1 Transfer time    500
12.2.2 Issues    501

Index    503

# PREFACE

Internetworking can be defined as the creation of networks of networks. Representing probably the most interesting and perhaps the most practical area of communications technology for small and large corporations, academia and government agencies, internetworking provides the electronic highway necessary to link separate islands of connectivity.

Since the original edition of this book was published in 1993, significant advances in communications technology have occurred. The use of the Internet has increased at a near-exponential rate, and Web servers and the application of Internet technology to form intranets are now a reality rather than an idea. This new edition expands coverage of TCP/IP, adds coverage of ATM, Fast Ethernet, LAN switches, Windows NT and network security in the form of router access lists, and the features and functions performed by different types of firewalls. In addition, the operation and utilization of virtual LANs based upon the use of LAN switches, virtual networking based upon the creation of tunnels routed through the Internet, and the use of several relatively new types of network servers are included, to provide readers with the latest information required for performing internetworking. Whether you are a network analyst, communications specialist, LAN administrator, or just need a comprehensive reference to internetworking, this book was written for you.

Similar to a brick mason, we need a good foundation prior to mastering internetworking concepts and techniques. This foundation is presented in the first six chapters of this book. Those chapters provide a detailed examination of the operation and utilization of different types of networks, performance issues and the constraints and limitations imposed upon many networks due to technology. In addition, due to the importance of *de facto* and *de jure* standards we must also become aware of applicable networking standards which are presented in the first part of this book.

Once a foundation of information has been presented in the first six chapters of this book, we are ready to focus our attention upon the major focus of this book—internetworking. In the remainder of this book we will examine a variety of internetworking topics, ranging in scope from basic concepts to the operation and utilization of different types of communications equipment and communications carrier line facilities. In doing so we will examine several key performance issues that will assist you in determining the minimum level of performance required to avoid internetwork degradation. In addition, we will create several mathematical models that you can adapt to your specific communications environment to project different types of performance prior to actually ordering hardware or communications facilities. By using these models you may be able to avoid selecting the wrong equipment or communications carrier facilities based upon intuition or a salesperson's educated guess.

As a long time communicator, as both a networking manager and an author, I welcome your comments. If you would like to see future editions of this book expand upon a specific area or cover a presently omitted area, or if you have any other comments, please feel free to write me. You can write to me through my publisher at the address listed in this book or you can send a message directly to me on the Internet at 235-8068@mcimail.com.

**Gilbert Held**
*Macon, Georgia*

# ACKNOWLEDGEMENTS

Although this fact is sometimes overlooked, a book is a team effort in which the author's manuscript is just one portion of a considerable amount of work required by many individuals. From the issuance of a contract based upon a market analysis to the typing of the manuscript and through the movement of the manuscript into the production process many persons contribute their skills. I would be remiss if I did not take the opportunity to acknowledge the efforts of several individuals whose work was essential in enabling you to read this book. However, prior to doing so I would like to thank my family for their patience and understanding as I developed the manuscript for this book.

I would like to thank Ann-Marie Halligan for her efforts in arranging for the review of my proposal, and for providing guidance and arranging for the contract that enabled this writing project to go forward. Once again, Mrs Linda Hayes deserves a considerable 'thank you' for converting my hand-written notes and diagrams into a professional manuscript. Last but not least, I would like to thank Mr Robert Hambrook and the members of his production team for their effort in converting the manuscript into the book you are reading.

# 1

# NETWORK CONCEPTS

In this introductory chapter, we will focus our attention upon the key concepts behind the construction of wide area networks (WANs) and local area networks (LANs). In doing so we will first examine each type of network to obtain an understanding of its primary design goal. Next, we will compare and contrast their operation and utilization as well as examine the primary *de facto* and *de jure* standards that govern the operation of different types of networks. As this is an introductory chapter, we will cover LAN and WAN networking concepts without concern for specific details which are presented in later chapters in this book.

## 1.1 WIDE AREA NETWORKS

The evolution of wide area networks can be considered to have begun in the mid to late 1950s, commensurate with the development of the first generation of computers. Based upon the use of vacuum tube technology, the first generation of computers were physically relatively large, power-hungry devices whose placement resulted in a focal point for data processing and the coining of the term 'data center'.

### 1.1.1 Computer-communications evolution

Originally, access to the computational capability of first generation computers was through the use of punched cards. After an employee of the organization used a keypunch to create a deck of cards, that card deck was submitted to a window in the data center, typically labeled input/output (I/O) control. An employee behind the window would accept the card deck and complete a form which contained instructions for running the submitted job. The card deck and instructions would then be sent to a person in production control who would schedule the job and turn it over to operations for execution at a predefined time. Once the job was completed, the card deck and any resulting output would be sent back to I/O control, enabling the job originator to return to the window in the data center to retrieve his or her card deck and the resulting output. With a little bit of luck, programmers might see the results of their efforts on the same day that they submitted their job. Since the computer represented a considerable financial investment for most organizations, it was understandable that they would be receptive to methods that would enable an extension of access to its computational capability. By the mid-1960s, several computer manufacturers had added remote access capabilities to one or more of their computers.

*Remote batch transmission*

One method of providing remote access was obtained by the installation of a batch terminal at a remote location. That terminal was connected via a telephone company supplied analog leased line and a pair of modems to the computer in the corporate data center.

The first type of batch terminal developed to communicate with a data center computer contained a card reader, printer, serial communications adapter, and hard-wired logic in one housing. The serial communications adapter converted the parallel bits of each internal byte read from the card reader into a serial data stream for transmission. Similarly, the adapter performed a reverse conversion process by converting a sequence of received serial bits into an appropriate number of parallel bits to represent a character internally within the batch terminal. Since the batch terminal was located remotely from the data center, it was often referred to as a remote batch terminal, while the process of transmitting data was referred to as remote batch transmission. In addition, the use of a remote terminal as a mechanism to group a number of card decks representing individual jobs to be executed at the remote data center resulted in the term 'remote job entry terminal' being used as a synonym to reference this device.

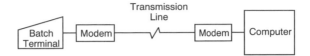

**Figure 1.1** Remote batch transmission. The transmission of data from a remote batch terminal represents one of the first examples of wide area data communications networks

Figure 1.1 illustrates in schematic form the relationship between a batch terminal, transmission line, modems, and the data center computer. Since the transmission line connected a remote batch terminal in one geographic area to a computer located in a different geographic area, Figure 1.1 represents one of the earliest types of wide area data communications networks (WAN).

Paralleling the introduction of remote batch terminals was the development of a series of terminal devices, control units, and specialized communications equipment which resulted in the rapid expansion of interactive computer applications. One of the most prominent collections of products was introduced by the IBM Corporation under the trade name 3270 Information Display System.

## IBM 3270 Information Display System

The IBM 3270 Information Display System was a term used to originally describe a collection of products ranging from interactive terminals, referred to as display stations that communicate with a computer, through several types of control units and communications controllers. Later, through the introduction of additional communications products from IBM and numerous third party vendors and the replacement of previously introduced products, the IBM 3270 Information Display System became more of a networking architecture and strategy rather than a simple collection of products. First introduced in 1971, the IBM 3270 Information Display System was designed to extend the processing power of the data center computer to remote locations. Since the data center computer typically represented the organization's main or primary computer, the term 'mainframe' was coined to refer to a computer with a large processing capability. As the mainframe was primarily designed for data processing, its utilization for supporting communications degraded its performance.

### Communications controller

To offload communications functions from the mainframe, IBM and other computer manufacturers developed hardware whose primary function was to sample communications lines for incoming bits, group bits into bytes, and pass a group of bytes to the mainframe for processing as well as performing a reverse function for data destined from the mainframe to remote devices. When first introduced, such hardware was designed using fixed logic circuitry and the resulting device was referred to as a communications controller. Later, minicomputers were developed to execute communications programs; the ability to change the functionality of communications support by the modification of software was a considerable enhancement to the capabilities of this series of products. Because both hard-wired communications controllers and programmed minicomputers performing communications offloaded communications processing from the mainframe, the term 'front-end processor' evolved to refer to this category of communications equipment. Although most vendors refer to a minicomputer used to offload communications processing from the mainframe as a front- end processor, IBM has retained the term communications controller', even though their fixed logic hardware products were replaced over 20 years ago by programmable minicomputers.

### Control units

To reduce the number of controller ports required to support terminals as well as the cabling between controller ports and terminals, IBM developed 'poll and select' software to support its 3270 Information Display System. Doing so enabled the communications controller to transmit messages from one port that could be destined to one or more terminals in a predefined group of devices. To share the communications controller port IBM developed a product called a control unit which acts as an interface between the communications controller and a group of terminals.

In general terms, the communications controller transmits a message to the control unit. The control unit examines the terminal address and retransmits the message to the appropriate terminal connected to the control unit. Thus, control

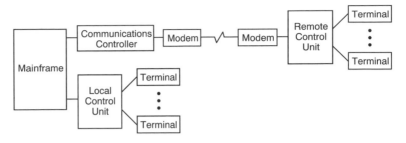

**Figure 1.2**  Relationship of 3270 Information Display products

units can be considered as devices which economize on the number of lines required to link display stations to mainframe computers. Both local and remote control units are available, with the key difference between the two primarily pertaining to the method of attachment to the mainframe computer and the use of intermediate devices between the control unit and the mainframe. Local control units are usually attached to a channel on the mainframe, whereas remote control units are connected to the mainframe's front-end processor, which is also known as a communications controller in the IBM environment. Since a local control unit is within a limited distance of the mainframe, no intermediate communications devices, such as modems, are required to connect a local control unit to the mainframe. In comparison, a remote control unit can be located in another building or in a different city, and it normally requires the utilization of intermediate communications devices, such as a pair of modems, for communications to occur between the control unit and the communications controller. The relationship of local and remote control units to display stations, mainframes, and a communications controller is illustrated in Figure 1.2.

### 1.1.2 Modern mainframe access

The introduction of the original IBM PC in 1981 resulted in the gradual displacement of terminals by PCs that provided a local processing capability and used coaxial cable adapters and special terminal emulation software to support the use of a personal computer to access a mainframe. Within a few years Ethernet and Token-Ring LANs were being used in organizations to provide client-server processing; however, client work-

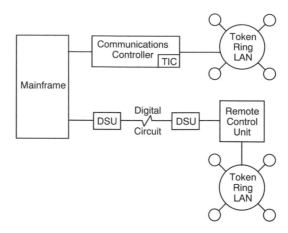

**Figure 1.3** Initial methods developed to link 3270 networks to LANs

stations still required access to corporate mainframes. At first the primary method of linking LAN-based workstations to a mainframe was accomplished through the use of special adapter cards installed in communications controllers and control units. Figure 1.3 illustrates the initial method used to provide the integration of LAN-based workstations into a 3270 type network, and it is still in use by many organizations.

In the upper portion of Figure 1.3 a Token-Ring Interface Coupler (TIC) is shown installed in the communications controller which allows it to become a participant on a Token-Ring LAN. Under the communications controller a pair of Data Service Units (DSUs) which can be considered to represent digital modems required for transmission on digital circuits enable a remote control unit to be connected at a high data rate to the mainframe. The remote control unit uses a network adapter card similar to the TIC in the communication controller to become a participant on the remote Token-Ring network.

In addition to special adapter cards allowing communications controllers and control units to become participants on a LAN, special software is required on each workstation. Another key difference between the initial 3270 network and more modern LAN connections to mainframes is the reliance of the latter upon digital circuits that operate at 56 Kbps and above. In comparison, the initial 3270 networks were primarily constructed using analog transmission facilities limited to data rates up to 19.2 Kbps.

As LANs proliferated, a specialized communications device known as a router was developed to transport data between

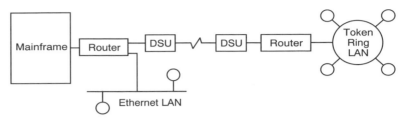

**Figure 1.4**   Modern LAN workstations' access to mainframes

networks. Routers were also developed with a channel interface to mainframes, enabling router-based networks and LAN workstations to replace the use of communications controllers and control units as illustrated in Figure 1.4.

In the example shown in Figure 1.4, a router with a mainframe interface is shown replacing both the communications controller and control unit. By supporting local and wide area interfaces, a single router can be used to provide both local and remote LAN access. As we will note later in this book, through the use of routers and leased lines we can create complex private networks or use routers with public networks to move traffic between LANs and from workstations on LANs to distant mainframes.

In addition, the basic operation of a router, which is to move data originating on one network and destined to another network off the source network, provides the routing capability which the device obtains its name. As we will note later in this book, the router is a key communications device which enables geographically separated LANs to be interconnected and whose operation enables the network of interconnected networks known as the Internet to function as intended.

Regardless of the method used to link geographically separated locations to one another, data are transported over wide area networks. Thus, let us turn our attention to WAN network construction and the general characteristics of this type of network.

### 1.1.3 Network construction

To provide batch and interactive access to the corporate mainframe from remote locations, organizations began to build sophisticated networks. At first, communications equipment such as modems and transmission lines was only obtainable from AT & T and other telephone companies. Commencing in 1974 in the United States with the well-known Carterphone decision, competitive non-telephone company sources for the supply of communications equipment became available. The divestiture of AT & T during the 1980s and the emergence of many local and long distance communications carriers paved the way for networking personnel being able to select from among two to hundreds of vendors for transmission lines and communications equipment.

As organizations began to link additional remote locations to their mainframes, the cost of providing communications began to escalate rapidly. This in turn provided the rationale for the development of a series of line sharing products referred to as multiplexers and concentrators. Although most organizations operated separate data and voice networks, beginning in the mid-1980s communications carriers began to make available for commercial use high-capacity circuits known as T1 in North America and E1 in Europe. Through the development of T1 and E1 multiplexers, voice, data, and video transmission can share the use of common high-speed circuits. Since the interconnection of corporate offices via the use of communications equipment and facilities normally covers a wide geographical area outside the boundary of one metropolitan area, the resulting network is known as a wide area network.

Figure 1.5 illustrates an example of a wide area network spanning the continental United States. In this example, regional offices in San Francisco and New York are connected with the corporate headquarters located in Atlanta via the use of T1 multiplexers and T1 transmission lines operating at 1.544 Mbps. Assuming each T1 multiplexer is capable of supporting the direct attachment of a private branch exchange (PBX), both voice and data are carried by the T1 circuits between the two regional offices and corporate headquarters. In addition, the San Francisco and Atlanta location have LANs that require communications connectivity with one another. Rather than install a separate leased line to interconnect the two locations, routers are connected to input ports on the T1 multiplexers in each location. This enables the T1 circuit between San Francisco and Atlanta to support inter-LAN connectivity as well as voice and data terminal traffic from tail circuits which we will shortly discuss. Thus, the three T1 circuits can be considered as the primary data highway or backbone of the corporate network.

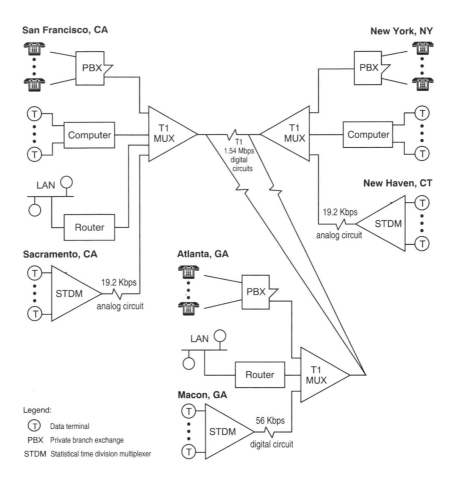

**Figure 1.5** Wide area network example. A wide area network uses telecommunications lines obtained from one or more communications carriers to interconnect geographically dispersed locations

In addition to the three major corporate sites that require the ability to route voice calls and data between locations, let us assume that the corporation also has three smaller area offices located in Sacramento, CA; Macon, GA; and New Haven, CT. If those locations only require data terminals to access the corporate network for routing to the computers located in San Francisco and New York, one possible mechanism to provide network support is through the installation of tail circuits. Those tail circuits could be used to connect a statistical time division multiplexer (STDM) in each area office serving a group of data terminals to the nearest T1 multiplexer, using either analog or digital circuits. The T1 multiplexer would then be configured to route data terminal traffic over the corporate backbone portion of the network to its destination.

### 1.1.4 Network characteristics

There are certain characteristics we can associate with wide area networks. First, the WAN is typically designed to interconnect two or more dispersed geographical areas. This interconnection is accomplished by the lease of transmission facilities from one or more communications vendors. Secondly, most WAN transmission occurs at or under a data rate of 1.544 Mbps or 2.048Mbps, which are the operating rates of T1 and E1 transmission facilities. However, it should be noted that other popular WAN transmission facilities include T3 circuits that operate at approximately 45 Mbps and fractional T3 that operates at fractions of the T3 operating rate. In addition, communications carriers have deployed ATM as a transport mechanism that can be accessed at data rates from the T1 1.544 Mbps to direct ATM operating rates ranging up to 622 Mbps.

A third characteristic of WANs concerns the regulation of transmission facilities used for their construction. Most, if not all, transmission facilities marketed by communications carriers are subject to a degree of regulation at the federal, state, and possibly at the local government level. Even though we now live in an era of deregulation, carriers must seek approval for many offerings prior to making new facilities available for use. In addition, although many of the regulatory controls governing the pricing of services were removed, the communications market is still not a truly free market. Thus, regulatory agencies at the federal, state, and local level still maintain a degree of control over both the offering of new services as well as the pricing of existing and new services.

## 1.2 LOCAL AREA NETWORKS

The origin of local area networks can be traced, in part, to IBM terminal equipment introduced during 1974. At that time, IBM introduced a series of terminal devices designed for use in transaction processing applications for banking and retailing. What was unique about those terminals was their method of connection, with a common cable that formed a loop being used to provide a communications path within a localized geographical area. Unfortunately, limitations in the data transfer rate, incompatibility between each IBM loop system, and other problems precluded the widespread adoption of this method of networking. The economics of media sharing and the ability to provide common access to a centralized resource were, however, key advantages that resulted in IBM and other vendors investigating the use of different techniques to provide a localized communications capability between different devices. In 1977, Datapoint Corporation began selling its Attached Resource Computer Network (Arcnet), considered by most persons to be the first commercial local area networking product marketed. Since then, hundreds of companies have developed local area networking products, and the installed base of terminal devices connected to such networks has exponentially increased until they now number in the tens of millions.

## 1.2.1 Comparison to WANs

Local area networks can be distinguished from wide area networks by geographic area of coverage, data transmission and error rates, ownership, government regulation, and data routing, and, in many instances, by the type of information transmitted over the network.

*Geographic area*

Concerning the geographic area of coverage, the name of each network provides a general indication of the scope of the area in which it can support the interconnection of devices. As its name implies, a LAN is a communications network which covers a relatively small local area. This small local area can range in scope from a department located on a portion of a floor in an office building to the corporate staff located on several floors in the building, to several buildings on the campus of a university.

Regardless of the LAN area of coverage, its geographic boundary will be primarily restricted by the physical transmission limitations of the local area network. Those limitations are primarily in the area of cable distance between devices connected to the LAN and the total length of the LAN cable. In comparison, a wide area network can provide communications support to an area ranging in size from a town or city to a state, country, or even the entire world. Here the major factor governing transmission is the availability of communications facilities in different geographic areas that can be interconnected to route data from one location to another.

To better grasp the differences between LANs and WANs, we can view the LAN as being analogous to our local telephone or cable TV company, while the WAN can be considered to be the long distance communications carrier. Then, communications support in different cities is provided by the local telephone company in each city. However, for calls between cities, the local telephone companies must interconnect to the long distance carrier. Similarly, we can have separate LANs in different cities or within different buildings in the same city; however, to interconnect those LANs we would require the use of a wide area network.

## Data transmission and error rates

Two additional areas that both differentiate LANs from WANs as well as explain the physical limitation of the LAN geographic area of coverage are the data transmission and error rate for each type of network. LANs normally operate at the low megabit-per-second rate, typically ranging from 4 Mbps to 16 Mbps, with relatively short distance (100 meter) copper wire based LANs and extended distance fiber optic-based LANs operating at 100 Mbps. At data rates above 100 Mbps ATM based LANs can operate at 155 Mbps and 622 Mbps. In comparison, the communications facilities used to construct a major portion of most WANs provide a data transmission rate at or under the T1 and E1 data rates of 1.544 Mbps and 2.048 Mbps. Although most communications carriers now operate on ATM infrastructure the cost of access to that infrastructure at data rates above T1 or E1 rates can be prohibitive for many organizations as carriers will have to install high speed access lines to subscribers. Due to this, most organizations use T1 or E1 lines to connect their ATM networks via WANs; however, within a few years it is probably reasonable to expect the cost of ATM WAN transmission to decrease as the ATM infrastructure is extended to corporate access points via fiber into buildings, enabling greater use of high speed end-to-end ATM transmission.

Since LAN cabling is primarily within a building or extends over a small geographical area, it is less susceptible to the impairments of nature, such as thunderstorms, lightning, and other acts of God. This in turn enables transmission at a relatively high data rate resulting in a relatively low error rate. In comparison, since wide area networks are based upon the use of communications facilities that are much more distant in length and always exposed to the elements, they have a much higher probability of being disturbed by changes in the weather, or electronic emissions generated by equipment, as well as such unforeseen problems as construction workers tearing up a street or paving a highway and accidentally causing harm to a communications cable. It is due to the greater exposure to the elements, the higher probability of accidental eruptions, and the greater change of electrical interference that the error rate on WANs is considerably higher than the rate experienced on LANs. On most WANs you can expect to experience an error rate of 1 in a million to 1 in 10 million $(1 \times 10^6)$ to $1 \times 10^7)$ bits. In comparison, the error rate on a typical LAN may exceed that range by one or more orders of magnitude, resulting in an error rate of 1 in 10 million to 1 in 100 million bits.

## Ownership

The construction of a wide area network requires the leasing of transmission facilities from one or more communications carriers. Although your organization can elect to purchase or lease communications equipment, the transmission facilities used to connect diverse geographical locations are owned by the communications carrier. In comparison, an organization which installs a local area network normally owns all of the components used to form the network, including the cabling used to form the transmission path between devices.

## Regulation

Since wide area networks require transmission facilities that may cross local, state, and national boundaries, they may be subject to a number of governmental regulations at the local, state, and national level. Most of those regulations will govern the services that communications carriers can provide customers and the rates they can charge for those services, with the latter referred to as a tariff. In comparison, regulations affecting local area networks are primarily in the areas of building codes.

Such codes regulate the type of wiring that can be installed in a building and whether or not the wiring must run in a conduit.

## Data routing and topology

In a local area network, data are routed along a path which defines the network. That path is normally a bus, ring, tree, or star structure and data always flow on that structure. The topology of a wide area network can be much more complex than the network structure of a local area network. In fact, many wide area networks may resemble a mesh structure, with equipment used to reroute data in the event of the failure of a communications circuit or equipment, or when too much traffic flows between two locations. Thus, the data flow on a wide area network can dynamically change, while the data flow on a local area network primarily follows the same basic route.

One exception to the preceding involves the use of LAN switches to include those that support Ethernet, Token-Ring, FDDI, and ATM. Through the use of such switches it becomes possible to construct local mesh structured networks that can become as complex as mesh structured WANs; however, unlike wide area networks that can span the globe, mesh structured LANs developed through the use of switches are restricted to transmission distances measured in hundreds of feet between switches.

## Type of information carried

The last major difference between local and wide area networks concerns the type of information carried by each network. Many wide area networks support the simultaneous transmission of voice, data, and video information. In comparison, most local area networks are limited to carrying data. In addition, although all wide area networks can be expanded to transport voice, data, and video, many local area networks are restricted by design to the transportation of data. The one exception to the preceding is ATM that can operate from the desktop onto LANs and from LANs to WANs. Although ATM is in use by communications carriers to support voice, data, and video transmission in a WAN environment, it is currently used as a backbone switching mechanism and is limited to transporting data. In the future as prices decline we can reasonably expect ATM acceptance for use at the desktop which will enable voice, data, and video support

**Table 1.1** Comparing LANs and WANs

| Characteristic | Local Area Network | Wide Area Network |
|---|---|---|
| Geographic area of coverage | Localized to a building, group of buildings, or campus | Can span an area ranging in size from a city to the globe |
| Data transmission rate | Typically 4 Mbps to 16 Mbps, with some limited distance copper pair based and extended distance fiber optic-based networks operating at 100 Mbps | Normally operate at or below T1 and E1 transmission rates of 1.54 Mbps and 2.048 Mbps and T3 at 45 Mbps |
| Error rate | 1 in $10^7$ to 1 in $10^6$ | 1 in $10^6$ to 1 in $10^7$ |
| Ownership | Usually with the implementor | Communications carrier retains ownership of the facilities |
| Data routing | Normally follows fixed route or mesh structure for limited distance | Switching capability of network allows dynamic alteration of data flow for long distance |
| Topology | Usually limited to bus, ring, tree, and star | Virtually unlimited design capability |
| Type of information carried | Primarily data | Voice, data, and video commonly integrated |

from LANs onto WANs. Table 1.1 summarizes the similarities and differences between local and wide area networks.

## 1.2.2 Utilization benefits

In its simplest form, a local area network can be considered as a cable that provides an electronic highway for the transportation of information to and from different devices connected to the network. By providing the capability to route data between devices connected to a common network within a relatively limited distance, numerous benefits can accrue to users of the network. Such benefits can include the ability to share the use of peripheral devices, obtain common access to data files and programs, communicate with other people on the LAN by electronic mail, and obtain access to the larger processing capability of mainframes or minicomputers through common gateways that link a local area network to larger computer systems. Here the gateway can be directly cabled to the mainframe or minicomputer if they reside at the same location or it may be connected remotely via the use of the corporate wide area network.

Peripheral sharing allows network users to access high speed color laser printers, CD-ROM jukebox systems, and other devices whose utilization may only be required a small portion of the time a workstation is in operation. Thus, users of a LAN can obtain access to resources that would probably be too expensive to justify for each individual workstation user.

The ability to commonly access data files and programs can substantially reduce the cost of software. In addition, shared access to database information allows network users to obtain access to updated files on a real-time basis.

One popular type of application program used on LANs enables users to transfer messages electronically. Commonly referred to as electronic mail, this type of application program can be used to supplement and, in many cases, eliminate the need for paper memorandums. Another of the more popular uses for LANs combines the ability to access data files and programs as well as the ability to transmit and receive electronic mail beyond the confines of the local area network. This is accomplished by connecting a LAN to the Internet, enabling each workstation on the network to access a variety of Internet sites and services through a common wide area network communications circuit routed to an Internet Service Provider.

For organizations with mainframe or minicomputers, a local area network gateway can provide a common method of access to those computers. In comparison, without the use of a LAN gateway, each personal computer requiring access to a mainframe or minicomputer would require a separate method of access. This might increase both the complexity of providing access as well as the cost of providing access.

## 1.3 STANDARDS ORGANIZATIONS AND THE OSI REFERENCE MODEL

The importance of standards and the work of standards organizations have proved essential for the growth of both local and worldwide communications. In the United States and many other countries, national standards organizations have defined physical and operational characteristics that enable vendors to manufacture equipment compatible with line facilities provided by communications carriers, as well as equipment produced by other vendors and which may be connected to a local or wide area network. At the international level, standards organizations have promulgated several series of communications-related recommendations. These recommendations, while not mandatory, have become highly influential on a worldwide basis for the development of equipment and facilities and have been adopted by hundreds of public companies and communications carriers.

In addition to national and international standards, a series of *de facto* standards has evolved through the licensing of technology among companies. Such *de facto* standards, as an example, have facilitated the development of communications software for use on personal computers. Today, consumers can purchase communications software that can control modems manufactured by hundreds of vendors since most modems are now constructed to respond to a core set of uniform control codes.

In this section we will focus our attention upon one national and three international standards organizations. The national standards organization we will discuss is the Institute of Electrical and Electronic Engineers (IEEE), whose work has been a guiding force in the rapid expansion in the use of local area networks due to a series of standards developed by that organization. In the international area, we will discuss the role of the International Telecommunications Union Telecommunications (ITU-T) standardization body, formerly known as the Consultative Committee for International Telephone and Telegraph (CCITT) and the International Standards Organization (ISO), both of which have developed numerous standards which facilitate the operation of wide area networks. In addition, we will discuss the role of the ATM Forum, a non-profit organization tasked with developing ATM standards.

Due to the importance of the ISO's Open Systems Interconnection (OSI) Reference Model in data communications, we will focus our attention upon the operation and general utilization of this model. This examination will provide an overview of the seven layers of the OSI model, and will serve as a foundation for a detailed investigation of several layers of that model presented in later chapters.

## 1.3.1 International standards organizations

Three important international standards organizations are the International Telecommunications Union Telecommunications

(ITU-T) standardization body formerly known as the Consultative Committee for International Telephone and Telegraph
(CCITT), the International Standards Organization (ISO) and
the ATM forum. The ITU-T can be considered as a governmental
body as it functions under the auspices of an agency of the
United Nations. Although the ISO is a non-governmental
agency, its work in the field of data communications is well
recognized. In comparison, the ATM Forum is an international
non-profit organization that focuses its efforts on ATM issues to
include standards.

## ITU-T

The International Telecommunications Union Telecommunications (ITU-T) standardization body is a group within the
International Telecommunications Union (ITU), the latter being
a specialized agency of the United Nations headquartered in
Geneva, Switzerland. The ITU-T is tasked with direct responsibility for developing data communications standards and
consists of 15 Study Groups, each tasked with a specific area
of responsibility.

The work of the ITU-T is performed on a four-year cycle which
is known as a Study Period. At the conclusion of each Study
Period, a Plenary Session occurs. During the Plenary Session,
the work of the ITU-T during the previous four years is reviewed,
proposed recommendations are considered for adoption, and
items to be investigated during the next four-year cycle are
considered.

The ITU-T's Tenth Plenary Session met in 1992 and its
eleventh session occurred during 1996. Although approval of
recommended standards is not intended to be mandatory, ITU-T
recommendations have the effect of law in some Western
European countries and many of its recommendations have
been adopted by both communications carriers and vendors in
the United States.

## ISO

The International Standards Organization (ISO) is a non-
governmental entity that has consultative status within the
UN Economic and Social Council. The goal of the ISO is to

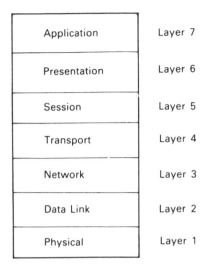

**Figure 1.6** ISO Reference Model

'promote the development of standards in the world with a view to facilitating international exchange of goods and services'.

The membership of the ISO consists of the national standards organizations of most countries, with approximately 100 countries currently participating in its work.

Perhaps the most notable achievement of the ISO in the field of communications is its development of the seven-layer Open Systems Interconnection (OSI) Reference Model.

### The ISO Reference Model

The International Standards Organization (ISO) established a framework for standardizing communications systems called the Open Systems Interconnection (OSI) Reference Model. The OSI architecture defines the communications process as a set of seven layers, with specific functions isolated and associated with each layer. Each layer, as illustrated in Figure 1.6, covers lower layer processes, effectively isolating them from higher layer functions. In this way, each layer performs a set of functions necessary to provide a set of services to the layer above it.

Layer isolation permits the characteristics of a given layer to change without impacting the remainder of the model, provided that the supporting services remain the same. One major advantage of this layered approach is that users can mix and match OSI conforming communications products to tailor their communications systems to satisfy a particular networking requirement.

The OSI Reference Model, while not completely viable with many current network architectures, offers the potential to directly interconnect networks based upon the use of different vendor equipment. This interconnectivity potential will be of substantial benefit to both users and vendors. For users, interconnectivity will remove the shackles that in many instances tie them to a particular vendor. For vendors, the ability to easily interconnect their products will provide them with access to a larger market. The importance of the OSI model is such that it has been adopted by the ITU-T as Recommendation X.200.

## Layered Architecture

As previously discussed, the OSI Reference Model is based upon the establishment of a layered, or partitioned, architecture. This partitioning effort can be considered as being derived from the scientific process whereby complex problems are subdivided into functional tasks that are easier to implement on an aggregate individual basis than as a whole.

As a result of the application of a partitioning approach to communications network architecture, the communications process was subdivided into seven distinct partitions, called layers. Each layer consists of a set of functions designed to provide a defined series of services which relate to the mission of that layer. For example, the functions associated with the physical connection of equipment to a network are referred to as the physical layer.

With the exception of layers 1 and 7, each layer is bounded by the layers above and below it. Layer 1, the physical layer, can be considered to be bound below by the interconnecting medium over which transmission flows, while layer 7 is the upper layer and has no upper boundary. Within each layer is a group of functions which can be viewed as providing a set of defined services to the layer which bounds it from above, resulting in layer $n$ using the services of layer $n-1$. Thus, the design of a layered architecture enables the characteristics of a particular layer to change without affecting the rest of the system, assuming the services provided by the layer do not change.

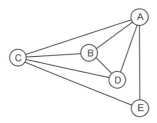

**Figure 1.7**  Network structure and components. The path between a source and destination node established on a temporary basis is called a logical connection

An understanding of the OSI layers is best obtained by first examining a possible network structure that illustrates the components of a typical wide area network. Figure 1.7 illustrates a network structure which is only typical in the sense that it will be used for a discussion of the components upon which networks are constructed.

The circles in Figure 1.7 represent nodes which are points where data enter or exit a network or is switched between two paths. Nodes are connected to other nodes via communications paths within the network where the communications paths can be established on any type of communications media, such as cable, microwave, or radio.

From a physical perspective, a node can be based upon the use of one of several types of computers, including a personal computer, minicomputer, mainframe computer, or specialized computer, such as a front-end processor gateway or router. Connections to network nodes into a wide area network can occur via the use of terminals directly connected to computers, computers connected to other computers, terminals connected to a node via the use of one or more intermediate communications devices, or paths linking one network to another network. Although terminals were originally fixed logic devices with little or no intelligence, the replacement of those devices by personal computers resulted in many persons continuing to refer to devices that interact with mainframes and minicomputers as terminals regardless of their processing capability. When used on a local area network we again modify terminology, referring to personal computers attached to LANs as workstations. When those workstations communicate with servers we refer to the communications method as client-server communications.

The routes between two nodes, such as C–E–A, C–D–A, C–A, and C–B–A, which could be used to route data between nodes A and C, are information paths. Due to the variability in the flow of information through a network, the shortest path between nodes may not be available for use or may represent a non-efficient path with respect to other paths constructed through intermediate nodes between a source and destination node. A temporary connection established to link two nodes whose route is based upon such parameters as current network activity is known as a logical connection. This logical connection represents the use of physical facilities, including paths and node switching capability on a temporary basis. Now that we have an appreciation of the general structure of networks, let us turn our attention to the layers of the OSI Reference Model.

The major functions of each of the seven OSI layers are described in the following seven paragraphs.

*Layer 1—the physical layer*  At the lowest or most basic level, the physical layer (level 1) is a set of rules that specifies the electrical and physical connection between devices. This level specifies the cable connections and the electrical rules necessary to transfer data between devices. Typically, the physical link corresponds to previously established interface standards, such as the RS-232/V.24 interface which governs the attachment of data terminal equipment, such as the serial port of personal computers, to data communications equipment, such as modems, at data rates below 19.2 Kbps. Included in the physical layer rules is the encoding method used to place data on the transmission medium. In a LAN environment common coding methods include Manchester coding, differential Manchester coding, and techniques that encode different numbers of data bits in a group of bits.

*Layer 2—the data link layer*  The next layer, which is known as the data link layer (level 2), denotes how a device gains access to the medium specified in the physical layer; it also defines data formats, including the framing of data within transmitted messages, error control procedures, and other link control activities. From defining data formats, including procedures to correct transmission errors, this layer becomes responsible for the reliable delivery of information. At the data link layer information is grouped into entities referred to as frames. As a minimum, each frame includes control information which enables the receiver to synchronize itself to an incoming frame, addressing information that identifies the source and destination, a field containing the actual information being transmitted from the source to the destination, and a field used for verifying the integrity of the data. Data link control protocols such as Binary Synchronous Communications (BSC) and High- level Data Link Control (HDLC) reside in this layer.

Since the development of OSI layers was originally targeted towards wide area networking, its applicability to local area networks required a degree of modification. Under the IEEE 802 standards, the data link layer was divided into two sublayers, logical link control (LLC) and media access control (MAC). The LLC layer is responsible for generating and interpreting commands which control the flow of data and perform recovery operations in the event of errors. In comparison, the MAC layer is responsible for providing access to the local area network, which enables a station on the network to transmit information. Later in this chapter we will examine the IEEE 802 standards in detail, including the functions and operation of the LLC and MAC layers.

*Layer 3—the network layer* The network layer (level 3) is responsible for arranging a logical connection between a source and destination on the network, including the selection and management of a route for the flow of information between source and destination based upon the available data paths in the network. Services provided by this layer are associated with the movement of data packets through a network, including addressing, routing, switching, sequencing, and flow control procedures. In a complex network, the source and destination may not be directly connected by a single path, but instead require a path to be established that consists of many subpaths. Thus, routing data through the network onto the correct paths is an important feature of this layer.

Several protocols have been defined for layer 3, including the ITU-T X.25 packet switching protocol and the ITU-T X.75 gateway protocol. X.25 governs the flow of information through a packet network, while X.75 governs the flow of information between packet networks. Other popular network layer protocols include the Internet Protocol (IP) and Novell's Internet Packet Exchange (IPX).

*Layer 4—the transport layer* The transport layer (level 4) is responsible for guaranteeing that the transfer of information occurs correctly after a route has been established through the network by the network level protocol. Thus, the primary function of this layer is to control the communications session between network nodes once a path has been established by the network control layer. Error control, sequence checking, and other end-to-end data reliability factors are the primary concern of this layer.

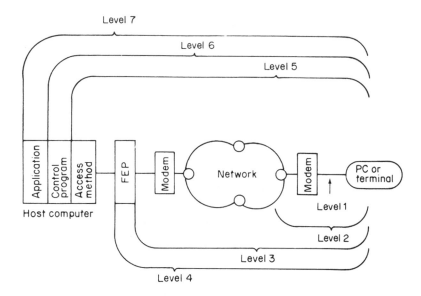

**Figure 1.8** OSI model schematic

Two popular transport layer protocols are the Transport control Protocol (TCP) and the User Datagram Protocol (UDP).

*Layer 5 — the session layer*   The session layer (level 5) provides a set of rules for establishing and terminating data streams between nodes in a network. The services that this session layer can provide include establishing and terminating node connections, message flow control, dialogue control, and end-to-end data control.

*Layer 6 — the presentation layer*   The presentation layer (level 6) services are concerned with data transformation, formatting, and syntax. One of the primary functions performed by the presentation layer is the conversion of transmitted data into a display format appropriate for a receiving device. Data encryption/ decryption and data compression and decompression are examples of the data transformation that could be handled by this layer.

*Layer 7 — the application layer*   Finally, the application layer (level 7) acts as a window through which the application gains access to all of the services provided by the model. Examples of functions performed at this level include file transfers, resource sharing, and database access. While the first four layers are fairly well defined, the top three layers may vary considerably, depending upon the network used. In fact, many protocols tend to group the higher

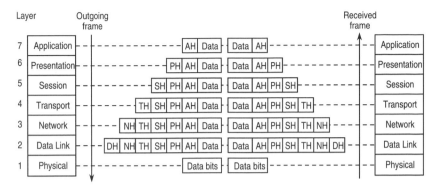

Legend:
DH, NH, TH, SH, PH and AH and appropriate headers Data Link, Network Header, Transport Header, Session Header, Presentation Header and Application Header added to data as the data flows through an ISO reference Model network

**Figure 1.9**   Data flow within an ISO Reference Model network

levels into one functional layer. Thus, such popular Internet protocols as the File Transfer Protocol (FTP), Telnet, and the HyperText Transport Protocol (HTTP) represent a blend of layer 5 through 7 functions. Later in this book we will examine the use of each of those Inernet protocols. Figure 1.8 illustrates the OSI model in schematic format, showing the various levels of the model with respect to a terminal accessing an application on a host computer system.

*Data flow*

As data flows within an ISO network each layer appends appropriate heading information to frames of information flowing within the network while removing the heading information added by a lower layer. In this manner, layer $(n)$ interacts with layer $(n-1)$ as data flow through an ISO network.

Figure 1.9 illustrates the appending and removal of frame header information as data flow through a network constructed according to the ISO Reference Model. Since each higher level removes the header appended by a lower level, the frame traversing the network arrives in its original form at its destination.

As the reader will surmise from the previous illustrations, the ISO Reference Model is designed to simplify the construction of data networks. This simplification is due to the eventual standardization of methods and procedures to append appropriate heading information to frames flowing through a network, permitting data to be routed to the appropriate destination following a uniform procedure.

## 1.3.2 IEEE

The Institute of Electrical and Electronic Engineers (IEEE) is a US-based engineering society that is very active in the development of data communications standards. In fact, the most prominent developer of local area networking standards is the IEEE, whose subcommittee 802 began its work in 1980 prior to the establishment of a viable market for the technology.

The IEEE Project 802 efforts are concentrated upon the physical interface of equipment and the procedures and functions required to establish, maintain, and release connections among network devices, including defining data formats, error control procedures, and other control activities governing the flow of information. This focus of the IEEE actually represents the lowest two layers of the ISO model, physical and link data.

IEEE 802 standards were originally limited to communications at data rates up to 20 Mbps within a local area up to 4 km, or a metropolitan area with a data path length up to 50 km. Additions to the 802 standards in the form of Fast Ethernet in all its flavors and 100Vg-AnyLAN resulted in specifications for data rates up to 100 Mbps, while work on a gigabit Ethernet can be expected to result in a specification for a LAN operating at 1000 Mbps.

### 802 Committees

Table 1.2 lists the organization of IEEE 802 committees involved in local area networks. In examining the lists of committees in Table 1.2 it is apparent that the IEEE early on noted that a number of different systems would be required to satisfy the requirements of a diverse end-user population. Accordingly, the IEEE adopted the CSMA/CD, Token Bus and Token-Ring as standards 802.3, 802.4 and 802.5, respectively.

The 802.1 committee responsible for Architecture and Overviews defines standards for enabling an IEEE 802 local or metropolitan area network station to communicate with another station on a different LAN or MAN or on a wide area network. Included under the 802.1 arena are such standards as 802.1D

**Table 1.2**  IEEE Series 802 committees

| | |
|---|---|
| 802.1 | Architecture and Overview |
| 802.2 | Logical Link Control |
| 802.3 | CSMA/CD |
| 802.3$\mu$ | Fast Ethernet |
| 802.4 | Token Bus |
| 802.5 | Token-Ring |
| 802.6 | Metropolitan Area Networks |
| 802.7 | Broadband Technical Advisory Group |
| 802.8 | Fiber Optic Technical Advisory Group |
| 802.9 | Integrated Voice and Data Networks |
| 802.10 | Network Security |
| 802.11 | Wireless LANs |
| 802.12 | 100VG AnyLAN |

which defines transparent bridging between two or more 802.X local area networks, 802.1H which defines Token-Ring bridging, and 802.li which defines the specifications for FDDI bridging.

The IEEE Committee 802 published draft standards for CSMA/CD and Token Bus local area networks in 1982. Standard 802.3, which describes a baseband CSMA/CD network similar to Ethernet, was published in 1983. Since then, several addenda to the 802.3 standard were adopted which govern the operation of CSMA/CD on different types of media. Those addenda include 10BASE-2 which defines a 10 Mbps baseband network operating on thin coaxial cable, 1BASE-5 which defines a 1 Mbps baseband network operating on twisted-pair, and 10BROAD-36, a broadband 10 Mbps network that operates on thick coaxial cable.

The next standard published by the IEEE was 802.4, which describes a token passing bus oriented network for both baseband and broadband transmission. This standard is similar to the Manufacturing Automation Protocol (MAP) standard developed by General Motors.

The third LAN standard published by the IEEE was based upon IBM's specifications for its Token-Ring network. Known as the 802.5 standard, it defines the operation of Token-Ring networks on shielded twisted-pair cable at data rates of 1 and 4 Mbps.

Once Token-Ring had been standardized for operation at 4 Mbps, the 802.5f committee specified changes to the 4 Mbps ring for operations at 16 Mbps. Recognizing the development of Fast Ethernet and a competitive technology that uses a demand priority access method instead of Ethernet's CSMA/CD protocol, the IEEE standardized both competitive methods after a

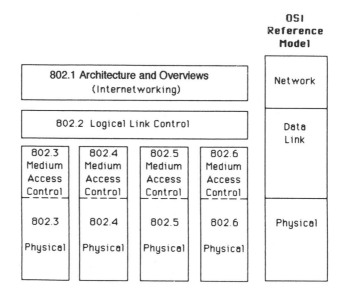

**Figure 1.10**  Relationship between IEEE standards and the OSI Reference Model

prolonged battle by various industry groups. As Fast Ethernet uses the CSMA/CD protocol similar to other versions of Ethernet, the resulting standard was promulgated as 802.3 $\mu$. The second 100 Mbps network, which also operates at 100 Mbps but uses a demand priority access protocol, was promulgated as 802.12. Since this standard supports either Ethernet or Token-Ring at 100 Mbps and operates on voice grade copper pair, its trade name became 100Vg-AnyLAN.

At the time this book was written the IEEE had approved Project Authorization Request (PAR) for the formation of a committee to develop standards for virtual LANs. Work was progressing under the direction of the 802.1Q committee, and an initial standard may be promulgated by the time you read this book.

*Data link subdivision*

One of the most interesting facets of IEEE 802 standards is the subdivision of the ISO Open Systems Interconnection Model's data link layer into two sublayers, logical link control and medium access control. This separation enables the mechanism for regulating access to the medium to be independent of the method for establishing, maintaining and terminating the

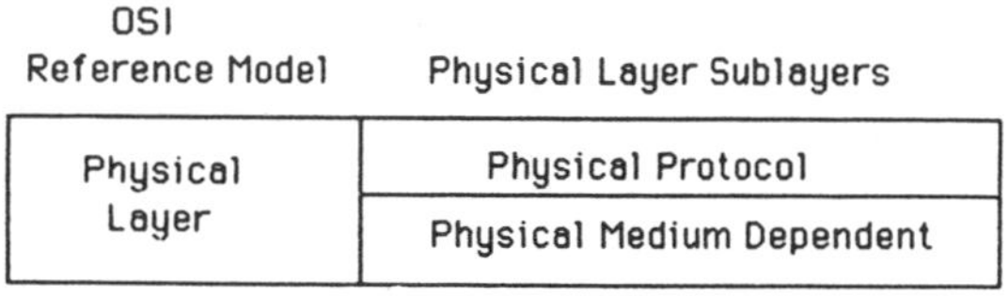

OSI
Reference Model        Physical Layer Sublayers

| Physical | Physical Protocol |
| Layer | Physical Medium Dependent |

**Figure 1.11**  The physical layer is subdivided for high speed LANs and MANs developed to operate on different types of media

logical link between workstations. Here the method of regulating access to the medium is defined by the medium access control portion of each local area network standard. This enables the logical link control standard to be applicable to each type of network. Figure 1.10 illustrates the relationship between IEEE 802 local area network standards and the first three layers of the OSI Reference Model.

### Physical layer subdivision

As local area networks gained acceptance it was soon recognized that the development of higher operating rate networks would require support for two or more distinct types of media such as unshielded twisted pair (UTP) and fiber, or even two or more types of fiber. This meant that a single physical layer would not be practical, and this resulted in the subdivision of the physical layer in a manner similar to the subdivision of the data link layer.

The actual method used to subdivide the physical layer is based upon the operating characteristics of the LAN or MAN and the media it will operate upon. One of the more common methods is to subdivide the physical layer into physical protocol and physical medium dependent sublayers as illustrated in Figure 1.11. The physical medium dependent layer will specify the type of connectors and their use with different types of media, while the physical protocol sublayer will define the signaling rate and method of encoding used with each type of physical medium dependent specification.

### 1.3.3 ATM Forum

The primary organization responsible for the development of ATM standards is the Technical Committee of the ATM Forum. The ATM Forum is a relatively new organization that was founded in 1991 as an international non-profit entity whose primary goal is to accelerate the use of ATM products and services via a rapid development of interoperability standards.

The ATM Forum's Technical Committee works with other standards bodies such as the American National Standards Institute (ANSI) and the International Telecommunications Union Telecommunications (ITU-T) standardization body to reconcile differences among standards as well as to recommend new standards when they are noted as being necessary or if existing ones are found inappropriate. Unlike the IEEE 802 committee which is tasked with LAN and MAN standards, the ATM Forum is responsible for both LAN and WAN standards, as ATM was developed as a universal technology that can run from an adapter in a workstation through LANs onto private and public WANs.

# 2

# LOCAL AREA NETWORKS

In the first chapter of this book we became acquainted with local and wide area networks, comparing the general characteristics of each. In this chapter we will focus our attention upon the technological characteristics of local area networks, examining in detail several types of LANs. In doing so we will examine a portion of the IEEE 802 series of standards applicable to Ethernet and Token-Ring local area networks as well as the operation of ATM as a local area network.

## 2.1 TECHNOLOGICAL CHARACTERISTICS

Although a local area network is a limited distance transmission system, the variety of options available for constructing such networks is anything but limited. Many of the options available for the construction of local area networks are based upon the technological characteristics which govern their operation. Those characteristics include different topologies, signaling methods, transmission media, access methods used to transmit data on the network and the hardware and software required to make the network operate. In this section we will primarily examine the topologies, signaling methods, transmission media and access methods used to transmit data on local area networks, deferring a discussion of most specific hardware and software to future sections in this chapter and later chapters in this book where discussion of those topics is more appropriate.

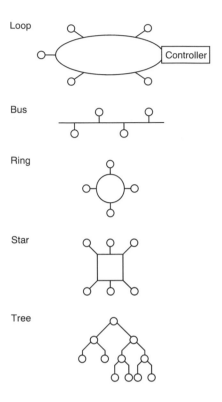

**Figure 2.1** LAN topology. The five most common geometric layouts of local area network cabling form a loop, bus, ring, star, or tree structure

## 2.1.1 Topology

The topology of a local area network means the structure or geometric layout of the cable used to interconnect work stations on the network. Unlike conventional data communications networks that can be configured in a variety of ways by the addition of hardware and software, most local area networks are designed to operate based upon the interconnection of work stations that follow a specific topology. The most common topologies used in LANs include the loop, bus, ring, star, and tree as illustrated in Figure 2.1.

*Loop*

As mentioned in Chapter 1, IBM introduced a series of transaction processing terminals in 1974 that communicated through the use of a common controller on a cable formed into a loop. This type of topology is illustrated at the top of Figure 2.1.

The controller employed a poll and select access method. That is, the controller would send a poll message to each terminal device in a predefined order. If the terminal had data to transmit it would wait until polled and upon being polled, transmit. Thus, terminal devices connected to the loop required a minimum of intelligence. Although this reduced the cost of terminals connected to the loop, the controller lacked enough intelligence to distribute the data flow evenly among terminals. A lengthy exchange between two terminal devices or between the controller and a terminal would thus tend to bog down this type of network structure. A second problem associated with this network structure was the centralized placement of network control in the controller. If the controller failed, the entire network would become inoperative. Due to these problems, the use of loop systems is restricted to several niche areas and is essentially considered as a derivative of a local area network. As such, we will eliminate this type of network from further consideration.

## Bus

In a bus topology structure, a cable is usually laid out as one long branch onto which branches are used to interconnect each station on the network to the main data highway. Although this type of structure permits any station on the network to talk to another station, rules are required to govern the action necessary to recover from situations such as when two stations attempt to communicate at the same time. Later in this chapter, we will examine the relationship between the network topology, the method employed to access the network and the transmission medium employed in building the network.

## Ring

In a ring topology, a single cable that forms the main data highway is shaped into a ring. Similar to the bus topology, branches are used to interconnect stations to one another via the ring. A ring topology can thus be considered to be a looped bus. Typically, the access method employed in a ring topology requires data to circulate around the ring, with a special set of rules governing when each station connected to the network can transmit data.

Both bus and ring topologies use access methods that enable only one device to transmit at a time. As this results in network devices sharing the media, another term commonly used to refer to bus and ring-based local area networks is 'shared media networks'.

*Star*

The fourth major local area network topology is the star structure illustrated in the lower portion of Figure 2.1. In a star network, each station on the network is connected to a network controller. Then, access from any one station on the network to another station can be accomplished through the network controller. Here the network controller can be viewed as functioning similarly to a telephone switchboard, since access from one station to another station on the network can occur only through the central device.

The most common form of star-based local area network involves the use of a LAN switch. LANs developed using bus and ring topologies are now supported by the use of applicable LAN switches. When this occurs, it becomes possible to initiate multiple client-server sessions if two or more servers are connected to a switch, alleviating the major constraint of shared media networks in which only one source to destination data flow can be supported at a time. In addition, as we will note later in this chapter, ATM is based upon the use of switches.

*Tree*

A tree network structure can be considered to represent a complex bus. In this topology the common point of communications at the top of the structure is known as the headend. From that location feeder cables radiate outward to nodes, which in turn provide workstations with access to the network or provide a feeder cable route to additional nodes from which workstations gain access to the network.

*Mixed topologies*

Some networks, from a topology perspective, are a mixture of topologies. For example, as previously discussed, a tree structure can be considered as a series of interconnected buses. Another example of the mixture of topologies is the IBM Token-Ring Network. That network can actually be considered to be a 'star–ring' topology, since up to eight workstations and servers are first connected to a common device known as a multistation access unit or MAU, which in turn is connected in a ring topology to other MAUs. Later in this chapter and in Chapter 4 we will examine the IBM Token-Ring Network in detail.

*Comparison of topologies*

Although there is a close relationship between the topology of the network, its transmission media, and the method used to access the net, we can examine topology as a separate entity and make several generalized observations. First, in a star network the failure of the network controller will render the entire network inoperative. This results from the fact that all data flow on the network must pass through the network controller. On the positive side, the star topology is normally in existence within most buildings in the form of telephone wires that are routed to a switchboard. This means that a local area network that can use in-place twisted-pair telephone wires is normally simple to implement and usually very economical.

In a ring network, the failure of any node connected to the ring normally inhibits data flow around the ring. Due to the fact that data travel in a circular path on a ring network, any cable break has the same effect as the failure of the network controller in a star-structured network. Since each network station is connected to the next network station, it is usually easier to install the cable for a ring network. In comparison, if existing telephone wires are not available you would have to cable each station in a star network to the network controller, which could result in the installation of very long cable runs.

In a bus-structured network, data are normally transmitted from one station to all stations located on the network, with a destination address appended to each transmitted data block. As part of the access protocol only the station with the destination address in the transmitted data block will respond to the data. This transmission concept means that a break in the bus may affect only network stations on one side of the break which wish to communicate with stations on the other side of the break. Thus, unless a network station functioning as the primary network storage device becomes inoperative, a failure in a bus-structured network is usually less serious than a failure in a ring network.

A tree-structured network is similar to a star-structured network in that all signals flow through a common point. In the tree-structured network the common signal point is the head-end. In addition to the failure of the headend rendering the network inoperative, this network structure requires the transmission of information between some workstations to traverse relatively long distances. For example, communications between two workstations at the most distant end of the network would require a signal to propagate twice the length of the longest network segment. Due to the propagation delay associated with the transmission of any signal, the use of a tree structure may result in a degree of response time delay when transmission occurs between two workstations located at the most distant node or pair of nodes from the headend.

## 2.1.2 Signaling methods

The signaling method used by a local area network references both how data are encoded for transmission and the use of the frequency spectrum of the media. To a large degree the signaling method is related to the use of the frequency spectrum of the media.

### Broadband versus baseband

Two signaling methods used by LANs are broadband and baseband. In broadband signaling the bandwidth of the transmission medium is subdivided by frequency to form two or more subchannels, with each subchannel permitting data transfer to occur independently of data transfer on another subchannel. In baseband signaling only one signal is transmitted on the medium at any point in time.

In comparison to baseband signaling, broadband is more complex. Broadband signaling requires information to be

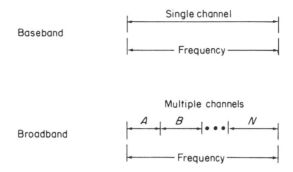

**Figure 2.2** Baseband versus broadband signaling. In baseband signaling the entire frequency bandwidth is used for one channel. In comparison, in broadband signaling the channel is subdivided by frequency into many subchannels.

transmitted via the modulation of a carrier signal, requiring the use of special types of modems discussed later in this section.

Figure 2.2 illustrates the difference between baseband and broadband signaling with respect to channel capacity. It should be noted that although a twisted-pair wire system can be used to transmit both voices and data, the data transmission is baseband since only one channel is normally used for data. In comparison, a broadband system on coaxial cable can be designed to carry voice and several subchannels of data as well as facsimile and video transmission.

**Broadband signaling**

A broadband local area network uses analog technology in which high frequency (HF) modems operating at or above 4 kHz place carrier signals onto the transmission medium. The carrier signals are then modified, a process known as modulation, which impresses information onto the carrier. Other modems connected to a broadband LAN reconvert the analog signal back into its original digital format, a process known as demodulation.

Figure 2.3 illustrates the three primary methods of data encoding used by broadband analog systems: amplitude, frequency and phase modulation. The most common modulation method used in broadband LANs is frequency shift keying (FSK), in which two different frequencies are used, one to represent a binary 'one' and another frequency to represent a binary 'zero'.

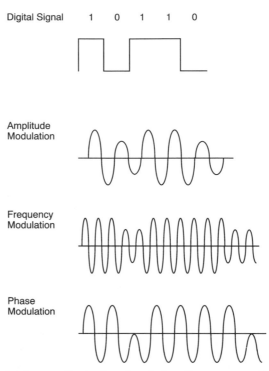

**Figure 2.3** Modulation methods. Baseband signaling uses amplitude, frequency or phase modulation, or a combination of modulation techniques to represent digital information

Another popular modulation method uses a combination of amplitude and phase shift changes to represent pairs of bits. Referred to as amplitude modulation phase shift keying (AM PSK), this method of analog signaling is also known as duobinary signaling as each analog signal represents a pair of digital bits.

As it is not economically feasible to design amplifiers that boost signal strength to operate in both directions, broadband LANs are unidirectional. To provide a bidirectional information transfer capability a broadband LAN will use one channel for inbound traffic and another channel for outbound traffic. These channels can be derived by frequency or obtained from the use of a dual cable.

## Baseband signaling

In comparison to broadband local area networks that use analog signaling, baseband LANs use digital signaling to convey information.

To understand the digital signaling methods used by base-band LANs let us first review the method of digital signaling used by computers and terminal devices. In that signaling method a positive voltage is used to represent a binary one, while the absence of voltage (zero volts) is used to represent a binary zero. If two successive one bits occur, two successive bit positions then have a similar positive voltage level or a similar zero voltage level. Since the signal goes from zero to some positive voltage and does not return to zero between successive binary ones, it is referred to as a unipolar non-return to zero signal (NRZ). This signaling technique is illustrated at the top of Figure 2.4.

Although unipolar non-return to zero signaling is easy to implement, its use for transmission has several disadvantages. One of the major disadvantages associated with this signaling method involves determining where one bit ends and another begins. To overcome this problem would require synchronization between a transmitter and receiver by the use of clocking circuitry, which can be relatively expensive.

To overcome the need for clocking, two popular types of baseband LANs, Ethernet and Token-Ring, use Manchester and Differential Manchester encoding, respectively. In Manchester encoding a timing transition always occurs in the middle of each bit while an equal amount of positive and negative voltage is used to represent each bit. This coding technique provides a good timing signal for clock recovery from received data due to its timing transitions. In addition, since the Manchester code always maintains an equal amount of positive and negative voltage, it prevents direct current (DC) voltage buildup, enabling repeaters to be spaced further apart from one another.

The lower portion of Figure 2.4 illustrates an example of Manchester coding. Note that a low to high voltage transition represents a binary one, while a high to low voltage transition represents a binary zero. Under Differential Manchester encoding the voltage transition is used only to provide clocking. The encoding of a binary zero or one is represented by the presence or absence of a transition at the beginning of each bit period.

## 2.1.3 High speed encoding techniques

Although Manchester and Differential Manchester coding have proven to be suitable for Ethernet and Token-Ring networks,

Unipolar non-return to zero

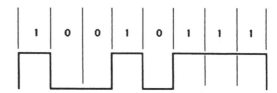

Manchester coding

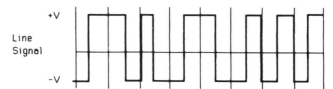

**Figure 2.4** Manchester coding. In Manchester coding, a timing transition occurs in the middle of each bit and the line code maintains an equal amount of positive and negative voltage

both require two transitions per bit. This means that their signaling rate in terms of cycles or Hertz per second (c.p.s. or Hz/s) is twice the bit rate. Thus, a 16 Mbps Token-Ring LAN requires a signaling of 32 MHZ.

The necessity to develop local area networks operating at higher data rates would require expensive circuitry if a bi-phase signaling technique such as Manchester or Differential Manchester coding was retained. Rather than attempt to develop circuitry to operate at a signaling rate of 200 MHZ to support a LAN operating rate of 100 Mbps, network designers turned to the use of different encoding schemes. Some of those schemes include MLT-3, 4B5B, 8B6T, 5B6B and 8B10T coding methods.

## *MLT-3*

MLT-3 represents a coding scheme used to support two types of LANs that operate at 100 Mbps. Those LANs include a twisted pair version of the Fiber Distributed Data Interface (FDDI) fiber optic based LAN commonly referred to as Copper Distributed Data Interface (CDDI) and a version of Fast Ethernet standardized as 100BASE-T.

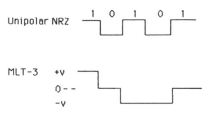

**Figure 2.5** MLT-3 encoding

Under MLT-3 encoding, three levels are used for encoding a binary 1: a positive voltage (+v), a negative voltage (−v) and no voltage (0v). The encoding rules are summarized below and illustrated in Figure 2.5. Under MLT-3, encoding occurs based upon the following rules:

1. If the next input bit is 0, then the next output value is the same as the preceding value.
2. If the next input bit is 1, the next output value results in a translation. The translation process examines the preceding output value.
   - If the preceding value was either +v or −v, then the next output value is 0.
   - If the preceding output was 0, then the next output will be non-zero and have the opposite sign to the last non-zero output.

Under MLT-3 encoding bits are encoded as one of three voltage levels. This means that the signaling rate is one-third of the operating rate. Thus, a baud rate of 33.33 MHZ will support a LAN operating rate of 100 Mbps. In comparison, the use of a bi-phase signaling technique would have required a baud rate of 200 MHZ. Thus, MLT-3 coding significantly lowers the signaling rate required to support certain types of high speed local area networks.

*Bit transformation*

In addition to altering the signaling method, LAN designers use a variety of bit transformation methods to ensure the frequent transition between the two binary digits. The rationale for the use of bit transformation is to obtain synchronization without requiring the use of a bi-phase code. By combining a bit

**Table 2.1** Popular LAN encoding schemes

| Type of LAN | Encoding |
| --- | --- |
| IEEE 802.3 Ethernet (CSMA/CD) | |
|    10BASE-5, 10BASE-2, 10BASE-T | Manchester |
|    100BASE-TX | 4B5B/MLT-3 |
|    100BASE-T4 | 8B6T |
|    100BASE-FX | 4B5B/NRZI |
| IEEE 802.5 Token-Ring | Differential Manchester |
| FDDI | 4B5B/NRZI |
| CDDI | 4B5B/IMLT-3 |
| 100VG-AnyLAN | 5B6B/NRZ |
| Fiber Channel | 8B10B/NRZ |

transformation scheme with a coding method LAN designers developed numerous encoding schemes. Table 2.1 lists 11 more popular LANs and the encoding schemes they use.

*4B5B*

Under 4B5B coding each four bits of data are first encoded into a 5 bit symbol. When used with 200 Mbps Ethernet and FDDI LANs, the 5 bit symbol is then treated on an individual bit by bit basis and encoded using a Non Return to Zero Inverted (NRZI) signaling method. Here NRZI represents a variation of NRZ. Under NRZI a constant voltage pulse is maintained for the duration of the bit time, with a transition from low to high or high to low at the beginning of the bit time used to denote a binary 1, while no transition is used to represent a binary 0. Figure 2.6 provides a comparison of the operation of NRZ and NRZI for encoding a sequence of 8 bits. Note that NRZI is a differential coding method similar to Differential Manchester, in that the signal is decoded by comparing the polarity of adjacent signal elements instead of determining the absolute value of each signal element.

Through the use of 4B5B coding only 16 ($2^4$) of the 32 ($2^5$) possible patterns are required for the actual encoding of data. This enabled the codes selected to represent the 16 four-bit data blocks to provide two transitions for each 5-code block. Thus, by

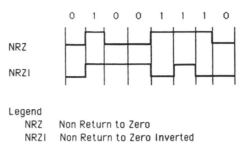

**Figure 2.6** NRZ versus NRZI coding

the appropriate selection of data blocks, a sufficient number of transmissions will occur to provide synchronization.

*Other coding techniques*

In addition to 4B5B, other popular coding methods used by LAN designers include 8B6T, 5B6B and 8B10B. Two of these coding methods are similar to 4B5B, in that a group of *n* bits are used to form an *m* bit symbol, resulting in a coding technique we can classify as nBmB. The exception is 8B6T, which results in 8 bits being mapped into a code group represented by six ternary symbols. As we focus our attention upon specific types of LANs, later in this book we will discuss their coding and signaling method, when appropriate, in additional detail.

## 2.1.4 Transmission medium

The transmission medium used in a local area network can range in scope from 'twisted-pair' wire, such as is used in conventional telephone lines, to coaxial cable, fiber optic cable and the atmosphere which is used by some transmission schemes to include FM radio and infrared. Each transmission medium has a number of advantages and disadvantages associated with its use in comparison to other media. The primary differences between media concern their cost and ease of installation, the bandwidth of the cable which may permit only one or several transmission sessions to occur simultaneously, the maximum speed of communications permitted and the geographic scope of the network that the medium supports.

*Twisted-pair wire*

In addition to being the least expensive medium available for LAN installations, twisted-pair wire is very easy to install. Since this wiring uses the RJ45 modular connectors used with the telephone system, once a wire is cut and a connector fastened the attachment of the connector to network devices is extremely simple. Normally, a screwdriver and perhaps a pocket knife are the only tools required for the installation of twisted-pair wire. Anyone who has hooked up a pair of speakers to a stereo set normally has the ability to install this transmission medium.

Although inexpensive and easy to install, unshielded twisted-pair (UTP) wire is very susceptible to noise generated by fluorescent light ballasts and electrical machinery. In addition, a length of twisted-pair wire acts as an antenna. Thus, the longer the wire length the greater the noise it gathers. At a certain length the received noise will obliterate the signal which attenuates or decreases in strength as it propagates along the length of the wire. This noise can affect the error rate of data transmitted on the network, although the utilization of lead-shielded twisted- pair (STP) cable can be employed to provide the cable with a high degree of immunity to the line noise and enable extended transmission distances.

Since the bandwidth of twisted-pair cable is considerably less than that of coaxial or fiber optic cable, normally only one signal is transmitted on this cable at any point in time. As previously explained, this signaling technique is known as baseband signaling and should be compared to the broadband signaling capability of coaxial and fiber optic cable.

It should be noted that, although a twisted-pair wire system can be used to transmit both voice and data, the data transmission is baseband since only one channel is normally used for data. In comparison, a broadband system on coaxial or fiber optic cable can be designed to carry voice and several subchannels of data as well as facsimile and video transmission. Another constraint of unshielded twisted-pair wire is the rate at which data can flow on the network and the distance they can flow. Although data rates up to 155 megabits per second (Mbps) can be achieved, normally local area networks employing data rates beyond 10 Mbps are limited to a transmission distance of 100 meters or less.

In comparison, coaxial and fiber optic cable based systems may be limited in terms of miles. To extend transmission distances over twisted-pair wire, both use shielded wire and periodically insert repeaters into the cable. The repeater receives a digital signal and then regenerates it; hence it is also known as a data regenerator.

Most high speed twisted-pair based local area networks are hub based, with a maximum cabling distance of 100 meters from the hub port to a participant on the network. In actuality, under cabling standards developed jointly by the Electronic Industries Association and the Telecommunications Industry Association (EIA/TIA), a maximum distance of 90 meters is permitted from a hub port to a wall outlet and 10 meters from the wall outlet to the network device. If cabling is directly from a hub port to a network device, a cabling distance of up to 100 meters is permitted. Later in this book we will examine the EIA/TIA cabling standard as well as the transmission properties of several types of transmission media.

*Coaxial cable*

Coaxial cable consists of a center conductor copper wire which is then covered by an insulator known as a dielectric. An overlapping woven copper mesh surrounds the dielectric and the mesh which, in turn, is covered by a protective jacket which can consist of polyethylene or aluminum. Figure 2.7 illustrates the composition of a typical coaxial cable; however, it should be noted that over 100 types of coaxial cable are currently marketed. The key differences between such cables involve the number of conductors contained in the cable, the diclectric employed and the type of protective jacket and material used to

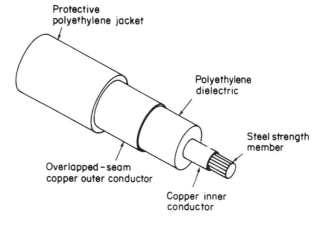

**Figure 2.7**  Coaxial cable

provide strength to the cable which allows it to be pulled through conduits without breaking.

Two basic types of coaxial cable are used in local area networks, with the type of cable based upon the transmission technique employed: baseband or broadband signaling. Both cable types are much more expensive than twisted-pair wire; however, the greater frequency bandwidth of coaxial cable permits higher data rates for longer distances than can be obtained over twisted-pair wire.

Normally, $50\,\Omega$ coaxial cable is used in baseband networks, while $75\,\Omega$ cable is used in broadband networks. The latter coaxial is identical to that used in cable television (CATV) applications, including the coaxial cable used in a home. Data rates on baseband networks using coaxial cable range upward to between 50 and 100 Mbps. With broadband transmissions, data rates up to and including 400 Mbps are obtainable.

### Hardware interface

A coaxial cable with a polyethylene jacket is normally used for baseband signaling. Data is transmitted from stations on the network to the baseband cable in a digital format and the connection from each station to the cable is accomplished by the use of a simple coaxial T-connector. Figure 2.8 illustrates the hardware interface designed to connect a personal computer to a coaxial cable of a typical baseband local area network. Here the network adapter card is a hardware device that contains the logic to control network access and is inserted into one of the expansion slots in the system unit of the computer. At the rear

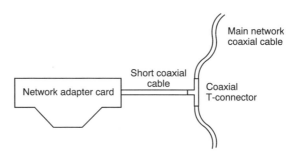

**Figure 2.8** Hardware interface to coaxial cable. The network adapter card is installed in the system unit of the PC and connected to the main coaxial cable of the network via a short coaxial cable interfaced to a T-connector

of the computer's system unit a short section of coaxial cable is used to connect the network adapter card to the baseband cable via a T-connector.

Since data on a baseband network travel in a digital form, those signals can be easily regenerated by the use of a device known as a line driver or data regenerator. The line driver or data regenerator is a low-cost device that is constructed to look for a pulse rise; upon detecting the occurrence of the rise, it will disregard the entire pulse and regenerate an entirely new pulse. Thus, you can install low-cost line drives into a baseband coaxial network to extend the distance over which transmission can occur on the cable. Typically, a coaxial cable baseband system can cover several miles and may contain hundreds to thousands of stations on the network.

### Broadband coaxial cable

To obtain independent subchannels derived by frequency on coaxial cable broadband transmission requires a method of translating the digital signals from workstations into appropriate frequencies. This translation process is accomplished by the use of radio-frequency (RF) modems which modulate the digital data into analog signals and convert or demodulate received analog signals into digital signals. Since signals are transmitted at one frequency and received at a different frequency, a 'head end' or frequency translator is also required for broadband transmission on coaxial cable. This device is also known as a remodulator as it simply converts the signals from one subchannel to another subchannel.

The requirement for modems and frequency translators normally makes broadband transmission more expensive than baseband. Although the ability of broadband to support multiple channels provides it with an aggregate data transmission capacity that exceeds baseband, in general baseband transmission permits a higher per-channel data flow. While this is an important consideration for mainframe-to-mainframe communications when massive amounts of data must be moved, for most personal computer interactive screen sessions and file transfer operations the speed of either baseband or broadband transmission should be sufficient. This fact may be better understood by comparing the typical transmission rates obtainable on baseband and broadband networks to drive a high-speed dot matrix printer and the differences between the time required to transmit data on the network and the time required to print the data.

Typical transmission speeds on commonly employed base-band and broadband networks range from 2 to 16 Mbps. In comparison, a high-speed dot matrix printer operating at 120 c.p.s. would require approximately 200 seconds to print 1 second's worth of data transmitted at 2 Mbps and 1600 seconds to print 1 second's worth of data transmitted at 16 Mbps.

Turning our attention to a more modern laser printer capable of printing 8 pages per minute (p.p.m.), if each page contains 200 words with an average of five characters, then in one minute the printer would print 8000 characters. Using 8 bits per character, this would result in 64 000 bits in one minute. Thus, one second's worth of data transmitted at 100 Mbps on a high speed LAN could keep an 8 p.p.m. laser busy for approximately 26 hours!

Based upon the preceding you might question the need for high speed LANs. If your organization makes use of a limited amount of graphics, has no intention of using multimedia application on a network, and does not intend to interconnect a substantial number of devices to the LAN, you probably can use a conventional 10 Mbps Ethernet or 16 Mbps Token-Ring network. However, if your organization uses or intends to use a significant number of graphic intensive applications, multi-media applications, or plans to connect a substantial number of highly active network devices you will more than likely consider the use of a high speed LAN. To illustrate this, consider the use of a LAN to send print jobs to a color laser. One 3 by 5 inch graphic with a resolution of 600 dots per inch (d.p.i.) would require $3 \times 5 \times 600 \times 600$ or 5.4 Mbits without considering the color depth of the image. If the image was stored in what is referred to as true color then 24 bits or 3 bytes are used to represent the color of each bit position. Thus, the full image would require 16.2 Mbits. If your network users transmit a sequence of color print jobs, retrieve color images such as computer aided design (CAD) from network servers, and use or intend to use videoconferencing which can be considered to represent a sequence of 30 images per second, the transmission capacity of conventional local area networks can be expected to become severely taxed. For such situations you will more than likely consider either the use of LAN switches to acquire the ability to obtain multiple simultaneous transmissions or a high speed LAN, both of which will be covered in this book.

*Fiber optic cable*

Fiber optic cable is a transmission medium for light energy and as such provides a very high bandwidth, permitting data rates ranging up to Gigabits (Gbps) billions of bits per second. The fiber optic cable consists of a thin core of glass or plastic which is surrounded by a protective shield. Several shielded fibers in turn are bundled in a jacket with a central member of aluminum or steel employed for tensile strength.

Digital data represented by electrical energy must be converted into light energy for transmission on a fiber optic cable. This is normally accomplished by a low-power laser or through the use of a light emitting diode and appropriate circuitry. At the receiver, light energy must be reconverted into electrical energy. Normally, a device known as a photo detector, as well as appropriate circuitry to regenerate the digital pulses and an amplifier, are used to convert the received light energy into its original digital format.

In addition to the high bandwidth of fiber optic cables, they offer users several additional advantages in comparison to conventional transmission media. Since data travel in the form of light, they are immune to electrical interference, and building codes that may require expensive conduits to be installed for conventional cables are usually unnecessary. Similarly, fiber optic cable can be installed through areas where the flow of electricity could be dangerous since only light flows through such cables.

Since most fibers only provide a single, unidirectional transmission path, a minimum of two cables is normally required to connect all transmitters to all receivers on a network built using fiber optic cable. Due to the higher cost of fiber optic cable than coaxial or twisted-pair, the dual cable requirement of fiber cables can make them relatively expensive in comparison to other types of cable. In addition, until recently it was very difficult to splice such cable, which usually required sophisticated equipment and skilled installers to implement a fiber optic based network. Similarly, once this type of network was installed, until recently it was difficult to modify the network.

Currently, the cost of the cable, a degree of difficulty of installation and modification make the utilization of fiber optic based local area networks impractical for many commercial applications. Today, the primary use of fiber optic cable is to extend the distance between workstations on a network or to connect two or more networks to one another with the fiber optic network functioning as a backbone network. The device used to connect a length of fiber optic cable into the LAN or between LANs is a fiber optic repeater. The repeater converts the electrical energy of signals flowing on the LAN into light energy for transmission on the fiber optic cable. At the end of the fiber optic cable, a second repeater converts light energy back into electrical energy. With the cost of the fiber optic cable declining and improvements that simplify the installation and modification of networks using this type of cable continuing to be introduced, the next few years may witness a profound movement toward the utilization of this transmission medium throughout local area networks.

## 2.1.5 Cabling standards

The Electronics Industry Association/Telecommunications Industry Association Commercial Building Telecommunications Standard commonly referred to as EIA/TIA-568, was ratified in 1992. This standard specifies a variety of building cabling parameters, ranging from backbone cabling used to connect a building's telecommunication closets to an equipment room, to horizontal cabling used to cable individual users to the equipment closet. The standard defines the performance characteristics of both backbone and horizontal cables as well as different types of connectors used with different types of cabling.

*Backbone cabling*

Four types of media are recognized by the EIA/TIA-568 standard for backbone cabling. Table 2.2 lists the media options supported by the EIA/TIA-456 standard for backbone cabling.

*Horizontal cabling*

As previously indicated, horizontal cabling under the EIA/TIA-568 standard consists of cable that connects equipment in a telecommunications closet to a user's work area. The media options supported for horizontal cabling are the same as specified for backbone cabling, with the exception of coaxial cable for which 50 ohm thin cable is specified; however, cabling

**Table 2.2** EIA/TIA-568 backbone cabling media options

| Media type | Maximum cable distance |
|---|---|
| 100 ohm UTP | 800 meters (2624 feet) |
| 150 ohm STP | 700 meters (2296 feet) |
| 50 ohm thick coaxial cable | 500 meters (1640 feet) |
| 62.5/125 $\mu$m multimode optical fiber | 2000 meters (6560 feet) |

distances are restricted to 90 meters in length from equipment in the telecommunications closet to a telecommunications outlet. This permits a patch cord or drop cable up to 10 meters in length to be used to connect a user workstation to a horizontal cabling not exceeding the 10 meters restriction associated with many LAN technologies that use UTP cabling.

*UTP categories*

One of the more interesting aspects of the EIA/TIA-568 standard is its recognition that different signaling rates require different cable characteristics. This resulted in the EIA/TIA-568 standard classifying UTP cable for five categories. Those categories and their suitability for different types of voice and data applications are indicated in Table 2.3.

In examining the entries in Table 2.3, note that categories 3 through 5 support transmission with respect to indicated signaling rates. This means that the ability of those categories of UTP to support different types of LAN transmission will depend upon the signaling method used by different LANs. For example, consider a LAN encoding technique that results in 6 bits encoded into 4 signaling elements that have a 100 MHZ signaling rate. Through the use of category 5 cable, a data transmission rate of 150 Mbps ($(6/4) \times 100$) could be supported.

**Table 2.3** EIA/TIA-568 UTP cable categories

| | |
|---|---|
| Category 1 | Voice or low-speed data up to 56 Kbps; not useful for LANs. |
| Category 2 | Data rates up to 1 Mbps. |
| Category 3 | Supports transmission up to 16 MHZ. |
| Category 4 | Supports transmission up to 20 MHZ. |
| Category 5 | Supports transmission up to 100 MHZ. |

Category 3 cable is typically used for 10 Mbps for Ethernet and 4 Mbps Token-Ring LANs. Category 4 is normally used for 16 Mbps Token-Ring LANs, while category 5 cable supports 100 Mbps Ethernet LANs, such as 100BASE-T and ATM to the desktop at a 155 Mbps operating rate.

## 2.1.5 Access method

If the topology of a local area network can be compared to a data highway, then the access method might be viewed as the set of rules that enable data from one workstation to successfully reach its destination via the data highway. Without such rules, it is quite possible for two messages sent to the same or a different address by two different workstations to collide, with the result that neither message reaches its destination. There are four access methods primarily used in local area networks, three of which are associated with shared media networks. The three access methods primarily employed in shared media local area networks are Carrier-Sense Multiple Access/Collision Detection (CSMA/CD), Carrier- Sense Multiple Access/Collision Avoidance (CSMA/CA) and token passing. Each of these access methods is uniquely structured to address the previously mentioned collision and data destination problems. A fourth access method involves the creation of a path or channel between the source and destination. This access method is completely different from the preceding methods since it represents a connection-oriented protocol in which data are explicitly transmitted between two stations without other stations receiving the same data and having to check the destination address to determine if they are the recipient. Thus, we can classify CSMA/CD, CSMA/CA, and Token-Ring as connectionless protocols while a fourth access method can be classified as a connection oriented protocol. As connection oriented protocols are usually based upon the use of switches, we will refer to this access method as a switch-based connection-oriented access protocol.

Prior to discussing how access methods work, let us first examine the two basic types of device that can be attached to a local area network to gain an appreciation of the work a shared media access method must accomplish.

*Listeners and talkers*

We can categorize the operating mode of each device as being a 'listener' or a 'talker'. Some devices, like printers, only receive data and thus operate only as a listener. Other devices, such as personal computers, can either transmit or receive data and are capable of operating in both modes. In a baseband signaling environment where only one channel exists or on an individual channel on a broadband system, if several talkers wish to communicate at the same time a collision will occur unless a scheme is employed that defines when each device can talk and, in the event of a collision, what events must transpire to avoid its recurrence.

For data to correctly reach its destination, each listener must have a unique address and its network equipment must be designed to respond to a message on the net only when it recognizes its address; thus the primary goals in the design of an access method are to minimize the potential for data collision and to provide a mechanism for corrective action when data collide as well as to ensure that an addressing scheme is employed to enable messages to reach their destination.

*Carrier-Sense Multiple Access with Collision Detection (CSMA/CD)*

Carrier-Sense Multiple Access with Collision Detection can be categorized as a 'listen' then 'send' access method. CSMA/CD is one of the earliest developed access techniques and is the technique used in Ethernet, which is the Xerox Corporation developed local area network whose technology was licensed to many companies and standardized by the IEEE.

Under the CSMA/CD concept, when a station has data to send it first listens to determine if any other station on the network is talking; the fact that the channel is idle is determined in one of two ways based upon whether the network is broadband or baseband.

If a broadband network, the fact that a channel is idle is determined by noting the absence of a carrier tone on the cable. Carrier-sensing thus provides the mechanism to determine whether or not the channel is busy.

Ethernet, like other baseband systems, uses one channel for data transmission and does not employ the use of a carrier. Instead, Ethernet encodes data using a Manchester code in which a timing transition always occurs in the middle of each bit as previously illustrated in Figure 2.4. Although Ethernet does not transmit data via the use of a carrier, the continuous transitions of the Manchester code can be considered as equivalent to a carrier signal. Carrier-sensing on a baseband network is thus performed by monitoring the line for activity.

In a CSMA/CD network, if the channel is busy, the station will wait until it becomes idle prior to transmitting data. Since it is possible for two stations to listen at the same time and discover an idle channel, it is also possible that the two stations could then transmit at the same time. When this situation arises, a collision will occur. Upon sensing that a collision has occurred, a delay scheme will be employed to prevent a repetition of the collision. Typically, each station will use either a randomly generated or predefined time-out period prior to attempting to retransmit the message that previously collided. Since this access method requires hardware capable of detecting the occurrence of a collision, it is usually more expensive than the hardware required for a similar method that uses collision avoidance.

Figure 2.9 illustrates a CSMA/CD bus-based local area network. Here each workstation is attached to the transmission medium, such as coaxial cable, by a device known as a bus interface unit (BIU). To illustrate the operation of a CSMA/CD network, assume that workstation A is currently using the channel and workstations C and D wish to transmit. The BIUs connecting workstations C and D to the network would listen to the channel and note it was busy. Once workstation A completes its transmission, workstations C and D would attempt to gain

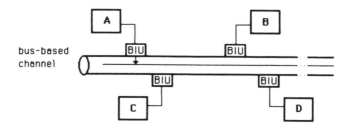

BIU = bus interface unit

**Figure 2.9** CSMA/CD network operation. In a CSMA/CD network, as the distance between workstations increases the resulting increase in propagation delay time increases the probability of the occurrence of collisions

access to the channel. Since workstation A's signal takes longer to propagate down the cable to workstation D than to C, C's BIU notices that the channel is free slightly before workstation D's BIU. However, as workstation C gets ready to transmit, workstation D now assumes the channel is free. Within an infinitesimal period of time C starts transmission followed by D, resulting in a collision. Here the collision is a function of the propagation delay of the signal and the distance between two competing workstations. Due to this, CSMA/CD networks work better as the main cable length decreases.

Although several versions of CSMA/CD are marketed, by far the most common version is based upon licensed technology from Xerox Corporation, which was standardized by the IEEE.

When the IEEE developed its 802.3 standard for CSMA/CD systems it did not precisely follow Xerox's original Ethernet specifications, although there is an extremely high degree of similarity between the original Ethernet specifications and the IEEE 802.3 standard. Recognizing the value of the CSMA/CD access protocol, it forms the basis for the operation of Fast Ethernet that operates at 100 Mbps as well as the evolving Gigabit Ethernet that operates at one billion bits per second (Gbps).

The CSMA/CD access technique is best suited for networks with intermittent transmission, since an increase in traffic volume causes a corresponding increase in the probability of the cable being occupied when a station wishes to talk. In addition, as traffic volume builds under CSMA/CD throughput may decline, since there will be longer waits to gain access to the network as well as additional time-outs required to resolve collisions that occur.

*Carrier-Sense Multiple Access with Collision Avoidance (CSMA/CA)*

Carrier-Sense Multiple Access with Collision Avoidance represents a modified version of the CSMA/CD access technique. Under the CSMA/CA access technique, each of the hardware devices attached to the talkers on the network estimates when a collision is likely to occur and avoids transmission during those times. Since this technique eliminates the requirement for collision-detection hardware, the cost of hardware to implement this access technique is usually less than that of CSMA/CD hardware. Although this access method appeared to have promise for adoption it was displaced by the rapid acceptance of Ethernet and its CSMA/CD access protocol.

## Token passing

In a token passing access method, each time the network is turned on a token is generated. Consisting of a unique bit pattern, the token travels the length of the network, either around a ring or along the length of a bus. When a station on the network has data to transmit it must first seize a free token. The token is then transformed to indicate that it is in use, and information is added which represents data being transmitted from one station to another. During the time the token is in use the other stations on the network remain idle, eliminating the possibility of collisions occurring. Once the transmission is complete the token is converted back into its original form by the workstation that transmitted the frame and becomes available for use by the next station on the network.

Figure 2.10 illustrates the general operation of a token passing network using a ring topology. Since a station on the network can only transmit when it has a free token, token passing eliminates the requirement for collision-detection hardware. Due to the dependence of the network upon the token, the loss of a station can bring the entire network down. To avoid this, several vendors initially included special backup circuitry in their hardware. When the Token-Ring standard was developed it specified a mechanism whereby the loss of a station results in its disconnection from the network. This enables a failing or purposely powered-off station to be gracefully disconnected from the network without adversely affecting other network devices.

## Switch-based, connection-oriented

A switch-based, connection-oriented access protocol requires network devices to request the establishment of a route or path through one or more switches to the recipient. Once a path is established, data are routed on the established path either on a frame or packet basis or for the entire transmission session, with the type of switch used determining the method by which the connection-oriented access between source and destination address occurs.

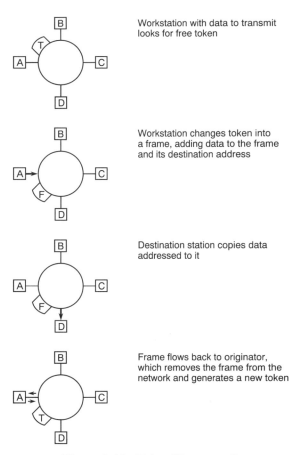

Workstation with data to transmit looks for free token

Workstation changes token into a frame, adding data to the frame and its destination address

Destination station copies data addressed to it

Frame flows back to originator, which removes the frame from the network and generates a new token

**Figure 2.10**   Token-Ring operation

The most popular form of switch-based, connection-oriented access protocol is the one used by the Asynchronous Transfer Mode (ATM) protocol. ATM is a switch based LAN and WAN that supports both permanent and switched virtual circuits for the routing of data. A Switched Virtual Circuit (SVC) represents a logical connection established for the routing of data between two endpoints for a transmission session, and a Permanent Virtual Circuit (PVC) represents a similar connection that is established by a network administrator and remains intact until the administrator removes or tears down the connection.

Figure 2.11 illustrates a switch-based, connection-oriented network formed by connecting three switches in a two-tiered hierarchy. In this example note that workstations 1 and 2 connected to a common switch are shown accessing the same

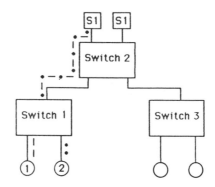

Legend _ _ channel from workstation 1 to server 1
• • channel from workstation 2 to server 2

**Figure 2.11**   Switched-based, connection oriented access

server on a different switch at the same time. This is accomplished by switches subdividing the connection to other switches by time, a technique known as Time Division Multiplexing (TDM). Under ATM terminology the route from switch 1 to switch 2 is referred to as a Virtual Path (VP), and each workstation's connection on the common path is referred to as a Virtual Channel (VC).

Due to the variety of transmission media, network structures and access methods, there is no one best network for all users. Table 2.4 should be used by the reader to obtain a generalized comparison of the advantages and disadvantages of the technical characteristics of local area networks, using the transmission medium as a frame of reference.

## 2.2 POPULAR TYPES OF LANs

In this section we will examine three popular types of local area networks and one type of LAN whose use can be expected to significantly increase in the near future. The three currently popular types of networks we will examine in this section are Ethernet, Token-Ring and FDDI. Each of these networks presently provides connectivity for millions of workstations. The network whose usage is rapidly increasing and which we will also examine in this section is ATM.

**Table 2.4**   Technical characteristics of LANs

| Characteristic | Transmission medium | | | |
| --- | --- | --- | --- | --- |
| | Twisted-pair wire | Baseband coaxial cable | Broadband coaxial cable | Fiber optic cable |
| Topology | Bus, star or ring | Bus or ring | Bus or ring | Bus, ring or star |
| Channels | Single channel | Single channel | Multi-channel | Single, multi-channel |
| Data rate | Normally up to 16 Mbps, with 100 and 155 Mbps obtainable at distances up to 100 meters | Normally 2 to 10 Mbps, up to 100 Mbps obtainable | Up to 400 Mbps | Up to Gbps |
| Maximum nodes on net | Usually <255 | Usually <1024 | Several thousand | Several thousand |
| Geographical coverage | In hundreds or thousands of feet | In miles | In tens of miles | In tens of miles |
| Major advantages | Low cost, may be able to use existing wiring | Low cost, simple to install | Supports voice, data, video applications simultaneously | Supports voice, data, video applications simultaneously |
| Major disadvantages | Limited bandwidth, requires conduits, low immunity to noise | Low immunity to noise | High cost, difficult to install, requires RF modems and headend | Cable cost, difficult to splice |

## 2.2.1 Ethernet

Ethernet is a local area network that uses the CSMA/CD access protocol on a bus structure. The concept behind Ethernet was developed at Xerox Corporation's Palo Alto Research Center (PARC) in Palo Alto, California during the late 1970s. That research center is also considered as the developer of such technological innovations as the graphic interface and the concept of laptop and notebook computers.

Originally Ethernet was developed to provide a mechanism for linking computers located at Xerox's Office Products Division.

Since the intent of Ethernet was to provide a method of connectivity for linking different vendor products, Xerox enlisted Digital Equipment Corporation and Intel Corporation in the development of specifications for the network. In 1980, those three companies jointly published a specification for the Ethernet local area network. That specification was later presented to the IEEE 802 committee and, after several modifications, resulted in the 802.3 standard. Although Ethernet and the 802.3 standard differ in some signaling and formatting methods, many vendors originally introduced equipment capable of supporting both specifications.

Today, when we talk about Ethernet, we typically refer to the IEEE 802.3 standard and the vast majority of Ethernet products currently manufactured support the specifications in that standard. In fact, the terms Ethernet and IEEE 802.3 are considered to be synonymous, although in actuality they are not. In addition, the term Ethernet, as we will shortly note, collectively refer to a family of CSMA/CD access protocol networks that operate on different types of media at data rates from 10 Mbps to 1 Gbps.

## Ethernet frame

The transportation of information on an Ethernet local area network occurs in packets formed by eight-bit bytes that are more commonly referenced as frames since data transmission occurs at the data link layer. Figure 2.12 compares the general format of Ethernet and IEEE 802.3 frames. Both are variable in length, since the data field can range in size from a minimum of 46 bytes to a maximum of 1500 bytes.

The frame's preamble provides synchronization and consists of either a seven- or eight-byte sequence of alternating binary ones and zeros. In an IEEE 802.3 frame the start of Frame Delimiter is similar to the preamble; however, its last two bits are always ones. Those bits announce the coming frame and provide additional synchronization for all receivers on the network.

In both the Ethernet and IEEE frame formats the first eight bytes are followed by two six-byte addresses, the first representing the frame's destination, while the second address identifies the originator and is known as the source address. The destination address can specify a single host (unicast), multiple hosts (multicast) or all hosts on the network (broadcast). When

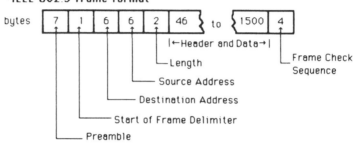

**Figure 2.12** Ethernet/IEEE 802.3 frame formats. Both Ethernet and IEEE 802.3 frames can vary in length from 72 to 1526 eight-bit bytes

the first bit in the destination address is set to zero this indicates a unique address. If that bit is set to a one, it indicates either a multicast address to a group or a broadcast to all stations, in which all address bits are then set to one. To ensure the worldwide uniqueness of network addresses the IEEE has assumed the responsibility for assigning the first three bytes of the six-byte address to hardware vendors. Those vendors use that assignment to develop unique addresses in read only memory (ROM) in each network interface card (NIC) they manufacture. The values of the last three bytes are assigned by the network administrator.

The two-byte type field specifies how the data is to be interpreted by the receiver. Under the IEEE 802.3 standard, the type field is replaced by a length field which is also two bytes in length. This field indicates the number of bytes in the data field that are non-pad bytes. Pad bytes are used to fill the data field to its minimum 46-byte size and are also covered by the frame check sequence. Both the type and length fields are followed by the data field, which varies in length from a minimum of 46 bytes to a maximum of 1500 bytes. The last field is the four-byte Frame Check Sequence (FCS). This field contains a cyclic redundancy check (CRC) that covers the destination field through the data field and provides the error-detection and correction mechanism to ensure data reach the destination correctly.

Although there is a slight difference in frame composition between Ethernet and IEEE 802.3 formats, the key difference between the two is in their support of the network layer. Ethernet specifies the entire link layer through the use of a type field. In comparison, IEEE 802.3 only specifies the lower half of the OSI Reference Model link layer. Readers are referred to Section 2.3 for information on how the link layer is specified under the IEEE 802 series of standards.

From Figure 2.12 it is apparent that both Ethernet and IEEE 802.3 frames can vary in size from a minimum of 72 bytes to a maximum of 1526 bytes. This variance in frame size as well as the fact that both Ethernet and IEEE 802.3 standards require a dead time of 9.6 ms between frames enables us to compute the maximum number of different sized frames that can be transmitted on this type of network per unit of time. From this calculation we can calculate various performance measurements as well as determine such information as the minimum frame processing rate required by bridges and routers that will not degrade network performance and the time required to transfer files between two local area networks connected by a wide area network transmission facility. Readers are referred to Chapter 7 in which several mathematical models of local area network performance are developed and used to compute a variety of performance and throughput statistics.

## Types of Ethernet

Ethernet was originally developed as a baseband signaling mechanism in which digital signals are transmitted on a 50 Ω coaxial cable at a data rate of 10 Mbps. The CSMA portion of the access mechanism is built into electronics that reside on a network interface card (NIC) which normally is represented by an adapter card installed in the system unit of a personal computer. The NIC determines whether or not the channel is available for use and either holds the frame in a buffer until the channel is available or transmits the information. Data is transmitted from the NIC to a transmitter/receiver known as a transceiver. The transceiver maintains a balanced electrical

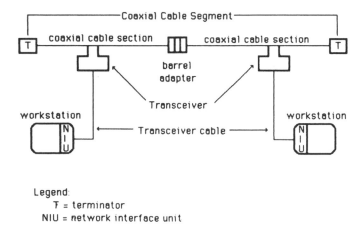

Legend:
 T = terminator
 NIU = network interface unit

**Figure 2.13** Ethernet 50 Ω coaxial cable network structure. An Ethernet LAN using a 50 Ω coaxial bus-based cable has several restrictions. The maximum length of a cable segment is 500 m, the minimum distance between transceivers is 2.5 m, and when segments are joined together by repeaters the maximum separation between nodes is 2.8 km. In addition, there is a maximum of 1024 nodes allowed on this network

signal between the NIC and the coaxial cable and by examining the balance detects collisions, relaying this fact to the NIC.

Figure 2.13 illustrates the relationship between a segment on a main bus-based coaxial cable Ethernet LAN, and its coaxial cable sections, transceivers, NICs and workstations. The maximum length of a 50 Ω coaxial cable segment is 500 m, with no more than 100 transceivers or nodes allowed per segment. The minimum distance between transceivers is 2.5 m, while the total number of nodes on the entire LAN must be less than or equal to 1024 regardless of the number of segments. Although an Ethernet can be extended by joining segments together through the use of repeaters, the maximum separation between nodes is 2.8 km, which represents the maximum length of an Ethernet 50 Ω coaxial cable-based local area network.

An Ethernet LAN using a 50 Ω coaxial bus-based cable has several restrictions. The maximum length of a cable segment is 500 m, the minimum distance between transceivers is 2.5 m and when segments are joined together by repeaters the maximum separation between nodes is 2.8 km. In addition, there is a maximum of 1024 nodes allowed on this network.

The use of 50 Ω coaxial cable was expensive and resulted in several constraints and limitations. In addition to being difficult to bend when installing the cable, a break in the cable would affect all users on a segment. To overcome those limitations

**Table 2.5**   IEEE 1 Mbps and 10 Mbps Network 802.3 specifications

| Feature | 10BASE-5 | 10BASE-2 | 10BROAD-36 | 1BASE-5 | 10BASE-T |
|---------|----------|----------|------------|---------|----------|
| Medium | 'Thick' 50 Ω coaxial | 'Thin' coaxial cable | CATV coaxial cable | Twisted-pair wire cable | Twisted-pair wire |
| Topology | Bus | Bus | Bus | Star | Star |
| Segment distance | 500 m | 200 m | 3.6 km | 500 m | 100 m |
| Data rate | 10 Mbps | 10 Mbps | 10 Mbps | 1 Mbps | 10 Mbps |

several variations of the original 50 Ω coaxial cable-based Ethernet have been standardized by the IEEE 802.3 committee. Those new versions of the CSMA/CD access protocol involve changes to the media used for the network, its topology, the maximum distance per segment and the operating rate of the network. Table 2.5 summarizes the IEEE 802.3 specifications with respect to media, topology, maximum segment length and data rate for CSMA/CD Networks that operate at 1 Mbps and 10 Mbps. Since there are several types of fast Ethernet networks, we will examine them as a separate entity later in this chapter. Note that the prefix to 'BASE' or 'BROAD' defines the operating rate of the LAN in Mbps. The term BASE or BROAD indicates baseband or broadband, while the suffix denotes the maximum segment length in 100 m multiples. Also note that 10BASE-5 represents the original Ethernet specification based upon the use of 50 Ω coaxial cable referred to as 'thick' coaxial, in comparison to thinner coaxial cable used with 10BASE-2.

**Coaxial versus twisted-pair**

Although the growth in the use of 50 Ω coaxial cable-based Ethernet networks has substantially diminished, the cause of its decline is not the network but the availability of twisted-pair wire. As a result of the development of 1BASE-5 and 10BASE-T specifications, inexpensive twisted-pair cable that costs less than one-tenth the cost of coaxial cable can be used. In addition, the simplicity of installing twisted-pair in comparison to coaxial cable can halve the cost of installing a network.

Perhaps the key advantage associated with the use of twisted-pair is the greater degree of reliability it provides network users in comparison to a coaxial cable bus-based network. Twisted-

Coaxial bus-based cable

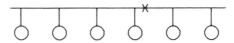

Twisted-pair

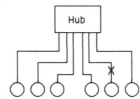

**Figure 2.14** Coaxial versus twisted-pair reliability. A twisted-pair-based Ethernet is normally more reliable than a coaxial bus-based network. A cable failure on a star topology only affects one workstation, while the failure of a bus-based cable can affect many users or bring down the entire network

pair based networks use a point-to-point topology in which workstations are connected to a hub to form a star. The resulting star-based network permits both centralized administration and maintenance. To better understand this consider Figure 2.14 which compares a break in a coaxial bus-based Ethernet with a twisted-pair-based Ethernet.

Depending upon where the break occurs on the bus-based cable, the entire network or a portion of the network may become inopcrative. In comparison, the failure of a cable on a star-based network only affects the workstation cabled to the hub.

### 2.2.2 Fast Ethernet

Fast Ethernet is not actually a local area network but a term commonly used to reference a series of three 100 Mbps physical layer LAN specifications in the IEEE 802.3$\mu$ addendum. Those specifications include 100BASE-TX, 100BASE-FX, and 100BASE-T4. Each specification maintains the use of the Media Access Control (MAC) protocol used by earlier Ethernet/IEEE 802.3 standards, CSMA/CD.

100BASE-T specifies 100 Mbps operations using the CSMA/ CD protocol over two pairs of category 5 unshielded twisted-pair

| SSD<br>1 byte | Preamble<br>7 bytes | SFD<br>1 byte | Destination<br>Address<br>6 bytes | Source<br>Address<br>6 bytes | L/T<br>2 bytes | Data<br>46 to 1500<br>bytes | FCS<br>1 byte | ESD<br>1 byte |
|---|---|---|---|---|---|---|---|---|

The 100BASE-TX frame differs from the IEEE 802.3 MAC frame through the addition of a byte at each end to mark the beginning and end of the stream delimiter.

SSD   Start of stream delimiter
SFD   Start of frame delimiter
L/T   Length (IEEE 802.3)/Type (Ethernet)
ESD   End of stream delimiter

**Figure 2.15**  Fast Ethernet frame

(UTP) cable. 100BASE-FX changes the LAN transport media to two pairs of fiber, and 100BASE-T4 supports four pairs of category 3, 4, and 5 UTP or shielded-pair (STP) cable.

*Frame format*

The frame composition associated with each of the three Fast Ethernet standards is illustrated in Figure 2.15. In comparing the composition of the Fast Ethernet frame to Ethernet and IEEE 802.3 frame formats previously illustrated in Figure 2.12, you will note that, other than the addition of starting and ending stream delimiters, the Fast Ethernet frame duplicates the older frames. A third difference between the two is not shown as it is not actually observable from a comparison of frames since this difference is associated with the time between frames. Ethernet and IEEE 802.3 frames are Manchester encoded and have an interpacket gap of 9.6 µs between frames. In comparison, the Fast Ethernet 100BASE-TX frame is transmitted using 4B5B encoding, and IDLE codes (refer to Table 2.7) representing sequences of I (binary 11111) symbols are used to mark a 0.96 µs interpacket gap. Now that we have an overview of the differences between Ethernet/IEEE 802.3 and Fast Ethernet frames, let us focus upon the new fields associated with the Fast Ethernet frame format.

### Start of stream delimiter

The Start of Stream Delimiter (SSD) is used to align a received frame for subsequent decoding. The SSD field consists of a sequence of J and K symbols, which defines the unique code 11000 10001. This field replaces the first octet of the preamble in Ethernet and IEEE 802.3 frames whose composition is 10101010.

### End of stream delimiter

The End of Stream Delimiter (ESD) is used as an indicator that data transmission terminated normally and a properly formed stream was transmitted. This one-byte field is created by the use of T and R codes (see Table 2.7) whose bit composition is 01101 00111. The ESD field lies outside of the Ethernet/IEEE 802.3 frame and for comparison purposes can be considered to fall within the interframe gap of those frames.

## 100BASE-T overview

The standardization of 100BASE-T required an extension of previously developed IEEE 802.3 standards. In the definition process of standardization development, both the Ethernet Media Access Control (MAC) and physical layer required adjustments to permit 100 Mbps operational support. For the MAC layer, scaling its speed to 100 Mbps from the 10BASE-T 10 Mbps operational rate required a minimal adjustment, since in theory the 10 BASE-T MAC layer was developed independently of the data rate. For the physical layer, more than a minor adjustment was required, since Fast Ethernet was designed to support three types of media. Using work developed in the standardization process of FDDI in defining 125 Mbps full-duplex signaling to accommodate optical fiber, UTP, and STP through Physical Media Dependent (PMD) sublayers, Fast Ethernet borrowed this strategy. Since a mechanism was required to map the PMD's continuous signaling system to the start-stop half-duplex system used at the Ethernet MAC layer, the physical layer was subdivided. This subdivision is illustrated in Figure 2.16. The PMD sublayer supports the appropriate media to be used, while the convergence sublayer (CS), which was later renamed the physical coding sublayer,

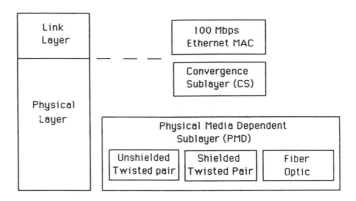

**Figure 2.16** Fast Ethernet physical layer subdivision overview

performs the mapping between the PMD and the Ethernet MAC layer.

Although Fast Ethernet represents a tenfold increase in the LAN operating rate from 10BASE-T, to ensure proper collision detection the 100BASE-T network span was reduced to 250 meters, with a maximum of 100 meters permitted between a network node and a hub. The smaller network diameter reduces potential propagation delay. When coupled with a tenfold operating rate increase and no change in network frame size, the ratio of frame duration to network propagation delay for 100BASE-T network is the same as for a 10BASE-T network.

**Physical layer**

The physical layer subdivision previously illustrated in Figure 2.16, as indicated in the title of the figure, presents an overview of the true layer subdivision. In actuality, a number of changes were required at the physical layer to obtain a 100 Mbps operating rate. Those changes include the use of three wire pairs for data (the fourth is used for collision detection), 8B6T ternary coding (for 100BASE-T4) instead of Manchester coding, and an increase in the clock signaling speed from 20 MHZ to 25 MHZ. As indicated in Table 2.6, in comparison to 10BASE-T the difference at the physical layer resulted in a tenfold increase in the 100BASE-T operating rate.

When the specifications for Fast Ethernet were being developed, it was recognized that the physical signaling layer would incorporate medium dependent functions if support was extended to two pair cable (100BASE-TX) operations. To

**Table 2.6**   100BASE-T system throughput compared to 10BASE-T

| | |
|---|---|
| Transmit on 3 pairs versus 1 pair | × 3.00 |
| 8B6T coding instead of Manchester | × 2.65 |
| 20 to 25 MHZ clock increase | × 1.25 |
| Total throughout increase | 10.00 |

separate medium dependent interfaces to accommodate multiple physical layers, a common interface referred to as the Medium Independent Interface (MII) was inserted between the MAC layer and the physical encoding sublayer. The MII represents a common point of interoperability between the medium and the MAC layer. The MII can support two specific data rates, 10 Mbps and 100 Mbps, permitting older 10BASE-T nodes to be supported at Fast Ethernet hubs. To reconcile the MII signal with the MAC signal, a reconciliation sublayer was added under the MAC layer, resulting in the subdivision of the link layer into three parts: a logical link control layer, a media access control layer, and a reconciliation layer. The top portion of Figure 2.17 illustrates this subdivision.

That portion of Fast Ethernet below the MII, which is the new physical layer, is now subdivided into three sublayers. The lower portion of Figure 2.17 illustrates the physical sublayers for 100BASE-T4 and 100BASE-TX.

The physical coding sublayer performs the data encoding, transmit, receive, and carrier sense functions. Since the data coding method differs between 100BASE-T4 and 100BASE-TX, this difference requires distinct physical coding sublayers for each version of Fast Ethernet.

The Physical Medium Attachment (PMA) sublayer maps messages from the physical coding sublayer (PCS) onto the twisted-pair transmission media, and vice versa.

The Medium-Dependent Interface (MDI) sublayer specifies the use of a standard RJ-45 connector. Although the same connector is used for 100BASE-TX, the use of two pairs of cable instead of four results in different pin assignments.

*100BASE-T4*

Figure 2.18 illustrates the RJ-45 pin assignments of wire pairs used by 100BASE-T4. Note that wire pairs D1 and D2 are unidirectional. As indicated in Figure 2.18, three wire pairs are

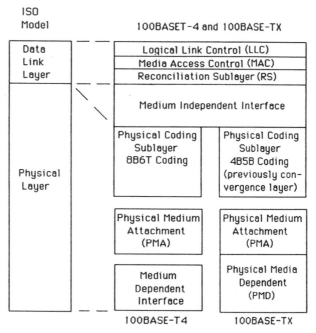

**Figure 2.17**    100BASE-T4 versus 100BASE-TX physical and link layers

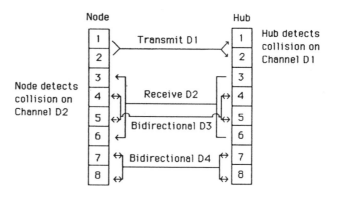

**Figure 2.18**    100BASE-T4 pin assignments

available for data transmission and reception in each direction, while the fourth pair is used for collision detection.

The 100BASE-T4 Physical coding sublayer implements 8B6T block coding. Under this coding technique, each block of 8 input bits is transformed into a unique code group of 6 ternary symbols. Figure 2.19 provides an overview of the 8B6T coding process used by 100BASE-T4.

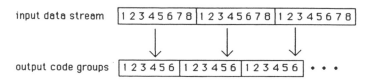

**Figure 2.19**  8B6T coding process

The output code groups resulting from 8B6T coding flow out to three parallel channels that are placed on three twisted pairs. Thus, the effective data rate on each pair is 100 Mbps/3, or 33.33 Mbps. As 6 bits are represented by 8 bit positions, the signaling rate or baud rate on each cable pair becomes 33 Mbps × 6/8, or 25 MHZ, which is the clock rate used at the MII sublayer.

*100BASE-TX*

100BASE-TX represents 100BASE-T which supports the use of two pair of category 5 UTP cabling with RJ-45 connectors. A 100BASE-TX network requries a hub, and the maximum cable run is 100 meters from hub port to node, with a maximum network diameter of 250 meters.

Figure 2.20 illustrates the cabling of two pairs of UTP wires between a hub and node to support 100BASE-TX transmission. One pair of wires is used for transmission, while the second pair is used for collision detection and reception of data. The use of a 125 MHZ frequency requires the use of a data grade cable. Thus 100BASE-TX is based upon the use of category 5 UTP.

Although the 100BASE-TX physical layer structure resembles the 100BASE-T4 layer, there are significant differences between the two to accommodate the differences in media used. At the physical coding sublayer, the 100 Mbps start-stop bit stream from the MII is first converted to a full-duplex 125 Mbps bit stream. This conversion is accomplished by the use of the FDDI PMD as the 100BASE-TX PMD. Next, the data stream is encoded

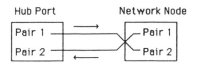

**Figure 2.20**  100BASE-TX cabling

using a 4B5B coding scheme. The 100BASE-TX PMD decodes symbols from the 125 Mbps continuous bit stream, and converts the stream to 100 Mbps start-stop data bits when the data flow is reversed.

### 4B5B coding

The use of a 4B5B coding scheme enables data and control information to be carried in each symbol represented by a 5-bit code group. In addition, an inter-stream fill code (IDLE) is defined, as well as a symbol used to force signaling errors. As 4 data bits are mapped into a 5-bit code, only 16 symbols are required to represent data. The remaining symbols not used for control or to denote an IDLE condition are not used by 100BASE-TX and are considered as invalid. Table 2.7 lists the 4B5B 100BASE-TX code groups.

*100BASE-FX*

100BASE-FX represents the third 100BASE-T wiring scheme, defining Fast Ethernet transmission over fiber optic media. 100BASE-FX requires the use of two-strand 62.5/125 micron multimode fiber media and supports the 4B5B coding scheme, identical to the one used by 100BASE-TX. The use of fiber optics results in longer cable runs than permissible with UTP. This enables 100BASE-FX to be used for connections between bridges, routers, and switches separated by distances greater than supported by UTP cable.

### 2.2.3 Token passing

Although we normally associate a token-passing local area network with a ring topology, this technology is also standardized for use on a bus.

*Bus operation*

When used with a bus topology the token bus LAN provides access to the network as if it were a ring. Under the IEEE 802.4 specification for a token bus network a token circulates from end-to-end on the bus and provides a workstation with the

**Table 2.7**  4B/5B code groups

| PCS code group 43210 | Name | MII (TXD/RXD) 3210 | Interpretation |
|---|---|---|---|
| DATA | | | |
| 11110 | 0 | 0000 | Data 0 |
| 01001 | 1 | 0001 | Data 1 |
| 10100 | 2 | 0010 | Data 2 |
| 10101 | 3 | 0011 | Data 3 |
| 01010 | 4 | 0100 | Data 4 |
| 01011 | 5 | 0101 | Data 5 |
| 01110 | 6 | 0110 | Data 6 |
| 01111 | 7 | 0111 | Data 7 |
| 10010 | 8 | 1000 | Data 8 |
| 10011 | 9 | 1001 | Data 9 |
| 10110 | A | 1010 | Data A |
| 10111 | B | 1011 | Data B |
| 11010 | C | 1100 | Data C |
| 11011 | D | 1101 | Data D |
| 11100 | E | 1110 | Data E |
| 11101 | F | 1111 | Data F |
| | | | |
| IDLE | | | |
| 1111 | I | | IDLE: |
| | | | Used as inter-Stream fill code |
| | | | |
| CONTROL | | | |
| 11000 | j | | Start-of-Stream Delimiter, Part 1 of 2; always used in pairs with K |
| 10001 | K | | Start-of-Stream Delimiter, Part 2 of 2; always used in pairs with J |
| 01101 | T | | End-of-Stream Delimiter, Part 1 or 2; always used in pairs with R |
| 00111 | R | | End-of-Stream Delimiter, Part 2 of 2; always used in pairs with T |
| | | | |
| INVALID | | | |
| 00100 | H | | Transmit Error; used to force signaling errors |
| 00000 | V | | Invalid code |
| 00001 | V | | Invalid code |
| 00010 | V | | Invalid code |
| 00011 | V | | Invalid code |
| 00101 | V | | Invalid code |
| 00110 | V | | Invalid code |
| 01000 | V | | Invalid code |
| 01100 | V | | Invalid code |
| 10000 | V | | Invalid code |
| 11001 | V | | Invalid code |

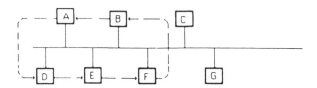

**Figure 2.21** Logical ring formation on a physical bus. Token passing on a physical bus enables a logical ring to be formed which may or may not include all stations on the bus

ability to use the bus for a predefined period of time to send or receive data. Under this standard all stations on the network can receive all signals transmitted, a condition known as broadcasting. However, the token access method can be structured to form a logical ring which bypasses one or more workstations as illustrated in Figure 2.21. In this illustration all stations can receive frames; however, stations C and G will not be able to initiate a transmission as they will never receive a token. Here a logical ring is formed consisting of workstations A, D, E, F and B. During normal operations a station which completes its use of a token passes it on to a designated station known as the successor. By passing the token from station to station the logical ring was formed as illustrated in Figure 2.21.

The IEEE 802.4 standard for a physical bus employing token passing as the access method is quite similar to the manufacturing automation protocol (MAP) developed by General Motors. Although this standard has achieved a high degree of usage in industrial applications, its use is considerably overshadowed by the use of a physical ring for token passing and the higher level of requirements to interconnect that type of network. Due to this we will focus our attention upon the Token-Ring.

*Ring operation*

Each device on a Token-Ring network obtains its connection to the network via a multistation access unit (MAU). The MAU is a passive device that commonly contains 10 connector receptacles as illustrated in Figure 2.22. Eight connectors are used to provide wiring connectivity between network stations, while the connectors on each end of the MAU provide the capability to connect one MAU to another, thus extending the Token-Ring.

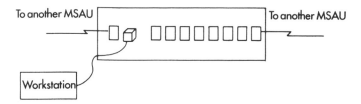

**Figure 2.22**  MAU connectivity

The MAU functions as a central control point for Token-Ring workstations. Its use facilitates the addition and removal of workstations from a Token-Ring network since the only cabling required is from the workstation to the MAU.

The cable from each workstation to the MAU is known as a lobe. The MAU contains relays that are operated by the voltage supplied by the Token-Ring adapter in each workstation. Thus, if a Token-Ring adapter should fail, the MAU can detect this by the loss of voltage which then opens the relay, in effect shedding the failing lobe from the remainder of the network.

### Data flow

Transmissions on a Token-Ring network follow a unidirectional path. Messages flow from one workstation adapter through other workstation adapters on a bit-by-bit basis until they reach their destination, with each intermediate workstation adapter receiving, regenerating and retransmitting each bit that flows on the network. Thus, workstation adapters function as repeaters in addition to performing many other activities that are discussed later in this section.

The MAU functions as a passive device, using the voltage provided by a workstation adapter to switch a relay. If an adapter fails, the relay is opened, disconnecting the lobe from the network.

### Network access, token and frame formats

A uniquely coded symbol known as a token is used to provide a workstation with permission to transmit data. To understand how network access is accomplished, let us first examine the token and frame formats used on a Token-Ring network.

Three types of transmission formats are supported on a Token-Ring network: token, abort and frame. The token format as illustrated in the top of Figure 2.23 is the mechanism by

(a)  Token format

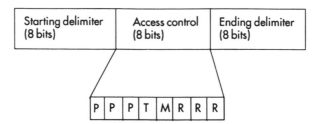

(b)  Abort token format

| Starting delimiter | Ending delimiter |
|---|---|

(c)  Information frame format

| Starting delimiter (8 bits) | Access control (8 bits) | Frame control (8 bits) | Destination address (48 bits) | Source address (48 bits) | Routing Information (optional) |
|---|---|---|---|---|---|

| Information variable | Frame check sequence (32 bits) | Ending delimiter (8 bits) | Frame status (8 bits) |
|---|---|---|---|

**Figure 2.23**  Token, abort, and frame formats. (P priority bits, T token bit, M monitor bit, R reservation bits)

which access to the ring is passed from one computer attached to the network to another device connected to the network. Here the token format consists of three bytes, of which the starting and ending delimiters are used to indicate the beginning and end of a token frame. The middle byte of a token frame is an access control byte. Three bits are used as a priority indicator, three bits are used as a reservation indicator, while one bit is used for the token bit and another bit position functions as the monitor bit.

When the token bit is set to a binary zero it indicates that the transmission is a token. When it is set to a binary one it indicates that data are being transmitted.

The second Token-Ring frame format signifies an abort token. In actuality there is no token, since this format is indicated by a starting delimiter followed by an ending delimiter. The transmission of an abort token is used to abort a previous transmission. The format of an abort token is illustrated in Figure 2.23b.

The third type of Token-Ring frame format occurs when a workstation seizes a free token. At that time the token format is converted into an information frame which includes the addition of frame control, addressing data, an error detection field and a frame status field. The format of the information frame is illustrated in Figure 2.23c. By examining each of the fields in the information frame we will also examine the token and token abort frames due to the commonality of fields between each frame.

### Starting/ending delimiters

The starting and ending delimiters mark the beginning and ending of a token or frame. Each delimiter consists of a unique code pattern which identifies it to the network.

### Access control

The second field in both token and frame formats is the access control byte. As illustrated at the top of Figure 2.23, this byte consists of four subfields and serves as the controlling mechanism for gaining access to the network. When a free token circulates the network the access control field represents one-third of the length of the frame since it is prefixed by the start delimiter and suffixed by the end delimiter.

The lowest priority that can be specified by the priority bits in the access control byte is zero (000), while the highest is seven (111), providing eight levels of priority. Workstations have a default priority of three, while bridges have a default priority of five. To reserve a token a workstation inserts its priority level in the priority reservation subfield. Unless another workstation with a higher priority bumps the requesting workstation, the reservation will be honored and the requesting station will obtain the token. If the token bit is set to one, this serves as an indication that a frame follows instead of the ending delimiter. The monitor bit is used to prevent a token with a priority exceeding 0 or a frame from continuously circulating on the Token-Ring. This bit is transmitted as a 0 in all tokens and frames, except for a device on the network which functions as an active monitor and thus obtains the capability to inspect and modify that bit.

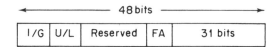

**Figure 2.24** Destination address subfields (I/G individual or group bit address identifier, U/L universally or locally administered bit identifier, FA functional address)

The active monitor is the device that has the highest address on the network. All other stations on the network are considered as standby monitors and watch the active monitor.

The function of the active monitor is to determine if a token has been lost, and if so, generate a new one. To accomplish this the active monitor sets the monitor count bit as a frame goes by. If a destination workstation fails or has its power turned off the frame will circulate back to the active monitor, where it is then removed from the network. In the event that the active monitor should fail or be turned off, the standby monitors watch the active monitor by looking for an active monitor frame. If one does not appear within 7 s the standby monitor that has the highest network address then takes over as the active monitor. The last field in the access control byte, reservation bits, enables devices on the network to request the next token to be issued at the priority level of the device.

*Frame control*

The frame control field informs a receiving device on the network of the type of frame and how it should be interpreted. Frames can be either logical link control (LLC) or reference physical link functions according to the IEEE 802.5 media access control (MAC) standard. As previously noted in this chapter, a logical link control frame includes control information, while a media access control frame carries data.

*Destination address*

The destination address field is made up of five subfields as illustrated in Figure 2.24. The first bit in the destination address identifies the destination as an individual workstation or as a group of one or more workstations. The latter provides the capability for a message to be broadcast to a group of workstations.

The universally administered address is a unique address permanently encoded into an adapter's ROM. Similar to

**Figure 2.25** Source address field. (RI routing information bit identifier, U/L universally or locally administered bit identifier)

Ethernet, the IEEE assigns blocks of addresses to each vendor manufacturing Token-Ring equipment, which ensures that Token-Ring adapter cards manufactured by different vendors are uniquely defined.

A key problem with the use of universally administered addresses is the requirement to change software coding in a mainframe computer whenever a workstation connected to the mainframe via a gateway is added or removed from the network. To avoid constant software changes, locally administrated addressing can be used. This type of addressing temporarily overrides universally administrated addressing; however, the user is now responsible for insuring the uniqueness of each address.

The functional address subfield in the destination address identifies the function associated with the destination address, such as a bridge, active monitor or configuration report server.

### Source address

The source address field always represents an individual address which specifies the adapter card responsible for the transmission. The source address field consists of three subfields as illustrated in Figure 2.25.

The routing information bit identifier identifies the fact that routing information is contained in the routing information field. This bit is set when a frame will be routed across a bridge.

### Routing information

The Routing Information Field (RIF) is optional and is included in a frame when the RI subfield of the source address field is set. The RIF is of variable length and contains a control subfield and one or more route fields when included in a frame. This is used to control the flow of frames across one or more bridges.

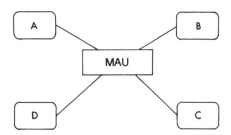

**Figure 2.26** Sample network

*Information field*

The information field is used to contain Token-Ring commands and responses as well as carry user data. This field is of variable length and can be considered to represent the higher level protocol enveloped in a Token-Ring frame.

In the IBM implementation of the IEEE 802.5 Token-Ring standard the maximum length of the information field depends upon the Token-Ring adapter used and the operating rate of the network. Token-Ring adapters with 64 Kbytes of memory can handle up to 4.5 Kbytes on a 4 Mbps network and up to 18 Kbytes on a 16 Mbps network.

*Frame check sequence*

The frame check sequence field contains four bytes which provide the mechanism for checking the accuracy of frames flowing on the network. The cyclic redundancy check data included in the frame check sequence field covers the frame control, destination address, source address, routing information and information fields. If an adapter computes a cyclic redundancy check that does not match the data contained in the frame check sequence field of a frame, the destination adapter discards the frame information and sets an error bit indicator. This error bit indicator actually represents a ninth bit position of the ending delimiter and serves to inform the transmitting station that the data was received in error.

*Frame status*

The frame status field contains three subfields that are duplicated for accuracy purposes since they reside outside of CRC checking. One field is used to denote if an address was recognized, while a second field indicates if the frame was copied at its destination. Each of these fields is one bit in length. The third field, which is two bit positions in length, is currently reserved for future use.

### Data flow example

Now that we have examined the token and frame formats, let us examine the flow of data on a Token-Ring network. For simplicity, let us assume our network consists of four work-stations labeled A, B, C and D as indicated in Figure 2.26.

Let us assume that station A wants to send data to station C. First, station A must wait until it receives a free token. Then, that workstation changes the token bit from a 0 to a 1 to indicate that a full frame is to flow over the network. Station A then adds destination and source addressing information into those fields and data into the information field, after which station A transmits the frame.

Since data flow is unidirectional, the frame bit flows from the lobe connecting station A to the MAU to station B. Since the destination address contained in the frame is C, the adapter in station B regenerates the frame back to the MAU, from which it flows on the lobe to workstation C.

Station C recognizes its address in the destination address field and copies the frame. To signify this operation, station C changes the address recognized and frame copied subfields in the frame status field and then retransmits the frame back onto the network. When the originating station, which was A, receives the frame it originated, it notes the frame's address recognized and frame copied subfields are set. Then station A removes the frame from the network and transmits a free token onto the network. This enables the next station with data to transmit to grab the token. Since a transmitting station follows frame removal with the generation of a free token, this eliminates a workstation from monopolizing traffic on the network.

#### Early token release

When IBM introduced its 16 Mbps Token-Ring network in 1988 it introduced a new token passing technique which considerably improves network performance. Known as early token release, this technique is restricted to IBM 16 Mbps Token-Ring networks and was standardized as an extension to the original IEEE 802.5 standard. The basis for early token release is the fact that a

16 Mbps network that has only one frame circulating the network at a time can be considered to have a large amount of unused idle time on the ring. Hence, there is actually room for two different users' sets of data to simultaneously circulate the ring. In recognition of this a station that captures a token and transmits a frame can then generate a free token. This process, known as early token release, improves the performance level obtainable on 16 Mbps networks. However, the use of early token release requires a ring length of approximately 3000 feet to ensure that there is a sufficient delay in circulation time so the token released early does not interfere with a previously transmitted token.

### 2.2.4 FDDI

Fiber Distributed Data Interface (FDDI) is a local networking standard which provides a 100 Mbps operating rate. In addition, due to the design of FDDI networks which incorporate counter-rotating rings, reliability is increased, since one ring functions as a backup to the other.

Work on FDDI dates from 1982, during which both vendors and standard bodies recognized the need for higher speed LAN products and standards to govern the operation of those products. The FDDI standard was developed by the American National Standards Institute (ANSI) X3T9.5 Task Group.

The original intention of FDDI standards organizations was for the development of specifications for fiber optic media, optical transmitters and receivers, frame formats, protocols, and media access. However, recent developments in the use of twisted-pair have expanded the operation of FDDI to operate over that transmission medium. Known as CDDI, with the C referring to copper, this technique generated a considerable amount of interest. Several vendors now market FDDI over twisted-pair products, however, the use of such products results in a significant limitation on cable distance in comparison with FDDI that can support a ring distance of approximately 100 miles, sufficient to more than cover a large campus or industrial complex.

*Advantages*

The major advantages of FDDI relate to its operating rate and reliability. FDDI provides an approximate eight- to ten-fold increase in operating rates over previously developed local area networks. This makes an FDDI network an attractive mechanism to provide an interconnection capability to link lower speed networks as well as to interconnect minicomputers and mainframes via an attachment to their high speed channels. When functioning as a mechanism to interconnect lower speed local area networks, an FDDI LAN serves as a backbone net. One example of its use would be the situation where each floor in a building has its own local area network. An FDDI LAN might then be routed vertically within the building, providing a high speed link between individual networks on each floor.

As previously mentioned, the FDDI standard specified dual fiber optic counter-rotating rings. The dual rings provide an architecture which permits redundancy which can negate the effect of a network failure. In fact, the FDDI standard defines a ring self-heading mechanism which enables stations to identify a failure and take corrective action. In doing so a station that identifies a cable fault would wrap an incoming signal on its healthy side onto an outgoing fiber. Its neighbor on the other side of the fault would also wrap away from the failure, resulting in a dual ring being converted into a single ring which maintains network connectivity. This mechanism will be illustrated later in this section once we review the basic components of an FDDI network. Other advantages of FDDI primarily relate to its use of optical media. Those advantages include the ability to install optical cable without the use of a conduit, the extended transmission distance of an optical system, its immunity to electrical interference, and a high degree of security, since an optical cable is almost impossible to tap.

## Hardware components

An FDDI network uses a ring–star topology. Similar to the IEEE 802.5 Token-Ring standard, a rotating token is used to provide stations with permission to transmit data. When an FDDI station wants to transmit information it waits until it detects the token and captures it. Once the station controls the token it can transmit either until it has no more data to send or until a token holding timer expires. When either situation occurs, the station then releases the token onto the ring so that it can be used by the next station that has data to transmit. This token passing technique is more formally known as a timed-token passing technique and uses bandwidth more efficiently than the 802.5 token passing method. This is because only one token and one frame can be present on a Token-Ring network. In comparison, although only one token is present on an FDDI network at any time, multiple frames from one or more stations can be traversing an FDDI network.

Access to an FDDI network is accomplished through the use of three types of station: a Single Attached Station (SAS) and two types of Dual Attached Station (DAS).

### Dual Attached Station

A Dual Attached Station connects to both counter rotating rings used to form an FDDI ring. Each DAS contains two defined optical connection pairs. One pair, called the A interface, contains one primary ring input and the secondary ring output. The second pair, called the B interface, contains the primary ring output and the secondary ring input. Through the use of two optical transceivers each DAS can transmit and receive data on each ring.

A second type of DAS is known as a concentrator. In addition to the previously described A and B interfaces, a DAS concentrator contains a series of extra ports that are called M, or Master ports. The M ports on a DAS concentrator provide connectivity to Single Attached Stations.

### Single Attached Station

In comparison to Dual Attached Stations that provide a connection to the dual FDDI rings, a Single Attached Station can only be connected to a single ring. The connection of Single Attached Stations to a DAS concentrator can resemble a star topology, even though the interconnection of DAS and DAS concentrators forms a ring. Since a Single Attached Station only contains a single optical transceiver, its cost is less than that of a Dual Attached Station. However, its inability to connect to the dual ring lowers its reliability in comparison to the connection of workstations to an FDDI network through a Dual Attached Station.

Figure 2.27 illustrates the major components of an FDDI network as well as how a ring can be reconfigured in the event of a cable fault or DAS failure. In this example, it was assumed that a cable fault occurred between the upper right and extreme right Dual Attached Stations. Each of those stations has the

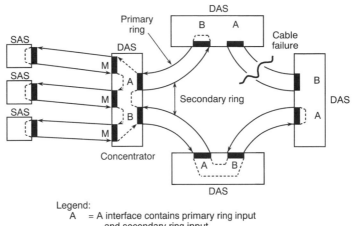

Legend:
A    = A interface contains primary ring input
        and secondary ring input
B    = B interface contains primary ring output
        and secondary ring input
M    = Master port
DAS = Dual attached station
SAS = Single attached station

**Figure 2.27** FDDI ring operation during cable fault failure. Two dual attched stations can perform a wrap operation to convert a dual ring into a single ring which bypasses a cable or device failure

capability to monitor light levels and recognize a cable failure. By two adjacent stations wrapping away from the failure, the dual ring becomes converted into a single ring and connectivity is restored. When the failure condition is corrected the restoration of an appropriate light level causes each DAS to remove the previously implemented wrap and restores the network to its dual ring operation.

### Encoding and signaling

FDDI was the first LAN to use 4B5B encoding with NRZI signaling, enabling a signaling rate of 125 MHZ as well as ensuring that a transition occurs twice for each five bit code. The success of the use of 4B5B encoding with NRZI signaling resulted in the FDDI physical layer being adapted by 100BASE-TX and other local area networks. Although each implementation of 4B5B coding results in the ability to specify 32 unique codes, FDDI's use of this coding technique slightly differs from 100BASE-TX, and other LANs also implement the coding interpretation with slight differences. Table 2.8 lists the FDDI implementation of 4B5B coding. In examining the entries in

**Table 2.8**   FDDI 4B/5B codes

| Function/4-bit group | 5B code | Symbol |
|---|---|---|
| Starting delimiter | | |
| First symbol of sequential SD pair | 11000 | J |
| Second symbol of sequential SD pair | 10001 | K |
| Ending delimiter | 01101 | T |
| Data symbols | | |
|   0000 | 11110 | 0 |
|   0001 | 01001 | 1 |
|   0010 | 10100 | 2 |
|   0011 | 10101 | 3 |
|   0100 | 01010 | 4 |
|   0101 | 01011 | 5 |
|   0110 | 01110 | 6 |
|   0111 | 01111 | 7 |
|   1000 | 10010 | 8 |
|   1001 | 10011 | 9 |
|   1010 | 10110 | 10 |
|   1011 | 10111 | 11 |
|   1100 | 11010 | 12 |
|   1101 | 11011 | 13 |
|   1110 | 11100 | 14 |
|   1111 | 11101 | 15 |
| Control indicators | | |
|   Logical ZERO (reset) | 00111 | R |
|   Logical ONE (set) | 11001 | S |
| Line status symbols | | |
|   Quiet | 00000 | Q |
|   Idle | 11111 | I |
|   Halt | 00100 | H |

Table 2.8 you will note that 24 4B5B codes are defined. In comparison, if you examine Table 2.7 you will note that 22 codes are defined. In addition, a comparison of the two tables indicates slight differences in the function of certain codes. When we next examine the FDDI frame formats we will also examine the use of certain 4B5B code functions.

## Frame formats

Similarly to Token-Ring networks, there are distinct frames and frame formats that are used on FDDI networks for information transfer. Figure 2.28 illustrates two FDDI frame formats used to transfer information. Like Token-Ring networks, the basic FDDI

**a. FDDI Token**

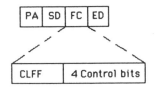

**b. FDDI Frame**

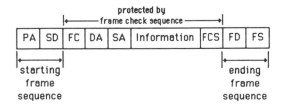

PA – Preamble
SD – Starting delimiter
FC – Frame control
ED – Ending delimiter
DA – Destination address
SA – Source address
FCS – Frame check sequence
FS – Frame status
C – Class bit
L – Length of address fields
FF – Format
Control bits – depend upon frame type

**Figure 2.28** FDDI frame formats

frame can convey MAC control data and LLC information. In addition, a station management frame permits management information to be transported between stations and higher level processes. As defined by ANSI, the station management (SMT) standard is used to control the FDDI PMD, PHY, and MAC layers. Services provided by SMT include fault detection, fault isolation, and ring reconfiguration. Data carried by SMT frames can be used by such higher level processes as Simple Network Management Protocol (SNMP) services to permit network administrators to monitor and control each FDDI network node from a central console. In addition to collecting data, SMT provides network administrators with the ability to dynamically alter the network by adding or removing predefined stations. Thus, SMT frames carry both monitoring and control information.

**FDDI token**

As illustrated in the top portion of Figure 2.28, the FDDI token consists of five fields. The preamble field is variable in length and is formed by 16 or more 5B I symbols. The starting delimiter field consists of the 5B J symbol followed by the 5B K symbol. That field is followed by the frame control field which identifies the type of frame.

The frame control field is eight bits in length, with the class and length of address fields bit positions used to indicate one of two possible settings per bit position. When the class bit is set to 0, this indicates an asynchronous class of transmission, whereas setting the class bit to 1 indicates a synchronous class of transmission. The length of address fields bit indicates the use of 48 bit addressing fields when set to 0 and the use of 16 bit addressing fields when set to 1. The two format bits are used to indicate a MAC or SMT frame when set to 00 or an LLC frame when set to 01. A setting of 10 is implementation dependent, whereas a setting of 11 is currently reserved for future use. The second half of the frame control field consists of four control bits whose values are dependent upon the type of frame defined by the format bits.

There are two special values that can be assigned to the frame control field: hex 80 and hex C0. If the frame control field is set to hex 80 it indicates an unrestricted token, while a value of hex C0 in this eight-bit field indicates a restricted token. The restricted token is generated by a station on an FDDI network that wishes to communicate with another station using all the asynchronous bandwidth available on the network. At the end of this section we will examine the allocation of bandwidth on an FDDI network and the two classes of traffic on that network, asynchronous and synchronous.

When the frame control field is directly followed by the ending delimiter an FDDI token is formed. Here the ending delimiter is the 4B5B T symbol.

**FDDI frame**

As indicated in Figure 2.28, the first three fields of the FDDI token and frame are the same. Thereafter, the frame contains destination and source address fields which identify the frame recipient and frame originator, respectively. Each address field can be either 16 or 48 bits in length but must be of similar length.

The source address field is followed by a variable information field that can range in length from 0 to 4472 bytes. That field is followed by a frame check sequence (FCS) field 32 bits in length which protects all data from the frame control field through the information field. The ending delimiter and frame status fields function as the ending FDDI frame sequence, with the ending delimiter formed by the use of the 4B5B T symbol which consists of the bit pattern 01101.

*Bandwidth allocation*

In a Token-Ring network, access is obtained by the setting of priority and reservation bits which enables a station to acquire a token. Once a token has been acquired, it is converted into a single frame to transport a unit of information. In comparison, a token flowing on an FDDI network is removed from the network by a station that has data to transmit, a process referred to as absorption. Once a token is absorbed, the absorbing station can transmit one or more frames prior to returning the token onto the network, with the number of frames that can be transmitted based upon the frame size and the setting of timers within the station. Thus, any discussion of FDDI bandwidth allocation must consider the timers supported by each station in an FDDI network. As those timers, as well as the frame control field of an FDDI token, govern the two classes of traffic that can be carried by an FDDI network, a logical place to initiate an explanation of FDDI bandwidth allocation is by explaining the two classes of traffic supported by this network. Once we have done this we will then examine the timers supported by each FDDI station and then use the preceding to discuss how an FDDI network allocates bandwidth capacity.

**Classes of traffic**

FDDI defines two classes of traffic, asynchronous and synchronous. These classes of transmission should not be confused with an asynchronous and synchronous mode of transmission. The asynchronous class of transmission is transmission that occurs when the token holding rules of an FDDI network permit transmission. In comparison, the synchronous class of transmission results in a guaranteed percentage of the ring's bandwidth allocated for a particular transmission. Once synchronous bandwidth is allocated, the remaining bandwidth becomes available for asynchronously transmitted frames. That bandwidth is shared by all stations in a fair and equitable manner based upon the use of timers.

**Timers**

The control of the amount of asynchronous and synchronous traffic that can be transmitted by a station is governed by FDDI's timed token access protocol. This protocol is based upon the use of timers used by each station to regulate their operation. These timers include a token rotation timer (TRT), token holding timer (THT), and valid transmission timer (TVX).

*Token rotation timer*

The TRT is used to time the period between the receipt of tokens. Under the timed token access protocol, stations expect to see a token within a specified period of time, referred to as the target token rotation time (TTRT). The value for the TTRT is set when a station initializes itself on the ring and is the same for all stations on the ring.

When a token passes a station, the station sets its TRT to the value of the TTRT and then decrements its TRT timer. If the TRT timer expires prior to the token returning to the station, a counter known as the late counter is incremented. The decision on whether a station can transmit a synchronous or asynchronous class of traffic depends upon the value of the TRT and the value of a counter known as the late counter.

When a token arrives at a station three events occur which govern the allocation of bandwidth. First, upon receiving a token a station can initiate the transmission of synchronous frames. Whether or not it does so, and the number of frames it can transmit, depend upon several factors that will be discussed shortly.

*Token holding timer*

If the token is received earlier than expected, the token rotation time (TRT) timer will be positive and the station will store that value in its token holding timer (THT). Thus, the value of the THT timer represents the amount of time by which the token was received earlier than expected. Finally, the station resets the TRT timer to the value assigned to the target token rotation timer (TTRT) and begins to decrement that timer.

### Synchronous transmission

As previously mentioned, the receipt of a token enables a station to initiate the transmission of synchronous frames. The ability of a station to transmit synchronous frames depends upon whether or not the station was enabled by an application for synchronous transmission. If enabled, the number of synchronous frames that the station can transmit is based upon the size of each frame to be transmitted and the time allocated for synchronous transmission. The frame size governs the amount of time required to place a frame on the ring, while the total time over which the station can transmit synchronously is based upon the value of the station's synchronous allocation timer. That timer is set to zero when a station is not enabled by an application for synchronous transmission. When enabled for synchronous transmission, the value of the synchronous allocation timer can be different for each station on the ring; however, the sum of all synchronous allocation timers on the active stations on the ring must always be less than the target token rotation time.

If enabled for synchronous transmission, a station will either transmit all the frames it has synchronously, or only those frames that can be transmitted within the allocated synchronous allocation timer value. When that timer expires, or all synchronous frames are transmitted and the timer has not expired, the station may then be able to transmit asynchronous frames.

### Asynchronous transmission

The decision on whether or not a station can transmit asynchronous frames is based upon the value of the late counter. If the value of the late counter is zero, which means that the TRT timer did not expire, asynchronous frames can be transmitted for the length of time stored in the token holding timer (THT). When the value of that timer reaches zero the token must then be placed back onto the ring.

During both synchronous and asynchronous transmission, the token rotation timer (TRT) continues to decrement. If both synchronous and asynchronous transmissions were stopped due to the expiration of the synchronous allocation timer and the token holding timer, and other stations have data to send, the TRT can be expected to expire prior to the token reappearing at the station. When this occurs, the token will be late, the TRT will be zero, and the THT will also be set to zero. With a value of zero in the token holding timer the station cannot transmit any asynchronous frames the next time it receives a token. Thus, the timed token access protocol penalizes a station that transmitted its fully allocated amount of traffic; however, the penalty only applies to asynchronous traffic and a station can always transmit synchronous traffic when it receives a token.

If the station is penalized, the next token will arrive early and the station's late counter will be decremented. Once the value of the late counter has reached zero, the station can again begin to transmit asynchronous traffic.

The preceding bandwidth allocation method guarantees an amount of ring capacity to synchronous traffic. Asynchronous traffic is only transmitted when there is spare capacity on the ring, and the use of the previously described counters and timers provides a level of fairness for asynchronous transmission.

In discussing the composition of the frame control field, we indicated that a setting of hex 80 indicates a restricted token. The use of this type of token provides another mechanism for allocating asynchronous transmission by permitting two stations to use all the asynchronous bandwidth available on the ring. When one station wishes to communicate with another station using all of the available asynchronous bandwidth, it transmits its asynchronous frames and then releases a restricted token. Due to FDDI rules, only the last station that receives an asynchronous frame can use a restricted token for asynchronous transmission, thus, this enables two stations to continue transmitting to one another. As the restricted token is only applicable to asynchronous transmission, any station that has synchronous traffic can use that token, ensuring that the guaranteed level of synchronous bandwidth remains available to all stations on the ring.

### Transmission example

To illustrate the FDDI capacity allocation algorithm, let us assume that the target token rotation timer was set to 100 milliseconds for all stations, while the synchronous allocation timer was set to 10 milliseconds for our station. Table 2.9 lists the settings of the different station timers and the occurrence of different events during the capacity allocation process for a station on an FDDI network based upon several predefined events occurring on the ring. By examining the entries in Table

**Table 2.9** FDDI capacity allocation process example

1. Token arrives at station.
2. TRT is set to value of TTRT (100 ms).
3. Token absorbed by station.
4. Synchronous traffic transmitted for 10 ms (synchronous allocation timer value).
5. Token released onto ring.
6. Token reappears 50 ms later.
7. Token absorbed.
8. TRT now 40 ms due to the 10 ms transmission of synchronous traffic and 50 ms on ring.
9. Token holding timer set to TRT value (40 ms).
10. TRT reset to 100 and begins to decrement.
11. Synchronous traffic again sent for 10 ms.
12. Asynchronous traffic sent for 40 ms (THT value).
13. TRT now has a value of 50 (100 − 10 − 40).
14. Token released.
15. Assume that other stations transmit data and token reappears after 70 ms.
16. TRT expires and late counter incremented to a value of 1.
17. THT set to a value of 0.
18. Assume no synchronous traffic to be sent. Asynchronous traffic cannot be sent since TRT expired and THT now has a value of 0.
19. TRT reset to 100.
20. Assume that token reappears in 30 ms.
21. TRT now set to 70 ms. Although token is early the late count has a value of 1. Thus, token is considered to be late and the station can only transmit synchronous traffic.
22. Token absorbed.
23. Station transmits synchronous traffic for 10 ms (synchronous allocation timer value).
24. Late count value decremented to 0.
25. Token placed back on ring.
26. Assume token reappears 40 ms later.
27. TRT now set to 70 − 40, or 30 ms. Since late count is 0, station can transmit asynchronous traffic for up to 30 ms.

2.9, readers will obtain an appreciation of the method by which timers and the late counter govern the ability of stations to transmit asynchronous and synchronous traffic.

*Status*

FDDI can be considered to represent a mature backbone LAN technology that has received a high degree of acceptance by industry, academia, and government agencies. Although the use of Fast Ethernet, LAN switches, and ATM reduced the market for FDDI, its allocation of bandwidth and token rotation predictability will result in a continued market for this product. In addition, as we will shortly note when we next discuss ATM, the use of that technology as a backbone for Ethernet or Token-Ring networks requires a process known as LAN emulation which can have certain performance limitations that are not associated with the use of FDDI.

### 2.2.5 Logical link control frame format

As mentioned earlier in this chapter, the IEEE subdivided the Data Link Layer of the ISO Reference Model into Media Access Control (MAC) and Logical Link Control (LLC) sublayers.

The logical link control (LLC) sublayer was defined under the IEEE 802.2 standard to make the method of link control independent of a specific access method. Thus, the 802.2 method of link control spans Ethernet (IEEE 802.3), Token Bus (IEEE 802.4), and Token-Ring (IEEE 802.5) local area networks. Functions performed by the LLC include generating and interpreting commands to control the flow of data, including recovery operations, for when a transmission error is detected.

Under the 802.5 Token-Ring standard each type of frame is specified by an appropriate setting in the Token-Ring Access Control Field. When an LLC frame is specified it is transported in the Information field as a sequence of four subfields. Under the 802.3 standard link control information is carried in the data field as an LLC Protocol Data Unit. Although Ethernet does not provide a direct mechanism to identify that the frame transports LLC data, similarly to Token-Ring the Ethernet LLC Protocol Data Unit (PDU) also contains the same four fields. Since Ethernet frame determination requires the examination of the contents of the Length field and the composition of LLC PDUs and LLC frames which are the same, we will primarily focus our attention upon Ethernet's LLC although the discussion of LLC types and classes of service presented in this section is applicable to both networks.

Link control information is carried within the data field of an IEEE 802.3 frame as an LLC Protocol Data Unit. Figure 2.29 illustrates the relationship between the IEEE 802.3 frame and the LLC Protocol Data Unit.

Service Access Points (SAPs) function much like a mailbox. Since the LLC layer is bound below by the MAC sublayer and

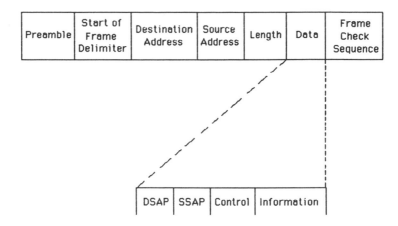

**Figure 2.29** Formation of LLC protocol data unit. Control information is carried within a MAC frame

bound above by the network layer, SAPs provide a mechanism for exchanging information between the LLC layer and the MAC and network layers. For example, from the network layer perspective, a SAP represents the place to leave messages about the services requested by an application.

The Destination Services Access Point (DSAP) is one byte in length, and is used to specify the receiving network layer process. As an IEEE 802.3 frame does not include a type field, the DSAP field is used to denote the destination upper-layer protocol carried within the frame. For example, the DSAP hex value EO indicates that the data field contains NetWare data.

The Source Service Access Point (SSAP) is also one byte in length. The SSAP specifies the sending network layer process. Since the destination and source protocols must be the same, the value of the SSAP field will always match the value of the DSAP field. Both DSAP and SSAP addresses are assigned by the IEEE. For example, the hex address FF represents a DSAP broadcast address.

The control field contains information concerning the type and class of service being used for transporting LLC data. For example, a hex value of 03 when NetWare is being transported indicates that the frame is using an unnumbered format for connectionless services.

### Types and classes of service

Under the 802.2 standard, there are three types of service available for sending and receiving LLC data. These types are

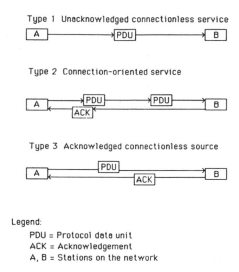

**Figure 2.30**  Local link control service types

discussed in the next three sections. Figure 2.30 provides a visual summary of the operation of each LLC service type.


### Type 1

Type 1 is an unacknowledged connectionless service. The term connectionless refers to the fact that transmission does not occur between two devices as if a logical connection were established. Instead, transmission flows on the channel to all stations; however, only the destination address acts upon the data. As the name of this service implies, there is no provision for flow control or for error recovery. Therefore, this is an unreliable service.

Despite those shortcomings, Type 1 is the most commonly used service for IEEE 802 LANs since most protocol suites use a reliable transport mechanism at the transport layer, thus eliminating the need for reliability at the link layer. In addition, by eliminating the time needed to establish a virtual link and the overhead of acknowledgments, a Type 1 service can provide a greater throughput than other LLC types of service.


### Type 2

The Type 2 connection-oriented service requires that a logical link be established between the sender and the receiver prior to information transfer. Once the logical connection has been established, data will flow between the sender and receiver until either party terminates the connection. During data transfer, a Type 2 LLC service provides all the functions lacking in a Type 1 service, using a sliding window for flow control. When IBM's SNA data is transported on a LAN, it uses connection-oriented services. Type 2 LLC is also commonly referred to as LLC 2.

### Type 3

The Type 3 acknowledged connectionless service contains provisions for the setup and disconnection of transmission; it acknowledges individual frames using the stop-and-wait flow control method. Type 3 service is primarily used in an automated factory process-control environment, where one central computer communicates with many remote devices that typically have a limited storage capacity.

### Classes of service

All logical link control stations support Type 1 operations. This level of support is known as Class I service. The classes of service supported by LLC indicate the combinations of the three LLC service types supported by a station. Class I supports Type 1 service, Class II supports both Type 1 and Type 2, Class III supports Type 1 and Type 3 service, and Class IV supports all three service types. Since service Type 1 is supported by all classes, it can be considered a least common denominator, enabling all stations to communicate using a common form of service.

## Other Ethernet frame types

Two additional frame types that warrant discussion are Ethernet-802.3 and Ethernet-SNAP. In actuality, both types of frames represent a logical variation of the IEEE 802.3 frame in which the composition of the data field varies from the composition of the LLC protocol data unit previously illustrated in Figure 2.29.

### Ethernet-802.3

The Ethernet-802.3 frame represents a proprietary subdivision of the IEEE 802.3 data field to transport NetWare. Ethernet-

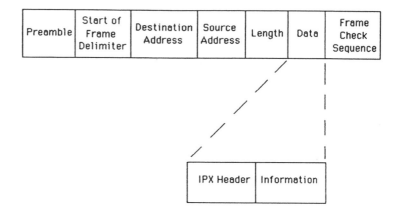

An Ethernet-802.3 frame subdivides the data field into an
IPX header field and an information field.

**Figure 2.31**   Novell's NetWare Ethernet-802.3 frame

802.3 is one of several types of frame that can be used to
transport NetWare. The actual frame type used is defined at
system setup by binding NetWare to a specific type of frame.

Figure 2.31 illustrates the format of the Ethernet-802.3
frame. Due to the absence of LLC fields, this frame is often
referred to as raw 802.3.

For those using or thinking of using NetWare, a word of
caution is in order concerning frame types. Novell uses the term
Ethernet-802.2 to refer to the IEEE 802.3 frame. Thus, if you set
up NetWare for Ethernet-802.2 frames, in effect your network is
IEEE 802.3-compliant.

### Ethernet-SNAP

The Ethernet Subnetwork Access Protocol (Ethernet-SNAP)
frame, unlike the Ethernet-802.3 frame, can be used to
transport several protocols. AppleTalk Phase II, NetWare, and
TCP/IP protocols can be transported due to the inclusion of an
Ethernet type field in the Ethernet-SNAP frame. Thus, SNAP can
be considered as an extension that permits vendors to create
their own Ethernet protocol transports. Ethernet-SNAP was
defined by the IEEE-802.1 committee to facilitate interoperability between IEEE 802.3 LANs and Ethernet LANs. This was
accomplished, as we will soon note, by the inclusion of a type
field in the Ethernet-SNAP frame.

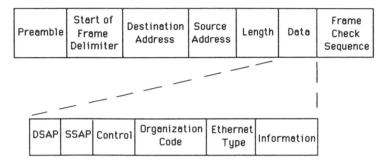

**Figure 2.32** Ethernet-SNAP frame format

Figure 2.32 illustrates the format of an Ethernet-SNAP frame. Although the format of this frame is based upon the IEEE 802.3 frame format, it does not use DSAP and SSAP mailbox facilities and the control field. Instead, it places specific values in those fields to indicate that the frame is a SNAP frame.

The value hex AA is placed into the DSAP and SSAP fields, and hex 03 is placed into the control field to indicate that a SNAP frame is being transported. The hex 03 value in the control field defines the use of an unnumbered format, which is the only format supported by a SNAP frame.

The organization code field refers to the organizational body that assigned the value placed in the following field, the Ethernet type field. A hex value of 00-00-00 in the organization code field indicates that Xerox assigned the value in the Ethernet type field. Through the use of the Ethernet-SNAP frame you obtain the ability to transport multiple protocols in a manner similar to the original Ethernet frame that used the type field for this purpose.

**Frame determination**

Through software, a receiving station can determine the type of frame and correctly interpret the data carried in the frame. To accomplish this, the value of the two bytes that follow the source address is first examined. If the value is greater than 1500, this indicates the occurrence of an Ethernet frame. If the value is less than or equal to 1,500, the frame can be either a pure IEEE 802.3 frame or a variation of that frame. Thus, more bytes must be examined.

If the next two bytes have the hex value FF:FF, the frame is a NetWare Ethernet-802.3 frame. This is because the IPX header has hex FF:FF in the checksum field contained in the

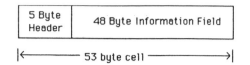

The ATM cell is of fixed length, consisting of a 48-byte
information field and five-byte header.

**Figure 2.33**   The ATM cell

first two bytes in the IPX header. If the two bytes contain the
hex value AA:AA, this indicates that it is an Ethernet-SNAP
frame. Any other value determined to reside in those two
bytes then indicates that the frame must be an Ethernet-
802.3 frame.

## 2.3 ATM

Previously in this chapter we briefly discussed the basic
operation of Asynchronous Transfer Mode (ATM), noting that it
normally represents a switch-based, connection-oriented technology. In this section we will examine the rationale for the
operation and utilization of ATM. In doing so, we will focus our
attention upon the use of ATM for both desktop to desktop data
transfer as well as its use as a backbone transmission
mechanism to interconnect connectionless LANs, such as
Ethernet and Token-Ring.

### 2.3.1 Rationale

ATM was developed as a transmission technology that can
support both voice and data on a common network infrastructure. To accomplish this, ATM uses a fixed size transmission unit known as a cell.

*The ATM cell*

The ATM cell is relatively short, containing a 48 byte information
field and a 5 byte header. Figure 2.33 illustrates the basic
composition of the ATM cell.

The selection of a relatively short 53 byte cell was based upon the necessity to minimize the effect of data upon such time dependent transmissions as voice and real-time video. For example, if a variable frame length technology such as Ethernet or Token-Ring is used, it becomes possible for a lengthy data transmission that fills a frame to its maximum length and which gains access to a network between a sequence of digitized voice filled frames to delay the receipt of succeeding frames so that, upon their receipt, the converted voice sounds distorted by time. ATM is designed to eliminate such problems as cells are relatively short, resulting in cells transporting voice being able to arrive on a regular basis.

A second significant advantage associated with the use of fixed length cells concerns the design of switching equipment. ATM logic can be developed as firmware embedded in hardware, enabling faster processing at a lower cost than if software was used to perform ATM operations.

In addition to its relatively short cell length facilitating the integration of voice and data, ATM provides three additional benefits. Those benefits are in the areas of scalability, transparency, and traffic classification.

*Scalability*

ATM cells can be transported on LANs and WANs at a variety of operating rates. This enables different hardware, such as LAN and WAN switches to support a common cell format, a feature lacking with other communications technologies. Within a few years, an ATM cell generated on a 25 Mbps LAN will be able to be transported from the LAN via a T1 line at 1.544 Mbps to a central office where it might be switched onto a 2.4 Gbps SONET network for transmission on the communications carrier infrastructure, with the message maintained in the same series of 53 byte cells, with only the operating rate scaled for a particular transport mechanism.

*Transparency*

The ATM cell is application-transparent, enabling it to transport voice, data, images, and video. Due to its application transparency, ATM enables networks to be constructed to support any type of application or application mix instead of requiring organizations to establish separate networks for different applications.

*Traffic classification*

Five classes of traffic are supported by ATM, including one constant bit rate, three types of variable bit rate, and a user-definable class. As ATM standards were further developed, supports for two traffic classes were merged together into a common ATM adaptation layer (AAL) protocol. Later in this section we will discuss the role of the AAL and its support for different classes of traffic.

By associating such metrics as cell transit delay, cell loss ratio, and cell delay variation to a traffic class, it becomes possible to provide a guaranteed Quality of Service on a demand basis. This enables a traffic management mechanism to adjust network performance during periods of unexpected congestion to favor traffic classes based upon the metrics associated with each class.

The Quality of Service (QoS) is one of the key features of ATM which enables the technology to provide a predefined level of support to different types of data streams. An end point requesting the setup of a connection through an ATM network can request a QoS from the network. Once granted, the end point will be assured that the network will provide the selected QoS for the life of the connection. The ATM Forum presently defines five traffic classes that are summarized in Table 2.10. That table includes the type of each traffic class, a description of its intended use, and an example of its potential utilization.

As we probe further into ATM we will note that the only priority field within an ATM cell is used to indicate whether or not a cell can be dropped. Thus, the method used by an ATM network to provide a QoS is not priority-based. Instead, it is based by a set of traffic parameters that define such metrics as the Peak Cell Rate (PCR), Cell Delay Variation Tolerance (CDVT), Sustainable Cell Rate (SCR), Burst Tolerance (BT), and Minimum Cell Rate (MCR). Only some of these metrics are applicable for certain traffic classes. For example, only the Peak Cell Rate which specifies how often data samples are transmitted and the Cell Delay Variation Tolerance (CDVT) which determines the amount of displacement of a signal from its intended location are applicable for CBR traffic. Later in this

**Table 2.10**  ATM traffic classes

| Traffic class | Description |
|---|---|
| Continuous Bit Rate (CBR) | Constant bit traffic with a fixed timing relationship between data samples, such as an emulated voice circuit. |
| Variable Bit Rate—Real Time (VBR/RT) | Variable bit rate traffic that has a fixed timing relationship between data samples, such as compressed video. |
| Variable Bit Rate—Non-Real Time (VBR/NRT) | Variable bit rate traffic that has no timing relationship between data samples but for which a guarantee of a Qos is required, such as Frame Relay. |
| Available Bit Rate (ABR) | Variable data transmission that has no timing relationship and can be handled on a best effort basis, such as electronic mail. |
| Unspecified Bit Rate (UBR) | A class of traffic for which there is no service guarantee. The user can transmit any amount of data up to a specified maximum but the network does not guarantee delay or a cell loss rate. |

section we will examine the relationship between ATM Adaption Layers, traffic classes, and traffic definition metrics.

## 2.3.2 The ATM Protocol Stack

Similar to other networking architectures, ATM is a layered protocol. The ATM protocol stack is illustrated in Figure 2.34 and consists of three layers: the ATM Adaptation Layer (AAL), the ATM Layer, and the Physical Layer. Both the AAL and

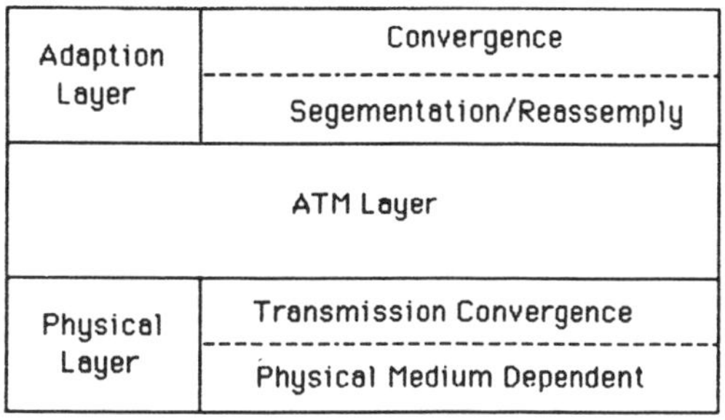

| Adaption Layer | Convergence |
|---|---|
|  | Segementation/Reassemply |
| ATM Layer | |
| Physical Layer | Transmission Convergence |
|  | Physical Medium Dependent |

**Figure 2.34**  The ATM protocol stack

Physical Layers are subdivided into two sublayers. Although the ATM protocol stack consists of three layers, as we will shortly note, those layers are essentially equivalent to the first two layers of the ISO Reference Model. However, since ATM possesses many of the characteristics of a layer 3 or network layer protocol such as a hierarchical address space and a complex routing protocol, some persons consider it to represent a network protocol.

## ATM Adaptation Layer

As illustrated in Figure 2.34, the ATM Adaptation Layer consists of two sublayers: a convergence sublayer and a segmentation and reassembly sublayer. The function of the AAL is to adapt higher level data into formats compatible with ATM Layer requirements. To accomplish this task the ATM Adaptation Layer subdivides user information into segments suitable for encapsulation into the 48 byte information fields of cells. The actual adaptation process depends upon the type of traffic to be transmitted, although all traffic winds up in similar cells. Currently there are four different AALs defined, referred to as AAL classes, which are described later in this chapter.

When receiving information, the ATM Adaptation Layer performs a reverse process. That is, it takes cells received from the network and reassembles them into a format the higher layers in the protocol stack understand. This process is known as reassembly. Thus, the segmentation and reassembly processes result in the name of the sublayer that performs those processes.

## The ATM Layer

As illustrated in Figure 2.34, the ATM Layer provides the interface between the AAL and the Physical Layer. The ATM Layer is responsible for relaying cells both from the AAL to the Physical Layer and to the AAL from the Physical Layer. The actual method by which the ATM Layer performs this function depends upon its location within an ATM network. As an ATM network consists of endpoints and switches, the ATM Layer can reside at either location. Similarly, a Physical Layer is required at both ATM endpoints and ATM switches.

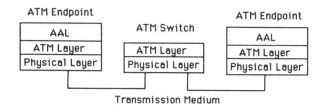

The ATM Adaption Layer is only required at endpoints within an ATM network.

**Figure 2.35**   The ATM protocol stack within a network

As a switch examines the information within an ATM cell to make switching decisions, it does not perform any adaptation functions. Thus, the ATM switch operates at layers 1 and 2, while ATM endpoints operate at layers 1 through 3 of the ATM protocol stack as shown in Figure 2.35.

When the ATM Layer resides at an endpoint, it will generate idle or empty cells whenever there are no data to send, a function not performed by a switch. Instead, in the switch the ATM Layer is concerned with facilitating switching functions, examining cell header information which enables the switch to determine where each cell should be forwarded to. For both endpoints and switches, the ATM Layer performs a variety of traffic management functions to include buffering incoming and outgoing cells as well as monitoring the transmission rate and conformance of transmission to service parameters that define a Quality of Service (QoS). At endpoints the ATM Layer also indicates to the AAL whether or not there was congestion during transmission, permitting higher layers to initiate congestion control.

*Physical Layer*

Although Figures 2.34 and 2.35 illustrate an ATM Physical Layer, a specific physical layer is not defined within the protocol stack. Instead, ATM uses the interfaces to existing physical layers defined in other protocols, which enables organizations to construct ATM networks on different types of physical interfaces which in turn connect to different types of media. Thus, the omission of a formal physical layer specification results in a significant degree of flexibility which enhances the capability of ATM to operate on LANs and WANs.

### 2.3.3 ATM operation

As previously discussed, ATM represents a cell-switching technology that can operate at speeds ranging from the T1 1.544 Mbps to the gigabit per second rate of SONET. In doing so the lack of a specific physical layer definition means that ATM can be used on many types of physical layers, which makes it a very versatile technology.

*Components*

ATM networks are constructed upon the use of five main hardware components. Those components include ATM network interface cards, LAN switches, ATM routers, ATM WAN switches and ATM service processors.

#### ATM network interface cards

An ATM network interface card (NIC) is used to connect a LAN based workstation to an ATM LAN switch. The NIC converts data generated by the workstation into cells that are transmitted to the ATM LAN switch and converts cells received from the switch into a data format recognizable by the workstation.

#### LAN switch

A LAN switch is a device used to provide interoperability between older LANs, such as Ethernet, Token-Ring or FDDI as well as from those networks to ATM. To provide connectivity to ATM, the LAN switch supports a minimum of two types of interface, with one being an ATM interface which enables the switch to be connected to an ATM switch that forms the backbone of the ATM infrastructure. The other interface or interfaces represent connections to older types of LANs.

The LAN switch functions as both a switch and protocol converter. Data received on one port destined to the ATM network are converted from frames to cells and transferred to the switch port providing a connection to the ATM switch. One of the key functions that must be performed by the switch in conjunction with the ATM switch it is connected to is a mapping between the MAC addresses used on a LAN switch and the virtual path/virtual channel (VP/VC) identifiers used by ATM. This mapping process is accomplished through a technology

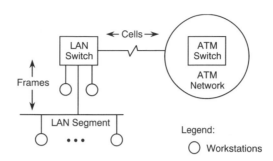

A LAN switch provides both a switching and protocol conversion function, allowing non-ATM devices to access an ATM network

**Figure 2.36**   Using a LAN swtich

known as LAN Emulation (LANE), which is described in Chapter 3 in the section which covers LAN switches.

As one LAN switch port can be capable of servicing a LAN segment, the use of a switch can minimize an organization's investment in ATM NICs. This is illustrated in Figure 2.36 which illustrates the use of a LAN switch with a single ATM port to provide access to an ATM network for individual workstations connected directly to individual switch ports as well as a group of workstations on a LAN segment. Through the use of the LAN switch, an organization can selectively upgrade existing LANs to ATM while obtaining a connection to the ATM network.

### ATM router

An ATM router, or perhaps a more correct terminology, an ATM supportable router, is a router containing one or more ATM NICs. As such, it can provide a direct or indirect capability for LAN workstations to access an ATM network or for two ATM networks to be interconnected. For example, a network segment or individual workstations could be connected to a router which in turn is connected to a LAN switch or directly to an ATM switch.

### ATM switches

An ATM switch is a multi-port device which forms the basic infrastructure for an ATM network. Unlike a LAN switch, an ATM switch only permits a single end station to be connected to each switch port. By interconnecting ATM switches an ATM network can be constructed to span a building, city, country, or the globe.

**Table 2.11** ATM communications operating rates

| Operating rate (Mbps) | Transmission media |
|---|---|
| 25–31 | unshielded twisted pair category 3 |
| 100 | multi-mode fiber |
| 155 | shielded twisted pair |
| 622 | single-mode fiber |

The basic operation of an ATM switch is to route cells from an input port onto an appropriate output port. To accomplish this the switch examines fields within each cell header and uses that information in conjunction with table information maintained in the switch to route cells. Later in this section we will examine the composition of the ATM cell header in detail.

One of the key features of ATM switches reaching the market during the late 1990s is their rate adaptation capability which in general is a function of the transmission media used to connect endpoints and to connect switches to other switches. Table 2.11 lists some of the communications rates associated with different transmission media.

### ATM service processor

An ATM service processor is a computer operating software or firmware embedded in an ATM switch which performs services required for ATM network operations. For example, an ATM network address can have one of three formats, with one format similar to a telephone number. In comparison, the NIC in an IEEE 802 standardized LAN has a hardware (MAC) address burnt into the adapter. Stations on a LAN can register their addresses using the facilities of a LAN Emulation Server (LES). That server would then act as a translator between the burnt-in LAN specific hardware addresses and ATM public or private network addresses that could considerably differ from the LAN addressing scheme. The LAN Emulation process, including a description of the operation of the LES, is described in the LAN switch section in Chapter 3.

### 2.3.4 Network interfaces

ATM support two types of basic interface: User-to-Network Interface (UNI) and a Network-to-Node Interface (NNI).

*User-to-network interface*

The UNI represents the interface between an ATM switch and an ATM endpoint. As the connection of a private network to a public network is also known as a UNI, the terms Public and Private UNI were used to differentiate between the two types. That is, a Private UNI refers to the connection between an endpoint and switch on an internal private ATM network, such as an organization's ATM-based LAN. In comparison, a Public UNI would refer to the interface between either a customer's endpoint or switch and a public ATM network.

*Network-to-node interface*

The connection between an endpoint and switch is simpler than the connect between two switches. This results from the fact that switches communicate information concerning the utilization of their facilities as well as passing setup information required to support endpoint network requests.

The interface between switches is known as a Network-to-Node or Network-to-Network Interface (NNI). Similarly to the UNI, there are two types of NNI. A Private NNI describes the switch-to-switch interface on an internal network such as an organization's LAN. In comparison, a Public NNI describes the interface between public ATM switches, such as those used by communications carriers. Figure 2.37 illustrates the four previously described ATM network interfaces.

## 2.3.5 The ATM cell header

The structure of the ATM cell is identical in both public and private ATM networks, with Figure 2.38 illustrating the fields within the five byte cell header. As we will soon note, although the cell header fields are identical throughout an ATM network, the use of certain fields depends upon the interface or the presence or absence of data being transmitted by an endpoint.

*Generic flow control field*

The Generic Flow Control (GFC) field consists of the first four bits of the first byte of the ATM cell header. This field is used to

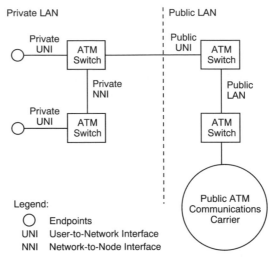

**Figure 2.37**  ATM network interfaces

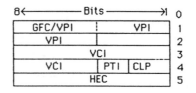

GFC   Generic Flow Control
VPI   Virtual Path Identifier
VCI   Virtual Circuit Identifier
PTI   Payload Type Identifier
CLP   Cell Loss Priority
HEC   Header Error Check

**Figure 2.38**  The ATM cell header

control the flow of traffic across the User-to-Network interface (UNI) and is used only at the UNI. When cells are transmitted between switches, the four bits become an extension of the Virtual Path Identifier (VPI) field, permitting a larger VPI value to be carried in the cell header.

*Virtual path identifier field*

The Virtual Path Identifier (VPI) identifies a path between two locations in an ATM network that provides transportation for a

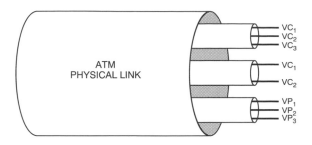

**Figure 2.39**   Relationship between virtual paths and virtual channels

group of virtual channels, where a virtual channel represents a connection between two communicating ATM devices. When an endpoint has no data to transmit, the VPI field is set to all zeros to indicate an idle condition. As previously explained, when transmission occurs between switches, the GFC field is used to support an extended VPI value.

### Virtual channel identifier field

The Virtual Channel Identifier (VCI) can be considered to represent the second part of the two-level routing hierarchy used by ATM, where a group of virtual channels are used to form a virtual path.

Figure 2.39 illustrates the relationship between virtual paths and virtual channels. Here the virtual channel represents a connection between two communicating ATM entities, such as an endpoint to a central office switch, or between two switches. The virtual channel can represent a single ATM link or a concatenation of two or more links, with communications on the channel occurring in cell sequence order at a predefined Quality of Service. In comparison, each virtual path (VP) represents a group of VCs transported between two points that can flow over one or more ATM links. Although VCs are associated with a VP, they are not unbundled nor processed. Thus, the purpose of a virtual path is to provide a mechanism for bundling traffic routed towards the same destination. This technique enables switches to examine the VPI field within the cell header to make a decision concerning the relaying of the cell instead of having to examine the entire three byte address formed by the VPI and the VCI. When an endpoint is in an idle condition, the VPI field is set to all zeros. Although the VCI field will also be set to all zeros to indicate the idle condition, other nonzero VCI values are reserved for use with a VPI zero value to indicate certain predefined conditions.

As we will note later in this section, all VPIs and VCIs have only local significance on a particular connection between an end point and switch or between two switches. At each switch in an ATM network, VPIs and VCIs can be remapped to different VPIs and VCIs. The actual route through an ATM network is established by signaling packets that are transmitted on a well known virtual channel, VPI=0, VCI=5.

### Payload type identifier field

The Payload Type Identifier (PTI) field consists of three bits in the fourth byte of the cell header. This field is used to identify the type of information carried by the cell. Values 0–3 are reserved to identify various types of user data, 4 and 5 denote management information, while 6 and 7 are reserved for future use.

### Cell loss priority field

The last bit in the fourth byte of the cell header represents the Cell Loss Priority (CLP) field. This bit is set by the AAL layer and used by the ATM layer throughout an ATM network as an indicator of the importance of the cell. If the CLP is set to 1, this indicates that the cell can be discarded by a switch experiencing congestion. If the cell should not be discarded due to the necessity to support a predefined quality of service, the AAL layer will set the CLP bit to 0. The CLP bit can also be set by the ATM layer if a connection exceeds the quality of service level agreed to during the initial communications handshaking process when setup information is exchanged.

### Header error check field

The last byte in the ATM cell header is the Header Error Check (HEC). The purpose of the HEC is to provide protection for the first four bytes of the cell header against the misdelivery of cells due to errors affecting the addresses within the header. To accomplish this the HEC functions as an error detecting and correcting code. The HEC is capable of detecting all single and certain multiple bit errors as well as correcting single bit errors.

### 2.3.6 ATM connections and cell switching

Now that we have a basic understanding of the ATM cell header to include the virtual path and virtual channel identifiers, we can turn our attention to the methods used to establish connections between endpoints as well as how connection identifiers are used for cell switching to route cells to their destination.

*Connections*

In comparison to most LANs that are connectionless, ATM is primarily a connection-oriented communications technology. This means that a connection has to be established between two ATM endpoints prior to actual data being transmitted between the endpoints. The actual ATM connection can be established as a Permanent Virtual Circuit (PVC) or as a Switched Virtual Circuit (SVC).

A PVC can be considered as being similar to a leased line, with routing established for long term use. Once a PVC has been established, no further network intervention is required any time a user wishes to transfer data between endpoints connected via a PVC. In comparison, a SVC can be considered as being similar to a telephone call made on the switched telephone network. That is, the SVC requires network intervention to establish the path linking endpoints each time a SVC occurs.

Both PVCs and SVCs obtain the V as they represent virtual rather than permanent or dedicated connections. This means that through statistical multiplexing, an endpoint can receive calls from one or more distant endpoints.

*Cell switching*

As previously mentioned, signaling packets are transmitted on the well-known virtual channel VPI=0, VCI=5 to make a connection. That connection results in each switch allocating a VPI and VCI to route data between switches or from a switch to an end point. As a switch can support numerous simultaneous connections as cells arrive, the switch examines the VIP and VCI fields in the cell header to determine the output port for relaying or transferring a cell. To determine the output port, the ATM switch first reads the incoming VPI, VCI, or both fields, with the field read dependent upon the location of the switch in the network. Next, the switch will use the connection identifier information to perform a table lookup operation. That operation uses the current connection identifier as a match criterion to determine the output port that the cell will be routed onto as well as a new connection identifier to be placed into the cell header. The new connection identifier is then used for routing between the next pair of switches or from a switch to an endpoint.

*Types of switch*

There are two types of ATM switch, with the differences between each related to the type of header fields read for establishing cross-connections through the switch. A switch limited to reading and substituting VPI values is commonly referred to as a VP switch. This switch operates relatively fast. A switch that reads and substitutes both VPI and VCI values is commonly referred to as a Virtual Channel switch (VC Switch). A VC switch generally has a lower cell operating rate than a VP switch as it must examine additional information in each cell header. You can consider a VP switch as being similar to a central office switch, while a VC switch would be similar to end office switches.

*Using connection identifiers*

To illustrate the use of connection identifiers in cell switching, consider Figure 2.40, which illustrates a three switch ATM network with four endpoints. When switch 1 receives a cell from device A connected to port 2 with VPI=0, VCI=10, it uses the VPI and VCI values to perform a table lookup, assigning VPI=1, VCI=12 for the cell header and switching the cell onto port 1. Similarly, when switch 1 receives a cell on port 3 with VPI=0, VCI=18 its table lookup operation results in the assignment of VPI=1, VCI=15 to the cell's header and the forwarding of the cell onto port 1. If we assume that switch 2 is a VP switch, it only

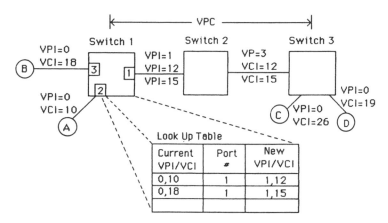

**Figure 2.40** ATM cell switching example

reads and modifies the VP; thus, the VCIs are shown exiting the switch with the same values they had upon entering the switch. At switch 3, the VPI is broken down, with virtual channels assigned to route cells to endpoints C and D that were carried in a common virtual path from switch 1 to switch 3.

The assignment of VPI and VCI values is an arbitrary process which considers those already in use, with the lookup tables being created when a connection is established through the network. Concerning that connection, it results from an ATM endpoint requesting a connection setup via the User-Network Interface through the use of a signaling protocol which contains an address within the cell. That address can be in one of three formats. One known as E.164 is the same used in public telephone networks, while the other two address formats include domain identifiers that allow address fields to be assigned by different organizations. The actual signaling method is based upon the signaling protocol used in ISDN, and it enables a Quality of Service to be negotiated and agreed to during the connection setup process. The quality of service is based upon metrics assigned to different traffic classes, permitting an endpoint to establish several virtual connections where each connection transports different types of data with different performance characteristics assigned to each connection. Figure 2.41 summarizing the relationship between the five types of specified ATM traffic classes, the ATM Adaption Layer (AAL) that will support each class, the timing relationship between source and destination, and bit rate per traffic class, as well as summarizes seven metrics used to provide a Quality of Service for each traffic class.

| | Traffic Classes | | | | |
|---|---|---|---|---|---|
| | Constant Bit Rate | Variable Bit Rate Real Time | Variable Bit Rate Now Real Time | Available Bit Rate | Unspecified Bit Rate |
| ATM Adaption Layer | AAL 1 | AAL 2 | AAL 3/4, 5 | AAL 3/4 | Unspecified |
| Timing Relationship Source-Destination | | | | | |
| Bit Rate | | | | | |
| Traffic Definition Metrics / Cell Loss Ratio | Specified | Specified | Specified | Specified | Unspecified |
| Cell Transfer Delay | Maximum Speficied | Maximum | Mean Specified | Unspecified | Unspecified |
| Cell Delay Variation | Specified | Specified | Unspecified | Unspecified | Unspecified |
| Peak Cell Rate | Specified | Specified | Specified | Specified | Specified |
| Sustainable Cell Rate | N/A | Specified | Specified | N/A | N/A |
| Minimum Cell Rate | N/A | N/A | N/A | Specified | N/A |

**Figure 2.41** Relationship of traffic classes, AAL support, and traffic definition metrics

## General operation

As indicated in the beginning of this section, ATM can be used as a desktop to desktop transport mechanism or can function as a backbone to connect existing IEEE 802 networks together and into an ATM infrastructure. Figure 2.40 illustrated an example of desktop to desktop or end point to end point ATM operation. In actuality the cost of ATM adapters as well as the considerable investment previously made in Ethernet, Token-Ring, and FDDI infrastructures will preclude the widespread adoption of ATM to the desktop for many years. In the interim the scalabilty of ATM as well as its ability to move from LAN to WAN to LAN has resulted in a growing use of the technology as a backbone for interconnecting older local area networks as well as providing for a migration strategy to ATM. Readers are referred to the LAN switch section in Chapter 3 for detailed information on how ATM is used as a backbone network.

# 3

# LOCAL AREA
# NETWORKING

In Chapter 2 we examined the technological concepts behind local area networks and focused our attention upon the operation of Ethernet, Fast Ethernet, Token-Ring, FDDI and ATM. In doing so we avoided an in-depth discussion of local area network hardware components used to interconnect and extend LANs as well as the role of software which governs the networking capability of LANs. In this chapter we will focus our attention upon those two areas. First we will describe the basic operation of several hardware components that are the building blocks of local area networks and enable their extension and the interconnection of repeaters, bridges, routers, brouters, gateways, servers, wiring hubs and switches. Next, we will discuss the role and operation of three major types of software required for local area network operations—computer operating systems, LAN operating systems, and application programs. By examining hardware and software, we will obtain an appreciation of the methods used to physically expand LANs and link LANs either directly or through a wide area network. In this chapter and throughout this book we will use the terms 'local area network' and 'network' synonymi ously. When we refer to the interconnection of local area networks, we will use the term 'internetwork' or just 'internet' to reference the joining of two or more networks. Readers should note that we will use the latter term to reference the combining of networks and not the specific network called the Internet, whose first letter is capitalized to denote its use as a proper noun.

## 3.1 HARDWARE COMPONENTS

In this section we will examine hardware products essential to the construction of local area networks and their interconnection.

These products provide us with the ability to extend the distance of local area network coverage, interconnect local and distant networks, and obtain access to centralized computational facilities.

### 3.1.1 Repeaters

A repeater represents the simplest type of hardware component in terms of design, operation, and functionality. This device operates at the physical layer of the ISO Open Systems Interconnection Reference Model, regenerating a signal received on one cable segment and then retransmitting the signal onto another cable segment. Figure 3.1 illustrates the operation of a repeater with respect to the ISO OSI Reference Model.

*Types*

There are two basic types of repeaters. An electrical repeater simply receives an electrical signal and then regenerates the signal. During the signal regeneration process a new signal is formed which matches the original characteristics of the received signal. This process is illustrated in the lower portion of Figure 3.1. By transmitting a new signal, the repeater removes any previous distortion and attenuation, enabling an extension in the permissible transmission distance. Although several network segments can be interconnected by the use of repeaters to extend the coverage of a network, there are constraints that govern the maximum permissible length of a LAN. For example, a 50 ohm coaxial bus-based Ethernet supports a maximum cabling distance of 2.8 km and that distance cannot be extended through the use of repeaters.

The second type of repeater commonly used is an electrical–optical device. This type of repeater converts an electrical signal into an optical signal for transmission and performs a reverse function when receiving a light signal. Similar to an electrical

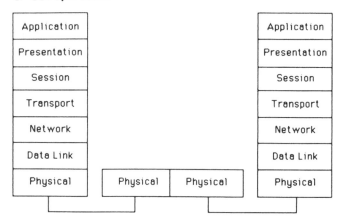

a. OSI operation

b. Signal regeneration process

**Figure 3.1** Repeater operation. A repeater connects two local area networks or network segments at the OSI physical layer (cable) by regenerating the signal received on one LAN or LAN segment onto the other network or network segment

repeater, the electrical–optical repeater extends the distance that a signal can be carried on a local area network.

Since a repeater is restricted to operating at the OSI physical layer, it is transparent to data flow. This restricts the use of a repeater to linking identical networks or network segments. For example, you could use repeaters to connect two Ethernet or two Token-Ring network segments but not an Ethernet to a Token-Ring.

*Utilization*

Figure 3.2 illustrates two examples of the use of repeaters. The top portion of Figure 3.2 illustrates the use of a repeater to connect two Ethernet bus-based LANs, one serving the accounting department while the other network serves the data processing department. In this situation all messages on one local area network are passed to the other, regardless of

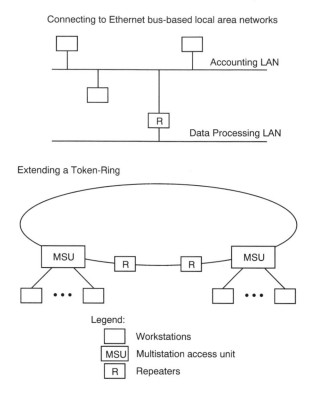

Connecting to Ethernet bus-based local area networks

Accounting LAN

R

Data Processing LAN

Extending a Token-Ring

MSU    R    R    MSU

Legend:

Workstations

MSU    Multistation access unit

R    Repeaters

**Figure 3.2**  Using repeaters. A repeater can be used to interconnect local area networks and extend the transmission distance of a LAN

their intended recipient. The use of repeaters in this manner increases the sum of the traffic on each LAN. If implemented without knowledge concerning the traffic flow and utilization levels on each network, performance problems may result when separate networks are interconnected through the use of repeaters.

In the lower portion of Figure 3.2, a pair of repeaters is shown being used to connect two multi-station access units (MAUs) used to form a Token-Ring network. In this example, the repeaters simply enable the placement of MAUs at wider distances from one another and regenerate traffic which only flows on one network. The use of repeaters in this manner does not add to the data flow on the network and requires little preplanning in comparison to the usage shown at the top of Figure 3.2.

*Repeater rules*

Different types of network have different constraints concerning the distance that a repeater can support and the number of repeaters that can be inserted between interconnected network segments or between a workstation and a network hub. Repeater constraints are based upon the type of LAN supported, including its access method, operating rate, and type of media used for the infrastructure. In addition, for Token-Ring networks additional constraints involve the number of hubs and wiring closets hubs are placed in. Specific repeater constraints for Ethernet, Fast Ethernet, and Token-Ring networks are presented in Chapter 4.

## 3.1.2 Bridges

In comparison to a repeater which lacks intelligence and is restricted to linking similar LANs and LAN segments, bridges are intelligent devices that can connect similar and dissimilar local area networks. To obtain an appreciation of the functions performed by bridges, let us examine the use of this type of networking product.

*Operation*

Figure 3.3 illustrates the operation of a bridge with respect to the OSI Reference Model as well as its use to connect two separate Ethernet local area networks. Although the use of the bridge in the lower portion of Figure 3.3 looks similar to the use of a repeater previously shown in Figure 3.1, as we will soon understand, the operation of each device includes a number of key differences.

When a bridge begins to operate, it examines each frame transmitted on connected local area networks at the data link layer—a process beyond the capability of a repeater which operates transparent to data. By reading the source address included in each frame, the bridge assembles a table of local addresses for each network. In addition to reading each source address, the bridge also reads the destination address contained in the frame. If the destination address is not contained in the local address table that the bridge constructs, this fact

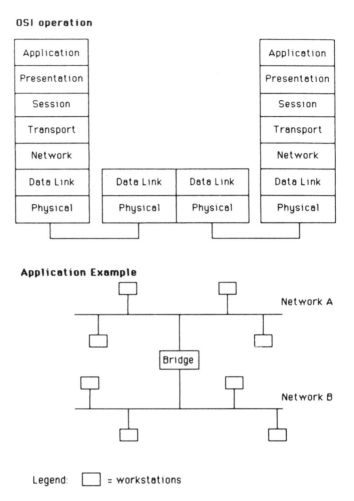

**Figure 3.3** Bridge operation. A bridge connects two local area networks or network segments at the data link layer

indicates that the frame's destination is not on the current network or network segment. In this situation, the bridge transmits the frame onto the other network or network segment. An exception to this process occurs when there are more than two bridge ports. If a frame has a destination address that is not in the bridge's address/port table, it would then transmit the frame onto all ports other than the port the frame was received on. The technical name for this situation is flooding. If the destination address is contained in the local address table, this indicates that the frame should remain on the local network. In this situation the bridge simply either repeats the frame if the network is a ring infrastructure, or discards it if the network is an Ethernet LAN, since the frame also flows to all stations on the network in addition to the bridge port.

The previously described method of bridging operation is referred to as transparent bridging. Readers are referred to Chapter 7 for detailed information concerning different methods of bridge operations.

We can summarize the operation of the bridge illustrated in the lower portion of Figure 3.3 as follows:

- Bridge reads all frames transmitted on network A.
- Frames with destination address on network A are repeated back onto that network or discarded.
- Frames with destination address on network B are retransmitted onto network B.
- The above process is reversed for traffic on network B.

*Flooding*

Figure 3.4 illustrates the operation of a four-port bridge that will also serve as a mechanism to discuss the effect of flooding. Instead of 48-bit MAC addresses we will use addresses A

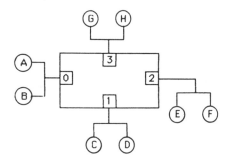

Address/port table entries.

| 1. Power-on state | | 2. Frame from A transmitted to E | | 3. Frame from G transmitted to A | |
|---|---|---|---|---|---|
| Address | Port | Address | Port | Address | Port |
| – | 0 | A | 0 | A | 0 |
| – | 1 | – | 1 | – | 1 |
| – | 2 | – | 2 | – | 2 |
| – | 3 | – | 3 | G | 3 |

**Figure 3.4**  Multiport bridge operation

through H for simplicity to indicate source addresses for each station on four networks connected to a common bridge.

Initially, when the bridge is powered on, its address/port table is empty. This situation is illustrated in the first address/port table entry at the bottom of Figure 3.4. Next, let us assume that the device with source address A transmits a frame to the device whose address is E. As a search of the address/port table provides no match for the destination address, the bridge transmits or floods the frame onto all ports other than the port it was received on. This means that the frame is forwarded onto the networks attached to ports 1, 2 and 3. Thus, the frame adversely affects the performance on the networks connected to ports 1 and 3 as it precludes other transmissions on those networks for the duration of the frame that will be discarded since its intended recipient is not on either network. In addition to flooding the frame, the bridge also updates its address/port table as it noted that the station with source address A is on port 0. This update is shown in the second entry at the bottom of Figure 3.4.

Next, let us assume that the workstation with address G transmits a frame to the station whose address is A. The bridge searches its address/port table, noting that address A is associated with port 0. Thus, the bridge forwards the frame onto the network connected to port 0. Note that the forwarding process depends upon the ability of a bridge to first learn the addresses of network devices. Thus, the forwarding process is sometimes referred to as a backward or reverse learning process. Returning to the bridge operation, once it notes address A is on port 0 and forwards the frame, it also notes that address G is not in the address/port table and updates the table. This update is indicated in the third entry at the bottom of Figure 3.4.

In addition to maintaining MAC addresses and their associated ports, a bridge time stamps each entry. The time stamp is used to purge aged entries and enables the finite memory of the bridge to hold the most recently noted addresses. Since many workstations have significant periods of network inactivity, it is quite common for entries to be purged from a bridge's address/port table. However, once purged the first frame with a destination address no longer in the address/port table will result in the bridge flooding the frame. Thus, flooding can be considered as a process associated with the use of bridges that will continue to periodically occur long after a bridge is powered on.

*Filtering and forwarding*

The process of examining each frame is known as filtering. The filtering rate of a bridge, is directly related to its level of performance. That is, the higher the filtering rate of a bridge, the lower the probability that it will become a bottleneck to network performance. A second performance measurement associated with bridges is their forwarding rate. The forwarding rate is expressed in frames per second and denotes the maximum capability of a bridge to transmit traffic from one network to another.

*Types*

There are two general types of bridge, transparent and translating. Each type of bridge can be obtained as a local or remote device, with a remote device including a wide area network interface as well as the ability to convert frames into a WAN transmission protocol. Readers are referred to Chapter 5 for information concerning wide area network transmission facilities, services, and protocols used for data transmission.

**Transparent bridge**

A transparent bridge provides a connection between two local area networks that employ the same data link protocol. Thus, the bridge shown in the lower portion of Figure 3.3 can be considered to be a transparent bridge. This type of bridge is used to connect two or more local area networks that employ identical protocols at the data link layer. At the physical layer, some transparent bridges have multiple ports that support different media. Thus, a transparent bridge does not have to be transparent at the physical level although the majority of such bridges are.

Although a transparent bridge provides a high level of performance for a small number of network interconnections, its level of performance decreases as the number of inter-connected networks increases. The rationale for this loss in performance is based upon the method used by transparent bridges to develop a route between LANs. Readers are referred to Chapter 7 for specific information concerning bridge routing and performance issues.

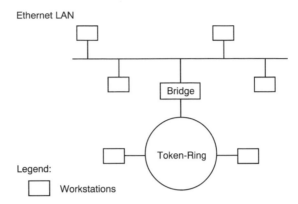

**Figure 3.5** Translating bridge operation. A translating bridge connects local area networks that employ different protocols at the data link layer. In this example the translating bridge is used to connect an Ethernet local area network to a Token-Ring network

### Translating bridge

A translating bridge provides a connection capability between two local area networks that employ different protocols at the data link layer. Since networks using different data link layer protocols normally use different media, a translating bridge will also provide support for different physical layer connections.

Figure 3.5 illustrates the use of a translating bridge to interconnect a Token-Ring and an Ethernet local area network. In this example, the bridge functions as an Ethernet node on the Ethernet and as a Token-Ring node on the Token-Ring. When a frame from one network has a destination on the other network, the bridge will perform a series of operations, including frame and transmission rate conversion. For example, consider an Ethernet frame destined to the Token-Ring network. The bridge will strip the frame's preamble and FCS, then it will convert the frame into a Token-Ring frame format. Once the bridge receives a free token the new frame will be transmitted onto the Token-Ring; however, the transmission rate will be at the Token-Ring network rate and not at the Ethernet rate. For frames going from the Token-Ring to the Ethernet the process would be reversed.

One of the problems associated with the use of a translating bridge is the conversion of frames from their format on one network to the format required for use on another network. As previously indicated in Chapter 2, the information field of an Ethernet frame can vary from 64 to 1500 bytes, while a Token-

Ring can have a maximum information field size of 4500 bytes when the ring operates at 4 Mbps and 18 000 bytes when the ring operates at 16 Mbps. If a station on a Token-Ring network has a frame whose information field exceeds 1500 bytes in length, the bridging of that frame onto an Ethernet network cannot occur. This is because there is no provision within either data link protocol to inform a station that a frame flowing from one network to another was fragmented and requires re-assembly. To effectively use a bridge in this situation requires software on each workstation on each network to be configured to use the smallest maximum frame size of any network to be connected together. In this example, Token-Ring workstations would not be allowed to transmit information fields greater than 1500 bytes.

*Features*

The functionality of a bridge is based upon the features incorporated into this device. Table 3.1 lists 11 major bridge features which define both the functionality and performance level of a bridge.

### Filtering and forwarding

The filtering and forwarding rate indicates the ability of the bridge to accept, examine, and regenerate frames on the same network (filtering) and transfer frames onto a different network (forwarding). A higher filtering and forwarding rate indicates a higher performing bridge.

**Table 3.1**  Bridge features

---

Filtering and forwarding rate
Selective forwarding capability
Multiple port support
Wide area network interface support
Local area network media interface support
Transparent operation at the data link layer
Translating operation to link dissimilar networks
Encapsulation operation to support wide area network usage
Standalone and adapter based fabrication
Self-learning (transparent) routing
Source routing

---

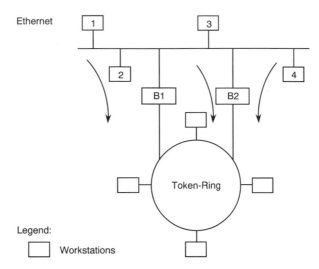

**Figure 3.6** Using bridge selective forwarding capability. Using the selective forwarding capability of bridges enables the data flow between networks to be distributed based upon source or destination addresses

**Selective forwarding**

Some bridges have a selective forwarding capability. Bridges with this feature can be configured to selectively forward frames based upon predefined source and destination addresses. Through the use of a selective forwarding capability you can develop predefined routes for frames to take when flowing between networks as well as enable or inhibit the transfer of information between predefined workstations.

Figure 3.6 illustrates the use of the selective forwarding capability of two bridges to provide two independent routes for data transfer between an Ethernet and a Token-Ring network. In this example, you might enable all workstations with source address 1 and 2 to have data destined to the Token-Ring flow over bridge 1, while workstations with a source address of 3 and 4 that are transmitting data to the Token-Ring are configured to use bridge 2.

For readers familiar with Ethernet bridging, you are probably aware of a constraint referred to as the spanning tree path which precludes the ability to form a closed loop when bridging. The reason for the spanning tree is to prevent the continuous forwarding of frames in a circular manner that would adversely effect network performance. Although the spanning tree algorithm would require one of the two bridges shown in Figure

3.6 to be placed into a standby state of operation, since the two bridges are considered to be selectively forwarding by address, this is not required. That is, by forwarding only over single paths the integrity of the spanning tree is maintained on the Ethernet network. In Chapter 7 we will discuss the operation of the spanning tree algorithm in detail.

### Multiple port support

The multiple port support capability of a bridge is related to its local and wide area network media interface support. Some bridges support additional ports beyond the two that make up a basic bridge. Doing so enables a bridge to provide connectivity between three or more local area networks.

Figure 3.7 illustrates one potential use of a multiple port bridge to link an Ethernet network to two Token-Ring networks.

### Local and wide area interface support

Local area media interfaces supported by bridges can include thin and thick Ethernet coaxial cable, IEEE 10BASE-T, and other types of twisted-pair cable. Wide area network interfaces are incorporated into remote bridges that are designed to

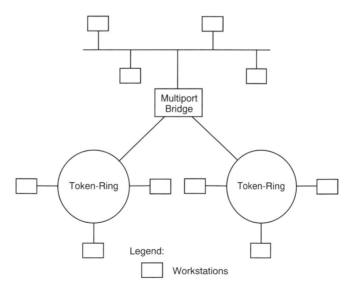

**Figure 3.7** Using a multiport bridge. Through the use of a multiport bridge you can interconnect three or more local area networks

provide an internetworking capability between two or more geographically dispersed LANs linked by a WAN. Common WAN media interfaces can include RS-232 for data rates at or below 19.2 Kbps, CCITT X.21 for packet network access at data rates up to 128 Kbps, CCITT V.35 for data rates between 48 Kbps and 128 Kbps, and a T1/E1 interface for operations at 1.544 Mbps and 2.048 Mbps, respectively.

### Transparent operation

Although bridges are thought of as transparent to data, this is not always true. For interconnecting different networks located in the same geographical area, bridges are normally transparent to data. However, some remote bridges use data compression algorithms to reduce the quantity of data transmitted between bridges connected via a wide area network. Such compression-performing bridges are not transparent to data, although they restore data to its original form.

### Frame translation

For interconnecting different types of local area networks, bridges must perform a translation of frames. For example, an Ethernet frame must be changed into a Token-Ring frame when the frame is routed from an Ethernet to a Token-Ring network. As previously mentioned, since frames cannot be fragmented at the data link layer you must set the workstations on the Token-Ring network to the smallest maximum frame size of the Ethernet, or 1500 bytes.

When data is transferred between colocated local area networks the frame format on one network is suitable for transfer onto the other network or modified for transfer when the media access control layers differ. When a bridge is used to connect two local area networks via a wide area network facility a WAN protocol is employed to control data transfer. The wide area network protocol is better suited for transmission over the WAN as it will normally incorporate error detection and correction, enable a large number of unacknowledged 'WAN' frames to exist to speed information transfer, support full-duplex data transfers, and is standardized. Examples of such wide area network protocols include IBM's SDLC, Digital Equipment Corporation's DDCMP, and the ITU-T HDLC and X.25.

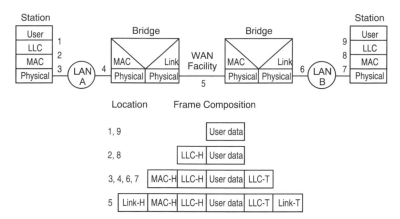

**Figure 3.8** Remote bridge operation. A remote bridge wraps the logical link control (LLC) and media access control (MAC) frames in another protocol for transmission over a wide area network. H represents a header and T a trailing field

### Frame encapsulation

Figure 3.8 illustrates the operation of a pair of remote bridges connecting two local area networks via a wide area network. For transmission from network A to network B, user data from a network A station is first converted into logical link control and media access control frames. The bridge then encapsulates one or more LAN frames into the bridging protocol frame used for communications over the wide area network. Since the local area network frame is wrapped in another protocol, we say the LAN frame is tunneled within the WAN protocol. At the opposite end of the wide area network the distant remote bridge performs a reverse operation, removing the WAN protocol header and trailer from each frame.

### Fabrication

Some bridges are manufactured as standalone products. Such devices can be considered as 'plug and play', as you simply connect the bridge to the media and power it on. Other bridges are manufactured as adapter cards for insertion into the system unit of a personal computer, workstation, or reduced instruction set computer (RISC). Through the use of software developed in conjunction with hardware you may obtain more flexibility in the use of this type of bridge than with a standalone device whose software is fixed in ROM.

**Routing method**

The routing capability of a bridge governs its capability to interconnect local area networks as well as its level of performance. A transparent bridge automatically develops routing tables. Thus, this device is known as a self-learning bridge and represents the most elementary type of bridge routing. In the IBM Token-Ring frame there is an optional routing field that can be used to develop routing information for frames routed through a series of bridges. Readers are referred to Chapter 7 for an in-depth discussion of bridge routing methods.

### 3.1.3 Routers

A router is a device that operates at the network layer of the ISO OSI Reference Model as illustrated in Figure 3.9. What this basically means is that a router examines network addresses and makes decisions about whether or not data on a local area network should remain on the network or should be transmitted to a different network. Although this level of operation may appear to be insignificant in comparison to a bridge which operates at the data link layer, in actuality there is a considerable difference in the routing capability of bridges and routers.

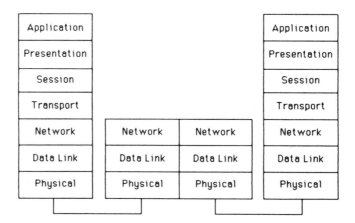

**Figure 3.9** Router operation. A router operates at the network layer of the ISO OSI Reference Model. This enables a router to provide network layer services, such as flow control and frame fragmentation

A bridge uses 48 bit MAC addresses that it associates with ports as a mechanism to determine whether a frame received on one port is ignored, forwarded onto another port, or flooded onto all ports other than the port it was received on. At the data link layer there is no mechanism to distinguish one network from another. Thus, the delivery of frames between networks requires bridges to learn MAC addresses and base their forwarding decisions on such addresses. Although this is an acceptable technique for linking a few networks together, as the number of networks increase and the number of workstations on inter-connected networks increase, bridges would spend a consider-able amount of time purging old entries and flooding frames, causing unacceptable performance problems. This resulted in the development of routers that prevent the flooding of frames between networks and operate by using network addresses.

To understand the concept behind routing, consider Figure 3.10 which illustrates two networks connected by a pair of routers. In this example, assume that addresses A, B, C and D represent MAC addresses of workstations, and E and F represent the MAC address of each router connected to each network. Assuming that workstation A has data to transmit to workstation C, an application program executing on work-station A assigns network 20 as the destination address in a packet it prepares at the network layer. That packet is transported via one or more MAC frames to MAC address E, which is the data link address of the network adapter card installed in router 1.

In actuality, each device on a network can have a unique network address, with a portion of the address denoting the network and the remainder of the address denoting each host or

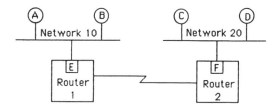

When a workstation on one network transmits data to a device on another network, an application program provides the destin-ation network address which is used by routers as a basis for their routing decisions.

**Figure 3.10**   Routing between two networks

router interface. This enables the application program on workstation A to transmit a packet destined to workstation C to router 1, with the data link layer passing the packet to MAC address E as a frame or sequence of frames. The router receives the frame or sequence of frames explicitly addressed to it and notes that the packet has the destination address for network 20. The router then searches its routing tables and determines that it should relay the packet to router 2. When the packet is received at router 2, it recognizes the fact that network 20 is connected to the router via its connection to the LAN by an adapter card using MAC address F. Thus, the router will transport the packet to its destination using one or more frames at the data link layer with a MAC source address of F.

The preceding description represents a simplified description of the routing process. A more detailed description will be presented later in this book after we investigate the TCP/IP protocol suite. We will examine the TCP/IP protocol suite in Chapter 6 and focus our attention upon router operations in Chapter 8.

The ability to operate at the network layer enables a router to extend internetworking across multiple data links in an orderly and predefined manner. This means that a router can determine the best path through a series of data links from a source network to a destination network. To accomplish this the router operates using a network protocol, such as the Internet Protocol (IP), Digital Equipment Corporation's DECnet Phase V, and Novell's IPX. This networking protocol must operate on both the source and destination network when protocol dependent routers are used. If protocol independent routers are used you can interconnect networks using different protocols. The protocol independent router can be considered as a sophisticated transparent bridge. Its operation and utilization are described in detail in Chapter 8. In comparison, since a bridge operates at the data link layer, it can always be used to transfer information between networks operating different network protocols. This makes a bridge more efficient for linking networks that only have one or a few paths, while a router is more efficient for interconnecting multiple network links via multiple paths.

### Network address utilization

Unlike a bridge which must monitor all frames at the media access control layer, a router is specifically addressed at the network layer. This means that a router only has to examine frames explicitly addressed to that device. In communications terminology, the monitoring of all frames is referred to as a promiscuous mode of operation, while the selective examination of frames is referred to as a nonpromiscuous mode of operation.

Another difference between the operation of bridges and routers is the structure of the addresses that they operate upon. Bridges operate at the data link layer, which means that they typically examine physical addresses that are contained in read- only memory on adapter cards and used in the generation of frames. In comparison, routers operate at the network layer where addresses are normally assigned by a network administrator to a group of stations having a common characteristic, such as being connected on an Ethernet in one area of a building. This type of address is known as a logical address and can be assigned and modified by the network administrator.

*Table operation*

Similar to bridges, routers make forwarding decisions using tables. Unlike a bridge that may employ a simple table look-up procedure to determine if a destination address is on a particular network, a router may employ much more sophisticated forwarding decision criteria. For example, a router may be configured to analyze several paths based upon an algorithm and dynamically select a path based upon the results of the algorithm. Routing algorithms and protocols are discussed in Chapter 8.

*Advantages of use*

The use of routers provides a number of significant advantages in comparison to the use of bridges. To illustrate those advantages we will examine the use of routers shown in Figure 3.11 in which four corporate offices containing seven local area networks are interconnected through the use of four routers. In this example networks A and B are located in a building in Los Angeles, networks C and D are located in New York, network E is located in Washington, DC, and networks F and G are located in Miami.

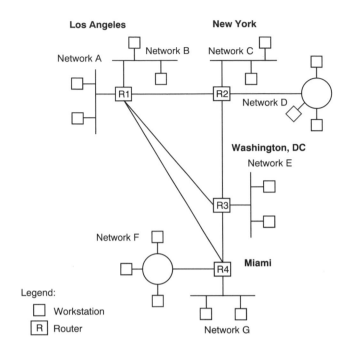

**Figure 3.11** Building an internet using routers. Routers can be used to establish complex networks in which traffic is varied over network facilities based upon the operational status and utilization of different network paths

### Multiple path transmission and routing control

Suppose that a station on network A in Los Angeles requires transmission to a station on network G in Miami. Initially, router R1 might use the path R1–R4 to transmit data between networks. If the path should fail or if an excessive amount of traffic flows between Los Angeles and Miami using that path, router R1 can seek to establish other paths, such as R1–R3–R4 or even R1–R2–R3–R4. In fact, many routers will consider each packet as a separate entity, routing the packet to its destination over the best available path at the time of transmission. Although this could conceivably result in packets arriving at R4 out of sequence, routers have the capability to resequence packets into their original order prior to passing data onto the destination network.

### Flow control

As data flows through multiple paths towards its destination it becomes possible for a link to become congested. For example, data from a station on network C and network E routed to network G might build up to the point where the path R3–R4 becomes congested. To eliminate the possibility of packet loss, routers will use flow control. That is, they will inhibit transmission onto a link as well as notify other routers to inhibit data flow until there is an available level of bandwidth for traffic.

### Frame fragmentation

As previously mentioned, bridges cannot break a frame into a series of frames when transmission occurs between networks with different frame sizes. This situation requires workstations to be configured to use the smallest maximum frame size of any network to be connected together. In comparison, most network protocols supported by routers include a provision for fragmentation of packets and their reassembly.

The higher level of functionality of routers over bridges is not without a price. That price is in terms of packet processing, software complexity, and cost. Since routers provide a more complex series of functions than bridges, their ability to process packets is typically one-half to two-thirds of the processing capability of bridges. In addition, the development time required to program a more complex series of functions adds to the cost of routers. Thus, routers are generally more expensive than bridges. Table 3.2 summarizes the major differences between bridges and routers in terms of their operation, functionality, complexity, and cost.

## 3.1.4 Brouters

A brouter can be considered as a hybrid device, representing a combination of bridging and routing capabilities.

*Operation*

When a brouter receives a frame it examines it to determine if it is destined for another local area network. If so, it then checks the protocol of the frame to determine if it is supported at the network layer supported by the router function. If supported, the brouter will route the frame similarly to the manner in which

**Table 3.2** Bridge/router comparison

| Characteristic | Bridge | Router |
|---|---|---|
| Routing based upon an algorithm or protocol | Normally no | Yes |
| Protocol transparency | Yes | Only protocol independent router |
| Uses network addresses | No | Yes |
| Promiscuous mode of operation | Yes | No |
| Forwarding decision | Elementary | Can be complex |
| Multiple path transmission | Limited | High |
| Routing control | Limited | High |
| Flow control | No | Yes |
| Frame fragmentation | No | Yes |
| Packet processing rate | High | Moderate |
| Cost | Less expensive | More expensive |

a router operates. However, if the brouter does not support the protocol it will bridge the frame using layer 2 information.

In comparison to routers, brouters provide an additional level of connectivity between networks, although that connectivity takes place at a lower level in the OSI Reference Model hierarchy. This is because a router would simply ignore a frame for which it does not support the network protocol, while a brouter would bridge the frame.

*Utilization*

The key advantage from the use of brouters is obtained from the ability of this device to both bridge and route data. Its ability to perform this dual function enables a brouter to replace the use of separate bridges and routers in some networking applications. For example, consider the use of a separate bridge and router in the top portion of Figure 3.10. In this example the bridge provides an interconnection capability between two relatively colocated networks, while the router provides an interconnection capability to distant networks. By replacing the separate bridge and router with a brouter the same level of functionality is obtained as illustrated in the lower portion of

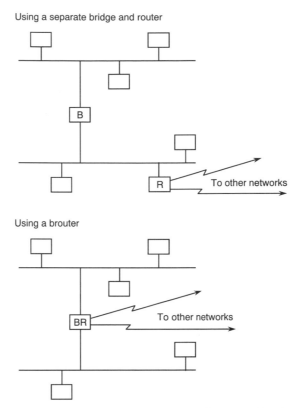

**Figure 3.12**  Replacing a separate bridge and router with a brouter

Figure 3.12. Of course, you want to ensure that the filtering and forwarding rate of the brouter is sufficient to be used in the manner illustrated, otherwise the replacement of separate bridges and routers by brouters may introduce delays that affect network performance. Readers are referred to Chapters 7 and 8 for information concerning the processing requirements of bridges and routers.

### 3.1.5 Gateway

The well known phrase 'one person's passion is another's poison' can in many ways apply to gateways. The term 'gateway' was originally coined to reference a device which provides a communications path between two local area networks or a LAN and a mainframe computer from the physical through the application layer. When applied to a device interconnecting

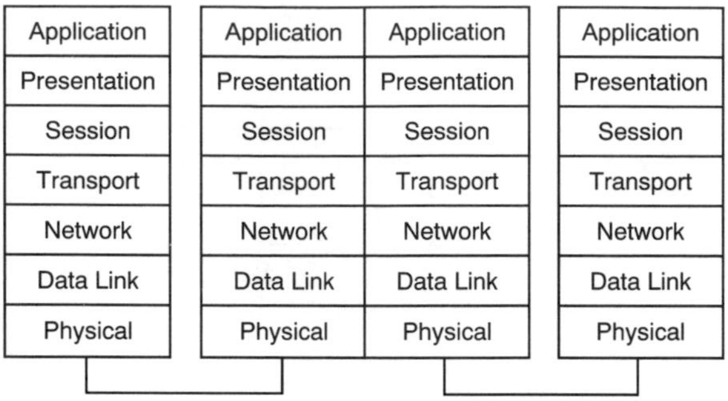

| Application | Application | Application | Application |
|---|---|---|---|
| Presentation | Presentation | Presentation | Presentation |
| Session | Session | Session | Session |
| Transport | Transport | Transport | Transport |
| Network | Network | Network | Network |
| Data Link | Data Link | Data Link | Data Link |
| Physical | Physical | Physical | Physical |

**Figure 3.13** Gateway operation. A gateway operates at all seven layers of the ISO OSI Reference Model

networks, the term gateway was originally used and is still commonly used to refer to a router. In fact, many programs used to configure workstation and server network operations request the entry of the gateway network address, even though it is more appropriate today to use the term router.

Figure 3.13 illustrates the operation of a gateway with respect to the ISO OSI Reference Model. Unfortunately the term 'gateway' has been used loosely to describe a range of products ranging from bridges and routers that interconnect two or more local area networks to protocol converters that provide asynchronous dial-up access into an IBM SNA network. Thus, a definition of the term is warranted.

*Definition*

In this book we will use the term 'gateway' to describe a product that performs protocol conversion through all seven layers of the ISO OSI Reference Model. As such, a gateway performs all of the functions of a router as well as any conversions required through the application layer.

One of the most common types of gateway is an electronic mail gateway. An electronic mail (email) gateway converts documents from one email format into another. For example, an internal corporate network might be operating Lotus Development Corporation's cc:MAIL. If they require connectivity with the Internet, the gateway must convert internal cc:MAIL documents so that they can be transported via the Simple Mail Transport Protocol (SMTP) which is a TCP/IP electronic mail application. Similarly, SMTP mail delivered via the Internet to the organization's gateway must be converted by the gateway into the format used by cc:MAIL. A second type of popular gateway enables workstations on a network to communicate with a mainframe as if the workstation was a specific type of terminal device. This type of gateway also operates at all seven layers of the ISO OSI Reference Model.

### Operation

Gateways are protocol specific in function, typically used to provide access to a mainframe computer. Some vendors manufacture multi-protocol gateways. Such products are normally manufactured as adapter cards containing separate processors that are installed in the system unit of a personal computer or a specially designed vendor hardware platform. When used in conjunction with appropriate vendor software, this type of gateway is actually an $N$-in-1 gateway, where $N$ refers to the number of protocol conversions and separate connections the gateway can perform.

Figure 3.14 illustrates the use of a multi-protocol gateway to link LAN stations to an IBM mainframe via an SDLC link and via an X.25 connection to a packet switching network. Once connected to the packet switching network, LAN traffic may be further converted by gateway facilities built into that network or traffic may be routed to a packet network node and transmitted from that node to its final destination in its X.25 packet format.

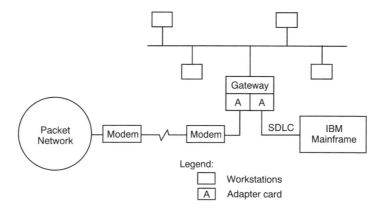

**Figure 3.14** Multi-protocol gateway operation. A multiprotocol gateway can be used to provide local area network stations access to different computational facilities, either directly or through the use of a packet network

Gateways are primarily designed and used for LAN–WAN connections and not for inter-LAN communications. Due to the more sophisticated functions performed by gateways, they are slower than routers in providing network throughput. In addition, due to the large number of protocol options that may require consideration when configuring a gateway, its installation is considerably more difficult than the setup of a router. Readers are referred to Chapter 9 for specific information concerning the operation and utilization of gateways.

### 3.1.6 File servers

The file server can be considered as the central repository of information upon which a local area network is normally constructed. The file server is normally a personal computer or workstation that has a very powerful microprocessor, such as an Intel 486, Pentium, Pentium Pro or a RISC chip, as well as a large amount of fast access on-line storage. The on-line storage is used to hold the local area network operating system and application programs that other stations on the network may use. In doing so some software vendors have split application programs, enabling portions of a program to be run on a network station, while other portions, such as the updating of a database, occur on the server. This technique is known as client-server processing. In comparison, the general term client-server operations refers to the access of one computer by another via a network. The computer being accessed, while normally considered to represent a file server, can also be a mainframe or minicomputer. For either situation, the client uses a network to access one or more features of the server. Those features can range in scope from a spreadsheet program stored on a file server to a database query program on a mainframe that provides access to tens or even hundreds of millions of records.

*Types of server*

The first type of server developed for use with local area networks primarily supported file and printer sharing. Thus, although referred to as a file server, the server also permitted a few printers to be connected to the computer as network accessible devices. As the concept of local area networking

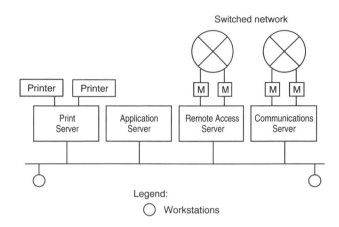

**Figure 3.15**  Servers can be acquired to perform specific functions

gained acceptance, servers were developed to perform specific functions. Today, popular types of server include application servers, communications servers, print servers, and remote access servers. Figure 3.15 illustrates an Ethernet network that contains four distinct types of servers.

The remote access server can be considered to represent a hybrid device that consists of a modem pool and router. This type of server permits the support of serial communications in the form of analog modems, digital ISDN calls, and the connection of a T1 circuit that contains 24 individual connections grouped together on a common circuit. Incoming communications are prompted for access validation, typically in the form of a User-ID and password, to gain access from the RAS onto the network. Once connected to the network, they then obtain access privileges commensurate with the network account they have.

Although a communications server also provides connectivity between a network and a serial communications facility, there are some distinct differences between this server and a remote access server. First, a communications server is primarily used for outbound traffic from network users. Thus, it may not support inbound traffic, and if it does, it probably just places the traffic onto the network without checking the validity of the user. Secondly, most communications servers function as replacements for users having individual modems. Thus, another popular name for a limited capability communications server is a modem pooler.

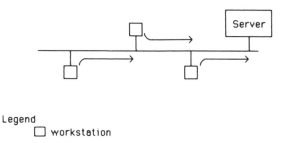

Legend
☐ workstation

**Figure 3.16** Server placement. The location of a server on a network is critical for insuring network performance. In this example, since each workstation requires access to the server its location requires the greatest transmission distance between individual workstations and the server. Thus, this is more than likely a poor server location

## Location considerations

Figure 3.16 illustrates the use of a file server in its traditional role as a repository for application programs as well as when used for modem pooling and gateway operations. The transmission of information between workstations and servers far exceeds transmission between workstations. Due to this, the location of file servers is critical for ensuring that the network performance remains at an acceptable level. In the example illustrated in Figure 3.16, the server is located at a point on a bus-based local area network in which the transmission distance between each workstation and the server is maximized. This location results in the greatest propagation delay for the transmission of data between each workstation and the server and more than likely represents a poor location with respect to network performance. The reason for this representing a poor placement is the fact that the longer the distance between two networks devices on a CSMA/CD access protocol network, the greater the probability that one station will listen to the network and not hear a signal while another has just begun transmitting. This in turn results in an increased number of collisions that adversely affects network performance. In comparison, on a Token-Ring or ATM network, the positioning of servers is irrelevant. This is because collisions cannot occur and the location of a server cannot enhance network performance with respect to reducing collisions. However, as we will note later in this book, in a switch-based network the location of a server can affect the quantity of traffic routed through switches and can result in some undesirable traffic patterns that can be easily corrected.

### 3.1.7 Wire hubs

As previously mentioned in Chapter 2, both Token-Ring and 10BASE-T Ethernet networks use wiring concentrators or hubs. In a Token-Ring network, the hub is referred to as a multistation access unit (MAU), which is normally located in telephone wiring closets. Wiring from individual stations to the MAU forms a star, with MAUs interconnected to form a ring. In a 10BASE-T Ethernet network, hubs are also typically located in telephone wiring closets, with stations cabled to the hub in the form of a star. Hubs are then connected to one another to form a bus.

*Advantages*

Both Token-Ring and Ethernet hubs employ standard wiring between stations and the hub in the form of twisted-pair cable. Since workstations are connected to a single point, administration of a hub-based network is normally simpler and less costly since a central point allows network configuration and reconfiguration, monitoring, and management. Due to the value of hubs in local area networking, several vendors have introduced products commonly referred to as intelligent hubs. This type of product provides users with the ability to build local area networks ranging in scope from a single LAN with a small number of nodes to mixed protocol LANs with several thousand nodes that can be monitored, modified, and analyzed from a single point.

*Intelligent hubs*

An intelligent hub represents an order of magnitude advance in functionality and capability over conventional wire hubs. The intelligent hub includes its own microprocessor and memory which not only provide a network management capability but, in addition, may provide the ability to interconnect separate networks through integrated bridges and routers.

Most intelligent hubs include a multibus backplane which enables bridges and routers to access and route data originating over multiple types of media. When operating in this manner, the intelligent hub can be viewed as a PBX, providing connectivity between any station on any network connected through the hub while providing a centralized management and control capability. Through the use of an intelligent hub the administrator can enable or disable network ports from a network management workstation, segment a network to better balance traffic and improve performance, and facilitate trouble-shooting and maintenance operations. As networks have become more sophisticated, intelligent hubs evolved to facilitate their operation and management. With the ability of some intelligent hubs to bring together various media flavors of different local area networks, this device also provides a mechanism for the integration of prior piece-by-piece planning or for the correction of a plan gone astray. Thus, the use of an intelligent hub may provide you with an umbrella mechanism to bring together separate networks and media previously installed in a building.

## 3.1.8 LAN switches

Until the early 1990s the primary method employed to overcome the effect of network congestion was segmentation, subdividing a network into two or more entities interconnected by a bridge or router. Today the network manager and administrator have several options: to include the use of a higher operating rate network such as Fast Ethernet or ATM or the use of LAN switches. In this section we will focus our attention on the latter, which are also referred to as switching hubs.

To obtain an appreciation for the role of LAN switches we will first review the operation of conventional hubs, including bandwidth constraints associated with their use. Once this is accomplished we will focus our attention upon the different operational methods supported by LAN switches including the basic switching methods supported by different products that fall into this class of networking device. Using this information as a foundation we will explore the use of both Ethernet and Token-Ring switches, including obtaining an understanding of the key features built into many products as well as why the presence of some features and the absence of other features can result in degraded performance instead of an expected improve-ment in performance. Owing to this, we will examine how the use of certain switch features can result in network problems and how those problems can be alleviated through the use of other device features.

*Conventional hub bottlenecks*

Conventional hubs, which were developed to facilitate the cabling of network devices, also function as a bottleneck with respect to the use of network bandwidth. This bottleneck is applicable to all types of shared media networks to include both Ethernet and Token-Ring networks. To illustrate why this occurs, let us examine the operation of both Ethernet and Token-Ring hubs.

**Ethernet hub operation**

In an Ethernet environment a single LAN is usually referred to as a segment, with large networks typically composed of multiple segments connected by a bridge or router. The early implementations of Ethernet in the form of 10BASE-5 and 10BASE-2 coaxial cable based networks resulted in the use of a common medium to which workstations are attached. This is illustrated in Figure 3.17 which shows the cabling structure of a coaxial-based Ethernet network.

Based upon the fact that the bandwidth of the media is shared with only one user able to transmit at any given time, the Ethernet LAN segment shown in Figure 3.17 is commonly referred to as a shared-media, shared-bandwidth network.

A change in the network topology and cabling structure of Ethernet resulted in the development of hub-centric 10BASE-T networks, in which cabling from individual network devices to dedicated ports on the hub resulted in a star-wiring configuration. When two or more hubs are interconnected to form a

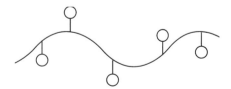

10BASE-5 and 10BASE-2 Ethernet networks consist of
a coaxial run to which network devices are attached

**Figure 3.17**   A shared media, shared bandwidth Ethernet LAN segment

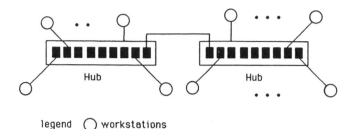

legend ◯ workstations

**Figure 3.18**  A two hub 10BASE-T Ethernet network

common network the wiring topology resembles a star-bus structure as illustrated in Figure 3.18. Although the wiring topology changed, the use of hubs did not alter the fact that the network remained a shared-media, shared-bandwidth network.

To illustrate the problem associated with the use of a shared-media, shared-bandwidth network, let us examine the operation of a conventional Ethernet hub. Figure 3.19 illustrates the data flow when one workstation (node 1) transmits a frame to another workstation, file server, gateway or another network device which is either connected to the same hub or to another hub which is connected to the hub that the data originator is connected to. As the hub functions as a data regenerator, the frame is repeated onto each connection to the hub to include interconnections to other hubs. This restricts data flow to one workstation at a time, since collisions occur when two or more attempt to gain access to the media at the same time.

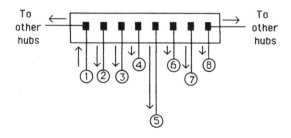

A conventional hub functions as a data regenerator, outputting an incoming frame received on one port onto all other ports.

**Figure 3.19**  Conventional hub dataflow

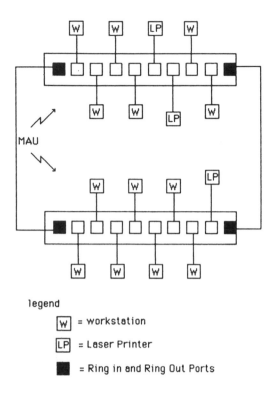

**Figure 3.20**   The connection of Token-Ring MAUs forms a star-ring topology

### Token-Ring hub operation

Although data flow on a Token-Ring network is circular, this type of network is also a shared-media, shared-bandwidth network. In a Token-Ring network environment hubs, referred to Multi-station Access Units or MAUs, are connected via their Ring In and Ring Out ports to form a star-ring topology similar to that shown in Figure 3.20. The actual data flow of a frame is from one device to the next, including flowing down the cable, called a lobe, connecting the device to the MAU port to an attached device and back to the port prior to flowing to the next port. Since only one frame can flow on the network at any point in time, access to the bandwidth is also shared. Thus, a Token-Ring network also represents a shared-media, shared-bandwidth network.

### Bottleneck creation

Conventional Ethernet hubs create network bottlenecks because all traffic flows through a shared backplane in the hub. Thus, every device connected to an Ethernet hub competes for a slice of the bandwidth of the backplane. In a Token-Ring environment devices compete to acquire a token, resulting in the sharing of network bandwidth in a similar manner. The end result of this bandwidth sharing is an average transmission rate per device that is many times below the operating rate of the network. For example, consider a departmental 10BASE-T network operating at 10 Mbps consisting of 12 interconnected 8 port hubs that supports a total of 96 devices. Then, the average slice of bandwidth available for each device is 10 Mbps/96 or approximately 104 Kbps. Note that although each device transmits and receives data at the LAN operating rate of 10 Mbps, their average data transfer capability is approximately 104 Kbps because each device must compete with 95 other devices to obtain access to the network. Similarly, a 96 node Token-Ring network would result in each device attached to that network having an average data transfer capability of 4 Mbps or 16 Mbps divided by 96, depending upon the operating rate of the network. This means that over a period of time the addition of network users, introduction of one or more graphic based applications or growth in the use of current applications can result in a severely taxed network. When this type of situation occurs, you can consider a variety of techniques to enhance network performance, including network segmentation through the use of a bridge or router, migrating your existing infrastructure to a different and higher operating rate technology, or employing LAN switches.

## Switching operations

The development of LAN switches has its foundation, similarly to many other areas of modern communications, in telephone technology. Shortly after the telephone was invented the switchboard was developed to enable multiple simultaneous conversations to occur without requiring telephone wires to be installed in a complex matrix between subscribers. Later, telephone office switches were developed to route calls based upon the telephone number dialed, followed in a similar manner by the development of bridges in a LAN environment. Bridges can be considered to represent an elementary type of switch due to their limited number of ports and simplistic switching operation. That switching operation is based upon whether or not the destination address in a frame read on one port is known to reside on that port.

A key limitation of a bridge is its common inability to perform more than one frame forwarding operation at any point in time. Recognizing this performance bottleneck, equipment designers developed a product that can perform multiple simultaneous frame forwarding operations. That device, which has evolved into a multi-billion dollar business, is the LAN switch. The LAN switch is based upon matrix switches which for decades have been successfully employed in telecommunications operations. By adding buffer memory to store address tables, frames flowing on LANs connected to different ports could be simultaneously read and forwarded via the switch fabric to ports connected to other networks.

### Basic components

Figure 3.21 illustrates the basic components of a four-port intelligent switch. Like a bridge that reads frames flowing on a network to construct a table of source addresses, the tables in a

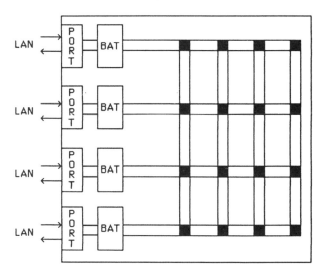

An intelligent switch consists of buffers and address tables (BAT),
logic and a switching fabric which permits frames entering
one port to be routed to any port in the switch. The destination
address in a frame is used to determine the associated port
with that address via a search of the address table, with the
port address used by the switching fabric for establishing the
cross connection.

**Figure 3.21**   Basic components of an intelligent switch

LAN switch can be created through a self-learning process. This allows the destination address in frames flowing on LANs connected to a switch port to be compared to a table of destination addresses and associated port numbers. When a match occurs between the destination address of a frame flowing on a network connected to a port and the address in the port's address table, the frame is copied into the switch and routed through the switch fabric to the destination port, where it is placed onto the network connected to that port. If the destination port is in use due to a previously established cross-connection between ports the frame is maintained in a buffer until it can be switched to its destination.

### Key advantages of use

A key advantage associated with the use of LAN switches results from their ability to support parallel switching, permitting multiple cross-connections between source and destination to occur simultaneously. For example, if four 10BASE-T networks were connected to the four port switch shown in Figure 3.21 two simultaneous cross-connections, each at 10 Mbps, could occur, resulting in an increase in bandwidth to 20 Mbps. Here each cross-connection represents a dedicated 10 Mbps bandwidth for the duration of a frame. Thus, from a theoretical perspective, an $N$ port LAN switch supporting a 10 Mbps operating rate on each port provides a throughput up to $N/2 \times 10$ Mbps. For example, a 128 port LAN switch would support a throughput up to $(128/2) \times 10$ Mbps or 640 Mbps, while a network constructed using a series of conventional hubs connected to one another would be limited to an operating rate of 10 Mbps, with each workstation on that network having an average bandwidth of 10 Mbps/128 or 78 Kbps.

Through the use of LAN switches you can overcome the operating rate limitation of a local area network. In an Ethernet environment, the cross-connection through a switching hub represents a dedicated connection so there will never be a collision. This fact enabled many switching hub vendors to use the collision wire-pair from conventional Ethernet to support simultaneous transmission in both directions between a connected node and hub port, resulting in a full-duplex transmission capability that will be discussed in more detail later in this section. In fact, a similar development permits Token-Ring switching hubs to provide full-duplex transmission since if there is only one station on a port there is no need to pass tokens and repeat frames, raising the maximum bi-directional throughput between a Token-Ring device and a switching hub port to 32 Mbps. Thus, the ability to support parallel switching as well as initiate dedicated cross-connections on a frame by frame basis can be considered the key advantages associated with the use of LAN switches. Both parallel switching and dedicated cross-connections permit higher bandwidth operations.

### Delay times

Switching occurs on a frame by frame basis, with the cross-connection torn down after being established for routing one frame. Thus, frames can be interleaved from two or more ports to a common destination port with a minimum of delay. For example, consider a maximum length Ethernet frame of 1526 bytes, including a 1500 byte data field and 26 overhead bytes. At a 10 Mbps operating rate each bit time is $1/10^7$ seconds or 100 ns. For a 1526 byte frame the minimum delay time if one frame precedes it in attempting to be routed to a common destination becomes:

$$1526 \text{ bytes} \times \frac{8 \text{ bits}}{\text{byte}} \times \frac{100 \text{ ns}}{\text{bit}} = 1.22 \text{ ms}$$

The previously computed delay time represents blocking resulting from frames on two service ports having a common destination and should not be confused with another delay time referred to as latency. Latency represents the delay associated with the physical transfer of a frame from one port via the switch to another port and is fixed based upon the architecture of the switch. In comparison, blocking delay depends upon the number of frames from different ports attempting to access a common destination port and the method by which the switch is designed to respond to blocking. Some switches simply have large buffers for each port and service ports in a round-robin fashion when frames on two or more ports attempt to access a common destination port. This method of service is not similar to politics as it does not show favoritism; however, it also does not consider the fact that some attached networks may have operating rates different from other attached networks. Other switch designs recognize that port buffers are filled based upon both the number of frames having a destination address of a different network and the operating rate of the network. Such switch designs use a priority service scheme based upon the occupancy of the port buffers in the switch.

## Switching techniques

There are three switching techniques used by intelligent switching hubs: cross-point, also referred to as cut-through or on the fly, store-and-forward, and a hybrid method which alternates between the first two methods based upon the frame error rate. As we will soon note, each technique has one or more advantages and disadvantages associated with its operation.

### Cross-point switching

The operation of a cross-point switch is based upon an examination of the destination of frames as they enter a port on the switching hub. The switch uses the destination address as a decision criterion to obtain a port destination from a look-up table as soon as the destination address in the frame is read. This technique enables the switch to initiate its table lookup and cross-connection operation without having to read the entire frame, providing a very fast switching operation that minimizes delay.

Figure 3.22 illustrates the basic operation of cross-point or cut-through switching. Under this technique the destination address in a frame is read prior to the frame being stored (1). That address is forwarded to a look-up table (2) to determine the port destination address which is used by the switching fabric to initiate a cross-connection to the destination port (3). As this switching method only requires the storage of a small portion of a frame until it is able to read the destination address and perform its table look-up operation to initiate switching to an appropriate output port, latency through the switch is minimized.

Latency functions as a brake on two-way frame exchanges. For example, in a client-server environment the transmission of a frame by a workstation results in a server response. Thus, the minimum wait time is $2 \times$ latency for each client-server exchange, lowering the effective throughput of the switch. As a cross-point switching technique results in a minimal amount of

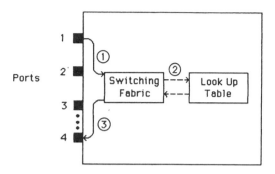

A cross-point or cut-through operating switch reads the
destination address in a frame prior to storing the entire
frame (1). It forwards that address to a look-up table (2) to
determine the port destination address which is used by the
switching fabric to provide a cross-connection to the
destination port (3).

**Figure 3.22**   Cross-point/cut-through switching

latency, the effect upon throughput of the delay attributable to a
LAN switch using this switching technique is minimal.

### Store-and-forward

In comparison to cut-through switching, a store-and-forward
LAN switch first stores an entire frame in memory prior to
operating on the data fields within the frame. Once the frame is
stored, the switching hub checks the frame's integrity by
performing a cyclic redundancy check (CRC) upon the contents
of the frame, comparing its computed CRC against the CRC
contained in the frame's Frame Check Sequence (FCS) field. If
the two match, the frame is considered to be error-free and
additional processing and switching will occur. Otherwise, the
frame is considered to have one or more bits in error and will be
discarded.

In addition to CRC checking, the storage of a frame permits
filtering against various frame fields to occur. Although a few
manufacturers of store-and-forward LAN switches support
different types of filtering, the primary advantage advertised
by such manufacturers is data integrity. Whether or not this is
actually an advantage depends upon how you view the
additional latency introduced by the storage of a full frame in
memory as well as the necessity for error checking. Concerning
the latter, switches should operate error-free, so a store-and-

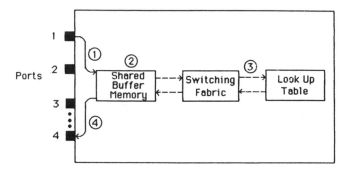

A store-and-forward LAN switch reads the frame destination
address (1) as it is placed in buffer memory (2). As the entire
frame is being read into memory, a look-up operation (3) is performed to obtain a destination port address. Once the entire
frame is in memory a CRC check is performed and one or more
filtering operations may be peformed. If the CRC check indicates
the frame is error-free, it is forwarded from memory to its
destination address (4), otherwise it is disregarded.

**Figure 3.23**   Store- and forward switching

forward switch only removes network errors which should be
negligible to start with.

When a switch removes an errored frame, the originator will
retransmit the frame after a period of time. As an errored frame
arriving at its destination network address is also discarded,
many persons question the necessity of error checking by a
store-and-forward LAN switch. However, filtering capability, if
offered, may be far more useful as you could use this capability,
for example, to route protocols carried in frames to destination
ports far more easily than by frame destination address. This is
especially true if you have hundreds or thousands of devices
connected to a large switch. You might set up two or three filters
instead of entering a large number of destination addresses into
the switch.

Figure 3.23 illustrates the operation of a store-and-forward
LAN switches. Note that a common switch design is to use shared
buffer memory to store entire frames which increases the latency
associated with this type of switch. As the minimum length of an
Ethernet frame is 72 bytes, then the minimum one way delay or
latency, not counting the switch overhead associated with the
look-up table and switching fabric operation, becomes:

$$96\,\mu s + 72 \text{ bytes} \times 8 \text{ bits/byte} \times 100 \text{ ns/bit}$$

$$\text{or} \quad 9.6 \times 10^{-6} + 576 \times 100 \times 10^{-9}$$

$$\text{or} \quad 67.2 \times 10^{-6} \text{seconds}$$

Here $9.6\,\mu s$ represents the Ethernet interframe gap, while 100 ns/bit is the bit duration of a 10 Mbps Ethernet LAN. Thus, the minimum one-way latency of a store-and-forward Ethernet switch is 0.0000672 seconds, while a round trip minimum latency is twice that duration. For a maximum length Ethernet frame with a data field of 1500 bytes, the frame length becomes 1526 bytes. Thus, the one way maximum latency becomes:

$$96\,\mu s + 1526 \text{ bytes} \times 8 \text{ bits/byte} \times 100 \text{ ns/bit}$$

$$\text{or} \quad 9.6 \times 10^{-6} + 12208 \times 100 \times 10^{-9}$$

$$\text{or} \quad 0.012304 \text{ seconds}$$

**Hybrid**

A hybrid switch supports both cut-through and store-and-forward switching, selecting the switching method based upon monitoring the error rate encountered by reading the CRC at the end of each frame and comparing its value to a computed CRC performed on the fly on the fields protected by the CRC. Initially the switch might set each port to a cut-through mode of operation. If too many bad frames are noted on a port, the switch will automatically set the frame processing mode to store-and-forward, permitting the CRC comparison to be performed prior to the frame being forwarded. This permits frames in error to be discarded without having them pass through the switch. As the switch, no pun intended, between cut-through and store-and-forward modes of operation occurs adaptively, another term used to refer to the operation of this type of switch is adaptive.

The major advantages of a hybrid switch are that it provides minimal latency when error rates are low and discards frames by adapting to a store-and-forward switching method so it can discard errored frames when the frame error rate rises. From an economic perspective, the hybrid switch can logically be expected to cost more than a cut-through or store-and-forward switch as its software development effort is more comprehensive. However, due to the competitive market for communications products upon occasion its price may be reduced below competitive switch technologies.

In addition to being categorized by their switching technique, LAN switches can be classified by their support of single or multiple addresses per port. The former method is referred to as port-based switching, while the latter switching method is referred to as segment-based switching.

### Port-based switching

A LAN switch which performs port-based switching only supports a single address per port. This restricts switching to one device per port; however, it results in a minimum amount of memory in the switch as well as providing for a relatively fast table look-up when the switch uses a destination address in a frame to obtain the port for initiating a cross-connect.

Figure 3.24 illustrates an example of the use of a port-based switch. In this example $M$ user workstations use the switch to contend for the resources of $N$ servers. If $M > N$, then a switch

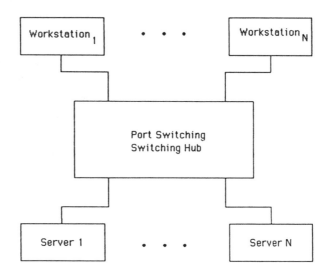

A port-based switch associates one address with each port, minimizing the time required to match the destination address of a frame against a table of destination addresses and associated port numbers.

**Figure 3.24** Port-based switching

connected to Ethernet 10 Mbps LANs can support a maximum throughput of $N/2 \times 10$ Mbps, since up to $N/2$ simultaneous client-server frame flows can occur through the switch.

It is important to compare the maximum potential throughput through a switch to its rated backplane speed. If the maximum potential throughput is less than the rated backplane speed, the switch will not cause delays based upon the traffic being routed through the device. For example, consider a 64 port switch that has a backplane speed of 400 Mbps. If the maximum port rate is 10 Mbps, then the maximum throughput assuming 32 active cross-connections were simultaneously established becomes 320 Mbps. In this example the switch has a backplane transfer capability sufficient to handle the worst case data transfer scenario. Now let us assume that the maximum backplane data transfer capability was 200 Mbps. This would reduce the maximum number of simultaneous cross-connections capable of being serviced to 20 instead of 32 and adversely affect switch performance under certain operational conditions.

As a port-based switch only has to store one address per port, search times are minimized. When combined with a pass-through or cut-through switching technique, this type of switch results in a minimal latency to include the overhead of the switch in determining the destination port of a frame.

### Segment-based switching

A segment-based switching technique requires a LAN switch to support multiple addresses per port. Through the use of this type of switch, you achieve additional networking flexibility since you can connect other hubs to a single segment-based switch port.

Figure 3.25 illustrates an example of the use of a segment-based switch in an Ethernet environment. Although two segments in the form of conventional hubs with multiple devices connected to each hub are shown in the lower portion of Figure 3.25, note that a segment can consist of a single device, resulting in the connection of one device to a port on a segment switch being similar to a connection on a port switch. However, unlike a port switch that is limited to supporting one address per port, the segment switch can, if necessary, support multiple devices connected to a port. Thus, the two servers connected to the switch at the top of Figure 3.25 could, if desired, be placed on a conventional hub or a high speed hub, such as a 100BASE-T

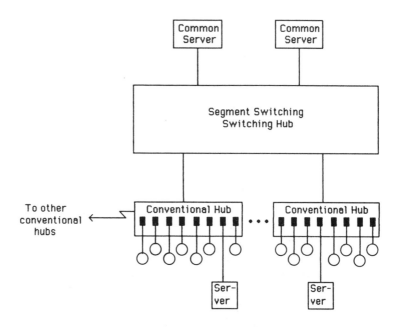

Through the use of a segment-based switching hub, you
can maintain servers for use by workstations on a common
network segment as well as provide access by all workstations to common servers.

**Figure 3.25**   Segment-based switching

hub, which in turn would be connected to a single port on a
segment switch.

In Figure 3.25 each conventional hub acts as a repeater and it
forwards every frame transmitted on that hub to the switch,
regardless of whether or not the frame requires the resources of
the switch. The segment switch examines the destination
address of each frame against addresses in its look-up table,
only forwarding those frames that warrant being forwarded.
Otherwise, frames are discarded as they are local to the
conventional hub. Through the use of a segment-based switching hub, you can maintain the use of local servers with respect
to existing LAN segments as well as installing servers whose
access is common to all network segments. The latter is
illustrated in Figure 3.25 by the connection of two common
servers shown at the top of the LAN switch. If you obtain a store-
and-forward segment switch which supports filtering, you could
control access to common servers from individual workstations

or by workstations on a particular segment. In addition, you can also use the filtering capability of a store-and-forward segment-based switch to control access from workstations located on one segment to workstations or servers located on another segment.

## Using LAN switches

Today you can acquire network specific switches that operate with a single type of LAN or switches with a translating capability that enable dissimilar networks to be serviced. In addition, some LAN switches incorporate a built-in routing feature that enables the switch to perform basic bridging and routing. Due to the almost infinite number of methods by which LAN switches can be employed, we will focus our attention upon several common generic methods; however, we will need to use specific types of LANs to illustrate and describe the operation of different switching methods.

### Network redistribution

Network redistribution involves the movement of bandwidth-intensive workstations off conventional hubs, connecting them directly to ports on a switch. Figure 3.26 illustrates an example of network redistribution through the use of a LAN switch.

In the left portion of Figure 3.26 a conventional hub is shown providing support for $n$ nodes to a common server. Assuming that two workstations require access to a visual database, transmit or receive large files, or perform other bandwidth-intensive applications, those workstations were redistributed onto a switch as shown in the right portion of Figure 3.26. Note that only one server is shown in the 'after' network schematic, with the server relocated from the conventional hub to the switch, with the server connected to the switch by either a fat pipe or high speed connection. Here the term fat pipe is used to refer to a group of switch ports that function as a single entity, providing a higher bandwidth than obtainable by a single connection of a switch to a network device. If a conventional connection were used the redistribution of workstations would have a negligible effect upon performance as access to the server would not increase,

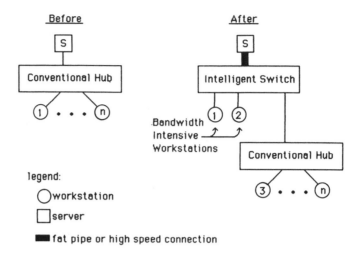

Through the movement of bandwidth intensive workstations off
conventional hubs, you can minimize the effect of bottlenecks
they cause on other workstations remaining connected to conventional hubs.

**Figure 3.26**  Network redistribution

only enhancing any peer-to-peer communications that may
occur.

### Server segmentation

As access to data on servers is normally the reason why
network performance degrades, another technique commonly
used is to segment servers. Figure 3.27 illustrates an example
of server segmentation obtained through the use of a LAN
switch.

In the top portion of Figure 3.27 two servers are shown on a
network consisting of interconnected conventional hubs. In
this example access to either server is constrained by the
operating rate of the network. For example, if the top portion
of Figure 3.27 represented a 10BASE-T network, the maximum bandwidth to a server would be 10 Mbps, which is the
operating rate of the LAN, while the average bandwidth would
be 10 Mbps/$n$, where $n$ represents the total number of nodes
on the network.

Through the use of a LAN switch, servers can be placed on
their own network segment as illustrated in the lower portion of

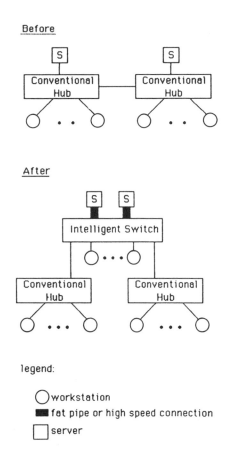

**Figure 3.27**  Server segmentation

Figure 3.27. In addition, through the use of a fat pipe or high speed connection between each server and the switch, you can enhance access to each server.

If you simply moved each conventional hub onto a port on the switch your ability to enhance network access would be limited. This limitation would result from the fact that the simultaneous access of workstations on different conventional hubs to different servers only provides the ability to double bandwidth. Thus, you would more than likely want to consider connecting high activity workstations directly to the switch, which is shown in the lower portion of Figure 3.27.

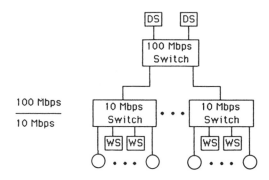

Legend:

    WS  Workgroup Server
    DS  Departmental Server

**Figure 3.28**  Using a high speed switch as a network backbone

### Backbone operation

A third common use of LAN switches is as a backbone to connect lower operating rate LANs or LAN switches. In doing so, you can create a tiered network hierarchy.

Figure 3.28 illustrates the use of one 100BASE-T switch to interconnect a group of 10BASE-T switches. Although individual stations are shown connected to each 10 Mbps switch port, this discussion is also applicable to the use of segment-based switches as well as segment-based switches that are used to connect individual workstations on some ports and network segments on other ports. In this example note that workgroup servers remain local to each 10 Mbps switch, resulting in a majority of 10 Mbps switch traffic remaining local to each switch. Only when communications are required to a departmental server or a workgroup server connected to another switch will traffic be routed to the 100 Mbps backbone switch.

An alternative to the use of a tiered structure backbone switch is the use of a conventional 100 Mbps LAN for backbone operations, such as a conventional 100BASE-T non-switching hub. Although the cost of a non-switching hub is considerably less than a switch, it only permits one frame at a time to flow through the hub between interconnected devices. In comparison, the use of a 100 Mbps switch with $n$ ports would support a throughput of $100 \times n/2$ as it permits $n/2$ simultaneous cross-connects.

### Handling speed incompatibilities

One of the main problems associated with the use of LAN switches occurs when a device connected on a high speed port requires communications with a device connected on a lower operating rate port. For example, assume that a server is connected to a switch at 100 Mbps while a workstation is connected via a 10 Mbps operating rate. Since buffer storage on each port is finite, it becomes possible for a client query followed by a long server response to result in the loss of frames once a buffer is filled. A similar problem can occur in the reverse direction when the cumulative operating rate of many clients attempting to access a common device exceed the operating rate of the connection between the switch and that device. Recognizing this problem, vendors developed several methods to regulate the transmission of information, a process referred to as flow control. Flow control is primarily applicable to Ethernet switches since the rotating token can be used to delay transmission on Token-Ring switches. Two popular methods used by switch vendors to regulate the transmission of information include backpressure and server software modules.

### Backpressure

Backpressure is a term used to represent the generation of a false collision signal. Because a collision signal causes an Ethernet workstation or server to delay further transmission based on an exponential backoff algorithm, it provides a mechanism for implementing flow control. That is, once buffer storage in the switch has reached a predefined level of occupancy, the switch will generate a false collision signal. As the transmitting device delays further transmission, the switch's destination port has the opportunity to empty the contents of its buffer, precluding the occurrence of data loss.

Although backpressure is an effective flow control mechanism, its use requires a second wire pair. This makes it mutually exclusive with full duplex-transmission (FDX) since workstations and servers directly cabled to switch ports never encounter a collision and can operate in a FDX mode by using the collision wire pair for transmission in the opposite direction. If you require full-duplex transmission and want to preclude the loss of frames via flow control, you must turn to the use of a server software module.

### Server software module

Several switch vendors developed software that operates on Windows NT and NetWare servers that regulate the flow of data between switch ports and those servers. To accomplish flow control the switch transmits a predefined signal to the module operating on the server, while a second signal is used to inform the module to resume transmission. The major difference between the use of backpressure and server software modules is that the latter can provide support for full-duplex transmission.

### ATM considerations

Although ATM equipment has been gaining considerable momentum for use for wide area networks, its use in a LAN environment is primarily as a backbone for interconnecting what many persons refer to as legacy LANs, such as Token-Ring and Ethernet, instead of as a replacement of those networks. The reason for the lack of ATM to the desktop is more than likely due to its cost, lack of multimedia desktop applications, and the fact that both Ethernet and Token-Ring LANs can continue to provide a reasonable level of performance by the segmentation and connection of segments via a high speed backbone.

The use of ATM switches as a backbone for connecting legacy LAN traffic results in a series of incompatibilities that must be overcome. The major incompatibilities between ATM and legacy LANs include their connection method, address, and transport mechanism. An ATM network uses a connection-oriented switching mechanism to route traffic in the form of 53 byte cells from source to destination using Virtual Path Identifiers (VPIs) and Virtual Channel Identifiers (VCIs). In comparison, legacy LANs are connectionless, transmitting variable length frames containing 48 bit MAC addresses to all stations on a network, with the addressed station then reading the frame. To overcome these incompatibilities, the ATM Forum developed a specification referred to as LAN Emulation (LANE). LAN Emulation represents a method whereby ATM's connection-oriented infrastructure provides a service which enables stations on legacy LANs to connect to other legacy stations, as well as devices connected to ATM switches by mimicking or emulating the connectionless operation of legacy networks.

*LAN emulation services*

ATM provides LAN Emulation through a client-server model. The client is commonly implemented on an ATM adapter installed in a legacy LAN switch. The server portion of the model which provides the emulation services is commonly implemented in an ATM switch; however, some vendors implement the emulation services in a router connected to an ATM switch.

LAN Emulation Services are performed by a LAN Emulation Server (LES), a Broadcast and Unknown Server (BUS), and a LAN Emulation Configuration Server (LECS). These three components can be provided either as a single centralized service or distributed and configured to provide redundancy. The LES is responsible for registering MAC addresses as well as for converting between MAC and ATM addresses.

Unlike legacy LANs that include a broadcast capability, ATM is a connection-oriented point-to-point network. Thus, a mechanism is required to facilitate obtaining unknown addresses by querying each station on an ATM network as well as for converting a legacy broadcast into appropriate ATM connections. The Broadcast and Unknown Server (BUS) assumes this responsibility by handling all of the broadcasting and multicasting functions.

The third component of LAN Emulation Services is the LAN Emulation Configuration Server (LECS). The LECS is responsible for providing configuration information about the ATM network and assigns individual LANE clients to emulated LANs by directing them to a LES.

*LAN emulation operation*

To illustrate the operation of LAN Emulation, consider Figure 3.29, which illustrates the use of an ATM backbone switch to provide communications between stations on two legacy LAN switches as well as from those stations to servers and a router connected to the ATM backbone. When a station on a legacy LAN first generates a frame that requires transportation via an ATM backbone, the LEC automatically locates the LECS via the use of a well-known ATM VPI,VCI address. This is denoted by the line labeled with the numerical 1 in Figure 3.29.

The LECS returns the address of the LES and the BUS. This is indicated by the line labeled with the numerical 2 in Figure 3.29. Once the address of the LES is known, the LEC can transmit an address resolution message to the LES. This is indicated by the

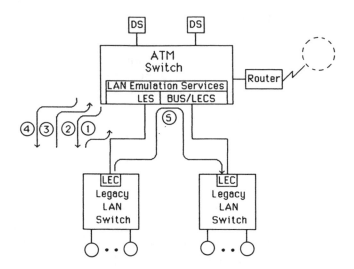

1. LEC locates the LECS.
2. LECS provides addresses of LES and BUS.
3. LEC requests ATM address of destination via an address resolution message to the LES.
4. LES provides ATM address.
5. LEC initiates connection.

Legend:

DS    Departmental Server                LES    LAN Emulation Server
◯    Workstations on legacy LANS    LECS  LAN Emulation Con-
BUS Broadcast and Unknown Server           figuration Server

**Figure 3.29** ATM Emulation enables legacy LANs to operate via an ATM backbone

line with the numerical 3 in Figure 3.29. If the LES previously resolved a MAC address into an ATM address, it can directly provide the ATM address from its cache memory, as indicated by the line associated with the numerical 4 in Figure 3.29. The LEC then uses the ATM address to establish a connection through the ATM switch to the destination legacy LAN switch, as indicated by the line labeled with the numerical 5 in Figure 3.29.

If the LES did not have the required ATM address, the LEC would send a request to the BUS. The BUS would broadcast the address resolution message to all end stations, with the LEC associated with the destination station returning its ATM address to both the LES and the originating LEC. This enables the LEC to initiate a connection to the appropriate ATM endpoint. In addition, the response is placed in both the LEC's and LES' cache memory so that subsequent requests via the same or different LECs can be expediently serviced.

*LAN emulation constraints*

One of the major problems associated with the use of ATM as a backbone for legacy LANs involves the LAN Emulation process. If the backbone switch performing emulation services should fail, all communications between legacy LANs also fail. Another problem is the temporary failure of an ATM switch due to a bad power supply causing previously learned addresses to be purged from cache memory. If a network using an ATM backbone has thousands of stations on legacy LANs, it can take 15 to 20 minutes or more until the MAC to ATM addresses are again resolved, adversely affecting the performance between legacy LANs during that learning period. For these reasons, many organizations using an ATM backbone continue to place workgroup servers on local switches instead of moving them to a 'server farm' on the backbone. This infrastructure enables local switches to continue to provide access to workgroup servers even if the backbone should fail.

## 3.2 SOFTWARE REQUIREMENTS

The installation of a local area network requires a variety of hardware and software products. As a minimum, each work-station on the network requires the installation of an interface card into its system unit. This interface card contains a number of ROM modules and specialized circuitry as well as a microprocessor that implements the access method used to communicate on the common cable.

In some local area networks, one personal computer must be reserved to process the network commands and functions. Since it services these commands and functions, it is normally called the network server. A combination of specialized software that overlays the operating system on each workstation connected to the network as well as software placed upon the server governs the operation of the network. To understand the role of the network server and the functions of LAN software, let us first review how a personal computer operates under a conventional version of the disk operating system (DOS) used in the IBM PC and compatible personal computer environment.

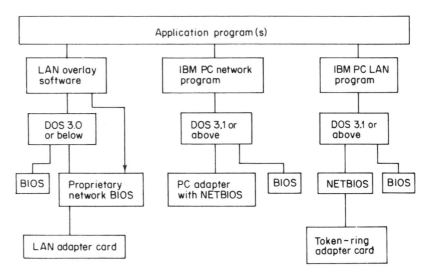

**Figure 3.30**   Original PC LAN hardware and software relationships in an IBM PC enviroment

## 3.2.1 DOS

DOS is a single-user operating system that is designed to provide access to peripherals attached to the system as well as control of those peripherals, the interpretation of commands to perform various functions on the system, management of disk storage and memory. Under DOS, your keyboard is the standard input device and your display is the standard output device, with the control of the personal computer limited to one user.

As soon as a networked personal computer is initialized, its network software routines are added to DOS, permitting the computer to interact with the rest of the network. Prior to the introduction of DOS version 3.1, this software was normally an overlay to DOS that served to filter commands. Thus, when a command was issued to perform a function on the PC the software overlay permitted the command to pass directly to DOS for execution. If a command is issued that references the network, the software overlay intercepts or filters the command from reaching DOS and in conjunction with the adapter board transmits the command onto the network. If the network is server based, the non-local commands must be sent to a server for additional processing. The left-hand portion of Figure 3.30 illustrates the hardware and software components required when LAN software was originally designed as an overlay to DOS.

Prior to the introduction of DOS 3.1, most LAN vendors either developed proprietary methods to lock files and records or ignored incorporating such features, in effect limiting their networks to simple file-swapping and printer-sharing applications. Since there was no Network Basic Input/Output System (NetBIOS), a proprietary network BIOS was developed and accessed via the vendor's LAN overlay software to send and receive data from the LAN adapter card. Here NetBIOS is the lowest level of software on a local area network, translating commands to send and receive data via the adapter card into the instructions that actually perform the requested functions.

With the introduction of IBM's first local area network, referred to as the PC Network, in August 1984, IBM released all three components required to implement an IBM local area network using IBM equipment: the IBM PC Network Program, PC DOS 3.1, and the IBM PC Network Adapter. The IBM PC Network Program was actually a tailored version of Microsoft Corporation's Microsoft Networks (MS-NET) software which is essentially a program that overlays DOS and permits workstations on a network to share their disks and peripheral devices. DOS 3.1, also developed by Microsoft, added file- and record-locking capabilities to DOS, permitting multiple users to access and modify data. Without file- and record-locking capability in DOS, custom software was required to obtain these functions, since their absence would result in the last person saving data onto a file overwriting changes made by other persons to the file. Thus, DOS 3.1 provided networking and application programmers with a set of standards they could use in developing network software.

Included on the IBM PC Network Adapter card in ROM is an extensive amount of programming instructions known as NetBIOS. The middle portion of Figure 3.30 illustrates the hardware and software components of an IBM PC LAN network.

When the IBM Token-Ring Network was introduced, NetBIOS was removed from the adapter card and incorporated as a separate software program which was activated from DOS. The right-hand column of Figure 3.30 illustrates the hardware and software relationship for the IBM Token-Ring local area network. Here, the network operating system for the Token-Ring was renamed as the IBM PC LAN Program from its former name of the IBM PC Network Program.

Due to the standardization of file and record locking under DOS 3.1, any multi-user software program written for DOS 3.1 or later versions of that operating system will execute on any

LAN that supports this version of DOS. Although DOS 3.1 supports many networking functions, it is not a networking operating system. In fact, a variety of networking operating systems support DOS 3.1 and later versions of DOS, including MS-NET, IBM's PC Network Program, IBM's Token-Ring Program, Microsoft's Windows NT and Novell's NetWare. This permits the user to select a third-party network operating system to use with IBM network hardware, or the user can consider obtaining both third-party hardware and software to construct his or her local area network.

## 3.2.2 Network operating system

A modern network operating system operates as an overlay to the personal computer's operating system, providing the connectivity which enables personal computers to communicate with one another, share such network resources as hard disks, CD-ROM jukebox drives and printers, and even obtain access to mainframes and minicomputers. Two of the more popular LAN operating systems are Microsoft Corporation's Windows NT, and Novell Corporation's NetWare.

Both Windows NT and NetWare are file server-based network operating systems. This means that most network modules reside on the file server. A shell program is loaded into each workstation and works in conjunction with the server modules. The shell program workstation filters commands, directing user- entered commands to DOS or to the network modules residing on the server. Communications between the shell and the server modules can be considered as occurring at the OSI Reference Model's Network Layer. Microsoft's Window's NT uses NetBIOS Extended User Interface, commonly referred to as NetBEUI, which is automatically installed when the operating system is installed, while Novell's NetWare uses its Internetwork Packet Exchange (IPX) protocol as the language with which the workstation communicates with the file server. Both Windows NT and NetWare support the concurrent use of multiple protocols. For example, Windows NT includes built-in support for TCP/IP, NWLink, and Data Link Control. Until the mid-1980s it was difficult to support more than one protocol at a time due to the manner by which network software residing on a workstation or server communicated with one or more software modules known as the protocol stack. Once we have examined the manner by which a client gains access to a server and obtained an overview of NetWare and Windows NT, we will then turn our attention to the method by which multiple stacks can be employed to support multiple protocols.

*Services*

The process by which the shell enables a workstation to communicate with a set of services residing on a server is known as a client/server relationship. Services provided by network modules on the server can range in scope from file access and transfer, shared printer utilization, and printer queuing to electronic mail. Other features available in most network operating systems include the ability to partition disk storage and allocate such storage to different network users, and the assignment of various types of security levels for individual network users and groups of users as well as on directories, files, and printers. Some network operating systems include a disk mirroring feature as well as a remote console dial-in capability.

As file information in the form of updated accounting, payroll, and engineering data can be critical to the health of a company, it is often very important to have duplicate copies of information in the event a hard disk should fail. Disk mirroring is a feature which duplicates network information on two or more disks simultaneously. Thus, if one disk should fail network operations can continue.

A remote console dial-in capability enables a network user to gain access to the network from a remote location. This feature can be particularly advantageous for persons who travel and wish to transmit and receive messages with colleagues back at the office or obtain access to information residing on the network. As the administration of a network can be a complex process, a remote dial-in feature may also make life less taxing for a network administrator. Working at home or at another location, the administrator can reassign privileges and perform other network functions that may not be possible in an eight-hour day.

*Looking at NetWare*

As the best way to obtain information concerning the relationship of a network operating system to network hardware is by

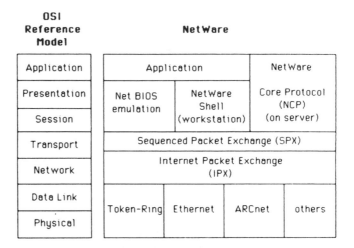

**Figure 3.31** NetWare and the OSI Reference Model

examining the software, we will do so. In doing so we will discuss Novell Corporation's NetWare, and Microsoft's Windows NT as those network operating systems (NOS) are by far the most popular of all NOSs used.

### Architecture

The architecture or structure of NetWare can be mapped to the OSI Reference Model; it provides an indication of the method by which this network operating system provides support for different types of hardware and includes the capability for the routing of packets between networks. Figure 3.31 illustrates the general relationship between NetWare and the OSI Reference Model.

In examining Figure 3.31, note that NetWare supports numerous types of local area networks. This means that you can use NetWare as the network operating system on Token-Ring, Ethernet, ARCnet, and other types of networks. In fact, NetWare also supports different types of operating systems, such as DOS, OS/2, UNIX, and Macintosh's Finder. This means that NetWare is capable of supporting different types of local area networks as well as workstations that use different operating systems.

At the network layer, Novell's IPX protocol performs addressing and internet routing functions. To accomplish this, an IPX packet contains both the source and destination network addresses. Those addresses are assigned by a network administrator and provide the mechanism for the routing of data between networks by routers which examine the network layer.

IPX is a connectionless network layer protocol that does not guarantee the delivery of data. To provide a reliable delivery mechanism, Novell developed its Sequenced Packet eXchange (SPX), a transport level interface which provides a connection-oriented packet delivery service.

At the session and presentation layers, NetWare uses a NetBIOS emulator which provides an interface between application programs written in compliance with NetBIOS and NetWare. As previously mentioned, the NetWare shell operates on each workstation and communicates with a core set of modules that reside on servers. That core set of modules is known as the NetWare Core Protocol (NCP). NCP provides such functions as workstation and network naming management, file partitioning, access and locking capability, accounting, and security.

### Looking at Windows NT

Windows NT, including the workstation and server, represents both a computer operating system and network operating system that can function together or independently. The basic networking protocol used by Windows NT is NetBEUI which provides a network user interface for local workstations and servers.

### NetBIOS

The NetBIOS Extended User Interface represents an extension of PC BIOS to the network. NetBIOS was originally developed by IBM as a simple network protocol for interconnecting PCS on a common network. The naming structure of the protocol results in names assigned to devices being translated into network adapter card (i.e. MAC) addresses. This results in NetBIOS operating at the data link layer. In addition, since the NetBIOS naming structure is non-hierarchical, there is no provision for specifying network addresses. Due to this, NetBIOS is considered to be non-routable. Thus, the initial method used to join two or more NetBIOS networks together was restricted to bridging.

*NetBEUI* Recognizing the routability problem of NetBIOS, the NetBIOS Extended User Interface (NetBEUI) allows data to be transported by a transport protocol to obtain the ability to interconnect separate networks. In fact, NetBEUI can be transported by TCP/IP and even IPX/SPX. To accomplish this, NetBEUI maintains a table of NAMES that are associated with TCP/IP addresses when TCP/IP is used as a transport protocol, and a similar table matched to NetWare network addresses and station MAC addresses when NetBEUI is transported via IPX/SPX.

To illustrate the operation of a few of the capabilities of Windows NT networking we will briefly use a Windows NT workstation to display the servers on both an NT and a NetWare network and transfer a file from an NT workstation to a Novell file server. In actuality, both NetWare and Windows NT can communicate on a common network since NT supports the NWLink protocol that provides compatibility with NetWare's IPX/SPX protocol.

### Network operations

Figure 3.32 illustrates the use of File Manager on a Windows NT workstation to view the names of devices on both a Windows network and a NetWare network. Figure 3.33 illustrates the result obtained by first selecting an appropriate NetWare server and then selecting a directory on that server which we wish to access. This action will result in the mapping of drive E on the local workstation to the path shown in Figure 3.33. Once we enter the appropriate connection information, drive E on the local Windows NT workstation will be mapped to the directory FRED located under the directory sys on the server MDPC-1.

After we correctly log onto the server, we can run network applications or transfer data to or from the server. Figure 3.34 illustrates how you could select 'Move' from the File menu and enter the command c:\funds\*.* to move all files under the subdirectory FUNDS on the local workstation to the network server.

### Multiple procotol support

The ability of an application program on a workstation to communicate via a local area network is dependent upon a group of communications software modules referred to as a protocol stack. The protocol stack can be thought of as an interface between an application and the network adapter which supports the orderly flow of information onto and from the network. Figure 3.35 illustrates the relationship between an

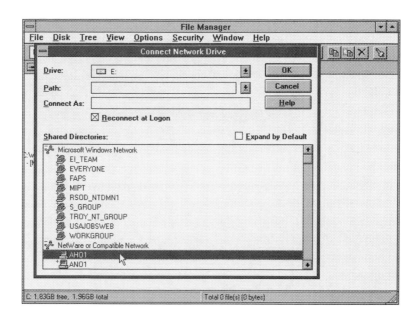

**Figure 3.32**  Viewing devices on both a Windows and a Novell network through the Windows NT File Manager

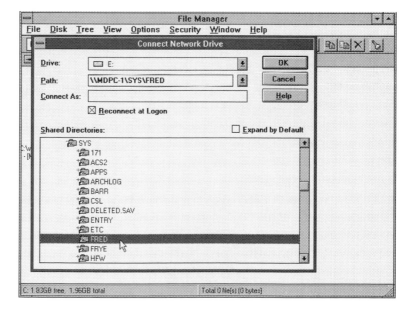

**Figure 3.33**  Selecting a path to a directory on a Novell server that will be mapped to drive E on a local workstation

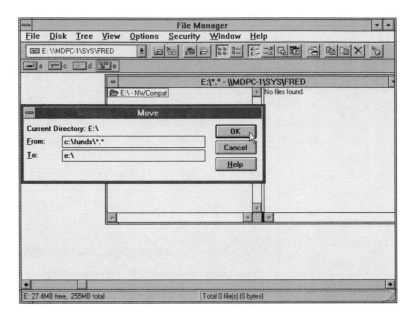

**Figure 3.34** Using File Manager to move all files in the directory FUNDS on the local workstation to the directory FRED on the file server

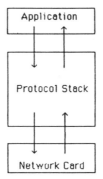

**Figure 3.35** Relationship between an application program, protocol stack and network card

application program running on a workstation, the communications software used to form a protocol stack and the network adapter card.

To access the network the application calls a procedure contained in the protocol stack. The protocol stack in turn sends a request to the network via the network adapter card. When the information flow is reversed, the adapter receives information from the network and generates an interrupt which informs the protocol stack to retrieve data from the card. The protocol stack then informs the application that information is available for its use and provides the information upon a request generated by the application.

A set of standards referred to as the application programming interface (API) governs the transfer of information between applications and protocol stacks. Another set of standards defines the composition of a protocol stack as well as how multiple stacks can be supported.

### Standards

Standards that define the composition of a protocol stack are based upon the operating system used by the workstation and the network operating system. Concerning the latter, the protocol stack operating on a workstation must support the data transport mechanism of the network operating system. Examples of data transport mechanisms include NetBIOS, IPX, TCP/IP and Logical Link Control (LLC). Standards that define the interface between multiple stacks fall into two major camps: Open Data-Link (ODI) jointly developed by Apple Computer and Novell, and the Network Driver Interface Specification (NDIS) jointly developed by 3Com and Microsoft. Two additional standard protocol managers are the Packet Driver Specification (PDS) from FTP Software and the Adapter Support Interface (ASI) from IBM.

PDS evolved from a series of hardware drivers developed at Clarkson University that are often referred to as the Clarkson Packet Drivers. The setup when a packet driver is used is relatively simple, requiring only the identification of the software interrupt when the driver is loaded. Then the protocol stack is loaded and interfaces with the packet driver through the software interrupt.

ASI is implemented in IBM's Token-Ring LAN Support Program. It uses a protocol manager and a hardware interface to support different protocol interfaces. In doing so ASI requires drivers to be written to the ASI interface which enables ASI and ODI or NDIS to be implemented on the same workstation.

### Rationale for multiprotocol stacks

To illustrate the rationale for the development of multiple protocol stack standards requires a review of single protocol stack arrangements as well as the limitations associated with this approach to networking. Most implementations of NetWare through version 3.11 required the network administrator to use the program WSGEN to generate IPX.COM which would include a network adapter card driver. Once this is accomplished the generated version of IPX.COM and another program known as NETx.COM, where x represents the version number, would be loaded onto a workstation. NETx.COM is a workstation shell which filters commands entered from the keyboard. This shell passes DOS commands to DOS and passes network commands to IPX for transmission onto the network. Since the shell sits atop IPX, the AUTOEXEC.BAT file of a DOS workstation connected to a NetWare LAN would contain the following statements:

C:\path\IPX
C:\path\NETX
F:

In the above statements the path normally represents a directory commonly named NETWORK or NETWARE, where the network files reside. The statement F: simply changes the user to drive F, which is normally the first network drive used by NetWare.

When used in this manner IPX, including its built-in network adapter card driver, retains exclusive control over the use of the adapter card. Although this may not be an inconvenience for many persons, if you have a requirement to execute an application that requires the use of a different network protocol problems would occur. You would have to create a different AUTOEXEC.BAT file with a new set of commands to load a different protocol stack, rename your existing AUTOEXEC.BAT file for later reuse and reboot your computer. As an alternative, you could install a second network adapter in your workstation and use a second protocol stack dedicated to that adapter card. For example, assume that your organization had a NetWare LAN which was connected to the Internet via an Internet access provider. The protocol used on the Internet is TCP/IP. Thus, you would either need to reconfigure your workstation's AUTOEXEC.BAT file and reboot your computer or obtain a second network adapter card and a separate protocol stack for TCP/IP operations, neither a pleasing answer to the problem. Concerning the TCP/IP protocol stack, it differs slightly from the protocol stack illustrated in Figure 3.35 in two primary areas. First, the

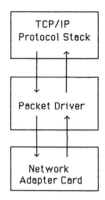

**Figure 3.36**  Typical layering of a TCP/IP protocol stack

stack can contain the application. Secondly, instead of a built-in network adapter card driver like IPX.COM, a separate packet drive is normally used. However, the packet driver functions in a similar manner to the built in network adapter driver in that it provides exclusive control over the operation of the adapter card so long as the TCP/IP protocol stack is memory-resident. Figure 3.36 illustrates the typical layering of a TCP/IP protocol stack which uses a separate packet driver to control the network adapter card.

Now that we have an appreciation of the role of single protocol stacks and the problems associated with operating multiple protocol stacks, let us focus our attention upon ODI and NDIS.

*ODI operation considerations*

The Open Data-Link Interface (ODI) standard was released by Novell and Apple Computer in 1989. With the growth in the use of the Internet the use of ODI correspondingly increased, as it provides a standard interface between a common network adapter card and multiple protocols. The ODI specification isolates the network adapter card from the protocol stacks, permitting multiple stacks to operate without specific knowledge of the hardware architecture of the network adapter card.

Figure 3.37 illustrates the ODI architecture for operating dual protocol stacks with a common network adapter card. In this illustration it was assumed that NetWare and TCP/IP protocol stacks are to use a common network adapter card.

*Link support layer*  In examining the ODI architecture illustrated in Figure 3.37 for running multiple stacks the Link Support Layer

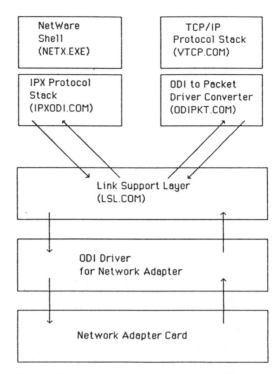

**Figure 3.37** ODI architecture shown supporting NetWare and TCP/IP protocol stacks

program (LSL.COM), which is the protocol manager, is supplied by Novell and is used to form a standard link for the simultaneous support of multiple protocols. Thus, LSL.COM must be loaded prior to loading the LAN driver normally provided by the vendor that manufactured the network adapter card, even though the driver sits below LSL in the stack.

*LAN drivers* Examples of LAN drivers include TOKEN.COM for an IBM Token-Ring adapter, MADGEODI.COM for a Madge Token-Ring adapter and NE2000.COM for an NE2000 Ethernet adapter. ODI LAN drivers are also known as Multi-Link Interface Drivers (MLIDs) because they can control multiple adapters at the physical layer while regulating communications between those network adapter cards and the protocol stacks resident in workstation memory.

*The NetWare stack*

In the NetWare stack shown in the left portion of Figure 3.37 IPXODI.COM provides the Network (IPX) and Transport (SPX is built into IPX) layers of the OSI reference model and resembles the IPX.COM single protocol stack, enabling NETx.EXE, the NetWare shell, to be layered on top of IPXODI.COM. The initialization sequence of commands included in a workstation's AUTOEXEC.BAT file to use ODI with a single NetWare protocol stack would become:

```
C:\path\LSL.COM
C:\path\LANDRIVER
C:\path\IPXODI.COM
C:\path\NETX.EXE
F:
LOGIN GHELD
```

Here LANDRIVER represents the ODI network adapter card driver that supports a specific vendor's adapter card, such as the previously mentioned TOKEN.COM, MADGEODI, or NE2000.COM.

*The TCP/IP protocol stack*

To add the TCP/IP protocol stack you would add the appropriate statements to your AUTOEXEC.BAT file. Those statements must follow the execution of LSL.COM but can either precede or succeed the statements used to invoke the NetWare protocol stack. For example, assume that the appropriate packet driver is contained in the file ODIPKT and the TCP/IP program is contained in the file TCPIP, while both files are located in the directory TCP. Then the AUTOEXEC.BAT file would contain the following statements with the REM(ark) statements optionally added for clarity.

```
REM *Install NetWare*
C:\NETWARE\LSL.COM
C:\NETWARE\LANDRIVER
C:\NETWARE\IPXODI.COM
C:\NETWARE\NETx.EXE
F:
LOGIN GHELD
REM *Install TCP/IP*
C:\TCP\ODIPKT
C:\TCP\TCPIP
```

*NET.CFG* One important file not shown in Figure 3.37 and until now not discussed is NET.CFG. This file describes the network adapter card configuration to the ODI driver and should be located in the same directory as the IPXODI and NETx files.

NET.CFG is an ASCII text file that can contain up to four main areas of information which describes the environment of a workstation. Those areas include a link support area, protocol area, link driver area, and parameter area.

*Link support area*  The link support area is used to define the number of communications buffers and memory set aside for those buffers. This area is required to be defined when running TCP/IP; however, since IPX does not use buffers or memory pools maintained by LSL you can skip this section if you are only using a NetWare protocol stack. The following illustration represents an example of the coding of the link support area in the NET.CFG file to support TCP/IP. The actual coding that you would enter depends upon the network adapter card to be used and you would obtain the appropriate information from the manual accompanying the adapter card.

```
LINK SUPPORT
     BUFFERS 8 1144
     MemPool 4096
     MaxStacks 8
```

*Protocol area*

The protocol area is used to bind one or more protocols to specific network adapter cards. By default, IPXODI binds to the network adapter in the lowest system expansion slot as it scans slots in their numeric order. If you have two or more network adapter cards in a workstation you can use the protocol area to specify which protocols you want to bind to each card. You can also accomplish this at the link driver area by specifying Slot $n$ where $n$ is the slot number of the network adapter card you are configuring. Assuming that you wish to bind IPX to a 3Com adapter card whose address is 3C5X9, you would add the following statements to the NET.CFG file.

```
Protocol
     PROTOCOL IPX
     BIND 3C5X9
```

As each computer using TCP/IP requires an IP address, the IP address information must be included in the NET.CFG file if you intend to use the TCP/IP protocol stack. For example, if the network administrator assigned your computer the IP address 133.49.108.05, the IP address information would be entered as follows:

> PROTOCOL TCP/IP
> ip_address 133.49.108.05

When using TCP/IP, each workstation on the network is assigned the address of a default router by the network administrator. Thus, another statement commonly added to the NET.CFG file includes the address of the router that the workstation will use. For example, if the router's address is 133.49.108.17, then you would add the following statement to the NET.CFG file in its protocol area.

> ip_router 133.49.108.17

The ip_address and ip_router statements can be avoided if the network administrator sets up a Reverse Address Resolution Protocol (RARP) server configured with IP and hardware addresses for workstations on the network. Then, when the workstation is powered on, it will broadcast an RARP packet that will contain its hardware address. The RARP server will respond with the workstation's IP address associated with the hardware address. In the next section we will examine the Madge Smart Plus Token-Ring card's Link Driver statements which support this addressing method.

*Link driver area*

The link driver area is used to set the hardware configuration of the network adapter card so that it is recognized by LAN drivers. If you are only using Novell's IPX, the first line of your NET.CFG file is a LINK DRIVER statement which tells NETX the type of LAN card installed in the workstation, such as

> Link Driver MADGEODI

The reason why this statement becomes the first statement is that the Link Support area is omitted and, if you only have one adapter card, you do not require a protocol area.

If you are using a Madge Smart Plus Token-Ring card your link driver area would appear as follows:

```
Link Driver MADGEODI
    Frame TOKEN-RING
    Frame TOKEN-RING_SNAP
    Protocol IPX EO TOKEN-RING
    Protocol IP 800 TOKEN-RING_SNAP
    Protocol ARP 806 TOKEN-RING_SNAP
    Protocol RARP 8035 TOKEN-RING_SNAP
```

The Frame statement tells LSL the types of frame that can be used by the adapter, while the protocol statements inform LSL of the protocol number associated with each protocol to be supported. In this example TCP/IP requires the addition of frame and protocol statements (TOKEN-RING_SNAP) to be added to the link driver area. If you were using an Ethernet NE2000 card, your link driver area in the NET.CFG file would appear as follows:

```
Link Driver NE2000
    INT 5
    PORT 300
    Frame Ethernet_802.3
    Frame Ethernet_II
    Protocol IPX 0 Ethernet_802.3
    Protocol IP 8137 Ethernet_II
```

In this example the frame statements define the types of frames that will be supported by the adapter cards. Although most adapter cards include software that automatically construct or modify the NET.CFG file, upon occasion you may have to customize the contents of that file. To do so you can use the manual accompanying the network adapter card which will normally indicate the statements required to be placed in the file.

### Virtual load modules

The introduction of NetWare 4.0 resulted in the replacement of NETX by Virtual Loadable Modules (VLMs) that sit behind DOS. In comparison, NETX sat in front of DOS and acted as a filter to identify and act upon network requests entered from the keyboard. VLMs are referred to as the NetWare DOS Requester as they use DOS redirection to satisfy file and print service requests. Since VLMs replace NETX.EXE, you would load VLM.EXE in the position previously used for NETX.EXE. That is, the sequence of commands placed in your AUTOEXEC.BAT file to initialize the NetWare protocol stack would appear as follows.

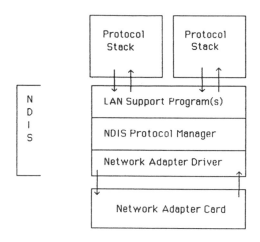

**Figure 3.38**  NDIS architecture

C:\NETWARE\LSL
C:\NETWARE\LANDRIVER
C:\NETWARE\IPXODI
C:\NETWARE\VLM.EXE
F:
LOGIN GHELD

To modify the AUTOEXEC.BAT file to support dual stack operations you could add the appropriate commands either after invoking LSL or after the Login statement.

*NDIS operation considerations*

Although the Network Driver Interface Specification (NDIS) provides a dual stack capability similar to that provided by ODI, its setup for operation varies considerably from the previously discussed dual stack mechanism. Figure 3.38 illustrates the relationship between NDIS software modules, upper layer protocol stacks and the network adapter card.

*CONFIG.SYS use*

Unlike ODI which represents a series of files loaded from an AUTOEXEC.BAT file, NDIS was designed as a series of device drivers which are loaded through the CONFIG.SYS file. In a DOS environment the first statement in the CONFIG.SYS file required for NDIS is:

DEVICE=drive:\path\PROTMAN.DOS

For OS/2, the file becomes PROTMAN.OS2. Both PROTMAN.-DOS and PROTMAN.OS2 are the NDIS Protocol Manager for each workstation operating DOS or OS/2. The Protocol Manager reads the file PROTOCOL.INI which contains initialization parameters and stores the contents of that file in memory for use by other NDIS drivers. Thus, a short discussion of PROTOCOL.INI file is in order.

*PROTOCOL.INI overview* The PROTOCOL.INI file can be considered to represent the NDIS equivalent of the NET.CFG file associated with ODI. Although most network products to include Windows NT will automatically create or modify the PROTOCOL.INI file, some products require users to create or modify that file. In addition, you may be able to enhance network performance by modifying an existing parameter set by a network program which does not consider your total user environment.

Entries in PROTOCOL.INI occur in sections, with each section name surrounded in brackets ([]). Under each section name are one or more named configuration entries which appear in the format name=value. Although configuration entries can appear anywhere in a line under the section name, normal practice is to indent each entry three character positions to enhance readability.

The first section in the PROTOCOL.INI file has the heading [PROTMAN_MOD]. The first configuration entry for both DOS and OS/2 is the device name PROTMAN$. Thus, the first section entry becomes:

```
[PROTMAN_MOD]
DriverName=PROTMAN$
```

Other entries in the [PROTMAN_MOD] section are optional and can include keywords Dynamic, Priority and Bindstatus in assignment statements. The Dynamic statement can be set to YES (Dynamic=YES) to support both static and dynamic binding or NO (Dynamic=NO) to set the Protocol Manager to operate only in static mode which is its default. In static mode protocol drivers are loaded once at system initialization and remain in memory. In the dynamic mode drivers load at the point in time when they are bound by Protocol Manager. In addition, if the drivers support a dynamic unloading capability they can be unloaded if the software unbinds them when they are not needed, freeing memory.

The Priority keyword is used to specify the order of priority of protocol processing modules. Under NDIS an incoming LAN packet is first offered to the protocol with the highest priority. Other protocols will see the packet only if a higher protocol does not first recognize and process the packet. Protocols not specified in a priority list are the last to inspect incoming packets.

The Bindstatus keyword is used to specify whether Protocol Manager can optimize memory and can be set to YES or NO. If the keyword is not used a default of NO is assumed.

The second communications statement included in a CONFIG.SYS file for NDIS operations invokes the network adapter card driver. For example, if you were using the Madge Token-Ring Smart Plus adapter you would include the following statement in the CONFIG.SYS file.

DEVICE=[drive:]\path\SMARTND.DOS

*NDIS adapter support*   The adapter driver which is compatible with the NDIS protocol manager is referred to as an NDIS MAC driver. The NDIS MAC driver is normally contained on a diskette that is included in a box in which your NDIS compatible network adapter is packaged. When using Windows NT the operating system includes built-in NDIS support for approximately 20 adapter cards. However, most of the built-in support is for Ethernet adapters. If the adapter you are using is not directly supported by Windows NT, you would select the Other option from the install adapter card entry from the network configuration display obtained from the Windows Control Panel. Then you would use the diskette that accompanies your adapter card to install the required driver. Once you have installed your adapter card and appropriate communications protocols under Windows NT, the operating system will automatically connect the software layers as required to form appropriate protocol stacks. Microsoft refers to this as network bindings, and Figure 3.39 illustrates an example of the NT Network Bindings display on the author's workstation after a large number of protocols were installed.

### 3.2.3 Application software

The third major component of software required for productive work to occur on a local area network is application software. In the form of programs which support electronic mail, multiple

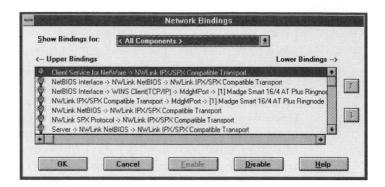

**Figure 3.39** Viewing an example of the Windows NT Network Bindings display on the author's workstation

access to database records, or the use of spreadsheet programs, application programs operate at the top layer of the OSI Reference Model.

Until the mid-1980s, most application programs used on LANs were not tailored to operate correctly in a multi-user environment. A large part of their inability to work correctly was due to the absence of file- and record-locking capability of PC operating systems, a situation that was corrected with the introduction of DOS 3.1. A second problem associated with application programs occurs when the program was written to bypass the personal computer's BIOS. Although this action in many instances would speed up screen displays, disk access, and other operations, it resulted in nonstandardized program actions. This made it difficult, if not impossible, for some network operating systems to support ill-defined programs as an interrupt clash could bring the entire network to a rapid halt. Today, most application programs use BIOS calls and can be considered as well defined. Such programs are easily supported by network operating systems. A few programs that bypass BIOS may also be supported due to the popularity of the application program which resulted in operating system vendors tailoring their software to support those applications.

# CONSTRUCTING LOCAL AREA NETWORKS

One of the better ways to become acquainted with the capabilities and limitations of local area networks is by examining specific types of network in detail. In this chapter we will do so, focusing our attention upon several types of Ethernet LAN including Fast Ethernet and IBM's Token-Ring network. For each network we will review the operation and utilization of some of the hardware products associated with the use of each network which serve as building blocks for their construction. As we construct each network we will also examine several of the constraints associated with building IEEE 802.3 and 802.5 networks as well as the use of different types of network products which enable both local and geographically dispersed networks to be interconnected.

## 4.1 10BASE-T ETHERNET

When we talk about Ethernet a degree of confusion can occur, since the term can be considered to represent a family of networks that use the CSMA/CD access protocol. As hub-based 10BASE-T and 100BASE-T networks currently represent the most popular types of Ethernet network, we will focus our attention upon both of these Ethernet networks. In doing so we will also discuss, when applicable, the methods by which hub-based networks can be connected to older coaxial cable media bus-based Ethernet networks. As the hub is the key to the operation of 10BASE-T and 100BASE-T networks, we will commence our examination of 10BASE-T Ethernet network construction with that networking device.

### 4.1.2 Wire hub

The main component of a 10BASE-T network is the wire hub. Each wire hub functions as a multi-port repeater and usually contains four, eight or twelve 10BASE-T wire ports that have modular jack connectors and may include one Attachment Unit Interface (AUI). The modular jack connectors enable the direct connection of twisted-pair cable to the hub, while the AUI enables the connection of external transceivers which permits the support of other types of cable connections, such as coaxial and fiber optic.

Under IEEE 802.3 terminology the hub port is referred to as a Medium Attachment Unit (MAU). Each MAU is designed to support a specific network medium specified by the IEEE 802.3 standard. Thus, a hub manufacturer can offer coaxial hubs and fiber hubs in addition to twisted-pair hubs. However, instead of separate types of media hub most hub vendors integrate coaxial and fiber support into a twisted-pair hub.

Cabling to a wire hub is accomplished through the use of unshielded twisted-pair (UTP). Any wire hub port supports up to 100 meters (328 feet) of UTP wire. This would appear to mean that if the wire hub is located in a central wiring closet two workstations can be up to 600 meters from one another. In actuality, this is only true as long as a wire distance limitation of 100 meters between any two devices on the network is maintained.

All hubs that conform to IEEE 10BASE-T specifications perform a core set of tasks in addition to receiving and regenerating signals. 10BASE-T hubs test each port connection, detect and handle excessive collisions, and ignore data that exceeds the maximum 802.3 frame size.

A 10BASE-T hub tests the integrity of the link from each hub port to a connected station by transmitting a special signal to the station. If the device does not respond, the hub will automatically shut down the port, and may illuminate a status light-emitting diode (LED) to indicate the status of each port.

Hubs monitor, record, and count consecutive collisions that occur on each individual station link. As an excessive number of consecutive collisions will prevent data transfer on all of the attached links, hubs are required to cut off or partition any link on which too many collisions have occurred. This partitioning enables the remainder of the network to operate in situations where a faulty NIC transmits continuously. Although the IEEE 802.3 standard does not specify a maximum number of consecutive collisions, the standard does specify that partitioning can be initiated only after 30 or more consecutive collisions occur. Thus, some hub vendors initiate partitioning when 31 consecutive collisions occur, while other manufacturers use a higher value.

Another operating function of 10BASE-T hubs is to ignore continuous data transmissions in which the frame length exceeds the maximum length of 1518 bytes. Such excessive length frames usually result from collisions, and are referred to as jabbering. Most hubs also partition a jabbering port, and some hubs include a jabber indicator LED in addition to a partition status LED on each port.

Although a wiring hub is commonly referred to as a concentrator, this term is not technically correct. A 10BASE-T wiring hub is a self-contained unit that typically includes 8, 10, or 12 RJ-45 ports for direct connection to stations, and a BNC and/or DB-15 AUI port for expanding the hub to other network equipment. The BNC and AUI ports enable the 10BASE-T hub to be connected to 10BASE-2 and 10BASE-5 networks, respectively. For the latter, the AUI port is cabled to a 10BASE-5 MAU (transceiver), which is tapped into thick 10BASE-5 coaxial cable. One 10BASE-T hub can be connected to another with a UTP link between RJ-45 ports on each hub.

When one hub is connected to another, a special cable must be used. In that cable, the transmit and receive wire pairs have to be crossed over; that is, the receive pair at one end (pins 1 and 2) must be connected to the transmit pair (pins 3 and 6) at the other end of the cable, and vice versa. The only exception to the use of a crossover cable is when a special hub port containing the crossover function is provided. On some hubs this type of port is labeled 'crossover', and enables a straight-through cable to be used to cascade one hub to another. On other hubs an X is placed over the crossover functioning port as a label to indicate pin reversals.

Unlike a hub, a concentrator consists of a main housing into which modular cards are inserted. Although some modular cards may appear to represent hubs, and do indeed function as 10BASE-T hubs, the addition of other modules permits the network to be easily expanded from one location and allows additional features to be supported. For example, the insertion of a fiber optic inter-repeater module permits concentrators to be interconnected over relatively long distances of approximately 3 km.

## *Interconnecting hubs*

One of the wire ports in a wire hub functions as an in/out wire port. This port is used to interconnect wire hubs to form an extended 10BASE-T network. Figure 4.1 illustrates a wire closet containing three wire hubs mounted in a rack and cabled to one another. Note that the cabling from each wire hub to attached workstations forms a star topology.

Due to the advantages of UTP cable most new IEEE 802.3 networks are designed using wire hubs. In addition to UTP being less expensive and easier to install than coaxial cable there are a large number of additional benefits associated with the use of this type of cable. UTP is both thinner and lighter than coax. This allows more cable pairs to be routed through a conduit than coax. In addition, if it becomes necessary to route cable over ceiling tiles UTP, unlike coax, will not cause ceilings to sag.

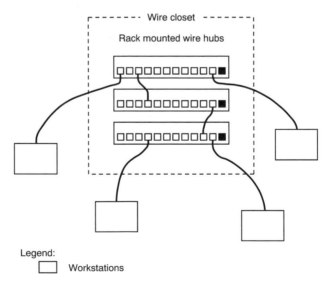

**Figure 4.1**  Using a wire closet. Wire hubs are normally installed in a rack mount in a wire closet. This provides a central point for the management and control of the network or network segment

Another advantage of UTP which builds the demand for wire hubs includes the fact that it is already installed in most buildings, making it readily available for use. Last but not least, twisted-pair is used as a point-to-point link. This means that a failure normally affects only one user. In comparison, the failure of a coaxial bus-based network can affect numerous users or the entire network.

### 4.1.2 Network access

Workstations and servers requiring access to a 10BASE-T network obtain a communications capability via the installation of a network interface card (NIC). The NIC is usually installed in a system expansion slot of a computer; however, laptops commonly use Ethernet PC cards to obtain access to a LAN. Regardless of the type of hardware used, the hardware is then called via the use of two-pair UTP cable on a point-to-point basis into a hub port, with the port termination accomplished via the use of a RJ-45 jack. That jack has eight pin connections; however, only four are actually used. Table 4.1 compares the 10BASE-T pin numbers to the RJ-45 jack numbers and indicates the signal names of the pins used with 10BASE-T UTP cable.

### 4.1.3 Attachment Unit Interface

The IEEE 802.3 standard defines an interface known as an Attachment Unit Interface (AUI). The AUI enables 10 Mbps IEEE

**Table 4.1**  10BASE-T wiring sequence

| 10BASE-T<br>Pin # | RJ-45<br>Pin # | 10BASE-T<br>Signal Name |
|---|---|---|
| 1 | 1 | Transmission Date + |
| 2 | 2 | Transmit Data − |
| 3 | 3 | Receive Data + |
| − | 4 | Not used |
| − | 5 | Not used |
| 6 | 6 | Receive Data − |
| − | 7 | Not used |
| − | 8 | Not used |

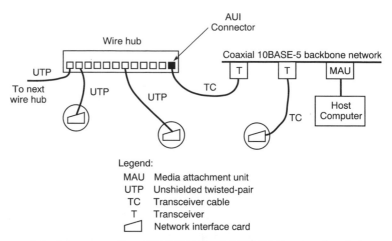

**Figure 4.2** Interconnecting 10BASE-T and 10BASE-5 networks. A transceiver cable can be wired to the AUI connector on a wire hub, permitting the interconnection of 10BASE-T and 10BASE-5 networks

802.3 end nodes to connect to medium attachment units and can be considered as the lowest common denominator for network connectivity. This enables each new media type supported by the IEEE 802.3 standard to obtain a MAU specification, since the MAU provides a media dependent interface of the AUI connection.

Figure 4.2 illustrates the relationship between a wire hub and NICs installed in the system unit of several computers to form a 10BASE-T network connected by an AUI to a coaxial cable (10BASE-5) backbone network. The coaxial cable backbone in turn provides a connection to a host computer.

To construct the hybrid network illustrated in Figure 4.2 the 10BASE-5 network must be attached to the wire hub via the hub's AUI port. This is accomplished by connecting a coaxial transceiver in the same way that workstations are cabled to a 10BASE-5 network. Then the transceiver is connected to the wire hub's AUI port through the use of a transceiver cable. Once this is accomplished any workstation connected to the backbone coaxial network as well as the mainframe computer can communicate with any workstation connected to the wire hub. The wire hub can be cabled using unshielded twisted-pair wire to another hub as previously indicated in Figure 4.1, if it is desired to extend the network.

Now suppose that you previously acquired NICs that only support coaxial cable media and you wish to connect

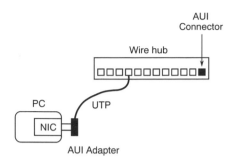

**Figure 4.3** Connecting a coaxial cable NIC to a wire hub. Through the use of an AUI adapter you can connect a network interface card (NIC) to a wire hub port using a UTP cable

workstations using those network interface cards to a wire hub. To accomplish this using UTP wire you would first connect an AUI adapter to the NIC card connector. Then you would wire the AUI to a wire hub connector using UTP. This is illustrated in Figure 4.3. For this example the AUI adapter becomes the functional equivalent of an Ethernet transceiver that has a UTP network medium interface instead of a coaxial cable interface.

## 4.1.4 Using fiber optic technology

An important addition to 10BASE-T Ethernet is known as FOIRL, an acronym which stands for fiber optic repeater link. Although FOIRL is not an Ethernet network, this specification governs the transmission of Ethernet across dual fiber cable in which one fiber is used for the transmission of data in the form of light pulses, while the second fiber is used for the reception of data in the form of light pulses.

The use of fiber permits you to support multiple Ethernet segments at distances up to 2000 meters (6600 feet) from one another. At a remote location connected through the use of FOIRL technology, you can directly connect a single station using a fiber transceiver or you can connect a 10BASE-T or fiber hub and support multiple stations. You would use the AUI port of the hub to provide a connection via a standard transceiver to different types of Ethernet networks, while you would use an optical transceiver to provide a connection to the dual fiber cable.

*Optical transceiver*

An optical transceiver consists of a pulse-generating light-emitting diode (LED), photodetector, and associated transmit and recieve circuitry. Transmit circuitry turns the LED ON and OFF to convert electrical voltages that represent data into a series of light pulses for transmission over the fiber. The photodetector recognizes received light pulses, while the receive circuitry generates electrical voltages and shapes pulses to correspond to the received light pulses.

Today you can purchase a 'fiber' network access unit (NAU), an optical transceiver mounted on an adapter card for installation in the system unit of a personal computer, for less than $1000. A second type of optical transceiver used on Ethernet networks is built into fiber hubs whose use will be covered next in this section. This type of optical transmitter may be designed to share the use of a common power source and circuitry, resulting in the per port hub cost usually being less than the cost of a fiber adapter.

## 4.1.5 Fiber hubs

A fiber hub is a special type of hub which contains a number of FOIRL ports, one AUI port, and usually one or more 10BASE-T ports. For example, AT&T's StarLAN fiber hub contains six FOIRL ports, one 10BASE-T port, and one AUI port. In comparison, Transition Engineering's Model 1050 fiber optic hub contains 12 FOIRL ports and one AUI interface port.

In effect, a fiber hub can be considered a grouping of fiber NAUs as well as one or more 10BASE-T and/or AUI ports. Thus, you can use a fiber hub to support several extended distance Ethernet connections and then directly link those connections to a 10BASE-T network through the use of a 10BASE-T port built into the fiber hub or indirectly to any type of Ethernet network through the use of an AUI port built into the fiber hub.

## 4.1.6 Fiber adapter

A third type of hardware product used with FOIRL is a fiber adapter. The fiber adapter can be considered a media conversion device which performs media conversion between twisted

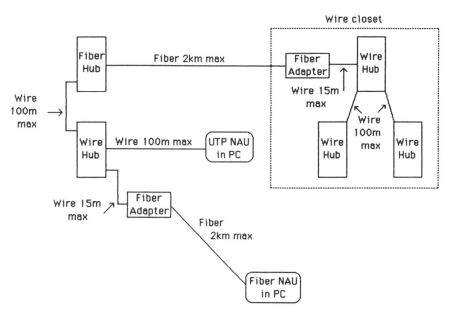

**Figure 4.4** Wire and fiber hub distance limits. The distance limits between 10BASE-T network components depend upon the media used, fiber or UTP

pair and fiber optic cable. This device extends the transmission distance between a wire hub and an attached workstation or another 10BASE-T wire hub from 100 meters (328 feet) to 2 km. Unless the fiber adapter is directly connected to a fiber hub, an adapter is required at both ends of an extended fiber link.

## Distance limits

Figure 4.4 illustrates the transmission distance limits associated with the use of 10BASE-T and fiber hubs and fiber adapters. Note that a fiber network access unit installed in the system unit of a PC can communicate over 2 km via fiber optic cable either directly into a fiber hub or to a fiber adapter connected to a wire hub. Also note that in the upper right corner of Figure 4.4 it was assumed that three 10BASE-T wire hubs were installed in a wire closet. If that wire closet is located on a low floor in a building and your organization leases another floor hundreds of feet above the wire closet floor, the use of fiber optic cable provides a mechanism to link two network segments together. Similarly, the wire closet shown in the illustration

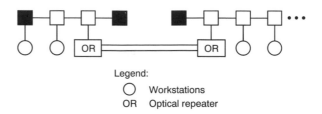

Legend:
○   Workstations
OR   Optical repeater

**Figure 4.5**   Connecting 10BASE-2 networks using a fiber optic inter-repeater link

could be in one building on a university campus, with fiber used to connect that building to another building. In doing so, the use of fiber optic cable not only extends the transmission distance of the network but eliminates the possibility of electromagnetic interference (EMI), since fiber cable is immune to EMI.

The distance limitation associated with the use of FOIRL has nothing to do with the transmission constraints associated with optical signals. Instead, the FOIRL distance limitation is related to the timing constraints in the IEEE 802.3 standard.

As the FOIRL standard is limited to point-to-point connections, when used to interconnect two 10BASE-2 networks you must consider the cable length of each segment. For example, assume you have two 10BASE-2 networks located in different areas on a large factory floor as illustrated in Figure 4.5. If segment A has a cable length of 300 meters and segment B has a cable length of 500 meters, what is the maximum FOIRL cable length? As the maximum cabling distance of a 10BASE-2 network is 2500 meters, subtracting the sum of the cable lengths from that cable constraint $(2500 - (300 + 500))$ results in a maximum fiber optic link of 1700 meters.

Another constraint that you must consider is the Ethernet repeater limitation. Ethernet limits any interconnected network to a maximum of four repeaters between any two nodes. Thus, when considering the use of fiber optic repeaters you must take into consideration the maximum network length as well as the number of repeaters that can be placed between nodes.

### 4.1.7 Coax adapter

Another 10BASE-T product that permits the connection of an existing coaxial based network to a wire hub is the coax adapter.

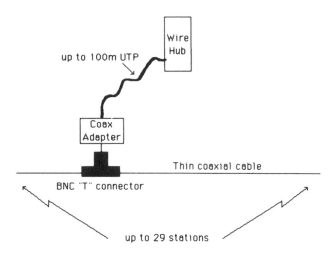

**Figure 4.6** Connecting 10BASE-T and 10BASE-2 networks. A 10BASE-2 network can be connected to a 10BASE-T network through the use of a coax adapter

This device is a two-port repeater, containing a single 10BASE-T port and a single BNC port for thin coaxial cable (10BASE-2).

Through the use of a coax adapter you can connect 10BASE-T and 10BASE-2 networks together to form one network. In doing so you can cable up to 100 meters of UTP wire from a coax adapter to a 10BASE-T wire hub as illustrated in Figure 4.6. Through the use of a coax adapter a thin coax cable up to 200 meters in length, with up to 29 stations, can be integrated into a 10BASE-T network. For organizations that previously installed a thin coax network, the use of a coax adapter enables that network to be used without modification including previously installed network access units and cabling.

### 4.1.8 Expanding a 10BASE-T network

A 10BASE-T network can be expanded with additional hubs once the number of stations serviced has used up the hub's available terminal ports. In expanding a 10BASE-T network, the wiring that joins each hub together is considered to represent a cable segment, while each hub is considered as a repeater. Thus, under the 802.3 specifications, no two stations can be separated by more than four hubs connected together by five cable segments.

Figure 4.7 illustrates the expansion of a 10BASE-T network through the use of five hubs. Note that the connection between

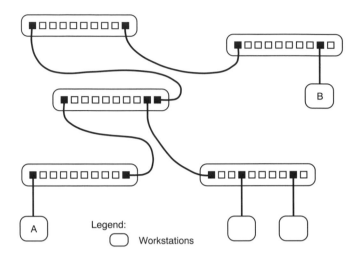

**Figure 4.7** Expanding a 10BASE-T network. No two stations can be separated by more than four hubs in a 10BASE-T network

station A and station B traverses five segments and four hubs, and so does not violate IEEE 802.3 connection rules.

As the maximum span of a 10BASE-T network is 100 meters per segment multiplied by five segments, or 500 meters, it is quite common for 10BASE-T networks to use a 10BASE-5 or even a 10BASE-2 cable backbone. Thus, either 10BASE-2 or 10BASE-5 cable can be used to support an extension of a 10BASE-T network. In such situations, the AUI port of a 10BASE-T hub is connected to a MAU (transceiver) connected to the 10BASE-5 (thick coaxial) cable, or the BNC connector is mated to a thin coaxial cable's T-connector. Another reason for using a thin or thick coaxial cable for a backbone is that you can thereby avoid the four-hub cascading limit of 10BASE-T. For example, if you cabled 10 hubs to a 10BASE-5 coaxial cable backbone, each station would traverse at most two hubs, and would thus comply with the IEEE rules. In comparison, you could not connect more than five hubs together in a conventional 10BASE-T network because of IEEE 802.3 rules.

*Segmentation options*

When traffic on an Ethernet network begins to exceed a 40 to 45% level of utilization, it is probably time to segment the

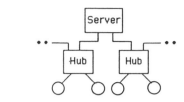

Bridge based segmentation

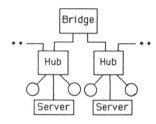

Legend:  ◯ workstation

**Figure 4.8**   Server and network based segmentation

network. To accomplish this you can consider the use of a server for network segmentation or install a second server on a segmented network connected together via a bridge. Figure 4.8 illustrates both segmentation methods. In the first method shown at the top of Figure 4.8 a server with dual NICs permits users on two networks to access the common server. In the bridged network example illustrated at the bottom of Figure 4.8 a bridge is used to connect two network segments. In this example a second server is installed in an attempt to distribute the workload between the two networks. Otherwise, without a second server all traffic on one segmented network would flow across the bridge to the network with the single server defeating the purpose of the segmentation effort.

*Bridge segmentation*

Through the use of a server or bridge to segment a network you can double your aggregate bandwidth. Unfortunately, this may not be sufficient for segments with a large number of network users, especially if some of those users require access to multimedia applications. Thus, server and bridge segmentation have practical limits since servers usually cannot support more than two or three segments, and complex bridge-based networks introduce flooding problems, learning delays, and an inability to direct bandwidth to individual stations on specific stations. When the use of a low cost server adapter card or bridge cannot overcome your organization's requirements for additional bandwidth, a practical next step is to consider the use of LAN switches.

Through the use of a LAN switch you can directly provide bandwidth-intensive devices with the bandwidth they require. In addition, through the use of port and segment-based switches, you can create a switch-based infrastructure to accommodate different organizational requirements. In doing so, it is important to note that a LAN switch with $n$ 10BASE-T ports provides a maximum bandwidth of $n/2 \times 10$ Mbps as it can support a maximum of $n/2$ cross-connections.

Figure 4.9 illustrates the use of an 8-port 10BASE-T segment switching switch that supports two Fast Ethernet connections. In this example, each of the 100 Mbps switch ports are used to provide a connection from the switch to a server because it is reasonable to expect that each server will be the most heavily accessed device on the switch-based network. Although each of the four segments is shown connected to the switch via 10 Mbps 10BASE-T ports, the actual bandwidth through the switch from clients to the two servers can reach 20 Mbps. This is because the servers are connected at 100 Mbps to the switch, enabling the

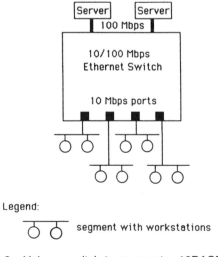

**Figure 4.9** Using a switch to segment a 10BASE-T network

server to respond quicker to a client query and then become available to service a subsequent query. In comparison, a 10 Mbps connect would delay the subsequent connection request.

Due to the significant decline in the price of 100BASE-T adapters, the cost of 100BASE-T switches has also declined. This makes the use of conventional Fast Ethernet as well as Fast Ethernet switches important to consider when 10BASE-T network utilization reaches a level that adversely effects a network. Thus, in the next section we will turn our attention to Fast Ethernet.

## 4.2 100BASE-T FAST ETHERNET

Fast Ethernet is very similar to Ethernet with respect to their hub-based design and use of the CSMA/CD access protocol. The primary difference between the two hub-based networking technologies are in the areas of operating rate, type of cabling used to form a network, and network span distance and repeater hop limitations.

Ethernet operates at 10 Mbps and 10BASE-T requires the use of category 3 UTP cable. In comparison, the 100BASE-TX version of Fast Ethernet that operates at 100 Mbps requires category 5 certified cabling to operate reliably. Concerning network span distance and repeater hop limitations, the so-called 3-4-5 rule which refers to a maximum of 3 populated segments, 4 repeater hops, and 5 total segments, is invalid in a Fast Ethernet environment. Instead, cable distance is limited to 100 meters and the maximum distance between your farthest nodes cannot exceed 205 meters without using fiber optic connections. Another limitation of Fast Ethernet is a maximum distance of 5 meters between two cascaded networks which, in effect, precludes the construction of a Fast Ethernet cascaded network.

### 4.2.1 Repeater rules

Similarly to 10BASE-T, you can use copper and fiber hubs with built-in repeaters to extend the transmission distance of a Fast Ethernet network. Fast Ethernet supports two types of hubs with built-in repeaters, Class I and Class II. Only one Class I hub-based repeater can be used in a network segment. In

**Table 4.2**  Fast Ethernet cable span distance

| Connection method | Cable type | | |
| --- | --- | --- | --- |
| | TX | TX fiber | Fiber |
| Direct connection | 100 m | n/a | 412 m |
| One Class I repeater | 200 m | 250.8 m | 272 m |
| One Class II repeater | 200 m | 308.8 m | 320 m |
| Two Class II repeaters | 205 m | 216.2 m | 228 m |

comparison, two Class II hub-based repeaters can be used to form a network segment so long as the inter-hub cable is limited to a length of 5 meters or less. Table 4.2 summarizes the cable span restrictions for Fast Ethernet based upon the direct connection of a station as well as the use of Class I and Class II hub-based repeaters to extend the network span distance.

In spite of the previously mentioned limitations, Fast Ethernet represents a viable networking technology either as a stand-alone network or as a backbone for connecting lower speed 10BASE-T networks. In addition, through the use of Fast Ethernet switches you can split a single Fast Ethernet collision domain into more manageable parts and extend the span of a single network by interconnecting multiple networks.

## 4.2.2 Segmentation methods

Similarly to a 10BASE-T network, a 100BASE-TX network can be segmented via the use of a server with multiple NICs or via the use of a bridge. Both methods result in the breaking of the Fast Ethernet collision domain in a manner similar to the breaking of an Ethernet collision domain, enabling the span of interconnected segments to increase. The use of a server with multiple NICs and a bridge for network segmentation was previously illustrated in Figure 4.8.

## 4.2.3 Backbone operation

Due to the significant decline in the cost of Fast Ethernet adapters and hubs, some network managers considered using 100BASE-T hubs as a low cost backbone for providing access to

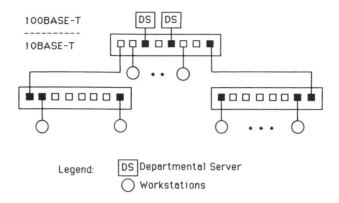

Figure 4.10   Using a 100BASE-T hub with auto-sensing ports as a backbone for conventional hubs does not enhance bandwidth utilization as it maintains one collision domain

departmental servers. When used in this manner, a 100BASE-T hub with auto-negotiation ports that operate at either 10 or 100 Mbps is used as a backbone to connect two or more 10BASE-T segments in a manner similar to the illustration in Figure 4.10. Unfortunately, the use of the network structure shown in Figure 4.10 results in one collision domain and does not actually improve performance with respect to users on the 10BASE-T hubs.

However, if some users from 10BASE-T hubs are moved to the 100BASE-T hub, those users will obtain 100 Mbps access to departmental servers. Thus, the network configuration shown in Figure 4.10 could provide an enhanced communications capability if users that primarily access departmental servers were to be moved to the 100BASE-T hub. In addition, you can gradually replace 10BASE-T hubs and use the initial 100BASE-T hub as a migration strategy as your organization moves to a full 100BASE-T network.

To obtain an enhanced level of performance for 10BASE-T network users, the 100BASE-T hub must be replaced by a backbone LAN switch. Here the switch separates collision domains, as well as providing simultaneous access from workstations on the two 10BASE-T segments to each departmental server, increasing the available bandwidth to departmental servers. This type of networking strategy is referred to as switch tiered networking and is gaining popularity as a backbone.

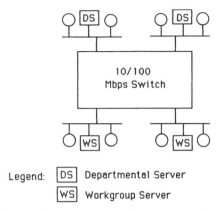

Legend:  DS  Departmental Server
         WS  Workgroup Server

**Figure 4.11**   Using a 10/100 Mbps switch

### 4.2.4 Switch segmentation

Through the use of a 10/100 Mbps Ethernet switch you obtain the ability to interconnect 10 and 100 Mbps segments or individual devices, permitting both interoperability between Ethernet and Fast Ethernet, as well as providing a migration path to Fast Ethernet. Figure 4.11 illustrates the use of a 10/100 Mbps segment switching LAN switch to connect two 10 Mbps Ethernet segments and two 100 Mbps Fast Ethernet segments. Note that workgroup servers local to Ethernet hubs serving small groups of employees are shown residing on each 10 Mbps segment, while departmental servers that can be accessed by individual users or users on a segment are shown either directly cabled to a 100 Mbps switch port or located on a 100 Mbps segment. This design technique provides additional bandwidth to the servers that you expect will obtain a high level of access. Also, note that if your organization migrates to a full 100 Mbps Ethernet infrastructure, you can either upgrade the switch ports to 100 Mbps and replace your existing 10 Mbps segments with Fast Ethernet, or consider using a repeater or bridge to chain one Fast Ethernet segment to another. Thus, the use of an upgradable 10/100 Mbps switch provides a considerable degree of network design flexibility.

In addition, many NICs manufactured since mid-1995 for stand-alone use in a computer or as a module for a switch port support an auto-negotiation feature. This feature allows the NIC or switch port to adaptively support either a 10 or 100 Mbps connection, providing another migration path for network managers.

## 4.3 IBM TOKEN-RING NETWORKS

Due to IBM's initial effort in developing the technology that resulted in the IEEE 802.5 Token-Ring standard, many persons continue to refer to the technology as an IBM Token-Ring network. In actuality, the IBM Token-Ring network can be considered as a family of hardware and software products manufactured and developed by IBM and hundreds of other vendors. Those products enable Token-Ring networks to be established, interconnected and attached locally or remotely to personal computers, mainframe computers and minicomputers. In addition to hubs, bridges, and network adapters, IBM developed specifications for a cabling system to include connectors and wallplates that can be used to develop the transmission media infrastructure to support a Token-Ring network.

In Chapter 2 we examined the basic operation of a Token-Ring network without considering specific products. In this section we will focus our attention upon a few Token-Ring products used to build Token-Ring networks. Although we will focus our attention upon IBM products for illustrative purposes, readers should note that today hundreds of vendors market similar products. Thus, one of the most difficult aspects of constructing a Token-Ring network may involve selecting between similar-functioning vendor products. Fortunately for this author, that is an acquisitions decision beyond the scope of this book.

### 4.3.1 Multistation access unit

As previously mentioned in Chapter 2, the topology of a Token-Ring network resembles a ring-star or a series of stars linked to form a ring. The rationale for this topology is the use of multistation access units (MAUs) which can be considered as the basic building blocks for the construction of Token-Ring networks.

The IBM Model 8228 MAU was originally developed as a ten port device, of which eight ports are used to connect devices to the Token-Ring. The remaining two ports, labeled Ring In (RI) and Ring Out (RO), are used to cable MAUs together to extend the number of stations supported by a Token-Ring network.

Figure 4.12a illustrates a single Token-Ring network formed by the use of one MAU. Figure 4.12b illustrates a single Token-

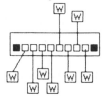

a.   Single Token-Ring network using one MAU

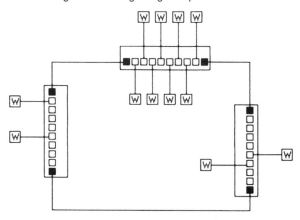

b.   Single Token-Ring using multiple MAUs

Legend:
■ Ring In (RI) or Ring Out (RO) port
W workstation

**Figure 4.12** Using the multistation access unit (MAU). The original IBM multistation access unit (MAU) contained 10 ports. Eight are used to service Token-Ring devices while the remaining two ports are used to interconnect MAUs to form a larger Token-Ring network

Ring formed by the interconnection of multiple MAUs. For the latter, the RI port of one MAU is cabled to the RO port of another MAU to interconnect MAUs into a ring.

A passive MAU is unpowered, requiring a voltage from a workstation connected to the network to operate. That voltage opens a relay and provides access to the network. When a workstation is powered off the flow of current to the MAU ceases. This causes the voltage at the relay on the MAU port to which the workstation is connected to be lowered, closing the relay and resulting in the workstation being bypassed. More modern MAUs contain a microprocessor and examine MAC source and destination addresses to develop network utilization statistics. This type of MAU can be considered to function as an intelligent hub. As this type of MAU requires power, it can also be considered as an active device.

### 4.3.2 IBM Cabling System

The IBM Cabling System was introduced in 1984 as a mechanism to support the networking requirements of office environments. By defining standards for cables, connectors, faceplates, distribution panels and other facilities, IBM's Cabling System is designed to support the interconnection of personal computers, conventional terminals, mainframe computers and office systems. In addition, this system permits devices to be moved from one location to another or added to a network through a simple connection to the Cabling System's wall plates or surface mounts.

Although IBM was responsible for developing the specifications for its cabling system, it left the manufacture and distribution of cabling products to other vendors. Although many organizations still retain IBM cabling system wiring, the development of the EIA/TIA cabling standard previously discussed in this book has resulted in most organizations now installing an EIA/TIA 568 category type of unshielded twisted pair cable. The most commonly used IBM Cabling system cable type, Type 1 cable, is equivalent to Category 3 cable. Category 3 cable uses four solid copper twisted pair 24 AWG conductors and supports a signaling rate up to 16 MHz, which enables Token-Ring's Differential Manchester encoding to provide an operating rate of 16 Mbps on Category 3 cable. Today most organizations installing new cabling commonly use Category 5 as it is tested to support a 100 MHz signaling rate, making it suitable to transport Fast Ethernet or ATM if an organization should later decide to migrate to a new and higher speed local area network infrastructure.

*Cable types*

The IBM Cabling System specifies eight different cabling categories. Depending upon the type of cable selected, one can install the selected wiring indoors, outdoors, under a carpet or in ducts and other air spaces.

The IBM Cabling System uses wire which conforms to the American Wire Gauge or AWG. AWG is a measure of wire diameter. As the wire diameter becomes larger the AWG number decreases, in effect resulting in an inverse relationship between wire diameter and AWG. The IBM Cabling System uses wire between 22 AWG (0.644 mm) and 26 AWG (0.405 mm). As a larger diameter wire has less resistance to current flow than a smaller diameter wire, a smaller AWG permits cabling distances to be extended in comparison to a higher AWG cable.

### Type 1

The IBM Cabling System Type 1 cable contains two twisted pairs of 22 AWG conductors. Each pair is individually shielded with a foil wrapping and both pairs are surrounded by an outer braided shield or with a corrugated metallic shield. The braided shield is used for indoor wiring, while the corrugated metallic shield is used for outdoor wiring. Type 1 cable provides the largest cable distance and is available in two different designs: plenum and non-plenum. Plenum cable can be installed without the use of a conduit but non-plenum cable requires a conduit. The impedance of a Type 1 cable is 150 ohms and it is rated at speeds up to 2 Mbps.

### Type 2

Type 2 cable is actually a Type 1 indoor cable with the addition of four pairs of 22 AWG unshielded conductors for telephone usage. Due to this, Type 1 cable is also referred to as data-grade twisted-pair cable while Type 2 cable is known as two data-grade and four voice-grade twisted-pair. Due to its voice capability, Type 2 cable can support PBX interconnections. Like Type 1 cable, Type 2 cable supports plenum and non-plenum designs. Type 2 cable is not available in an outdoor version. The shielded pairs in a Type 2 cable are rated at 20 Mbps, while the unshielded pairs are tested to support data rates up to 4 Mpbs.

### Type 3

Type 3 cable is conventional unshielded twisted-pair (UTP) telephone wire with a minimum of two twists per foot. Both 22 AWG and 24 AWG conductors are supported by this cable type. One common use of Type 3 cable is to connect PCs to MAUs in a Token-Ring network, however, since it is unshielded it is rated for supporting data rates up to 4 Mpbs.

### Type 5

Type 5 is a fiber optic cable. Two 100/140 mm optical fibers are contained in a Type 5 cable. This cable is suitable for indoor, non-plenum installation or outdoor aerial installation. Due to the extended transmission distance obtainable with fiber-optic cable, Type 5 cable is used in conjunction with the IBM 8219 Token-Ring network optical fiber repeater to interconnect two MAUs up to 6600 feet (2 km) from one another.

### Type 6

Type 6 cable contains two twisted-pairs of 26 AWG conductors for data communications with each pair individually shielded and both pairs then contained in a common shield. It is available for non-plenum applications only and its smaller diameter than Type 1 cable makes it slightly more flexible. The primary use of Type 6 cable is for short runs as a flexible path cord. This type of cable is often used to connect an adapter card in a personal computer to a faceplate which, in turn, is connected to a Type 1 to Type 2 cable which forms the backbone of a network. Type 6 cable has an impedance of 150 ohms and is rated for transmitting data at up to 20 Mbps.

### Type 7

Type 7 cable represents a single-pair version of Type 6 cable. Type 7 cable consists of a single pair of 26 AWG gauge conductors with a common shield, resulting in an impedance of 150 ohms and a data transmission capability up to 20 Mbps.

### Type 8

Type 8 cable is designed for installation under a carpet. This cable contains two individually shielded, parallel pairs of 26 AWG conductors with a plastic ramp designed to make under-carpet installations as unobtrusive as possible. Although Type 8 cable can be used in a manner similar to Type 1 and has an impedance of 150 ohms and supports an operating rate up to 20 Mbps, it provides only half the maximum transmission distance obtainable through the use of Type 1 cable.

**Type 9**

Type 9 cable is essentially a low-cost version of Type 1 cable. Like Type 1, Type 9 cable consists of two twisted-pairs of data cable; however, 26 AWG conductors are used in place of the 22 AWG wire used in Type 1 cable. As a result of the use of smaller-diameter cable, transmission distances on Type 9 cable are approximately two-thirds of those obtainable through the use of Type 1 cable.

*Connectors*

The IBM Cabling System includes connectors for terminating both data and voice conductors. The data connector has a unique design based upon the development of a latching mechanism which permits it to mate with another identical connector.

Figure 4.13 illustrates the IBM Cabling System data connector. Its design makes it self-shorting when disconnected from another connector. This provides a Token-Ring network with electrical continuity when a station is disconnected. Unfortunately, the data connector is very expensive in comparison to an RJ jack and plug connector; the typical retail price of the data connector is between $4 and $5, whereas jack and plug connectors cost approximately a dime.

*Cable distance*

As previously mentioned in Chapter 2, the cable connecting a workstation to a port on an MAU is known as a lobe. The

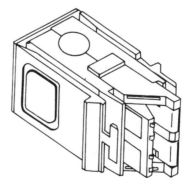

**Figure 4.13** IBM cabling system data connector

maximum lobe distance depends upon the type of cabling used and the data transfer rate of the network.

On a 4 Mbps Token-Ring network using Type 1 double-shielded pair cable the recommended maximum lobe distance without the use of repeaters is 100 meters or 330 feet. When Type 3 unshielded twisted-pair (UTP) telephone wire is used lobe distances can be extended to 300 meters or approximately 1000 feet. In a 16 Mbps network the use of Type 1 cable also restricts the lobe distance to 100 meters. Although the same maximum cabling distance for both 4 Mbps and 16 Mbps networks may appear strange, in actuality the 100 meter limit for 4 Mbps took into consideration a projected user requirement to keep previously installed Type 1 cable when a network is upgraded to 16 Mbps.

When Type 3 cable is used to connect a workstation to a 16 Mbps Token-Ring network the lobe distance is reduced to approximately 75 meters or 250 feet. This reduction in the maximum lobe length results from the fact that line noise increases in proportion to the square root of frequency. In addition, the Federal Communications Commission (FCC) limits on permissible radiated energy further reduce the maximum transmission distance when a Token-Ring network operates at 16 Mbps.

### 4.3.3 Network adapters

IBM and third-party vendors market a number of adapter cards that are designed for installation in PC, PS/2, EISA and PCI bus-based and Macintosh personal computer system units. Each adapter card is cabled to an MAU port and provides an interface to the Token-Ring network.

IBM Token-Ring adapters support both IEEE 802.2 and 802.5 protocols. Other manufacturers provide 802.2 LLC support in the form of downloadable software which is loaded into an adapter card's RAM from a server. Although technique for providing LLC support slightly reduces the cost of manufacturing an adapter and makes it easier to upgrade, it also increases traffic across the network. Other functions performed by a Token-Ring adapter include signal retiming, signal regeneration, the detection of error conditions, and the performance of certain types of ring tests.

IBM's first series of adapter cards operated at 4 Mbps and were restricted to being used with a 4 Mbps Token-Ring network. The original PC adapter card introduced with the Token-Ring product announcement in October 1985 was supplemented by a second offering known as the Adapter II. Containing double the 8-kbyte buffer of the original adapter, the Adapter II was designed to provide increased performance for network servers since its additional memory enabled the Adapter II to retrieve data from the network quicker than the original adapter.

Both the original Token-Ring adapter and the Adapter II operate at 4 Mbps. In early 1989, IBM introduced a new version of its Token-Ring network to include adapter cards and software that enable a Token-Ring network to operate at either 4 or 16 Mbps. For older PC bus computers, IBM introduced its 16/4 Adapter that allows computers on a Token-Ring to operate at 4 Mbps on older networks while obtaining the ability to operate at 16 Mbps if the network should be upgraded to that data rate. A similar adapter called the 16/4 Adapter/A was introduced for use with Micro Channel members of the PS/2 family of computers. Both adapters contain 64 kbytes of memory as opposed to the 16 kbytes for the Adapter II. The additional memory boosts Token-Ring performance since it enables the adapter to handle larger data frames, up to 4.5 kbytes on a 4 Mbps Token-Ring network and up to 18 kbytes on a 16 Mbps network. Within a few months of the introduction of the dual-speed Token-Ring adapters, IBM withdrew the previous adapters from sale.

The introduction of Pentium processor based computers was accompanied by the development of a new bus known as the Peripheral Component Interconnect (PCI) local bus. This bus provides a much higher data transfer capability than previously developed buses. To provide compatibility with the large base of previously developed adapter cards as well as to support adapter cards that do not require a high data transfer capability, such as serial port cards, Pentium-based computers commonly include both PCI and EISA buses, with the EISA bus also supporting the use of ISA adapter cards. Today both IBM and many third party vendors offer PCI 16/4 Token-Ring adapter cards that support IEEE 802.2 and 802.5 standards as well as the relatively recent 802.5r standard for dedicated Token-Ring, a standard for full-duplex Token-Ring operations that provides a total 32 Mbps bi-directional data transfer capability that will be described later in this section. One example of a PCI Token-Ring adapter is IBM's Auto LANStreamer which operates at either 4 or 16 Mbps over UTP or STP cabling via either an RJ-45 or an 9-pin D-shell connector, with the latter connector providing the adapter via an IBM Cabling System connector to a lobe cable routed to a MAU port. The PCI Token-Ring adapter provides the highest level of performance available from IBM's series of Token-Ring adapter cards.

### 4.3.4 Device and wiring constraints

The number of devices that can be connected to a Token-Ring network without the use of a bridge, router, or gateway depends upon several factors including the type of cabling used and the number of permissible MAUs. When Type 1 cable is used, up to 260 devices can be connected to a single Token-Ring using up to 33 MAUs. Here the maximum lobe length is 100 meters and the maximum distance between wiring closets without the use of repeaters is limited to 200 meters (660 feet). The use of Type 3 telephone twisted-pair (UTP) permits a maximum of 72 devices connected to a Token-Ring using nine MAUs.

*Ring size*

One of the key constraints in designing a Token-Ring network is the ring size, which is a function of the length of the main ring path, the length of the longest lobe and the number of MAUs in the ring. If all lobes terminate in a single wire closet you can interconnect up to 33 MAUs which can serve up to 260 devices, each of which can have a lobe length of 100 meters. Thus, a single wire closet supports the geographical dispersion of workstations in a 100 meter (330 foot) radius.

If two or more wire closets are used to locate MAUs the drive distance can be obtained from a series of tables published by IBM. Those tables indicate the allowable drive distance in feet based upon the number of MAUs and the number of wiring closets in the network. Here the allowable drive distance is the sum of the longest lobe length up to 100 meters (330 feet) and the adjusted ring length (ARL).

*Adjusted ring length*

The ARL is an adjustment to the ring length made necessary by problem determination procedures which require portions of a

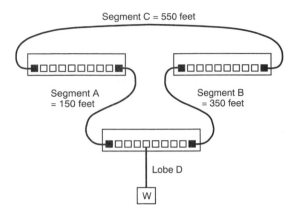

**Figure 4.14** Determining the adjusted ring length. The adjusted ring length (ARL) is the sum of the length of all wiring closet-to-wiring closed cable lengths less the length of the shortest of those cables. In this example, the ARL is $(550+350+150) - 150$, or 900 feet

ring to be removed. In doing so the ends of the main ring are wrapped around to allow tokens to complete their path around the ring which increases the drive distance. To determine the adjusted ring length the smallest portion of the main ring is mathematically removed. Figure 4.14 illustrates a three MAU Token-Ring network, showing the cabling distance between each MAU and the longest lobe distance.

If segment A is removed messages will wrap around the ends of the ring to return to a transmitting device. Since segment A is the shortest cable, the distance messages have to travel is maximized. Thus by subtracting the shortest segment from the ring distance we obtain the longest remaining path. Hence, the adjusted ring length (ARL) becomes:

$$ARL = (A + B + C) - A = 900 \text{ feet}$$

The adjusted ring length (ARL) is the sum of the length of all wiring closet-to-wiring closed cable lengths less the length of the shortest of those cables. In this example the ARL is $(550+350+150) - 150$ or 900 feet.

Once you obtain the allowable drive distance from the use of a table and compute the adjusted ring length you can determine the maximum allowable lobe length. For example, for three wiring closets, each containing one MAU, the allowable drive distance contained in IBM's set of tables is 1148 feet. Subtracting the ARL of 900 feet results in a maximum lobe length of 248 feet. If one or more of those distances are not sufficient to satisfy your networking requirements you can adjust the permissible cabling distances by reducing the number of MAUs, decreasing the number of wire closets, or using repeaters or bridges to extend the cabling distance.

The reduction in the number of MAUs allows longer ARLs and/or lobe lengths. Similarly, a decrease in the number of wiring closets can increase the allowable lobe length. If neither reduction can provide the desired cable distance you should examine the effect of using repeaters and bridges.

### 4.3.5 Token-Ring repeaters

IBM and other vendors market two basic types of repeaters, copper and fiber optic. A copper repeater regenerates the electrical signal as it passes through the main ring path. As IBM's copper repeater is not designed to pass the current generated by a Token-Ring adapter card used to operate an MAU relay, that device cannot be used on a lobe. Thus, the use of a copper repeater is restricted to extending inter-MAU cabling distances.

The actual distance supported by the use of a copper repeater depends upon the number of wiring closets and the number of MAUs in the Token-Ring. This distance, known as the ring segment drive distance, varies from 1235 feet when a ring uses one wiring closet and one MAU to 327 feet when a ring is formed using 12 wiring closets and 27 MAUs. IBM publishes a series of tables which define the maximum ring segment drive distance based upon the number of wiring closets and MAUs used to form a Token-Ring.

Figure 4.15 illustrates the placement of copper repeaters for a Token-Ring network formed by the use of two wiring closets, each containing one MAU. When two MAUs are in a network that contains two wire closets the maximum distance between copper repeaters is 1207 feet.

The fiber optic repeater (referred to as an optical fiber repeater by IBM) is a media converter and signal regenerator. The repeater performs copper-to-fiber media conversion, regenerating and converting the signal in both directions. IBM's fiber optic repeater supports a transmission distance of up to 2 km.

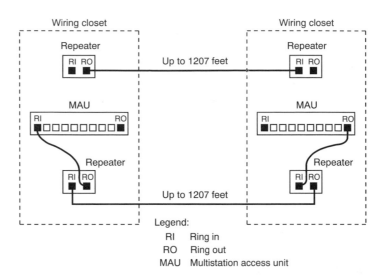

**Figure 4.15** Using copper repeaters. The use of copper repeaters permits a maximum cable distance of 1207 feet between two wiring closets when each closet contains one MAU

The use of both copper and fiber repeaters reduces the total number of devices that can be supported by a Token-Ring network. Each copper or optical repeater counts as an attached device, reducing by one the total number of other devices that can be attached to a Token-Ring network.

## 4.3.6 Bridge

IBM and third party vendors market a large number of hardware products which, when used in conjunction with a vendor's bridge program, provide customers with the ability to tailor hardware and software to satisfy most, if not all, bridging requirements.

One of the earliest examples of a Token-Ring bridge was the IBM Token-Ring network bridge program. That program could be configured to provide either a local or a remote bridging capability. Since users can have two types of Token-Ring networks the program provided three data rate combinations which provide linkage between every network combination: 16 Mbps to 16 Mbps, 16 Mbps to 4 Mbps, and 4 Mbps to 4 Mbps.

To build a local bridge a customer would obtain two Token-Ring adapter cards and the network bridge program. The adapter cards were installed in a wide range of IBM personal computers and resulted in the PC becoming a dedicated bridge. To construct a remote bridge requires the use of one Token-Ring adapter and a serial port adapter card, such as an X.25 interface co-processor card. The latter contains a serial port and packetizes Token-Ring frames into an X.25 packet format for transmission over a wide area transmission facility. IBM offered a wide range of interfaces for the X.25 co-processor board, to include RS-232, V.35 and several types of X.21 interfaces. The use of an RS-232 interface enables the attachment of a modem or DSU operating at a data rate of up to 19.2 Kbps, while the use of a V.35 interface permits the co-processor board to be connected to a DSU operating at 56 Kbps or to the port of a multiplexer operating at a data rate up to 1.344 Mbps.

Since the introduction of its Token-Ring network bridge program, IBM has introduced a series of bridge products that are plug-and-play devices that can connect two local rings, a local Token-Ring to a local Ethernet network, or two geographically separated Token-Ring networks via a serial connection at data rates up to T1 or E1 speeds. The most recent IBM Token-Ring bridge is the 8229. This bridge uses flash memory for its code and includes an RS-232 port to download software modifications directly into flash memory.

### 4.3.7 Controlled Access Unit

Recognizing that the use of individual MAUs could result in a significant use of space as well as time for cabling Ring In to Ring Out ports when Token-Ring networks have a large number of nodes, IBM introduced a series of Controlled Access Unit models to facilitate the cabling of clusters of nodes. A CAU can be considered to represent a series of modular MAU ports that can be expanded to provide a common housing to support a large number of Token-Ring network users. One of the more recent CAUs provides connectivity from 2 to 80 devices in 2-, 3- or 4-port increments through the use of Lobe Insertion Units (LIUs) that install into Lobe Attachment Modules (LAMs). In effect, you can view the LIUs as groups of MAU ports while LAMs can be considered to represent MAUs. Thus, the Controlled Access Unit can be considered to represent a concentration of MAUs and, in fact, is referred to as a Token-Ring workgroup concentrator.

The IBM model 8230 is that vendor's nomenclature for its controlled access unit. The 8230 is marketed in both desktop and rack-mountable models. Both models consist of a base unit and up to four lobe attachment modules (LAMs). Each LAM supports the connection of up to 20 devices to the ring using any combination of one to five 2-port, 3-port and 4-port LIUs, permitting one 8230 to attach up to 80 workstations to a Token-Ring network.

Similar to the IBM 8228, the 8230 contains one RI and one RO port. Those ports enable the 8230 to be connected to conventional eight-port MAUs, the latter used to satisfy the connectivity requirements of groups of users located in small clusters. In addition to providing the support formerly required through the use of up to ten 8228s, the 8230 works with IBM's LAN Network Manager program. That program enables an operator to list the adapter addresses connected to each 8230 in a network, set 8230 parameters, control access to the network through the 8230, and perform other functions.

The 8230 supports both 4 and 16 Mbps networks and can function as a repeater in both directions. This device is similar to the 8228 in that it can work with both copper and optical fiber cables in the IBM cabling system. In addition, 8230 lobe attachment modules are available with IBM Cabling System connectors as well as RJ45 connectors, the latter supporting twisted-wire lobe connections.

Figure 4.16 illustrates the use of the IBM 8230 in conjunction with a 8228 to construct a Token-Ring network. In this example, it was assumed that up to 20 network users were located in a relatively small clustered area in a corner of a floor and would be cabled to a one-LAM 8230. At the opposite end of the floor, a small group of eight or less users is located. Here you could use a single 8228 to service those users. By using the 8228 at the second location instead of expanding the 8230, you would minimize lobe runs and could both significantly reduce the cost of cabling devices to the network as well as ensure that you do not violate network cabling constraints.

### 4.3.8 Network processor

In early 1992 IBM introduced its long-awaited model 6611 network processor which can be considered as a sophisticated router. The 6611 is a multiprotocol router built on IBM's reduced instruction set computer (RISC) System/6000 platform. When introduced, two models of the 6611 were announced, four-slot and eight-slot models.

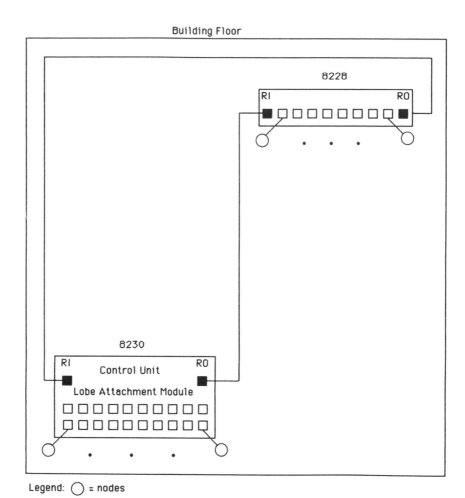

**Figure 4.16** Using IBM 8228 and 8230 devices to build a ring. The IBM 8230 Controlled Access Unit can be expanded to support the connection of up to 80 devices into a Token-Ring network, while the 8228 MAU supports up to 8 devices

Each 6611 slot can support a Token-Ring card, an Ethernet card, a serial T1 card with two ports, and an SDLC card with either two V.35 or four RS-232 ports. By selecting and using appropriate adapter cards the 6611 can be used for a variety of bridge and routing functions.

One of the more interesting features of the 6611 is its so-called 'firewall' capability. This feature can be used to prevent source routing bridge broadcasts from flowing across a wide area network link and can considerably improve WAN perfor-mance. The 6611 creates the firewall by internally maintaining a table of Token-Ring addresses mapped to their destination. This

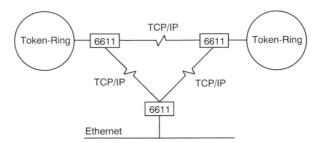

**Figure 4.17** IBM 6611 operations. The IBM 6611 router can be configured to transmit using a true TCP/IP protocol

enables the table to be used to route a broadcast message to its destination, rather than allowing broadcast messages to proliferate throughout the network. Readers are referred to Chapter 7 for detailed information concerning source routing and to Chapter 8 for information concerning the operation and utilization of routers.

In addition, it is suggested that readers turn to Chapter 10 for specific information concerning network devices known as firewalls which provide a more extensive protection facility than the firewall created by the 6611.

As the original introduction of the 6611 IBM has added a significant number of networking enhancements. Those enhancements include the ability to support frame relay WAN connections, IP and IPX at the network layer, as well as a networking technique known as Data Link Switching (DLSw). The latter enables SNA traffic to be transported over a TCP/IP backbone. DLSw and SNA are covered in Chapter 9. Another enhancement that warrants mention is the inclusion of a priority queuing capability in the 6611. Currently the 6611 supports the assignment of traffic types to one of three service queues: high, medium, and low. This allows users to assign priorities to different types of network traffic to satisfy organizational operational requirements. Figure 4.12 illustrates the potential use of the 6611 to interconnect three local area networks. Note that the data flow between 6611s is TCP/IP.

## 4.3.9 Connectivity overview

As previously mentioned Token-Ring networks can be interconnected through the use of bridges and routers. In addition to

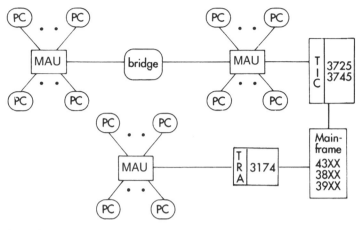

Legend:

TIC   Token-Ring Interface Coupler
TRA   Token-Ring Adapter
MAU  Multistation Access Unit

**Figure 4.18** Token-Ring connections options. (TIC Token-Ring interface coupler, TRA Token-Ring adapter, MAU multistation access unit)

those devices IBM markets an assortment of other connectivity products which enable Token-Rings to be connected to mainframe and minicomputers. Figure 4.18 illustrates a few of the basic Token-Ring connectivity options that users can consider to link Token-Ring workstations to a higher level of processing power.

Figure 4.18 illustrates two common methods to obtain a connection between local and remote Token-Ring networks and IBM mainframes. The top portion of that illustration shows the interconnection of two Token-Ring networks, one via a bridge, to an IBM 3725 or 3745 front-end processor. Either front-end processor requires the installation of a Token-Ring interface coupler (TIC), which is cabled to a port on an MAU. This enables the front-end processor to become an active participant on the Token-Ring and enables communications to the mainframe to occur via the front-end processor at 4 or 16 Mbps. Each PC on the network requiring access to the mainframe must operate the IBM PC 3270 emulation program which results in the PC emulating a 3X74 control unit with an attached type 3278/9 display and 3287 printer. What this means is that the program converts the PC into a terminal device capable of responding to the full screen codes generated by application programs executing on an IBM mainframe. Similarly, data entered at the

PC is transmitted in a form recognizable by the application program operating on the mainframe.

In the lower portion of Figure 4.18 a Token-Ring network connection via a 3174 control unit is illustrated. Connectivity to the Token-Ring is accomplished by the installation of a Token-Ring adapter (TRA) into the 3174. Then, the TRA is cabled to an MAU port and becomes an active participant on the ring.

Both local and remote 3174s support the addition of a TRA. This enables a Token-Ring located at a data center or at a remote location to be integrated to a mainframe via the use of a local or remote 3174 and a TRA. In comparison, a TIC used to provide connectivity between a Token-Ring network and a 3725 or 3745 front-end processor must be directly cabled to an MAU and is restricted to providing local connectivity.

## Gateways

The key to the connection of workstations on a Token-Ring network to a mainframe is a combination of hardware and software that provides a gateway to the mainframe. IBM and other vendors market a series of products that provide a variety of methods to obtain gateway connectivity from a Token-Ring network to a mainframe. In this section, we will focus our attention upon IBM products; however, readers should note that many third-party vendors market similar functioning equipment and software which are described in Chapter 9.

IBM gateways are personal computers and RISC based processors that can be considered equivalent to minicomputers that can be connected to a mainframe via the use of one of three types of communications adapter cards or via a channel directly to a mainframe. The three types of adapter cards that provide mainframe access include the IBM 3278/9, IBM SDLC and IBM Token-Ring network adapter card. Due to the importance of understanding the constraints and limitations associated with each method of connection, we will cover each method in detail based upon the type of adapter used in the gateway personal computer and the use of an interconnect controller for direct mainframe attachments. For each of the connectivity methods discussed in this section, it is assumed that IBM's workstation emulation program operates on the gateway computer.

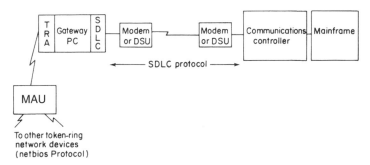

**Figure 4.19**   Using an SDLC adapter for gateway connectivity

### SDLC adapter connectivity

The use of an SDLC adapter permits a gateway PC to be connected directly to an IBM communications controller, such as a 3720, 3725 or 3745 device. As the SDLC adapter is used to obtain remote connectivity, the link between the gateway PC and the communications controller is obtained by the use of either a pair of modems or data service units. Modems are used if an analog communications facility is used, while data service units are used when a digital communications facility is employed. Figure 4.19 illustrates the use of an SDLC adapter in a gateway PC.

When a gateway PC uses an SDLC adapter, its data rate is limited to a maximum of 19.2 Kbps if the adapter has an RS-232 interface or 56 Kbps if the adapter has a CCITT V.35 interface. The gateway PC communicates with other workstations on the network via IBM's NetBIOS interface and a Token-Ring adapter board at 4 or 16 Mbps. One key limitation of this method of connectivity is the data rate between the gateway and mainframe, which can be a bottleneck with respect to the response time of other workstations on the network accessing mainframe applications.

When the PC is used as a gateway via an SDLC adapter, only the gateway PC is recognized as an SNA physical unit. Each of the workstation PCs on the network is designated as a logical unit (LU). As a maximum of 32 LUs can be associated with a PU, a second limitation associated with this method of connectivity concerns the number of workstations supported by this type of gateway which is 32.

### 3278/9 adapter connectivity

The use of a 3278/9 adapter card requires a gateway PC to be cabled to a 3X74 control unit via the use of a coaxial cable. The

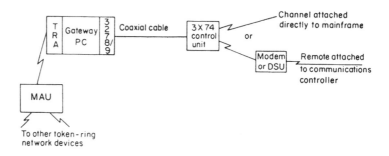

**Figure 4.20**   Using a 3278/9 adapter for gateway connectivity

control unit can be either locally attached to a host computer or remotely attached via the use of modems or DSUs. Figure 4.20 illustrates gateway connectivity obtained via the use of an IBM 3278/9 adapter.

A gateway using an IBM 3278 adapter is limited to supporting up to five concurrent network workstation communications sessions to the mainframe. This is because the port on the control unit must be configured as a distributed function terminal (DFT) port, which is limited to supporting five concurrent sessions. Thus, seven gateways using 3278/9 adapter cards would be required to provide an equivalent level of concurrent sessions obtained through the use of a SDLC adapter card.

Similarly to the use of an SDLC adapter, a throughput bottleneck can occur when a 3278/9 adapter card is used. This bottleneck resides in the 3X74 control unit to communications controller link. Unless special hardware modifications are made to the control unit and communications controller, their maximum data transfer rate is limited to 19.2 Kbps. With hardware modifications, a data transfer rate of 56 Kbps becomes obtainable.

### 4.3.10 The Interconnect Controller

The IBM 3172 Interconnect Controller can be viewed as a multi-protocol modular gateway as well as a specific functioning front-end processor. The 3172 can be attached to Systems/390 mainframes, communicating with either an SNA Virtual Tele-communications Access Method (VTAM) operating on the mainframe or a TCP/IP VTAM. For LAN and WAN connectivity,

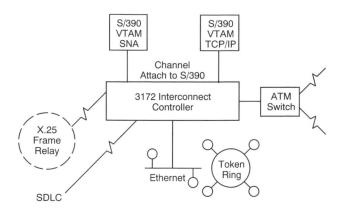

**Figure 4.21** Network connectivity via the use of an IBM 3172 Interconnect Controller

the 3172 supports a variety of connection methods. For example, through appropriate expansion modules the 3172 can connect to Ethernet, Token-Ring, FDDI and ATM networks. For WAN connectivity the 3172 can provide SDLC communications to SNA devices or can be interfaced to X.25 packet or frame relay networks, providing a mechanism to globally extend connectivity into a mainframe. Figure 4.21 illustrates the potential use of an IBM 3172 Interconnect Controller to provide LAN and WAN gateway services to IBM S/390 mainframes. Note that the 3172 Interconnect Controller uses LAN Emulation to provide the required conversion between Ethernet and Token-Ring networks and an ATM network. Also note that the 3172 has a TCP/IP for OS/2 feature which enables the off-loading of certain TCP/IP processing on the S/390. Thus, the Interconnect Controller can be considered to represent a front end processor as well as a bridge and gateway.

### 4.3.11 Token-Ring switching

Similarly to Ethernet, Token-Ring networks suffering from high levels of utilization can obtain a considerable degree of relief through the use of switches developed to segment rings, permit multiple simultaneous client-server sessions, and collapse ring backbones that adversely effect bridging performance. Token-Ring switches are similar to their Ethernet relatives in that some support a single node per switch port (port switching), while others support the connection of a ring to a switch port (segment

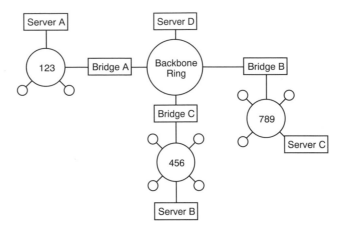

**Figure 4.22** Using a backbone ring

switching). One key difference between Token-Ring and Ethernet switches is the fact that the flow of a token provides a built-in flow control mechanism.

### Backbone ring performance

One of the more popular uses for Token-Ring switches is to collapse a backbone ring. Figure 4.22 illustrates the use of a backbone ring to interconnect three LANs. In this example it was assumed that rings 123, 456, and 789 were formed to support local workgroups, and servers A, B and C are primarily accessed by users on the networks they are attached to. Then server D represents a departmental server which users on each LAN periodically need to access.

Performance problems arise when stations on two or more rings contend for access to server D or another server other than their local server. For example, if a station on rings 123 and 456 attempt to access servers B and D, they must first gain access to the backbone ring. Thus, one client-server transportation request will delay another request. So long as a small portion of traffic on each LAN requires access to another LAN, a backbone network solution for linking rings provides an acceptable level of performance. However, as utilization increases and additional rings are bridged to the backbone, the backbone will become heavily utilized and will eventually

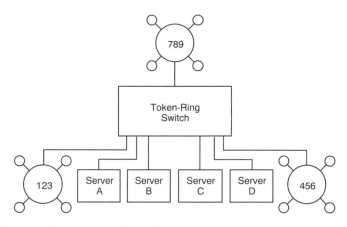

**Figure 4.23**  Using a Token-Ring switch as a collapsed backbone

introduce unacceptable delays. When this occurs or hopefully before it occurs, you will want to consider creating a collapsed backbone.

*Creating a collapsed backbone*

You can consider the use of routers or switches to form a collapsed backbone. Routers operate in a store-and-forward mode at the network layer, resulting in the addition of latency which exceeds that associated with switches that operate at the data link layer. In addition, on a per port basis, they are more expensive than switches.

As the transmission capacity of the backplane of a Token-Ring switch considerably exceeds many multiples of 16 Mbps, it can support multiple simultaneous connections from ring stations to servers. This permits nodes to communicate with servers as if the servers were directly connected to each ring. Figure 4.23 illustrates the use of a Token-Ring switch as a mechanism to collapse the backbone ring previously shown in Figure 4.22. Note that through the use of the switch shown in Figure 4.23 it becomes possible for three servers to be accessed simultaneously regardless of the relationship between the network where a client is located and the location of the network the server resides on.

*Token-Ring switch operations*

As previously discussed, Token-Ring switches are similar to Ethernet with respect to their ability to support port and segment switching. In addition, Token-Ring switches are also similar to Ethernet switches with respect to the types of switching method performed. Token-Ring switches can operate as cut-through, store-and-forward, and hybrid, with the latter method resulting in the switch toggling between cut-through and store-and-forward based upon the error rate noted by creating CRCs and examining their values against the CRC values in frames flowing through the switch. However, unlike Ethernet switches that do not have to contend with a beaconing condition nor source routing, a Token-Ring switch must take both into consideration. This means that when a Token-Ring switch is operating in a cut-through mode and a destination ring is beaconing, the switch cannot directly output a frame. Thus, it must then go into a store-and-forward mode of operation and wait for the beaconing condition to cease. Similarly, if data is routed between rings that operate at different speeds, the switch must act as a buffer and cannot directly perform cut-through operations. One additional difference between Ethernet and Token-Ring switches involves the fact that Token-Ring networks support the use of the Routing Information Field (RIF) as a mechanism to forward frames. Similarly, Token-Ring switches can perform switching based upon source routing information. Readers are referred to Chapter 7 for specific information concerning source routing.

*The dedicated Token-Ring standard*

Recognizing the necessity to standardize Token-Ring switching, the IEEE developed the 802.5r Dedicated Token-Ring (DTR) standard. Under this standard, a Token-Ring switch is referred to as a DTR concentrator which consists of C- (classical) ports and a Data Transfer Unit (DTU) that represents the switching fabric that connects C-ports within the concentrator. The C-ports provide basic connectivity to Token-Ring stations, classic concentrators, or other DTR concentrators.

Figure 4.24 provides a schematic of the major components of an IEEE 802.5r DTR concentrator. Note that the Transmit Immediate (TXI) protocol defines full duplex operations

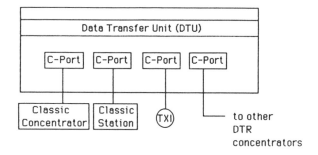

Transmit Immediate (TXI) protocol defines full duplex
operation to obtain simultaneous bi-directional 16 Mbps
data flow.

**Figure 4.24**  The dedicated Token-Ring concentrator

between a C-port and a single node, enabling a simultaneous
bi-directional 16 Mbps data flow that results in a 32 Mbps
data transfer capability. As servers are the most heavily
accessed devices on a network, C-ports supporting full duplex
transmission should normally be connected to network
servers.

## Recent developments

A recent capability added to some vendor Token-Ring switches
that deserves mention is token pipe support. A token pipe is a
logical linkage of two to four Token-Ring switch ports that
function as an entity. Through the formation of token pipes,
you can tune bandwidth between switch ports and other
switches and servers. Currently vendor switch products that
support token pipes are limited to four physical connections
between a switch and a server, and two physical connections
between a switch and another switch. As token pipe
connections can be full duplex, this provides a logically
developed 64 Mbps transmission capability between switches
and a 128 Mbps capability to servers. Figure 4.25 illustrates
the use of token pipes to tune bandwidth between a switch
and other switches and directly connected servers. This figure
illustrates the potential use of four token pipes in a multi-
switch networking environment. In this example, the use of
four links to each departmental server provides a 128 Mbps
connect to each server. As each tier 1 switch communicates

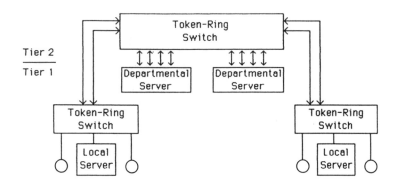

Legend ⟷ Full duplex connection

**Figure 4.25** Using token pipes to tune the allocation of bandwidth

with the tier 2 switch at 64 Mbps, it becomes possible for multiple requests from both tier 1 switches to the same departmental server to be serviced without delay. Thus, the use of token pipes can have a significant effect upon the ability to minimize delay when constructing a switch based Token-Ring network.

# 5

# WIDE AREA NETWORKS AND NETWORK FACILITIES

In Chapter 1 we examined the general characteristics of wide area networks and their utilization. In this chapter we will focus our attention upon the major types of wide area networks used for the transportation of information. In doing so we will examine the transmission facilities available for use and the data transmission rates that can be obtained from the use of different network facilities.

One of many methods that can be used to categorize wide area networks is with respect to the flow of information on a transmission facility. If we use this method to categorize wide area networks, we can group them into three basic types: circuit switched, leased line and packet switched.

## 5.1 CIRCUIT SWITCHED NETWORKS

The most popular type of network and the one almost all readers use on a daily basis is a circuit switched network. The public switched telephone network, in which the number you dial results in telephone company offices switching the call between offices to establish a connection to the dialed party, represents the most commonly used circuit switched network. However, circuit switching is not limited to the telephone company. By purchasing appropriate switching equipment, any organization can construct its own internal circuit switched network and, if

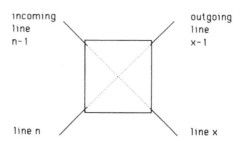

**Figure 5.1**  Generic switch operation. In a circuit switching system, an incoming line is cross-connected to an outgoing line

desired, provide one or more interfaces to the public switched network to allow voice and data transmission to flow between the public network and their private internal network.

In a circuit switching system, switching equipment is used to establish a physical path for the duration of a call. The path that is established is temporary and the facilities used to establish the call become available for another call after the conclusion of the first call. This type of connection in which a call is established by switching equipment over a temporary path is known as a switched virtual call (SVC). Figure 5.1 illustrates the operation of a generic switch used to establish a circuit switched call. In this illustration, any incoming line can be cross-connected to any outgoing line. This switching mechanism results in the establishment of a path between the caller/originator and the called party/destination.

Both the incoming and outgoing lines and the switching equipment illustrated in Figure 5.1 are shown in a generic representation. In actuality, both the type of line facilities and the switching equipment used to establish a circuit switched call can vary considerably.

The earliest circuit switched networks used a twisted-pair wire conductor to route calls from a telephone subscriber to a serving office, the latter commonly referred to as a local or end office. Depending upon the destination of the call it will be routed directly to another subscriber served by that office or into a trunk for transmission to another telephone company office. The first type of routing involves an intraoffice call, while the second type of routing involves an interoffice call.

The concept of the switched virtual call has been extended to packet switching networks, with a temporary connection between a data originator and recipient flowing on a fixed path setup for a transmission session. As we will note later in this chapter, this type of connection is referred to as a switched virtual circuit.

### 5.1.1 Types of facility

There are two types of circuit switched transmission facility that you can use to interconnect geographically dispersed locations, analog and digital. Analog circuit switched transmission facilities are available worldwide and are represented by the conventional telephone network. Digital circuit switched transmission facilities are available in most major metropolitan areas; however, only certain locations within a city may support this service.

*Analog*

The transmission of data over the analog circuit switched telephone network requires the use of modems. A modem is a contraction of the term modulator–demodulator and it converts digital data transmitted by business machines and computers into analog tones for transmission on the analog telephone network. The process of converting digital data into analog signals is known as modulation, while the reverse process is called demodulation.

Figure 5.2 illustrates the use of the telephone network to transmit data between a personal computer and a mainframe computer. The circle with the enclosed × is the symbol commonly used to represent a switched network.

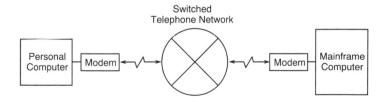

**Figure 5.2** Using the switched telephone network for data transmission. Through the use of modems, digital data can be transmitted over the analog public switched telephone network

**Modem utilization**

When transmission occurs over the public switched telephone network the type of modem used and its features govern the effective transmission rate. Here the type of modem refers to the modulation technique used and the data transmission rate in bits per second obtained from the use of a particular modulation technique. The features of a modem, such as data compression, can boost the effective transmission rate above the modem's data transmission rate. For example, a V.32 type modem provides a data transmission rate of 9600 bps. When a V.32 modem incorporates V.42 bis data compression the effect of this feature more than doubles the throughput of the modem, resulting in its effective data transmission rate exceeding 19 200 bps. Of course, to obtain this throughput you must communicate with a compatible modem that supports the same modulation technique and data compression feature.

The two most common types of data compression used in modems are Microcom Networking Protocol (MNP) Class 5 and the ITU-T V.42 bis. MNP Class 5 provides an approximate 1.5:1 compression ratio, meaning that it raises the effective rate of data transmission by 50% above the modem's operating rate. The more modern V.42 bis data compression technique provides an average compression ratio of 2:1, in effect doubling the modem's transmission rate.

Table 5.1 lists seven commonly available switched network modems, their operating rate in bps, and the type of data compression normally available as an option or included with the modem. Each of the modems listed in Table 5.1 operates full duplex, allowing the transmission of data in both directions to occur simultaneously. The first two modems listed in Table 5.1

**Table 5.1**  Common switched network modems

| Type | Operating rate (bps) | Compression offered | Effective data rate (bps) |
|------|------|------|------|
| Bell 212A | 1200 | None | 1200 |
| V.22 | 1200 | None | 1200 |
| V.22 bis | 2400 | MNP Class 5 | 2400–3600 |
| V.32 | 9600 | MNP Class 5, V.42 bis | 9600–19 200 |
| V.32 bis | 14 400 | MNP Class 5, V.42 bis | 14 400–28 800 |
| V.34 | 28 800 | MNP Class 5, V.42 bis | 28 000–57 600 |
| V.34 bis | 34 600 | MNP Class 5, V.42 bis | 34 600–69 200 |

were primarily designed for asynchronous transmission. Although the last five modems in the table can operate synchronously, their use in this manner is primarily restricted to leased lines. In addition, when used for synchronous transmission the modem's compression feature is disabled.

In examining Table 5.1 note that the effective data rate column represents the range of data transmission obtainable based upon the modem's operating rate and, if applicable, the effect of data compression. Although many vendors have advertised V.42 bis providing a 4:1 compression ratio, it is highly doubtful that this compression ratio is obtainable for a sustained period of time as different types of data are operated upon. Instead, a compression ratio of 2:1 can normally be expected to be achieved and it represents a more realistic expectation of the effect of V.42 bis technology.

Although the use of V.32, V.32 bis, V.34, and V.34 bis modems can provide an acceptable level of remote dial-in access to a LAN, their use is normally impractical for connecting geographically distributed networks via a wide area network. This is because most LAN interconnections occur on a permanent basis and the use of switched network modems results in long distance toll charges which even at a dime a minute can result in a substantial expenditure over a 40 hour work week, 52 weeks a year. In addition, the use of what we may consider to be high speed modems pale in comparison to the operating rates of newer digital services, as well as an evolving series of analog transmission methods that are referred to by the term digital subscriber line. Due to the transmission overhead associated with servers and routers that periodically broadcast their presence, many vendors rightly recommend that LANs should be interconnected at a minimum of 56 Kbps, a data rate more appropriately obtained from digital transmission facilities or the evolving DSL technology discussed next.

_DSL_

Digital Subscriber Line (DSL) represents a series of technologies developed to enhance the use of copper telephone lines from a communication carrier's central office to the subscriber. Through the use of different modulation techniques that use portions of the frequency spectrum beyond the 4 kHz used for normal telephone operations, both voice and high speed data

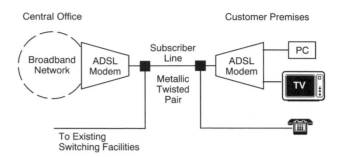

**Figure 5.3** Asymmetric digital subscriber line

transmission from the central office to the subscriber via an existing copper cable becomes possible. One of the more promising DSL technologies being introduced when this book was prepared is Asymmetric Digital Subscriber Line (ADSL). ADSL is implemented from the subscriber to the communications carrier's central office via the use of a pair of ADSL modems.

Each ADSL modem provides two data channels, with the return channel having a maximum operating rate of 576 Kbps, and results in the asymmetric operation of the modem. In actuality, an ADSL circuit with ADSL modems connected to each end of a twisted-pair line has three channels: a high-speed downstream channel, a medium-speed upstream channel, and a standard voice telephone channel. The latter is split off from the digital modem by filters, which ensures that subscribers can continue to obtain the use of a voice telephone channel on the existing twisted-pair connection even if one or both ADSL modems fail.

Figure 5.3 illustrates the basic operation of an ADSL circuit. The downstream operating rate depends on several factors, including the length of the subscriber line, its wire gauge, the presence or absence of bridged taps, and the level of interferences on the line. Based on the fact that line attenuation increases with line length and frequency, whereas it decreases as the wire diameter increases, we can note ADSL performance in terms of the wire gauge and subscriber line distance. Ignoring bridged taps, which represent sections of unterminated twisted-pair cable connected in parallel across the cable under consideration, various tests of ADSL lines provided a general indication of other operating rate capability. That capability is summarized in Table 5.2.

**Table 5.2** ADSL performance

| Operating rate | Wire guage | Subscriber line distance |
| --- | --- | --- |
| 1.5/2.0 Mbps | 24 AWG | 18 000 feet |
| 1.5/2.0 Mbps | 26 AWG | 15 000 feet |
| 6.1 Mbps | 24 AWG | 12 000 feet |
| 6.1 Mbps | 26 AWG | 9000 feet |

### Operation

ADSL operations are based on advanced digital signal processing and the employment of specialized algorithms to obtain high data rates on twisted-pair telephone wire. Currently there are two competing technologies used to provide ADSL capabilities: Discrete Multitone (DMT) modulation and Carrierless Amplitude/Phase (CAP) modulation. The first technology, DMT, represents an American National Standards Institute (ANSI) standard. In comparison, CAP represents a proprietary technology developed by AT&T; however, at the time that this book was prepared CAP had been licensed to a number of communications carriers throughout the world. Both DMT and CAP permit the transmission of high-speed data using Frequency Division Multiplexing (FDM) to create multiple channels on twisted pair. Through the use of FDM, the copper twisted-pair subscriber line is divided into three parts by frequency, as illustrated in Figure 5.4. FDM assigns one channel for downstream data and a second channel for upstream data, while the third channel from 0 to 4 kHz is used for normal telephone operations. The downstream path can be subdivided through time division multiplexing to derive

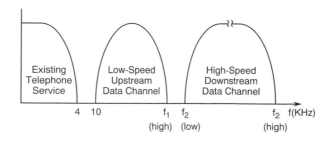

**Figure 5.4** ADSL frequency spectrum

several high- and low-speed subchannels by time. In a similar manner the upstream channel can be subdivided.

### Discrete multitone modulation

Under DMT modulation, the available bandwidth is split or subdivided into a large number of independent subchannels. As the amount of attenuation at high frequencies depends on the length of the subscriber line and wire gauge, a DMT modem at the central office must determine which subchannels are useable. To do so, that modem sends tones to the remote modem where they are analyzed. The remote modem responds to the central office modem subchannel scan at a relatively low speed, which significantly reduces the possibility of the signal analysis performed by the remote modem being misinterpreted. Based on the returned signal analysis, the central office modem will use up to 256 4 kHz wide subchannels for downstream transmission. Through a reverse measurement process, the remote modem will use up to 32 4 kHz wide subchannels for upstream transmission.

One of the key advantages of DMT is its ability to take advantage of the characteristics of twisted-pair wire, which can vary from one local loop to another. This makes DMT modulation well suited for obtaining a higher data throughput than obtainable through the use of a single carrier transmission technique.

### Carrierless amplitude/phase modulation

Carrierless amplitude/phase (CAP) modulation is a derivative of QAM that was developed by AT&T Paradyne. Unlike DMT, which subdivides the bandwidth of the wire into 4 kHz segments, CAP uses the entire bandwidth in the upstream and downstream channels. Under CAP, serial data is encoded by mapping a group of bits into a signal constellation point using two-dimensional eight-state trellis coding with Reed-Solomon forward error correction. The latter automatically protects transmitted data against impairments due to crosstalk, impulse noise, and background noise.

The ADSL unit developed by AT&T Paradyne uses a CAP-256 line code (256-point signal constellation) for downstream operations, using bandwidth from 120 kHz to 1224 kHz. The composite signaling rate is 960 kbaud and 7 bits are packed into each signal change to provide a downstream operating rate of 6.72 Mbps. However, the use of Reed–Solomon forward error correction reduces the actual payload to 6.312 Mbps plus a 64 Kbps control channel. In the upstsream direction the Paradyne device uses a CAP-16 line code in the 35 kHz to 72 kHz frequency band to obtain a composite signaling rate of 24 kbaud across 16 subchannels. Packing 3 bits per signal change, an upstream line rate of 72 Kbps is obtained, of which 64 Kbps is available for data.

Currently it appears that ADSL is more suitable for providing Internet Web browser access than connecting LANs. The reason for this is the fact that the asymmetric transmission in which the downstream operating rate is much higher than the upstream rate favors browser operations in which a click on a Universal Resource Locator (URL) that results in a location being transmitted to the Internet obtains a response in the form of a Web page or file representing considerably more downstream traffic than upstream. However, because the lowest ADSL rate exceeds that obtainable with modems, the true test of the usefulness of this emerging service will be its price and the carrier infrastructure that enables ADSL local loop transmission to flow on the carrier's backbone network to provide connectivity between central offices. Although ADSL requires a permanent connection from the subscriber to a carrier's central office similar to a leased line, it also supports switched telephone network calls. In addition, the manner by which its use will be priced remains to be determined. For example, its use could be priced on a per call basis, on a timed basis, on a per call and quantity of data basis, or on a monthly basis. Thus, although our description of ADSL was placed in the switched network section of this chapter, it may evolve into a leased line or packet service.

## Digital

Switched digital transmission became available in the late 1980s when AT&T introduced its Accunet Switched 56 service, a dial-up 56 Kbps digital transmission service. The use of Switched 56 and similar transmission facilities marketed by other communications carriers requires the use of a data service unit (DSU) in place of a modem.

### DSU utilization

The DSU is sometimes referred to as a digital modem as it converts unipolar digital signals produced by business

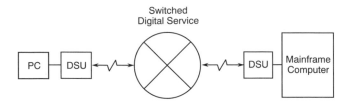

**Figure 5.5** Using switched digital transmission. Through the use of DSUs and digital access lines, data can be transmitted over a communications carrier's switched digital transmission facilities

machines and computers into bipolar digital signals suitable for transmission over a switched digital network. As data is transmitted over a digital network the signal is regenerated by the communications carrier numerous times prior to its arrival at its destination. In general, digital service gives data communications users improved performance and reliability when compared to analog service, owing to the nature of digital transmission and the design of digital networks. The improved performance and reliability are due to the fact that digital signals are regenerated, whereas analog signals are amplified, any distortion to the analog signal also being increased in magnitude due to the operation of the amplifiers.

Figure 5.5 illustrates the use of switched digital transmission. Similarly to analog switched networks, the DSU governs the operating rate obtainable on the transmission facility. However, unlike an analog switched service where the data rate can be increased by obtaining higher operating modems, you must normally obtain both higher operating DSUs and a new digital access line to obtain a higher switched digital transmission service capability. The digital access line connects the subscriber's location to a carrier's central office that supports switched digital transmission.

Several communications carriers offer switched 56 Kbps transmission. In November 1991, AT&T introduced switched 384 Kbps digital transmission. This was followed by the introduction of switched T1 service a few years later from AT&T and other vendors.

Switched 56 Kbps, 384 Kbps and T1 digital services can be used in a variety of internetworking applications. They can be used to supplement the interconnection of LANs via leased lines, provide a backup for leased lines, or provide the primary method of interconnection when transmission between two networks is relatively infrequent. Switched services are particularly useful in the latter situation since billing is primarily based upon usage. In comparison, leased lines are billed on a monthly basis regardless of usage.

*ISDN*

One of the key limitations associated with switched 384 Kbps and switch T1 services is their availability. Both services require the use of special central office switches as well as a good quality line from the subscriber to the central office. A more popular switched digital service that can be obtained at over 70% of all communications carrier service points is ISDN, an acronym for Integrated Services Digital Network.

ISDN represents a series of digital transmission protocols defined by the ITU-T that were developed to support the simultaneous transmission of voice, data, fax, and video over a common infrastructure. There are two types of commonly offered ISDN interface through which users gain access to a carrier's ISDN infrastructure. Those interfaces are referred to as the Basic Rate Interface (BRI) and the Primary Rate Interface (PRI).

### Basic Rate Interface

The ISDN Basic Rate Interface (BRI) consists of two Bearer (B) channels and a (D) channel used for call setup and signaling. All three channels flow on a common wire pair with time division multiplexing used to separate channels. Each B channel operates at 64 Kbps which represents the Pulse Code Modulation (PCM) rate required to digitize an analog voice conversation, while the D channel operates at 16 Kbps. Thus, the ISDN BRI is commonly referred to as a 2B+D Basic Rate Interface. Both PCM and time division multiplexing are explained in the next section as they were originally associated with leased lines. Although ISDN is a switched service it should be noted that it operates on a digital leased line infrastructure, with switching equipment at communications carrier offices connecting circuits to route calls to their destination.

Each ISDN B channel provides a separate dial-up transmission for either voice or data at 64 Kbps. Thus, the BRI interface enables simultaneous voice and data transmission to occur over

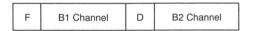

B channels are 64 Kbps each.
D channel is 16 Kbps.
2B+D Basic Access service is a 155 Kbps data stream which
operates at 192 Kbps due to framing and multiplexing overhead.

**Figure 5.6**   ISDN basic access channel format

a common wire pair. In addition, the 16 Kbps D channel uses packet switching for call setup and signaling, and can also be used for low speed functions such as turning appliances or machinery on and off, meter reading, and similar functions. Thus, the BRI can actually support three simultaneous operations on a common wire pair. Figure 5.6 illustrates the ISDN basic access channel frame format. As indicated in the illustration, the 2B+D service represents a 144 Kbps data stream which is transported at 192 Kbps due to framing and multiplexing overhead.

The use of ISDN's BRI is based upon a series of functional groupings and network interface reference points illustrated in Figure 5.7. The functional groupings are sets of functions that

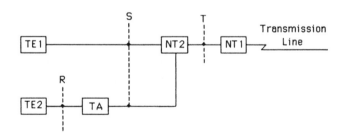

Legend:
    TE1 (Terminal Equipment 1) type devices comply with the
        ISDN's interface.
    TE2 (Terminal Equipment 2) type devices do not have an
        ISDN interface and must be connected via a TA
        (terminal adapter) functional grouping.
    NT2 (Network Termination 2) includes switching and con-
        centration equipment which performs functions similar
        to layers 1 and 3 of the OSI Reference Model.
    NT1 (Network Termination 1) includes functions equivalent
        to layer 1 of the OSI Reference Model.

**Figure 5.7**   ISDN reference points and network interfaces

may be required at an interface, whereas reference points are employed to divide the functional groups into distinct entities.

The Terminal Equipment (TE) functional grouping consists of TE1 and TE2 type equipment. Digital telephones, conventional data terminals, and integrated voice-data workstations are examples of TE equipment. TE1 equipment complies with the ISDN user-network interface and permits such equipment to be directly connected to an ISDN S type interface that supports multiple B and D channels.

TE2 devices represent equipment with non-ISDN interfaces, such as RS-232 or ITU-T V-series interfaces. This type of equipment must be connected through the use of a Terminal Adapter (TA) functional grouping which converts a non-ISDN interface (R) into an ISDN interface (S). The TA provides both a physical and a protocol conversion capability that enables TE2 devices to operate on ISDN.

The Network Termination 2 (NT2) functional group includes devices that perform switching and data concentration functions equivalent to the first three layers of the OSI Reference Model. Typical NT2 equipment can include PABXs, LAN routers, concentrators, and multiplexers.

The ISDN digital interface point that is equivalent to layer 1 of the OSI Reference Model is the Network Termination 1 (NT1) functional group. Functions of NT1 include the physical and electrical termination of the loop, line monitoring, timing and bit multiplexing. In some locations where carriers are government-owned monopolies, NT1 and NT2 functions may be combined into a common device, such as a PABX. In such situations, the equipment serves as an NT12 functional group. In the United States, a communications carrier may only provide the NT1, whereas third-party equipment would connect to the carrier equipment at the T interface.

### Primary Rate Interface

A second type of ISDN interface represents a large aggregation of B channels with one high speed 64 Kbps D channel. Referred to as a Primary Rate Interface (PRI), the number of B channels corresponds to the type of digital transmission circuit used to carry the aggregation. In North America an ISDN PRI consists of 23 B channels and one D channel that is transported on a T1 line operating at 1.544 Mbps. In Europe the ISDN PRI consists of 30 B channels and one D channel that is transported on an E1 circuit that operates at 2.048 Mbps. The installation of a PRI

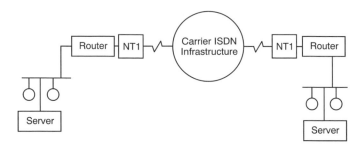

**Figure 5.8**  The temporary connection of two LANs via ISDN

instead of multiple BRIs is based upon economics, as it is less costly for a communications carrier to install one line to a subscriber that can provide 23 or 30 B channels than to install 23 or 30 individual twisted wire pairs to obtain 22 or 30 B channels. Thus, if you have a requirement to access multiple LANs at the same time from one location you may prefer to order a single PRI connection that can be provisioned to support up to 30 distinct calls at one time instead of ordering the installation of multiple circuits that can result in a considerable installation expenditure.

### Utilization

The use of the ISDN BRI provides a mechanism to initiate switched digital calls at 64 Kbps or two calls that can be aggregated at 128 Kbps. As the call setup time is very low, ISDN can be used for the temporary linking of geographically separated LANs on an on-demand basis. This method of utilization can include the specific use of ISDN to link geographically separated LANs several times a day to support email transfers, or its use as a supplement to an existing circuit connecting LANs when network utilization reaches a predefined level. In its second role, the cost of ISDN which averages approximately $0.06/minute at 64 Kbps for usage plus a nominal monthly access fee can be considerably less expensive than the installation of a second leased line or the upgrading of an existing leased line to a higher operating rate. Figure 5.8 illustrates the use of ISDN as a mechanism to interconnect two geographically separated LANs.

## 5.2 LEASED LINE NETWORKS

In the early days of circuit switching, groups of lines were routed between telephone company offices, with each line used to carry one conversation at a time that was switched onto the line. As the number of telephone subscribers proliferated, telephone companies quickly realized that this method of switching individual calls onto individual circuits was not economical.

To reduce the number of physical lines required to connect telephone company offices to one another, communications carriers implemented a technique called multiplexing. Originally, frequency division multiplexing (FDM) was used exclusively by communications carriers. Gradually, FDM was replaced by time division multiplexing (TDM) that utilizes the T-carrier as a digital transport mechanism. This evolution to TDM equipment and T-carrier facilities was based upon the advantages associated with digital signaling in comparison to analog signaling and has gradually led to the replacement of analog leased lines by digital leased lines.

### 5.2.1 Frequency division multiplexing

Employing frequency division multiplexing between carrier central offices requires the use of a communications circuit that has a relatively wide bandwidth. This bandwidth is then divided into subchannels by frequency.

When a communications carrier uses FDM for the multiplexing of voice conversations onto a common circuit, the 3 kHz passband of each conversation is shifted upward in frequency by a fixed increment of frequency. This frequency shifting places the voice conversation into a predefined channel of the FDM multiplexed circuit. At the opposite end of the circuit, another FDM demultiplexes the voice conversations by shifting the frequency spectrum of each conversation downward by the same increment of frequency by which it was previously shifted upward.

As previously mentioned, the primary use of FDM equipment by communications carriers was to enable those carriers to carry a large number of simultaneous voice conversations on a common circuit routed between two carrier offices. The actual process for allocating the bands of frequencies to each voice conversation has been standardized by the ITU-T. ITU-T FDM recommendations govern the channel assignments of voice multiplexed conversations based upon the use of 12, 60 and 300 derived voice channels.

### ITU-T FDM recommendations

The standard group as defined by ITU-T recommendation G.232 occupies the frequency band from 60 to 108 kHz. This group can be considered as the first level of frequency division multiplexing and contains 12 voice channels, with each channel occupying the 300 to 3400 Hz spectrum shifted in frequency.

The standard supergroup as defined by ITU-T recommendation G.241 contains five standard groups, equivalent to 60 voice channels. The standard supergroup can be considered as the second level of frequency division multiplexing and occupies the frequency band from 312 to 552 kHz.

The third ITU-T FDM recommendation, known as the standard mastergroup, can be considered as the top of the FDM hierarchy. The standard mastergroup contains five supergroups. As each supergroup consists of 60 voice channels, the mastergroup contains a total of 300 voice channels. The standard mastergroup occupies the frequency band from 812 to 2044 kHz. Figure 5.9 illustrates the three standard ITU-T FDM groups, as well as the relationship between groups.

By using one of the three types of groups illustrated in Figure 5.9, telephone companies were able to place up to 12, 60, or 300 simultaneous calls on one circuit routed between offices. Although originally used to carry voice conversations, this mechanism for sharing wideband circuits also supports the transmission of data. However, as FDM is an analog system, the transmission of data required its conversion into a modulated signal through the use of modems.

Originally FDM was used to route multiple circuit switched conversations between communications carriers' central offices. The connection of terminal devices to modems enabled the transmission of data to occur on the switched telephone network. Although communications carriers originally developed FDM for their internal use, the additional capacity obtained through its use enabled carriers to market channels to customers for their exclusive use. Doing so resulted in the commercial offering of analog leased lines.

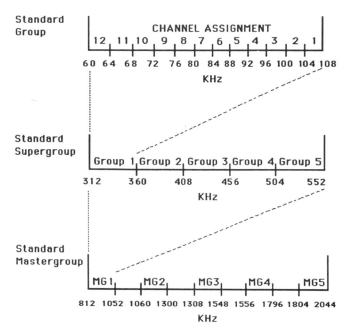

**Figure 5.9** Standard ITU-T FDM groups. ITU-T FDM recommendations govern the assignment of 12, 60, and 300 voice channels on wideband analog circuits

## Analog leased lines

In actuality the analog leased line was rarely a line dedicated to the exclusive use of a customer. Instead, the leased line represented a circuit routed from the customer's premises to the carrier's nearest office. At that location the circuit was multiplexed through the use of FDM equipment and routed onward towards its destination on a wideband circuit. At the carrier office nearest the customer's destination premises the wideband line was demultiplexed and the channel on the wideband circuit was connected to a line routed to the customer's premises.

### Modem utilization

Similar to the transmission of data over the switched network, the operating rate obtainable when data is transmitted over an analog leased line depends upon the operating rate of modems used on that transmission facility that can work within the approximate 3 kHz frequency spectrum. Two commonly used leased line modems follow the ITU-T V.29 and V.33 recommendations. The V.29 recommendation defines the modulation process for a synchronous modem operating at 9600 bps, while the V.33 recommendation defines the modulation process for a synchronous modem operating at 14 400 bps.

As previously discussed, more modern V.32, V.32 bis, V.34, and V.34 bis modems can be used in their synchronous mode of operation on leased lines. However, when doing so they do not support the use of V.42bis compression, resulting in a maximum transmission rate of 33.6 Kbps being obtainable when leased analog lines are used to interconnect geographically separated LANs. Although modems can be used to connect LANs with a relatively light internetwork transmission requirement, as previously mentioned, most internetworking equipment vendors recommend a minimum data transmission rate of 56 Kbps. This is primarily due to the overhead associated with transmitting server and router advertising frames between networks which precludes the use of a relatively large portion of the transmission capacity of an analog leased line.

If you use remote bridging instead of routing and are only interconnecting a few LANs with a handful of servers, you can probably obtain a reasonable level of performance via the use of high speed analog leased lines. However, when constructing a router-based network that connects many LANs and which cumulatively includes numerous servers, the higher transmission capabilities of digital services make them a preferred transmission medium.

Although analog leased lines are still used and marketed for use by communications carriers, the infrastructure of carriers has considerably changed. The backbone transmission facilities used to construct a carrier's network have changed from mostly analog to almost 100% digital equipment. As a result of this change almost all analog leased lines are converted into a digital transmission facility at a carrier's central office and then reconverted back into an analog format at the office serving the customer's destination premises. The construction of a digital backbone transmission facility was based upon the use of time division multiplexers and the development of high speed T-carrier transmission facilities. Originally their use was restricted to telephone company operations; however, by the early 1970s communications carriers began to market leased digital transmission facilities to commercial organizations and government agencies.

## 5.2.2 Time division multiplexing

In comparison to FDM in which a circuit is subdivided into derived channels by frequency, time division multiplexing (TDM) results in the use of a circuit being shared by time. Since TDM operates upon digital data, its utilization by communications carriers required voice conversations to be digitized prior to being transported on digital circuits routed between telephone company offices.

Voice digitization was accomplished using a technique known as pulse code modulation (PCM) in which an analog voice conversation is encoded into a 64 Kbps digital data stream for transmission on telephone company digital transmission facilities. Once a call was digitized and routed to a distant telephone company office serving the destination or called party, the 64 Kbps digital data stream was converted back into an analog voice signal and passed to the called party. Similarly, the voice conversation generated by the called party flowed in an analog form via the local loop to the telephone company office serving the subscriber. At that location, the conversation was digitized and was multiplexed using TDM equipment and placed onto a digital trunk linking that office to the office serving the call originator. At that office the call was removed from the trunk by the process known as demultiplexing, converted back into its analog format, and passed to the local subscriber.

The key to the successful use of time division multiplexing by telephone companies was the rapid growth in the use of T-carrier transmission facilities.

## 5.2.3 T-carrier evolution

T-carrier facilities were originally developed by telephone companies as a mechanism to relieve heavy loading on interexchange circuits. First employed in the 1960s for intracarrier communications, T-carrier facilities only became available to the general public during the early 1980s as a commercial offering.

The first T-carrier was placed into service by American Telephone & Telegraph in 1962 to ease cable congestion problems in urban areas. Known as T1 in North America, this wideband digital carrier facility operates at a 1.544 Mbps signaling rate.

The term T1 was originally defined by AT&T and referred to 24 64 Kbps PCM voice channels carried in a 1.544 Mbps wideband signal. Under the T1 framing format, each group of 24 eight-bit bytes representing 24 voice samples has a framing bit added for synchronization. As PCM sampling occurs 8000 times per second, this resulted in the use of 8000 frame bits. Thus, the T1 operating rate can be expressed as 24 channels × 64 Kbps/channel+8000 frame bits/second, resulting in an operating rate of 1.544 Mbps.

When AT&T initiated use of its T1 carrier, the company employed digital channel banks which were used to interface the analog telephone network to the T1 digital transmission facility.

### Channel banks

Channel banks used by telephone companies were originally analog devices. They were designed to provide the first step required in the handling of telephone calls that originated in one central office, but whose termination point was a different central office. The analog channel bank included frequency division multiplexing equipment, permitting it to multiplex, by frequency, a group of voice channels routed to a common intermediate or final destination over a common circuit. This method of multiplexing was previously illustrated in Figure 5.8.

The development of pulse code modulation resulted in analog channel banks becoming unsuitable for use with digitized voice. AT&T then developed the D-type channel bank which actually performs several functions in addition to the time division multiplexing of digital data.

The first digital channel bank, known as D1, contained three key elements as illustrated in Figure 5.10. The codec, an abbreviation for coder–decoder, converted analog voice into a 64 Kbps PCM-encoded digital data stream. The TDM multiplexes 24 PCM encoded voice channels and inserts framing information to permit the TDM in a distant channel bank to be able to synchronize itself to the resulting multiplexed data stream that is transmitted on the T1 span line. The line driver conditions the transmitted bit stream to the electrical characteristics of the T1 span line, ensuring that the pulse width, pulse height and pulse voltages are correct. In addition, the line driver converts the unipolar digital signal transmitted by the

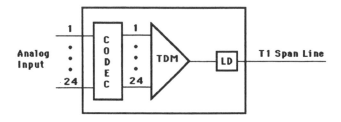

**Figure 5.10**  The D1 channel bank. (TDM time division multiplexer, LD line driver)

multiplexer into a bipolar signal suitable for transmission on the T1 span line.

Due to the operation of the digital channel bank, this equipment can be viewed as a bridge from the analog world to the digital world. To ensure the quality of the resulting multiplexed digital signal, AT&T installed repeaters at intervals of 6000 feet on span lines constructed between central offices. Although repeaters are still required on local loops to a subscriber's premises and on copper wire span lines, the introduction of digital radio and fiber optic transmission has added significant flexibility to the construction and routing of T-carrier facilities, since repeaters are not required on those facilities.

In addition to serving as the basic networking building block for the switched telephone network, T1 lines are available for use by organizations from a variety of communications carriers, including AT&T, MCI, US Sprint, and others. In Europe, the equivalent T1 carrier, which is known as E1 and CEPT PCM-30, is available in most countries under different names. As an example, in the United Kingdom E1 service is marketed under the name MegaStream.

### Digital transmission facilities

The introduction of T-carrier transmission facilities provided a digital highway which enabled communications carriers to introduce a series of digital transmission facilities for commercial use. In the 1970s AT&T introduced its Dataphone Digital Service (DDS). DDS service includes a series of leased line digital transmission facilities available at 2.4, 4.8, 9.6, 19.2 and 56 Kbps data rates. By the mid-1980s several communications carriers marketed similar leased line digital transmission facilities. Both AT&T and other carriers offering DDS and DDS equivalent leased lines require the use of DSUs at each end of the transmission facility.

Another digital transmission service based upon the use of the T-carrier resulted from carriers selling fractions of the T-carrier for the exclusive use of an organization. Known as fractional T1 (FT1), such service is usually available in multiples of 64 Kbps or 1/24th of the capacity of a T1 circuit.

The key difference between the use of DDS and DDS-equivalent services and fractional T1 involves the method used to access each transmission facility. DDS and DDS-equivalent services require the installation of an access line between the subscriber's premises and the carrier's serving office which operates at the desired data rate and is terminated by a DSU. An FT1 access line actually operates at the T-carrier rate although only a portion of the capacity of the T-carrier is used. At the carrier's serving office the fractional portion of the T1 line used by a subscriber is multiplexed along with other FT1 subscribers onto a T1 circuit. This is accomplished through the use of a T1 multiplexer located in the carrier's office serving the customer's premises.

A second difference between the use of DDS and FT1 leased lines concerns the terminating device required at each end of the leased line. As previously mentioned, DDS is terminated through the use of a DSU. In comparison, FT1 and T1 circuits are terminated at a subscriber's premises through the use of a Channel Service Unit (CSU). The CSU provides a line termination at 1.544 Mbps. For fractional T1 usage some CSUs contain a built-in multiplexer. The multiplexer provides FT1 subscribers with access to groups of 64 Kbps channels on the T1 span line. Otherwise, an FT1 subscriber must use a separate T1 multiplexer to obtain access to the fraction of the T1 line he or she is subscribing to. Table 5.3 lists three different types of commonly available digital leased line, their operating rate and the type of device used to terminate the line at the subscriber's premises.

## T3

Similarly to the manner by which T1 circuits were first developed for easing cable congestion in urban areas, communications carriers introduced the T3 carrier as a mechanism to combine multiple T1s onto a common circuit. A T3 carrier

**Table 5.3**  Digital leased lines

| Type | Operating rate (Kbps) | Terminating device |
|------|----------------------|--------------------|
| DDS | 2.4 | DSU |
| DDS | 4.8 | DSU |
| DDS | 9.6 | DSU |
| DDS | 19.2 | DSU |
| DDS | 56.0 | DSU |
| FT1 | 64 | CSU |
| FT1 | 128 | CSU |
| FT1 | 256 | CSU |
| FT1 | 384 | CSU |
| FT1 | 768 | CSU |
| T1 | 1544 | CSU |

represents an aggregate of 28 T1 circuits which, when framing is included for multiplexing, operates at 44.736 Mbps. When T3 was first introduced for commercial use during the late 1980s, its high cost coupled with its large transmission capacity resulted in a minimum amount of usage. Since then its cost has significantly decreased on a per monthly mileage basis, making it more affordable for large organizations. In addition, similarly to FT1, fractional T3 (FT3) service can be obtained in many locations.

The primary use of T3 during the late 1990s was by Internet Service Providers (ISPs) and Internet Network Service Providers (NSPs) as a high speed transport to interconnect ISPs and NSPs. In comparison, FT3 service is a more practical transmission facility for the large number of organizations that require more bandwidth than obtainable from the use of a single T1 circuit, but who cannot use anywhere near the capacity of a full T3.

A T3 carrier is formed by the use of an M13 multiplexer. This device combines four T1s into a T2 and then combines seven of the combined T2s into a T3. In technical terms, the T1 signal is referred to as a DS1, while the T2 and T3 carrier signals are referred to as DS2 and DS3 signals, respectively. Figure 5.11 illustrates the formation of a DS3 signal for transmission on a T3 circuit by an M13 multiplexer.

M13 multiplexers commonly reside at the carrier's central offices and use either fiber optic cable or microwave radio for transmission onto the carrier's backbone network. Network subscribers that need a full T3 are connected to the carrier's equipment using either fiber optic or coaxial cable. Similarly to

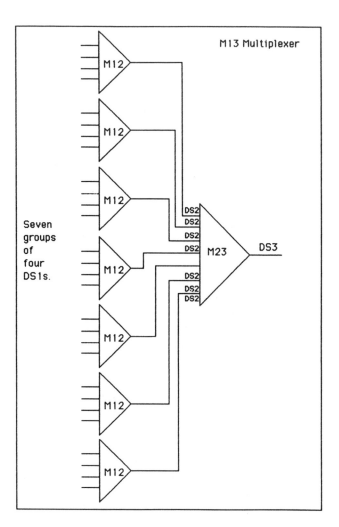

**Figure 5.11** Formation of a DS3 signal by an M13 multiplexer

T1, a CSU is required to interface the T3 line. On the Data Terminal Equipment (DTE) side, a DSU is required to provide a high speed interface to the communications device that will be interfaced to the T3 circuits. Commonly used DTE interfaces include V.35, RS 449, and EIA 530 for data rates of up to 6 Mbps and the High Speed Serial Interface (HSSI) for data rates up to a full T3.

Fractional T3 can be obtained by the routing of multiple T1 lines from a subscriber's premise to a carrier's central office or via the installation of a full T3 line. Concerning the latter, the subscriber would use a fraction of the capacity of the T3. At the carrier's central office the unused portion of the T3 would be used by other subscribers that would share the cost of the long distance portion of the T3 line.

## 5.3 PACKET SWITCHING NETWORKS

One of the major limitations associated with circuit switching is the permanent assignment of a path for the exclusive use of a communications session during the duration of that session. This means that regardless of whether a full circuit or a channel within a circuit is used to establish a path, that circuit or channel cannot be used to support other activities until the session in progress is completed. Recognizing this limitation, packet switching was developed as a technique to enable the sharing of transmission facilities among many users. Although multiplexing is also a mechanism which allows the sharing of transmission facilities, the two techniques are considerably different.

### 5.3.1 Multiplexing versus packet switching

In multiplexing, bandwidth (FDM) or time (TDM) is used to establish occupancy slots into which individual data sources are assigned the use of those slots. Thereafter, information in the form of voice or data uses the reserved slot for the duration of the voice call or data transmission session. In packet switching, specialized equipment divides data into defined segments that have addressing, sequencing, and error control information added. The resulting unit of data is called a packet and may represent a user message or a very small portion of a user message. The flow of packets between nodes in a packet network is intermixed with respect to the originator and destination of packets. That is, traffic in the form of packets from many users can share large portions of the transmission facilities used to form a packet network. Thus, packet network use is normally more economical than transmission over the public switched telephone network for long distance transmission.

### 5.3.2 Packet network construction

A packet network is constructed through the use of equipment that assembles and disassembles packets, equipment that routes packets, and transmission facilities used to route packets from the originator to the destination device. Some types of data terminal equipment (DTE) can create their own packets, while other types of DTE require the conversion of their protocol into packets through the use of a packet assembler/ disassembler (PAD) described later in this section. Packets are routed through the network by packet switches. Packet switches examine the destination of packets as they flow through the network and transfer the packets onto trunks interconnecting switches based upon the packet destination and network activity.

The transmission facilities used to interconnect packet switches are leased lines because the network must be available 24 hours per day. Some packet networks use analog leased lines operating at 19.2 Kbps to interconnect their switches however, most packet networks now use high speed digital transmission facilities, such as DDS, fractional T1, and T1 lines due to the growth in the use of packet networks.

### 5.3.3 Packet network recommendations

Most packet networks are illustrated by a drawing that resembles a cloud. A number of ITU-T recommendations govern the transmission of data both onto a packet network and between packet networks, as illustrated in Figure 5.12. In this illustration, two separate packet networks are shown, with a computer connected to each network.

ITU-T Recommendation X.25 controls the access from a packet mode DTE, such as a terminal device or computer system capable of forming packets, to the DCE at a packet node. Recommendation X.28 controls the interface between non-packet mode devices that cannot form packets and a PAD. Recommendation X.29 specifies the interface between the PAD and the host computer. Recommendation X.3 specifies the parameter settings on the PAD and X.75 specifies the interface between packet networks. Note that in Figure 5.6 there are two methods by which non-packet mode devices can be connected to a packet network. In packet network 1, the non-packet mode DTE communicates with a PAD located at the packet node, with terminal devices normally dialing the number of a modem connected to a port on the PAD. In packet network 2, the PAD is located with the non-packet mode devices. This allows a permanent connection from the PAD to the packet node

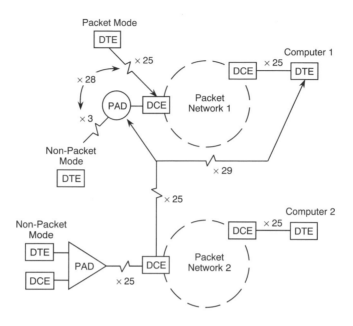

**Figure 5.12** CCITT packet network recommendations

as well as providing the capability to service multiple terminals on one line routed to the packet node.


### 5.3.4 The PDN and value-added networks

The term 'public data network' (PDN) is used to refer to a commercially available packet switching network. In the United States, BT Tymnet and Sprint's SprintNet are examples of PDNs. Outside the United States, PDNs are usually administered by government agencies, although divestiture has occurred overseas similar to the breakup of AT&T in the United States that has resulted in British Telecom's PSS and other PDNs now belonging to private companies. In addition to public PDNs, organizations can create their own private PDN. This is accomplished by purchasing appropriate packet switching equipment and leasing transmission facilities which results in the establishment of a packet switching network for the exclusive use of an organization.

Another term commonly used to reference packet switching networks is 'value-added'. Networks that provide such operational facilities as reverse charging (collect calls), alternate destination routing, and closed user groups are known as value-added networks due to the extra value they provide. As almost all packet switching networks now support one or more optional facilities, the term 'value-added network' is essentially synonymous with the term 'packet switching network'.

### 5.3.5 Packet network architecture

There are two major categories of packet network, with each category based upon the method by which packets are routed through the network: datagram and virtual circuit based networks.

*Datagram packet networks*

In a datagram network, each packet is transmitted independently of other packets, with packet switches routing each packet based upon such factors as the traffic currently carried on circuits linking network switches, and the error rate on those circuits, as well as whether or not specific circuits are available for use.

Figure 5.13 illustrates an example of the packet flow through a datagram packet network. In this example it was assumed that two devices creating packets have their data flow routed through a packet network consisting of four packet switches, with two computers connected to the network. Let us further assume that the packets labeled A, B, C, and D are routed to

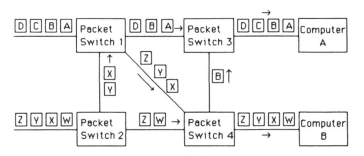

**Figure 5.13** Datagram packet network data flow. In a datagram packet network, packets are routed based upon the activity and availability of circuits connecting packet switches

computer A, while the packets labeled W, X, Y, and Z are routed to computer B.

As packets are routed through a datagram packet network, each switch examines the packet destination address (computer A or B) and routes the packet based upon criteria similar to that previously discussed, which results in the selection of an optimum route at a given time. As packets can traverse different paths, packets can be received at a destination switch out of sequence. Thus, destination switches must be capable of having sufficient memory to store packets until they can be sequenced into their appropriate order prior to their delivery to their ultimate destination. This resequencing would occur at packet switches 3 and 4 in Figure 5.13, with the result that although packets from each source routed to a common destination took different paths, they were reassembled into their original order at their destination nodes.

Although datagram packet networks permit transmission paths to be dynamically altered to correspond to network conditions and activity, they require a substantial amount of packet switch processing overhead. This is because each switch must know the state of circuits to other switches to implement appropriate routing algorithms. Although most packet switching networks were originally based upon datagram technology, a majority of those networks have been converted to the use of virtual circuit packet switching.

## Virtual circuit packet networks

In a virtual circuit packet network, a fixed path is established from the data originator to the recipient at the time a call is established. Thereafter, all packets flow over the same path, although the packets from two or more devices can share the use of circuits between packet switches that form a specific virtual circuit.

Figure 5.14 illustrates the data flow through a virtual circuit packet network. Note that although a route will be established based upon network activity, once established the route remains fixed for the duration of the call. Thus, packets will flow in sequence through each switch, which reduces both the amount of processing required to be performed at each switch and delays associated with waiting for out-of-sequence packets to arrive at a destination node prior to being able to pass an ordered sequence of packets to their destination.

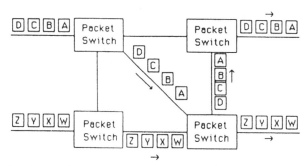

**Figure 5.14** Virtual circuit packet network data flow. In a virtual circuit packet network, packets are routed in sequence over a fixed path established at the time a call occurs

## 5.3.6 Packet formation

Although many devices have the ability to directly create packets, most devices rely upon the use of packet assembler/disassemblers (PADs). PADs are essentially protocol conversion devices that accept data from data terminal equipment (DTE) supporting one protocol and converting the data into packets based upon the ITU-T X.25 protocol.

The most common type of PAD converts an asynchronous teletype protocol into an X.25 data flow. Other common protocols supported by PADs include the IBM 2780 and 3780 bisynchronous protocols, IBM's SDLC protocol, and various protocols from Unisys and other computer manufacturers that resemble those IBM protocols.

PADs are currently manufactured on adapter boards designed for insertion into the system unit of a personal computer as well as in the form of standalone devices. Concerning the latter, some PADs perform a one-to-one conversion and as such are single input port devices. Other PADs may contain many ports and support different protocols on each port. Figure 5.15 illustrates a multi-protocol, multi-port PAD.

*X.25*

The transmission from a packet mode DTE or from a PAD to a packet switch node is based upon the ITU-T X.25 recommendation. The X.25 recommendation defines the interface between a terminal device and a packet network, including the physical, data link, and network layers which correspond to the first three

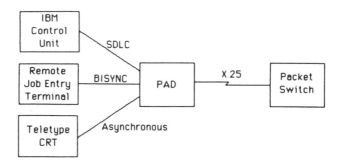

**Figure 5.15**  Multi-protocol multiport PAD

layers of the OSI Reference Model previously described in Chapter 1. The physical layer is defined by the X.21 and X.21 bis recommendations, the latter essentially RS-232. The X.25 data link layer consists of frames that are transported via the use of the HDLC protocol. The network layer of X.25 consists of packets which are carried within the information field of frames transported by the HDLC protocol. Figure 5.16 illustrates the structure of an X.25 frame.

Level 3 which is the packet level defines the procedures for establishing and clearing calls between users, describes packet formats, and defines the procedures for such functions as flow control, packet transfer, and error control.

*Packet format and content*

Every packet transmitted on an X.25 packet network contains a three- octet header which is illustrated in Figure 5.17.

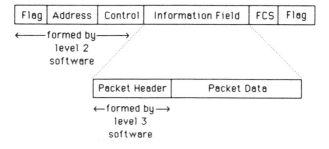

**Figure 5.16**  X.25 frame structure

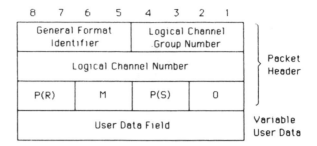

**Figure 5.17**  X.25 data packet format

X.25 packet switching networks use both virtual circuits and logical channels to allow many users to share the facilities of the network. As previously explained, a virtual circuit is a path established through the network for the duration of the call, similar to a direct physical circuit. The logical channel is a method which enables the multiplexing of a single subscriber access line to the packet network among several simultaneous virtual calls. For example, a PAD serving several terminals and connected to a packet network via a single access line would assign each terminal connected to the PAD to a different logical channel number. Thus, the logical channel number (LCN) identifies each packet as belonging to a particular logical connection.

The LCN is significant only at the interface between the subscriber and the local packet node. At the packet node, the LCNs are mapped to network paths and an independent set of LCNs are used between the destination packet node and the addressed device.

The third byte in the packet header is the packet type identifier. Currently, 20 packet types are defined in X.25, divided into six functional groups.

*Call establishment*

A virtual call through an X.25 packet network is initiated by the transfer of a call request packet to the network. The call request packet identifies the LCN selected by the call initiator as well as the addresses of the calling and called parties. This packet may also include any optional facilities desired as well as optionally contain call user data.

After the call request has been routed through the packet network to the destination node, a local LCN is selected and the destination node then transmits an incoming call packet to the called party. If the called party is available to accept the call it responds to the incoming call packet by transmitting a call-accepted packet to the network using the LCN that identified the incoming call. The network then responds to the call-accepted packet by transmitting a call-connected packet to the calling party on the LCN assigned to the initial call request. This action results in the establishment of a virtual call which allows data packets to be exchanged between users.

Once a virtual call has been established, the logical channel enters the data transfer phase. At this time, data packets consisting of the three-octet header field and the user data field carry the user information. The packet type identifier field (third octet) includes send ($P(S)$) and receive ($P(R)$) sequence numbers that are used to track and acknowledge packets in a manner similar to the $N(R)$ and $N(S)$ field in an HDLC frame. The More-Data (M) bit when set to a 1 notifies the network that the next packet to be transmitted is a logical continuation of the data in the current packet. The actual length of the user data field depends upon the packet network. Most networks support a default maximum user data field of 128 octets. Other maxima supported by most networks include 32, 64, 256, 512, 1024, 2048, and 4096 octets.

Once a called DTE has received the first data packet, it can authorize additional transmission by returning a Receiver Ready (RR) packet or it can delay transmission by returning a Receiver Not Ready (RNR) packet. Finally, when the calling DTE has completed its session, it transmits a Clear Request packet which is confirmed by the called DTE. At that time the virtual circuit is broken. Figure 5.18 illustrates the major packet flow used to establish a virtual connection, pass data, and break the virtual connection.

*Flow control*

Once data begins to flow through a packet network, delays can occur due to network congestion or transmission errors. Either situation can result in the inability of the X.25 packet network to accept the current rate of information transfer

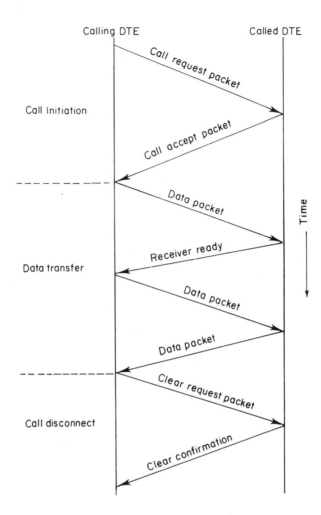

**Figure 5.18** Packet network session activity

through the network. Thus, a mechanism is required to regulate the flow of information. This mechanism is called flow control and is effected by the use of the receiver ready (RR) and receiver not ready (RNR) packets. The RR packet carries a receive sequence number (P(R)) which acknowledges packets previously received by the sending station. Conversely, the RNR packets are transmitted by the packet network or receiving station to halt the flow of incoming data packets. RNR packets indicate that the sender should stop transmitting data as soon as possible.

### 5.3.7 Advantages of X.25 packet networks

The design of X.25 packet networks results in the allocation of capacity only when stations have packets to transmit. Because almost all interactive transmission includes pauses, and because idle time on a circuit is essentially being wasted, packetizing and interleaving packets makes the most efficient use of a circuit. Thus, the more packets that can be carried on a circuit, the lower the cost per packet.

### 5.3.8 Internetwork utilization

The easy accessibility of packet network entry points (nodes) and the standardized X.25 protocol make this network very suitable for interconnecting dispersed local area networks as well as for obtaining access to remote mainframes. One of the more common methods used to connect a local area network into a packet network node is through the use of a dedicated access facility (DAF). The DAF is a leased line, either analog or digital, routed from a subscriber's premises to the packet node, where it is connected to a packet switch that supports the X.25 protocol. To provide protocol compatibility LAN traffic must be encapsulated into X.25 packets for routing through the packet network. This is normally accomplished by the installation of an X.25 adapter card in a gateway PC and the use of appropriate software. Although the PC is typically referred to as a gateway, in this situation it actually functions as a router. At the subscriber's other network location a similar gateway connected to the packet network via a DAF strips the X.25 packet encapsulation from arriving packets. Figure 5.19 illustrates the use of gateway PCs at each LAN location to interconnect two local area networks through the transmission facilities of a packet switching network.

A second common use of a packet switching network is to provide a transportation mechanism for a true gateway. Figure 5.20 illustrates the use of a true gateway on a LAN. In this example the gateway PC not only encapsulates LAN frames but, in addition, provides an emulation function which converts each LAN station accessing the mainframe through the gateway into a specific type of terminal whose screen attributes are compatible with the mainframe's application software.

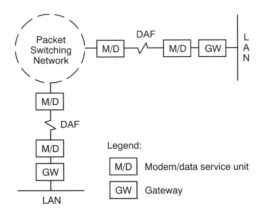

**Figure 5.19**  Using gateway PCs for interconnecting local area networks via a packet network

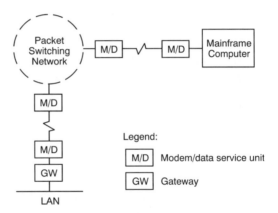

**Figure 5.20**  Using a packet network to provide LAN access to a mainframe. When a gateway performs a higher level function, such as terminal emulation, it operates as a true gateway

## 5.3.9 Remote access

A third common use of X.25 packet networks involves providing economical remote access to LANs. X.25 packet network dial-in nodes are located in just about every major metropolitan area in the world. This enables the traveling executive to obtain the ability to connect to a mail server on the corporate LAN while the traveling salesperson can connect to the order entry system to check the status of a previously placed order on the delivery schedule and cost for a possible new order. Each of these activities can be accomplished in an economical manner because the cost of using a packet network, especially from international locations, can be considerably less than the cost of a long distance call. In addition, when accessing the corporate LAN from many areas where the telephone infrastructure is less than modern, the ability to dial a local number and have your transmission flow error-free from the packet node entry point to its destination may be a significant improvement over an attempt to dial long distance.

As we will shortly note, the role of X.25 packet networks as a mechanism to interconnect geographically separated LANs has been to a significant degree superseded by the use of Frame Relay, a high speed packet switching technology. However, for remote access applications to include credit card verification, traveling executives requiring access to corporate mail servers, traveling salespersons needing access to corporate information systems, and similar remote access activities, X.25 packet networks can be expected to continue to provide a transmission system more suitable for such user requirements.

### 5.3.10 Technological advances

The growth in the use of fiber optic transmission facilities has resulted in a significant lowering of the error rate experienced on long distance transmission. This advance in communications transmission facilities in turn called into question the necessity of using conventional packet switching methods that support layers 1 through 3 of the OSI Reference Model and has resulted in the development of a series of new technologies called fast packet switching, frame relay, and cell relay. Prior to discussing these newer technologies, let us focus our attention upon the delays associated with conventional packet switching and the relevance of those delays in an era where the majority of trunks (leased lines) that interconnect packet nodes are now fiber optic cables.

*Packet network delay problems*

In a conventional packet switching network, each of the trunks linking the nodes in the network support layers 1 through 3 of the OSI model. This means that packets are error-checked (a layer 2 function) at each node. Although this was a necessity to ensure data integrity when trunks were primarily analog leased lines with a relatively high error rate, the use of fiber optic cable for transmission between nodes has reduced errors by several orders of magnitude. This means that most error checking within packet nodes only delays transmission through the network and is not actually beneficial for data integrity. In addition, the growth in intelligent terminal devices based upon microprocessors used in personal computers and workstations allows the integrity of data to be checked at each end of the link. Thus, error checking at each node can be considered as technically obsolete for many applications.

Flow control (layer 2 and layer 3) is greatly diminished when fiber optic cable is used; however, it is still applicable due to the processing delays encountered as packets are error checked at each node. Thus, the elimination of error checking at each node would substantially reduce the use of flow control in a packet network.

### Fast packet switching

Recognizing the previously described packet switching problems, AT&T's Bell Laboratories began experimenting with a technique during the 1980s to reduce the processing overhead in each packet node which would allow a packet to be forwarded with lower delay. AT&T's technique was based upon the use of Very Large Scale Integration (VLSI) hardware, with the technique referred to as fast packet switching.

AT&T's fast packet switching eliminated error checking at each node so the node could begin forwarding the packet as soon as its destination was decoded. To prevent a link error which could cause a packet to be routed to an unintended destination, a CRC was placed after the routing information. If a CRC error is detected, the packet node would simply drop the packet. If a transmission error occurred that affected other data in the packet, the node would not detect the error but would simply route the packet rapidly towards its destination. In this technique, it is assumed that the recipient will ask for a retransmission of missing or errored packets.

As all modern protocols have error detection and correction capability, as well as a timeout feature which results in a request for retransmission if a unit of data is not received within a predefined period of time, neither dropping packets nor carrying errored packets to their destination adversely affects modern equipment. In fact, by eliminating error detection processing at nodes, the flow of data through the network is substantially increased.

In general, the term 'fast packet' refers to the transmission of packets in which packet processing is streamlined to provide a much higher throughput than is obtainable on an X.25-based network. From the pioneering effort of AT&T, two new technologies have emerged that were standardized in the early 1990s: frame relay and cell relay in the form of ATM.

*Frame relay*

Frame relay is a data link protocol at the ISO layer 2 level which defines how frames of data are assembled and rapidly routed through a packet network. Frame relay is standardized by the ANSI T1S1 committee and by the ITU-T I.122 and Q.922 recommendations and represents the first packet mode interface to ISDN networks.

Under frame relay, a 2, 3 or 4-byte header is added to layer 2 information as illustrated in Figure 5.21. The Data Link Connection Identifier (DLCI) allows a packet network to route each frame through nodes along a virtual path established for a frame relay connection. The DLCI does not specify a destination address as in X.25. Instead, it specifies a connection resulting from the establishment of a virtual circuit. Then each device on the virtual circuit specifies the same DLCI to enable each device to transmit to the other device. Once the virtual circuit is cleared, the DLCI previously used can be reused on another virtual circuit establishment between two different subscribers.

### Comparison to X.25

Frame relay is very similar to X.25 packet switching; however, there are some distinct differences between the two transmission methods. Similarly to X.25 packet switching, a frame relay network represents both a public transmission facility operated by communications carriers as well as a private network facility that organizations can construct over a leased line infrastructure. Frame relay, like X.25, permits multiple communications sessions to share a single physical connection. To accomplish this, Frame relay, like X.25 packet switching, constructs multiple virtual circuits across a common physical connection between a frame relay access device (FRAD) and a frame relay

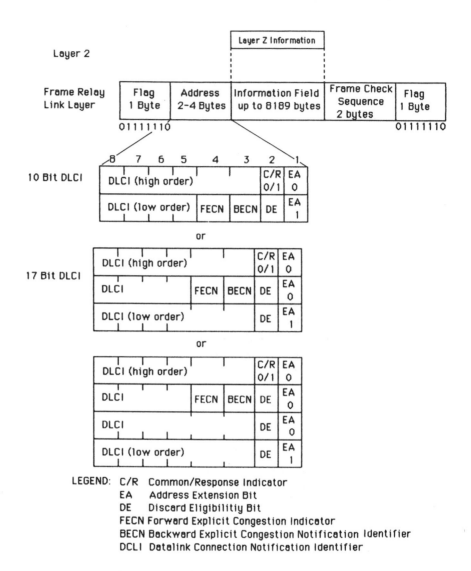

**Figure 5.21** Frame relay frame construction

network entry node. Here the FRAD can be viewed as performing a function similar to an X.25 PAD; however, instead of translation from a protocol other than X.25 to X.25, the FRAD provides a translation into the frame relay transmission protocol. Although there are many similarities between X.25 packet switching and frame relay, there are also some distinct differences. As those differences relate to the design goal of frame relay and its basic operation, let us turn our attention to those areas.

The design goal of frame relay assumes that data will be transferred, in its correct order, error-free. This design goal relies on the higher layers in the protocol stack to determine whether or not transmission errors occurred and, if so, to initiate a correction via retransmission. Another design goal of frame relay is to provide users with a guaranteed amount of transmission bandwidth referred to as a committed information rate (CIR), while letting users obtain the ability to burst their transmission above the CIR to the maximum rate of the connection without guaranteeing that the excess above the CIR will arrive at its destination. This means that frame relay has the ability to discard frames, and the upper layers of the protocol stack become responsible for retransmission when frames are dropped. This also means that by providing users with the ability to burst to high transmission rates, the physical access to a frame relay network can be much higher than access to an X.25 network.

As a frame relay network does not have to perform packet sequencing nor error checking, the flow of data through a network is considerably faster than through an X.25 network. Similarly, a frame relay switch will have a lower delay or latency, and the ability to process more packets or frames per unit time. Table 5.4 provides a general comparison between X.25 and frame relay network performance and operation.

### Utilization

Frame relay represents a high speed internetworking technology well suited for connecting geographically separated LANs and mainframes on an any to any connectivity basis via the mesh

**Table 5.4**  Comparing X.25 and frame relay

| Performance/operational feature | X.25 | Frame relay |
|---|---|---|
| Performs packet sequencing | yes | no |
| Performs error checking | yes | no |
| Performs flow control | yes | no, drops frames when congestion occurs |
| Network access | 300 bps–64 Kbps | 56 Kbps–2.048 Mbps, with T3 access being introduced |
| Switch delay | 10–40 ms | 2–6 ms |
| One-way delay | 200–500 ms | 40–150 ms |

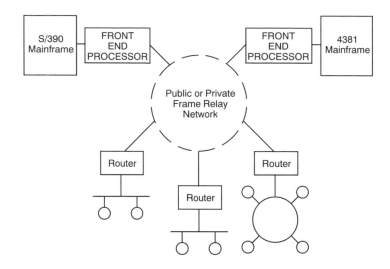

**Figure 5.22**  Frame relay transport application

structure of public frame relay providers. Figure 5.22 illustrates an example of how a public or private frame relay network could be used to interconnect three LANs and two mainframe computers. Note that a frame relay compliant router and front end processor only requires one connection to the network to obtain the ability to communicate with multiple destinations. To accomplish this, private virtual circuits (PVCs) must be established for each location that requires access to another location. For example, if the front-end processor connected to the S/390 mainframe requires the ability to communicate with each LAN, then three PVCs must be established.

In addition to reducing the port interface to one, frame relay can considerably reduce the cost of equipment required to interconnect geographically separated locations. This is because both router and front-end processor ports are relatively expensive. Thus, a few PVCs that a communications carrier may bill at $20 per month might eliminate a $3000 port upgrade.

### Operation

At each node, the switch supporting frame relay monitors the utilization of its buffers. If a predefined threshold is reached which indicates that congestion could occur if the data flow is not adjusted, this situation is indicated to the end-user devices in both directions. In the forward direction, the Forward Explicit

Congestion Notification (FECN) bit in the frame header is set. In the reverse direction, the switch sets the Congestion Backward Explicit Notification (BECN) bit in all frames transmitted in the opposite direction. When the devices at each end of the network receive a congestion notification, they are expected to reduce their information transfer rate until the congestion notification is cleared, in essence performing flow control. If the level of congestion should increase to a second threshold due to a slow response to FECN or BECN notifications, the frame handler at the packet node discards frames among all users in an equitable manner by the use of the Discard Eligibility (DE) bit. This bit, when set by customer-provided equipment, identifies frames from users that can be discarded if the network becomes overloaded. Thus, the DE bit enables user equipment to temporarily send more frames than it is allowed to send. The packet network will forward those frames if it has the capacity to do so; however, it will discard those frames first if the network becomes overloaded.

The CRC in the frame trailer is used to detect bit errors in the header and information fields. Unlike X.25 in which a node will delay transmission and request the originating node to retransmit the previously sent packet, a frame relaying network simply discards the errored frame. This places the burden of error recovery upon the end-user devices.

### The CIR

Most frame relay networks offer a committed information rate (CIR). The CIR denotes the minimum data transfer rate a subscriber is guaranteed upon the establishment of a permanent virtual call established through the network. It is important to note that the CIR is not an instantaneous measurement of transmission but an average rate over time. For example, consider the use of a T1 line operating at 1.544 Mbps used to provide access to a Frame Relay service. If the CIR is 256 Kbps, this does not mean that the user cannot transmit more than 256 Kbps. What it means is that the user will not transmit more than 256K bits in one second or 512K bits in two seconds. Although the distinction may appear trivial, it is extremely important and deserves a degree of elaboration, as CIRs can be assigned to each PVC and used to provide equitable access to the total bandwidth of a connection to a frame relay network.

To illustrate the use of CIRs, assume you are using a frame relay network to support inter-LAN and mainframe-to-mainframe communications. Let us further assume that you connect to a public frame relay network using a 512 Kbps fractional T1 line and have the carrier provision each PVC so that the mainframe-to-mainframe communications on one PVC has a CIR of 128 Kbps and LAN-to-LAN communications on another PVC has a CIR of 384 Kbps. This method of provisioning assigns a greater portion of the bandwidth to LAN-to-LAN communications; however, as that type of communication is bursty in nature it could shrink to 128 Kbps, 56 Kbps, or even 0 bps when a mainframe-to-mainframe communications session is in progress. Thus, enabling another PVC to transmit at a rate above its CIR has a degree of merit, especially when the other PVCs are operating below their CIRs. Therefore, the mainframe-to-mainframe session can burst its transmission above its CIR when the LAN-to-LAN session falls below its CIR; however, excess transmission above the mainframe-to-mainframe CIR is not guaranteed.

### Calculating the CIR

The CIR is computed based upon a measurement interval (Tc) and Committed Burst size (Bc). The measurement interval represents the period of time over which information transfer rates are computed and can vary from one frame relay service provider to another. The committed burst size (Bc) represents the maximum number of bits the network guarantees to deliver during the measurement interval (Tc). Thus, the CIR can be computed by dividing the committed burst size by the measurement interval, such that:

$$CIR = Bc/Tc$$

Carriers that use a small Tc value minimize the ability of users to burst transmission. In comparison, frame relay providers that use a relatively large value for Tc may be more suitable for users as they enable a higher degree of bandwidth aggregation over time by supporting longer bursts. Concerning transmission bursts, a third parameter known as the excess burst size (Be) is used by frame relay service providers to specify the maximum number of bits above the CIR that the network will attempt to deliver during the measurement interval, but for which delivery is not guaranteed.

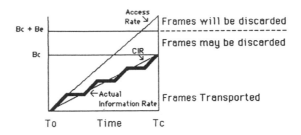

Legend:  Bc  committed burstsize
         Be  excess burst size
         Tc  measurement interval

**Figure 5.23**  Committed information rate (CIR) parameters

Figure 5.23 illustrates the relationship between Tc, Bc and Be. Note that Bc + Be represents the maximum amount of information that can be transmitted during the time interval Tc. If a user transmits more than Bc + Be bits during the interval Tc, the network will immediately discard the excess frames. Many frame relay service providers set Be as the difference between Bc and the interface access speed to the network. Thus, this setting then results in the avoidance of frame discards at the entry node to the network, and results in (Bc + Be)/Tc becoming equal to the access speed.

In examining Figure 5.23, note that the actual information rate can vary over the measurement interval. So long as there is a sufficient amount of data to transmit, the actual information rate can never fall below the CIR and can burst above it to a maximum of Bc + Be.

*Cost*

The cost associated with the use of a frame relay service can vary between access providers based upon the structure of their pricing for access port use, the CIR selected, and the number of PVCs. Most providers charge an increasing frame relay access port fee based upon the operating rate of the connection to the service provider. Similarly, the higher the CIR the higher the fee for providing a greater guarantee of available bandwidth. The last major frame relay provider fee is a surcharge for establishing PVCs. Typically the service provider will add a monthly charge for each PVC established through their network.

In addition to direct frame relay provider charges, you will also incur a local access charge that may be billed by the provider or a local communications carrier. The local access charge is a monthly charge for the circuit that connects your location to the nearest Point of Presence (POP) where the circuit becomes connected to the frame relay provider's network access port.

In spite of a considerable number of metrics upon which frame relay charges are based, its use may result in considerable savings in comparison to the cost associated with a private leased line based network. This potential cost savings results from the fact that similar to an X.25 network, a public frame relay network enables network resources to be shared among many users. This in turn provides greater transmission efficiencies and allows providers to set rates that can be 20 to 50% less than the cost associated with a private leased line network. Of course, if your organization has a substantial communications requirement between two locations and does not require the use of a mesh structure network topology, it is quite possible that a leased line will prove to be more economical. The only way to tell is to determine your transmission requirements and obtain price quotations for different transmission services.

### Voice over frame relay

Although not originally designed as a digitized voice transport mechanism, advances in voice digitization technology and the incorporation of prioritization techniques into vendor products resulted in many organizations turning to frame relay as a transmission scheme to support their voice, data, and fax requirements. To do so usually requires a separate device capable of presenting a voice or fax digitized data stream to a FRAD because most FRADS are limited to supporting data protocols. This conversion device commonly attaches to a PBX to accept an analog voice or fax or a digitized voice signal and compresses and digitizes the signal, generating a data flow in a protocol the FRAD supports. Concerning voice digitization, PCM produces a 64 Kbps digital data stream which is more susceptible to delays through a frame relay network when carried in a large number of time-dependent frames than a lower digitization rate carried in a lesser number of frames. Thus, many equipment developers now offer compression methods that can result in a voice conversation being carried by an 8 Kbps to 16 Kbps data stream.

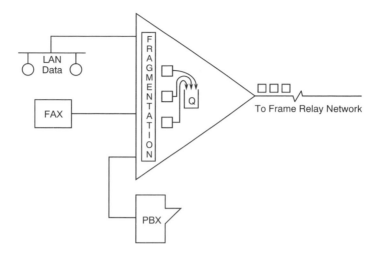

**Figure 5.24**   Using a multifunctional FRAD to support voice, data, and fax

In addition to stand-alone converters that provide an interface to FRADS, some vendors now market multifunctional FRADS that perform analog to digital conversion and compression. Included in many products is a silence-detection process which further enhances voice compression and a frame sizing algorithm which limits the length of digitized voice, fax, and data frames delivered to the network. This frame limiting algorithm minimizes end-to-end delay through the frame relay network being used and ensures that voice packets which are time-sensitive are not unacceptably delayed behind fax and data packets that can tolerate a relatively lengthy delay.

Figure 5.24 illustrates the use of a multifunctional FRAD to fragment and prioritize the flow of voice, data, and fax packets into a frame relay network. After a frame has been created based upon a maximum length associated with the data it transports, it is sent into a priority queue (labeled Q in Figure 5.24). As voice has the least tolerance for delay, frames carrying digitized voice would be placed at the top of the queue while more delay-tolerant fax and data carrying frames would be placed in lower priority areas in the queue. In 1997 the Frame Relay Forum was working on an Implementors' Agreement document for voice over frame relay. Once completed, this document will define agreements upon digitization, prioritization, fragmentation, and other methods required for vendors to build equipment that will be able to inter-operate with one another, and should contribute to a further growth in the use of frame relay as a voice transport mechanism.

Although frame relay has many advantages over X.25, it is not designed to replace X.25 networks. X.25 will remain the preferred method of data transportation for low speed, delay-insensitive transmission that requires the error correction capability afforded by an X.25 network. As most interactive transmissions such as personal computers used as a terminal to access a mainframe application, are insensitive to the short 100 millisecond delay of an X.25 network, such networks can be expected to remain viable data transportation facilities for the foreseeable future.

# 6

# NETWORK LAYER OPERATIONS

The primary method used to obtain communications between geographically separated LANs is based upon Network Layer operations. Thus, a detailed examination of the use of routers and gateways requires knowledge of network layer operations, which is the focus of this chapter.

In this chapter we will turn our attention to two popular Network Layer protocol suites, NetWare and TCP/IP. Although IBM's SNA represents a third Network Layer protocol suite, we will defer a description of that protocol until chapters 8 and 9 when we discuss routers and gateways in some detail. Although once very popular, separate SNA networks are now commonly being integrated into TCP/IP networks or transported via a peer-to-peer networking technique known as Data Link Switching, a topic also discussed later in this book.

Although the title of this chapter indicates that we will examine transmission at the third layer of the OSI Reference Model, since both protocol stacks extend beyond that layer we will also, when applicable, move up each protocol stack to obtain familiarity with how the higher levels of each stack interact with the third layer. In addition, since an understanding of IP addressing is important for obtaining an appreciation of the transportation of data under TCP/IP, we will also focus our attention upon a variety of addressing topics in this chapter, including IP address classes, subnetting, and the Domain Name Service (DNS), which provides the translation between English mnemonics, or words used to refer to a computer, and their dotted decimal IP address.

When discussing the size of fields in headers that reside at the Network and Transport layers, this author will normally use the term octet to refer to the number of bytes in different fields. This is because even though most of us use the term byte to refer to an 8-bit quantity, it is also used to refer to the smallest addressable unit of data stored in a computer. In the past, computer designers engineered computers with a variety of byte sizes. Thus, standards developers turned to the term octet to refer to an unambiguous 8-bit quantity. However, readers should note that this author, like most persons today, will use the terms byte and octet interchangeably to refer to an 8-bit quantity.

## 6.1 NETWARE IPX/SPX AND RELATED PROTOCOLS

NetWare primarily provides communications services using two protocols that are variations of the Xerox Network Systems (XNS) Internet Transport protocol: Internetwork Packet Exchange (IPX) and Sequence Packet Exchange (SPX). IPX is a best effort connectionless protocol, operating at the Network layer of the OSI Reference Model. In comparison, SPX is a connection-oriented protocol which supports reliable peer-to-peer communications and operates at the Transport layer of the OSI Reference Model.

### 6.1.1 IPX

Although IPX is a connectionless protocol it can be used in an implied verification mode. That is, file servers use IPX for request and reply packets. Thus, if a server responds to a request it is implied that it received the request. Conversely, if a station times out waiting for a response you can logically assume that the server never received the request. Figure 6.1 illustrates the format or structure of an IPX packet header.

*Checksum field*

The IPX Header contains a total of 30 octets, of which the Checksum field was included for compatibility with the XNS packet header. This field is always set to a value of hex FF-FF to indicate that a checksum has not been calculated. Normally,

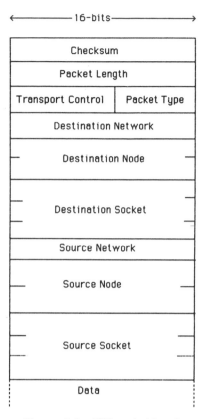

**Figure 6.1** IPX packet header

adapter cards perform a hardware checksum on the entire IPX packet which results in a sufficient level of protection when data flows on a LAN. However, under NetWare 4.0 Novell recognized that WAN transmission would require the use of the checksum field and allows the Virtual Loadable Module (VLM) based DOS Redirector to implement checksums in the IPX packet.

*Length field*

The Length field is set by IPX and denotes the length of the complete IPX packet, including the header and data. The data field can vary from zero to a maximum of 576 octets under NetWare 3.1. Under later versions of NetWare the 576 octet limitation was removed by the use of the vendor's Large Internet Packet Exchange (LIPX). LIPX enables workstations and servers to communicate more efficiently as well as reducing overall traffic since fewer packets are required to transport the same amount of information.

## Transport Control field

The Transport Control field is used by internetwork bridges and is initially set by IPX to zero prior to transmission. Thereafter, the Transport Control field contains the number of hops from source to destination.

## Packet Type field

The Packet Type field denotes the type of service either offered or requested by the packet. Under XNS, Xerox defined eight packet types. Those types and their values are listed in Table 6.1. Under IPX the Packet Type field value is set to either 0 or 4, and SPX sets the value to 5. Through the use of this field an application can quickly identify the type of data contained in the packet.

## Destination Network field

The Destination Network field contains the network number on which the station address in the Destination Node field resides. This is the administration assigned network number. NetWare uses four-octet network numbers as identifiers for servers on

**Table 6.1**  Packet Type field values.

| Value | Meaning |
| --- | --- |
| 0 | Unknown Packet Type |
| 1 | Routing Information Packet |
| 2 | Echo Packet |
| 3 | Error Packet |
| 4 | Internetwork Packet Exchange (IPX) Packet |
| 5 | Sequence Packed Protocol Packet |
| 16–31 | Experimental Protocols |
| 17 | NetWare Core Protocol |

the same network segment. If the value of the Destination Network field is 0, it is assumed that the Destination Node is on the same physical network as the source node and that the packet is not transmitted through an internetwork bridge. Together, the Destination Network field and the Destination Node field define a unique destination in a NetWare network, while a third field, known as the Destination Socket, identifies a process at the destination.

*Destination Node field*

The six-octet Destination Node field contains the physical address of the destination station which is its MAC address. A destination address of hex FF-FF-FF-FF-FF-FF represents a broadcast packet which is sent to all nodes on the destination network.

*Destination Socket field*

The Destination Socket field contains the address of the packet's destination process, a term referred to as the destination socket address which identifies the purpose of the packet. Table 6.2 lists socket numbers used by Xerox under XNS as well as socket numbers that Xerox assigned to Novell.

**Table 6.2** Destination Socket addresses.

| hex Value | Meaning |
| --- | --- |
| Reserved by Xerox | |
| 1 | Routing Information Packet |
| 2 | Echo Protocol Packet |
| 3 | Error Handler Packet |
| 20-3F | Experimental |
| 1-BB8 | Registered with Xerox |
| BB9- | Dynamically assignable |
| | |
| Assigned to Novell | |
| 451 | File Service Packet |
| 452 | Service Advertising Packet |
| 453 | Routing Information Packet |
| 455 | NetBIOS Packet |
| 456 | Diagnostic Packet |
| 4001-7FFF | Workstation Sockets dynamically assigned |

In examining the entries in Table 6.2, it is important to note that Novell also administers a list of sockets. Programmers can request Novell to register a socket number of their programs or can use the dynamic socket assignment of the NetWare shell. Dynamic socket numbers begin at hex 4000, whereas numbers assigned by Novell begin at hex 8000. One of the most frequently transmitted IPX packets contains a Packet Type field value of 4 and a Destination Socket Address field value of 452 hex. Those values identify a SAP packet used by servers to advertise their presence and the types of function they support. SAP packets are typically broadcast to all stations every 60 seconds.

### Source Network field

The next field of the IPX header which follows the Destination Socket field is the Source Network field. This field contains the network number of the station transmitting the IPX packet and serves to identify the originating network. Similarly to the Destination Network field, the Source Network field uses the four-octet network number given to servers on the same network segment. If this field has a value of zero, this indicates that the physical network is unknown. The combination of the Source Network field and the Source Node field results in a unique network address for the originator of network traffic.

### Source Node and Source Socket fields

The Source Node and Source Socket fields are set by IPX to indicate the physical MAC address of the source node and the socket address of the process sending the packet, respectively. Similarly to the Destination Socket, the Source Socket can be static or dynamic and the same numbering convention as described for destination socket numbers is followed.

### IPX Data field composition

As we will soon note, the structure of the IPX header provides a common foundation for the extension of information which converts an IPX header into a different transport mechanism. This extension occurs through the use of the data field as its composition results in the development of several types of transport mechanisms which Novell references as different types of NetWare protocols.

The Data field can contain Routing Information Protocol (RIP), Service Advertising Protocol (SAP), SPX, Echo, Error, or NetWare Core Protocol (NCP) information. In fact, via the extension of the previously described IPX header the packet can be converted into a different type of packet, such as an SPX packet.

Figure 6.2 illustrates the composition of the NetWare packet data field for RIP, SAP, SPX AND NCP information. In the remainder of this section I will discuss the contents of the SPX packet header in terms of its 12 octet extension of an IPX header as well as the operation of SAP, RIP, and NCP.

In comparison to IPX which operates as a connectionless protocol and takes a 'best effort' approach to delivering packets, SPX guarantees packet delivery. To do so, SPX allows stations to negotiate the establishment of a connection. The transmitting station then sends packets in their correct order to the receiving station which acknowledges their receipt. Thus, SPX guarantees both the sequencing and delivery of packets.

One common example of the use of SPX is the transmission of Remote Console (RCONSOLE) session data. RCONSOLE enables a remote user to perform file server operations as if they were located at the server's console. Thus, it is extremely important for each keystroke entered by the remote user to arrive at its correct sequence. Although SPX by default is used for RCONSOLE, most NetWare traffic is transported by IPX. This is because IPX avoids the overhead associated with acknowledging packets, and the error rates on LANs are essentially negligible.

## 6.1.2 SPX

In examining the composition of the data field which turns an IPX packet into an SPX packet you will note the addition of 12 octets to the IPX header. Thus, I will focus my attention upon those octets in discussing SPX.

### Connection Control field

The first new field, Connection Control, contains four bit flags used by the protocol to control the bidirectional flow of data.

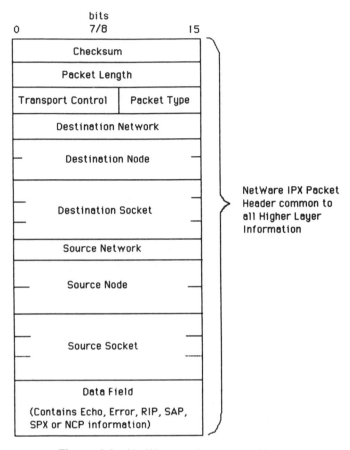

**Figure 6.2** NetWare packet composition

Table 6.3 lists the Connection Control field single-bit flags and their meanings.

### Datastream Type field

The second field in the SPX extension is a one-octet flag which indicates the type of data contained in the packet. Known as the Datastream Type field, possible values include hex 0-FD for client defined, hex FE for End-of-Connection, and hex FF for End-of-Connection Acknowledgment. A Client Defined setting results from an application and is ignored by SPX. An End-of-Connection is generated by SPX when a client requests the termination of an active connection and represents the last

| RIP Information | SAP Information | SPX Information | NCP Information |
|---|---|---|---|
| Operation (2) | Operation (2) | Connection Control(1) | Request Type |
| Network Number(4) | Server Type(2) | Datastream Type(1) | Sequence Number |
| Number of Hops(2) | Server Name(48) | Source Connection ID(2) | Connection Number |
| Number of Ticks(2) | Network Address(4) | Destination Connection(2) | Task Number |
| . . . | Node Address(6) | Sequence Number(2) | Reserved |
| | Socket Address(2) | Acknowledge Number(2) | Function Code |
| Maximum 50 sets of network information | Hops to Server(2) | Allocation Number(2) | Data |
| | . . . 0–534 octets of data | | (variable length) |

Maximum 7 sets of
server information          ( ) represents field length
in octets

**Figure 6.2**   (*Continued*)

message delivered on the connection. The third type of data, End-of-Connection Acknowledgment, is generated by SPX and is not delivered to connected clients.

## *Source and Destination Connection ID fields*

Following the Datastream Type field is the Source Connection ID field. This field contains a number assigned by SPX at the packet's source. That field is followed by the Destination Connection ID field which contains a number assigned by SPX at the packet's destination. As multiple connections active on a computer can use the same socket, the Destination Connect ID

**Table 6.3**  Connection Control bit flags

| Bit flag value | Meaning |
|---|---|
| 10h | (End-of-Message) A client sets this flag to signal its partner an end of connection. SPX passes it unaltered. |
| 20h | (Attention) A client sets this flag if a packet is an attention packet. SPX passes it unaltered. |
| 40h | (Acknowledgement Required) SPX sets this bit if an acknowledgment packet is required. |
| 80h | (System Packet) SPX sets this bit if the packet is a system packet. |

field provides a mechanism for de-multiplexing incoming packets arriving on the same socket from different connections.

### Sequence Number field

The Sequence Number field varies from hex 0 to FF-FF and is used to count packets exchanged in one direction on a connection. SPX wraps to 0 when the maximum value is reached.

### Acknowledgment Number field

The Acknowledgment Number field contains the sequence number of the next packet SPX expects to receive.

### Allocation Number field

The last field, Allocation Number, contains the number of listen buffers outstanding in one direction on the connection. SPX can only transmit packets until the sequence number equals the remote Allocation Number.

## 6.1.3 SAP and RIP

The Service Advertising Protocol (SAP) and Routing Information Protocol (RIP) govern the ability to have multiple servers on a common network or on geographically separated networks that can be recognized and then become accessible to client workstations. SAP and RIP are used to provide a request/reply sequence which provides a mechanism for workstations being able to locate and access servers.

### SAP operation

When a NetWare workstation loads NETX or VLM, the station transmits a SAP request onto the network. That request is a request for the nearest server unless altered by the use of the NetWare ATTACH command to request attachment to a specific server. Servers receiving the SAP request respond with SAP replies which include the server's network address. As the first response is considered to represent the nearest server, the workstation responds to the first SAP reply it receives by broadcasting a RIP request. The RIP request and the RIP reply sent from a router to the workstation enables the workstation to construct a table which associates the hardware address of the router with a network address for the requested service. This enables the workstation to correctly address its packets to the service it seeks.

In addition to supporting the connection of clients to servers when NETX or VLM is loaded SAPs support the ability of routers and certain network commands (SLIST) to know the presence of servers on a network. Every 60 seconds (default) servers broadcast a SAP to advertise their services as well as all known services. The SAP format which is shown in the third column in Figure 4.2 can contain up to seven sets of server descriptors whose contents specify information about the server.

*SAP fields*

The Server Type field specifies the type of server, such as file server or print server. The Server Name field contains the name of the server and explains how you can use the SLIST command to obtain a list of server names. The Network Address field is the internal network address.

In a NetWare environment there are two network addresses that you must consider: the network address assigned by the administrator and the internal network address. The first network address is assigned by the administrator when a file server is configured. The internal address is used to support file service requests as such requests are routed from a work-station's network address to a NetWare server's internal net-work address where the file service processes reside. The Node Address field is a 6-octet address which represents the data link address of the server, normally the Ethernet or Token-Ring adapter address. The two octet Socket Address field is similar to other IPX sockets, representing the internal address of a service, such as a Print Server.

The information carried in SAPs is used by servers and routers to construct Server Information Tables (SITs). SITs contain the information required to associate network services with network locations; however, they do not provide informa-tion required to send packets to a destination network. The information necessary to transmit packets to a destination network is contained in the Routing Information Table (RIT) which is constructed via RIP broadcasts which also occur every 60 seconds.

## RIP operation

The RIP packet shown in column 2 of Figure 6.2 is used by routers to construct RIP tables. RIP packets received on one port are updated via the incrementation of the hop and tick fields and transmitted to all other attached networks. In examining the IPX extension to construct a RIP packet, the Hop field contains the distance in routers that must be traversed to reach the destination network. In comparison, the Ticks field contains the time in one-eighteenth second increments required to reach the destination network.

Under RIP a network is considered to be unreachable if it is 16 hops away. This enables routers to gracefully exit a network and allow other routers to reconfigure themselves to provide a better route. Here the router exiting a route simply broadcasts that it is 16 hops away from the networks it no longer supports.

## Performance issues

Because SAP and RIP broadcasts occur every 60 seconds or whenever a change occurs in a network they can cause performance problems due to the bandwidth they consume. This is especially true when an internetwork consists of LANs connected by relatively slow 56 Kbps WAN links. Through the establishment of appropriate router filters, you can significantly reduce the effect of SAP and RIP broadcasts upon the bandwidth of a physical network.

## 6.1.4 NCP

The NetWork Core Protocol (NCP) packet format is illustrated in the right column in Figure 6.2. In actuality, there are two packet formats, one for an NCP request and a second for an NCP response. Most NCP requests and response packet fields are the same, with differences between the two denoted by two field labels separated by a slash in Figure 6.2. Here the name to the left of the slash indicates an NCP Request packet field, while a name to the right or below the slash indicates an NCP Response packet field.

NCP is used for all file and print services supported by NetWare. Due to this, it is the most commonly used IPX extension protocol. NCP is implemented on IPX using a Packet Type field value of 17 and Socket field value of 451 hex. The NCP packet header adds fields that define the type of NCP request, ensure the delivery of data, and maintain the sequence of packets. Some of the more common NCP header fields are described below.

### Request/Response Type fields

The NCP Request packet commences with a Request Type field while the NCP Response packet commences with a Response Type field. Both fields are two octets in length and define the type of service requested by the client and the type of replay from the server, respectively. Table 6.4 lists the field values assigned to each field and their meaning.

### Sequence Number field

The Sequence Number field is one octet in length and carries the sequential number assigned to the packet. Each request/response increments the sequence number and both

**Table 6.4**  Request and Response Type field values

| Request Type field | |
| --- | --- |
| Value | Definition |
| 1111 | Create Service Connection |
| 2222 | Service Request |
| 5555 | Destroy Connection |
| 7777 | Request Packet Burst |
| Reply Type field | |
| Value | Definition |
| 3333 | Request Processed |
| 7777 | Packet Burst Service |
| 9999 | Request Being Processed |

workstations and servers track and compare the value of this field to ensure they are receiving the correct packet.

## Connection Number fields

There are two connection number fields in an NCP packet. The first is the low order (LO) octet of the connection number which is assigned by a file server during the Create Service Connection request. The second is the high order (HO) octet of the connection number. Together, both octets enable connection numbers higher than 255 to support NetWare LANs with a large number of workstations.

## Task Number field

The Task Number field contains the number assigned by a file server to the current task. This field is one octet in length.

## Function and Completion Code fields

An NCP Request packet contains a one octet Function Code field that identifies file system operations, such as read, write, and lock. In comparison, an NCP Response packet contains a one octet Completion Code field which indicates the status of a requested operation, such as Oh for successful and FFh for failure.

## Packet bursting

As the most common type of IPX header extension any inefficiencies in NCP considerably decrease the efficiency of NetWare. As NCP is a request/response type protocol, every request must be accompanied by a response before the next request can occur. This transmission method works reasonably well on lightly and mediumly utilized LANs, but can result in significant inefficiencies when users on one network need to use file or print services on another LAN reached via a wide area network. Recognizing this problem, Novell modified NCP to enable one request to generate a sequence of responses. This modification is called Packet Burst and it uses a different NCP packet structure. The use of Packet Burst can significantly improve performance. For example, a long file transfer could be accomplished with one request followed by multiple responses representing sequences of file reads rather than requiring a request for each reply.

## 6.2 TCP/IP

TCP/IP represents a collection of network protocols that provide services at the Network and Transport layers of the ISO's OSI Reference Model. Originally developed based upon work performed by the US Department of Defense Advanced Research Projects Agency Network (ARPANET), TCP/IP is also commonly referred to as the DOD protocols or the Internet protocol suite.

### 6.2.1 Protocol development

In actuality, a reference to the TCP/IP protocol suite includes applications that use the TCP/IP protocol stack as a transport mechanism. Such applications range in scope from a remote terminal access program known as Telnet to a file transfer program appropriately referred to as ftp, as well as the Web browser transport mechanism referred to as the HyperText Transport Protocol (HTTP).

The effort behind the development of the TCP/IP protocol suite has its roots in the establishment of ARPANET. The research performed by ARPANET resulted in the development of three specific protocols for the transmission of information: the Transmission Control Protocol (TCP), the Internet Protocol (IP), and the User Datagram Protocol (UDP). Both TCP and UDP represent transport layer protocols. TCP provides end-to-end reliable transmission similar to NetWare's SPX, whereas UDP represents a connectionless layer-4 transport protocol. Thus, UDP operates on a best effort basis and depends upon higher layers of the protocol stack for error detection and correction and other functions associated with end-to-end reliable transmission. TCP includes such functions as flow control, error control, and the exchange of status information, and is based upon a connection being established between source and destination prior to the exchange of information occurring. Thus, TCP provides an orderly and error-free mechanism for the exchange of information.

ISO Layers

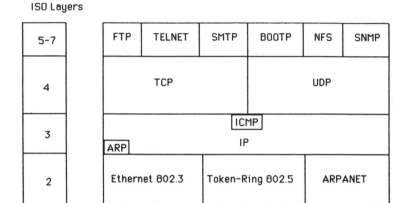

Legend

ARP    Address Resolution Protocol
BOOTP  Bootstrap Protocol
FTP    File Transfer Protocol
NSF    Network File System
SMTP   Simple Mail Transfer Protocol
SNMP   Simple Network Management Protocol

**Figure 6.3**   TCP/IP protocols and services

At the network layer, the IP protocol was developed as a mechanism to route messages between networks. To accomplish this task, IP was developed as a connectionless mode network layer protocol and includes the capability to segment or fragment and reassemble messages that must be routed between networks that support different packet sizes than the size supported by the source and/or destination networks.

## 6.2.1 The TCP/IP structure

TCP/IP represents one of the earliest developed layered communications protocols, grouping functions into defined network layers. Figure 6.3 illustrates the relationship of the TCP/IP protocol suite and the services they provide with respect to the OSI Reference Model. In examining Figure 6.3 note that only six of literally hundreds of TCP/IP application services are shown. As TCP/IP preceded the development of the OSI Reference Model, its developers grouped what are now session, presentation, and application layers that correspond to layers 5

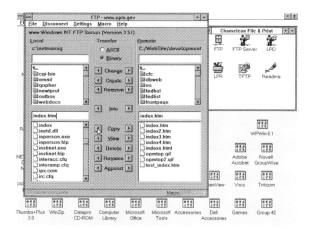

**Figure 6.4** Using a client FTP program to access a Windows NT FTP server

to 7 of the OSI Reference Model into one higher layer. Thus, TCP/IP applications, when compared to the OSI Reference Model, are normally illustrated as corresponding to the upper three layers of that model. Continuing our examination of Figure 6.3, you will note that the subdivision of the transport layer indicates which applications are carried via TCP and those that are transported by UDP. Thus, FTP, Telnet, HTTP, and SMTP represent applications transported by TCP.

Although many persons equate Web browsing with TCP/IP, that application is but one of many commonly supported by that protocol suite. In fact, many Web browsers support plug-in modules to provide file transfer, remote terminal access, and support for other applications, while other vendors market stand-alone TCP/IP applications as part of an application suite.

Figures 6.4 and 6.5 illustrate the use of the FTP and TN3270 applications from the NetManage Chameleon TCP/IP application suite. Figure 6.4 illustrates FTP access to a Windows NT FTP server with the file INDEX.HTM being prepared for copying from the server to the local computer. Figure 6.5 illustrates the use of the NetManage TN3270 program which is a Telnet derivative developed to provide remote terminal access to IBM mainframes. In this example the TN3270 program was used to enable a PC to obtain a connection as if it was a 3270 terminal device to an IBM OfficeVision application running on a S/390 mainframe which provides electronic mail, calendars, and even access to the Internet.

Returning to our examination of Figure 6.3, note that TCP/IP can be transported at the Data Link Layer by a number of

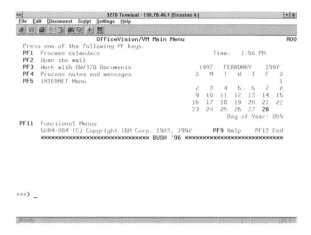

**Figure 6.5** Using a TN3270 client program to enable a PC to access an IBM mainframe as if it was a 3270 terminal

popular LANs, including Ethernet, Fast Ethernet, Token-Ring, and FDDI frames. Due to the considerable effort expended in the development of LAN adapter cards to support the bus structures used in Apple MacIntosh, IBM PCs and compatible computers, DEC Alphas and SUN Microsystem's workstations, and even IBM mainframes, the development of software-based protocol stacks to facilitate the transmission of TCP/IP on LANs provides the capability to interconnect LAN-based computers to one another whether they are on the same network, and only require the transmission of frames on a common cable, or if they are located on networks separated thousands of miles from one another. Thus, TCP/IP represents both a local and wide area network transmission capability. In the remainder of this section I will review IP and TCP packet headers, as well as discussing the use of several related network and transport layer protocols and higher level protocols implemented over TCP and its related protocol suite.

### 6.2.3 Datagrams versus virtual circuits

In examining Figure 6.3 you will note that the Internet Protocol (IP) provides a common Layer 3 transport for TCP and UDP. As briefly noted earlier in this section, TCP is a connection-oriented protocol which requires the acknowledgment of the existence of the connection and for packets transmitted once the connection has been established. In comparison, UDP, a mnemonic for User

Datagram Protocol, is a connectionless mode service that provides a parallel service to TCP. Here datagram represents a term used to identify the basic unit of information that represents a portion of a message and which is transported across a TCP/IP network.

A datagram can be transported either via an acknowledged connection-oriented service or via an unacknowledged, connectionless service, where each information element is addressed to its destination and its transmission is at the mercy of network nodes. IP represents an unacknowledged connectionless service; however, although it is an unreliable transmission method you should view the term in the context that delivery is not guaranteed instead of having second thoughts concerning its use. As a non-guaranteed delivery mechanism IP is susceptible to queuing delays and other problems that can result in the loss of data. However, higher layers in the protocol suite, such as TCP, can provide error detection and correction which results in the retransmission of IP datagrams.

Datagrams are routed via the best path available to the destination as the datagram is placed onto the network. An alternative to datagram transmission is the use of a virtual circuit, where network nodes establish a fixed path when a connection is initiated and subsequent data exchanges occur on that path. TCP implements transmission via the use of a virtual circuit, and IP provides a datagram-oriented gateway transmission service between networks.

The routing of datagrams through a network can occur over different paths, with some datagrams arriving out of sequence from the order in which they were transmitted. In addition, as datagrams flow between networks they encounter physical limitations imposed upon the amount of data that can be transported based upon the transport mechanism used to move data on the network. For example, the Information field in an Ethernet frame is limited to 1500 bytes, whereas a 4 Mbps Token-Ring can transport 4500 bytes in its Information field. Thus, as datagrams flow between networks, they may have to be fragmented into two or more datagrams to be transported through different networks to their ultimate destination. For example, consider the transfer of a 20 000 byte file from a file server connected to a Token-Ring network to a workstation connected to an Ethernet LAN via a pair of routers providing a connection between the two local area networks. The 4 MBPS Token-Ring network supports a maximum Information field of

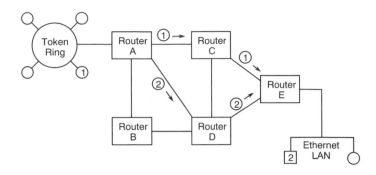

**Figure 6.6** Routing of datagrams can occur over different paths

4500 bytes in each frame transmitted on that network, while the maximum size of the Information field in an Ethernet frame is 1500 bytes. In addition, depending upon the protocol used on the wide area network connection between routers, the WAN protocol's Information field could be limited to 512 or 1024 bytes. Thus, the IP protocol must break up the file transfer into a series of datagrams whose size is acceptable for transmission between networks. As an alternative, IP can transmit data using a small maximum datagram size, commonly 576 bytes, to prevent fragmentation. If fragmentation is necessary, the source host can transmit using the maximum datagram size available on its network. When the datagram arrives at the router, IP operating on that communications device will then fragment each datagram into a series of smaller datagrams. Upon receipt at the destination, each datagram must then be put back into its correct sequence so that the file can be correctly reformed, a responsibility of IP residing on the destination host.

Figure 6.6 illustrates the routing of two datagrams from workstation 1 on a Token-Ring network to server 2 connected to an Ethernet LAN. As the routing of datagrams is a connection-less service, no call setup is required, which enhances transmission efficiency. In comparison, when TCP is used it provides a connection-oriented service regardless of the lower layer delivery system (e.g. IP).

TCP requires the establishment of a virtual circuit in which a temporary path is developed between source and destination. This path is fixed and the flow of datagrams is restricted to the established path. When the User Datagram Protocol (UDP), a different layer 4 protocol in the TCP/IP protocol suite, is used in place of TCP, the flow of data at the Transport layer continues to be connectionless and results in the transport of datagrams over available paths rather than a fixed path resulting from the establishment of a virtual circuit.

The actual division of a message into datagrams is the responsibility of the layer 4 protocol, either TCP or UDP while fragmentation is the responsibility of IP. In addition, when the TCP protocol is used, that protocol is responsible for reassembling datagrams at their destination as well as for requesting the retransmission of lost datagrams. In comparison, IP is responsible for routing of individual datagrams from source to destination. When UDP is used as the layer 4 protocol, there is no provision for the retransmission of lost or garbled datagrams. As previously noted by our discussion of IP, this is not necessarily a bad situation as applications that use UDP then become responsible for managing communications.

Figure 6.7 illustrates the relationship of an IP datagram, UDP datagram, and TCP segment to a LAN frame. The headers shown in Figure 6.7 represent a group of bytes added to the beginning of a datagram to allow a degree of control over the datagram. For example, the TCP header will contain information that allows this layer 4 protocol to track the sequence of the delivery of datagrams so they can be placed into their correct order if they arrive out of sequence. Prior to focusing our attention upon TCP and IP, let us briefly discuss the role of ICMP and ARP, two additional network layer protocols in the TCP/IP suite.

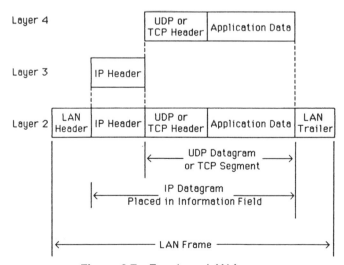

**Figure 6.7** Forming a LAN frame

## 6.2.4 ICMP and ARP

The Internet Control Message Protocol (ICMP) provides a mechanism for communicating control message and error reports. Both gateways and hosts use ICMP to transmit problem reports about datagrams back to the datagram originator. In addition, ICMP includes an echo request/reply that can be used to determine if a destination is reachable and if so, is responding. The Address Resolution Protocol (ARP) maps the high level IP address configured via software to a low level physical hardware address, typically the network interface card's (NIC) ROM address. The high level IP address is currently 32 bits in length and is commonly represented by four decimal numbers, ranging from 0 to 255 per number, separated from one another by decimals. Thus, another term used to refer to an IP address is dotted decimal address. The physical hardware address represents the MAC address. Thus, ARP provides an IP to MAC address resolution which enables an IP packet to be transported in a LAN frame to its appropriate MAC address. Later in this section we will examine IP addresses in detail.

## 6.2.5 TCP

The Transmission Control Protocol (TCP) represents a layer 4 connection-oriented reliable protocol. TCP provides a virtual circuit connection mode service for applications that require connection setup and error detection and automatic retransmission. In addition, TCP is structured to support multiple application programs on one host to communicate concurrently with processes on other hosts, as well as for a host to de-multiplex and service incoming traffic among different applications or processes running on the host.

Each unit of data carried by TCP is referred to as a segment. Segments are created by TCP subdividing the stream of data passed down by application layer protocols that use its services, with each segment identified by the use of a sequence number. This segment identification process enables a receiver, if required, to reassemble data segments into their correct order.

Figure 6.8 illustrates the format of the TCP protocol header. To obtain an appreciation for the functionality and capability of TCP, let us examine the fields in its header.

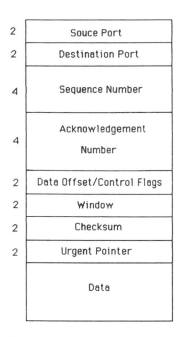

| | |
|---|---|
| 2 | Souce Port |
| 2 | Destination Port |
| 4 | Sequence Number |
| 4 | Acknowledgement Number |
| 2 | Data Offset/Control Flags |
| 2 | Window |
| 2 | Checksum |
| 2 | Urgent Pointer |
| | Data |

**Figure 6.8**  TCP protocol header

## Source and Destination Port fields

The source and destination ports are each 16 bits in length and identify a process or service at the host receiver. The Source Port field entry is optional and when not used is padded with zeros. Both Source and Destination Port values are commonly referred to as well-known ports as they typically identify an application layer protocol or process. Table 6.5 lists the well-known port numbers associated with eight popular TCP/IP application layer protocols. In examining the entries in the previously mentioned table, note that some protocols, such as FTP, use two port addresses or logical connections. In the case of FTP, one address (21) is used for the transmission of commands and responses and functions as a control path. In comparison, the second port address (20) is used for the actual file transfer.

## Sequence fields

The sequence number is used to identify the data segment transported. The acknowledgment number interpretation depends upon the setting of the ACK control flag which is not

**Table 6.5**  Examples of TCP/IP application layer protocol use of well-known ports

| Name | Acronym | Description | Well-known Port |
|------|---------|-------------|-----------------|
| Domain Name Protocol | DOMAIN | Defines the DNS | 53 |
| File Transfer Protocol | FTP | Supports file transfers between hosts | 20, 21 |
| Finger Protocol | FINGER | Provides information about a specified user | 79 |
| HyperText Trans-mission Protocol | HTTP | Transmits information between a Web browser and a Web server | 80 |
| Post Office Protocol | POP | Enables host users access mail from a mail server | 110 |
| Simple Mail Transfer Protocol | SNMP | Provides for the exchange of electronic mail | 161,162 |

directly shown in Figure 6.7. If the ACK control flag bit position is set, the acknowledgment field will contain the next sequence number the sender expects to receive. Otherwise the field is ignored.

## Control field flags

Six control field flags that are used to establish, maintain and terminate connections. Those flags include URG (urgent), SYN, ACK, RST (reset), PSH (push), and FIN (finish).

Setting URG=1 indicates to the receiver that urgent data is arriving. The SYN flag is set to 1 as a connection request and thus serves to establish a connection. As previously discussed, the ACK flag when set indicates that the acknowledgment flag is relevant. The RST flag when set means that the connection should be reset, and the PSH flag tells the receiver to immediately deliver the data in the segment. Finally, the setting of the FIN flag indicates the sender is done and the connection should be terminated.

## Window field

The Window field is used to convey the number of bytes that the sender can accept and functions as a flow control mechanism.

This 16-bit field indicates the number of octets, beginning with the one in the Acknowledgment field that the originator of the segment can control. As TCP is a full-duplex protocol, each host can use the Window field to control the quantity of data that can be sent to the computer. This enables the recipient to, in effect, control its destiny. For example, if a receiving host becomes overloaded with processing or another reason results in the inability of the device to receive large chunks of data, it can use the Window field as a flow control mechanism to reduce the size of data chunks sent to it. At the end of our review of TCP header fields we will examine a TCP transmission sequence to note the inter-related role of the Sequence, Acknowledgment and Window fields.

### Checksum field

The checksum provides error detection for the TCP header and data carried in the segment. Thus, this field provides the mechanism for the detection of errors in each segment.

### Urgent Pointer field

The Urgent Pointer field is used in conjunction with the URG flag as a mechanism to identify the position of urgent data within a TCP segment. When the URG flag is set the value in the urgent pointer field represents the last byte of urgent data.

When an application uses TCP, TCP breaks the stream of data provided by the application into segments and adds an appropriate TCP header. Next, an IP header is prefixed to the TCP header to transport the segment via the network layer. As data arrives at its destination network it is converted into a data link layer transport mechanism. For example, on a Token-Ring network TCP data would be transported within Token-Ring frames.

### TCP transmission sequence example

To illustrate the interrelationship between the Sequence, Acknowledgment, and Window fields, let us examine the transmission of a sequence of TCP segments between two

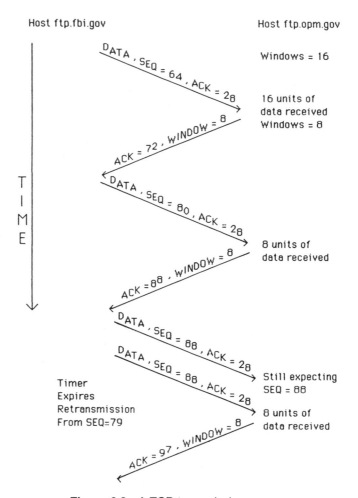

**Figure 6.9** A TCP transmission sequence

hosts. Figure 6.9 illustrates via the use of a time chart the transmission of a sequence of TCP segments.

At the top of Figure 6.9 it was assumed that a Window size of 16 segments is in use. Although TCP supports full-duplex transmission, for simplicity of illustration we will use a half-duplex model in the time chart.

Assuming that the host whose address is ftp.fbi.gov is transmitting a program or performing a similar lengthy file transfer operation, the first series of segments will have sequence numbers 64 through 79, assuming that sequence number 63 was just acknowledged. The ACK value of 28 acknowledges that segments through number 27 were received by the host ftp.opm.gov and that it next expects to receive segment 28.

Assuming that segments 64 through 79 arrive error free, the host with the address ftp.opm.gov returns an ACK value of 80 to indicate the next segment it expects to receive. At this point in time let us assume host ftp.opm.gov is running out of buffer space and halves the window size to 8. Thus, host ftp.opm.gov sets the Window field value in the TCP header it transmits to host ftp.fbi.gov to 8. Upon receipt of the TCP segment host, ftp.fbi.gov reduces the number of segments that it will transmit to eight and uses an initial SEQ value of 80, increasing that value by 1 each time it transmits a new segment until eight new segments are transmitted. Assuming that all eight segments were received error-free, host ftp.opm.gov then returns an ACK value of 88 which acknowledges the receipt of segments with sequence field numbers through 87.

Next, host ftp.fbi.gov transmits to host ftp.opm.gov another sequence of eight segments using sequence field values of 88 to 95. However, let us assume that a transmission impairment occurs that results in the segments being incorrectly received or perhaps not even received at all at their intended destination. If host ftp.opm.gov does not receive anything, it does not transmit anything back to host ftp.fbi.gov. Instead of waiting forever for a response, the TCP/IP protocol stack includes an internal timer which clicks down to zero while host ftp.fbi.gov waits for a response. When that value is reached, the timer expires and the transmitting station retransmits its sequence of eight segments. On the second time around the sequence of eight segments are shown acknowledged at the bottom of Figure 6.9. If the impairment continued, the transmitting station would attempt a predefined number of retransmissions after which it would terminate the session if no response was received.

The altering of Window field values provides a sliding window that can be used to control the flow of information. That is, by adjusting the value of the Window field a receiving host can inform a transmitting station whether or not an adjustment in the number of segments transmitted is required. In doing so there are two special Window field values that can be used to further control the flow of information. A Window field value of 0 means that a host has shut down communications, while a Window field value of 1 requires an acknowledgment for each unit of data transmitted, limiting transmission to a segment by segment basis.

## 6.2.6 UDP

The User Datagram Protocol (UDP) is the second layer 4 transport service supported by the TCP/IP protocol suite. UDP is a connectionless service which means that the higher layer application is responsible for the reliable delivery of the transported message. Figure 6.10 illustrates the composition of the UDP header.

### *Source and Destination port fields*

The Source and Destination port fields are each 16 bits in length and as previously described for TCP identify the port number of the sending and receiving process, respectively. Here each port number process identifies an application running at the corresponding IP address in the IP header prefixed for the UDP header. The use of a port number provides a mechanism for identifying network services as they denote communications points where particular services can be accessed. For example, a value of 161 in a port field is used in UDP to identify SNMP.

### *Length fields*

The Length field indicates the length of the UDP packets in octets to include the header and user data. The checksum, which is a one's complement arithmetic sum, is computed over a pseudo-header and the entire UDP packet. The pseudo-header is created by the conceptual prefix of 12 octets to the header previously illustrated in Figure 6.9. The first 8 octets are used by

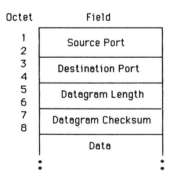

**Figure 6.10** The UDP header

source and destination IP addresses obtained from the IP packet. This is followed by a zero-filled octet and an octet which identifies the protocol. The last two octets in the pseudo-header denote the length of the UDP packet. By computing the UDP checksum over the pseudo-header and user data a degree of additional data integrity is obtained.

### 6.2.7 IP

As previously mentioned, IP provides a datagram-oriented gateway service for transmission between subnetworks. This provides a mechanism for hosts to access other hosts on a best effort basis but does not enhance reliability, as it relies on upper layer protocols for error detection and correction. As a Layer 3 protocol IP is responsible for the routing and delivery of datagrams. To accomplish this task IP performs a number of communications functions to include addressing, status information, management and the fragmentation and reassembly of datagrams when necessary.

*IP header format*

Figure 6.11 illustrates the IP header format and Table 6.6 provides a brief description of the fields in the IP header.

**Version field**

The four bit Version field identifies the version of the IP protocol used to create the datagram. The current version of the IP protocol is 4 and is encoded as 0100 in binary. The next generation IP protocol is version 6, which is encoded as 0110 in binary. In our discussion of IP we will focus on IPv4 in this section.

**Header Length and Total Length fields**

The Header Length field follows the Version field and is also four bits in length. This field indicates the length of the header in 32-bit words. In comparison, the Total Length field indicates the total length of the datagram to include its header and higher layer information. The use of 16 bits for the Total Length field

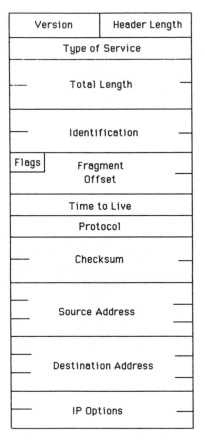

**Figure 6.11** IP header format

enables an IP datagram to be up to $2^{16}$ or 65 535 octets in length.

### Type of Service field

The Type of Service field identifies how the datagram is handled. Three of the eight bits in this field are used to denote the precedence or level of importance assigned by the originator. Thus, this field provides a priority mechanism for routing IP datagrams.

### Identification and Fragment Offset fields

The Identification field enables each datagram or fragmented datagram to be identified. If a datagram was previously

**Table 6.6**   IP header fields

| Field | Description |
| --- | --- |
| Version | The version of the IP protocol used to create the datagram. |
| Header Length | Header length in 32 bit words. |
| Type of Service | Specifies how the datagram should be handled. |

```
  0   1   2   3   4   5   6   7
┌─────────────┬───┬───┬───┬────────┐
│ PRECEDENCE  │ D │ T │ R │ UNUSED │
└─────────────┴───┴───┴───┴────────┘
```

| | |
| --- | --- |
| PRECEDENCE | indicates the importance of the datagram |
| D | When set requests low delay |
| T | When set requests high throughput |
| R | When set requests high reliability |

| Field | Description |
| --- | --- |
| Total Length | Specifies the total length, including header and data. |
| Identification | Used with source address to identify fragments belonging to specific datagrams. |
| Flags | Middle bit when set disables possible fragmentation. Low order bit specifies whether the fragment contains data from the middle of the original datagram or the end. |
| Fragment Offset | Specifies the offset in the original datagram of data being carried in a fragment. |
| Time to Live | Specifies the time in seconds that a datagram is allowed to remain in the internet. |
| Protocol | Specifies the higher level protocol used to create the message carried in the data field. |
| Header Checksum | Protects the integrity of the header. |
| Source IP Address | The 32 bit IP address of the datagram's sender. |
| Destination IP Address | The 32 bit IP address of the datagram's intended recipient. |
| IP Options | Primarily used for network testing or debugging. |

```
  0    1    2     3   4   5   6   7
┌──────┬────────────┬──────────────────┐
│ COPY │OPTION CLASS│   OPTION NUMBER   │
└──────┴────────────┴──────────────────┘
```

When the copy bit is set it tells gateways that the option should be copied into all fragments. When set to 0 the option is copied into the first fragment.

| Option Class | Meaning |
| --- | --- |
| 0 | Datagram or network control |
| 1 | Reserved for future use |
| 2 | Debugging |
| 3 | Reserved for future use |

The option number defines a specific option within a class.

fragmented, the Fragment Offset field specifies the offset in the original datagram of the data being carried. In effect, this field indicates where the fragment belongs in the complete message. The actual value in this field is an integer which corresponds to a unit of 8 octets, providing an offset in 64 bit units.

### Time To Live field

The Time To Live (TTL) field specifies the maximum time that a datagram can live. As an exact time is difficult to measure, almost all routers decrement this field by 1 as a datagram flows between networks, with the datagram being discarded when the field value reaches zero. Thus, this field more accurately represents a hop count field. You can consider this field to represent a failsafe mechanism, as it prevents misaddressed datagrams from continuously flowing on the Internet.

### Flags field

The Flags field contains two bits that indicate how fragmentation occurs while a third bit is currently unassigned. The setting of one bit can be viewed as a direct fragment control mechanism as a value of 0 indicates that the datagram can be fragmented, while a value of 1 denotes 'do not fragment'. The second bit is set to 0 to indicate that a fragment in a datagram is the last fragment, and set to a value of 1 to indicate more fragments follow the current protocol.

### Protocol field

The Protocol field specifies the higher level protocol used to create the message carried in the datagram. For example, a value of decimal 6 would indicate TCP, while a value of decimal 17 would indicate UDP.

### Source and Destination Address fields

The Source and Destination Address fields are both 32 bits in length. As previously discussed, each address represents both a network and a host computer on the network.

In examining the IP header a common network problem relates to the IP address carried in the source and destination address fields. Thus, a description of IP addressing is warranted, as it forms the basis for network addressing as well as the Domain

Name Service translation of English type mnemonics into what are known as dotted decimal IP addresses.

## *IP addressing*

The IP addressing scheme uses a 32 bit address which is divided into an assigned network number and a host number. The latter can be further segmented into a subnet number and a host number. Through subnetting you can construct multiple networks while localizing the traffic of hosts to specific subnets, a technique I will shortly illustrate.

IP addressing numbers are assigned by the InterNIC network information center and can fall into one of five unique network classes, referred to as Class A through Class E. Figure 6.12 illustrates the IP address formats for Class A, B and C networks. Class D addresses are reserved for multicast groups, and Class E addresses are reserved for future use.

In examining Figure 6.12, note that by examining the first bit in the IP address you can distinguish a Class A address from Class B and C addresses. Thereafter, examining the composition of the second bit position enables a Class B address to be distinguished from a Class C address.

An IP 32 bit address is expressed as a four decimal number, with each number ranging in value from 0 to 255 and separated from another number by a dot (decimal point). This explains why an IP address is commonly referred to as a dotted decimal address.

### Class A

In examining Figure 6.12, note that a Class A address has three bytes available for identifying hosts on one network or on subnets which provides support for more hosts than other address classes. Thus, Class A addresses are only assigned to large organizations or countries. As the first bit in a Class A address must be zero, the first byte ranges in value from 1 to 127 instead of to 255. Through the use of 7 bits for the network portion and 24 bits for the host portion of the address, 128 networks can be defined with approximately 16.78 million hosts capable of being addressed on each Class A network.

### Class B

A Class B address uses two bytes for the network identifier and two for the host or subnet identifier. This permits up to 65 636 hosts and/or subnets to be assigned; however, since the first two bits of the network portion of the address are used to identify a Class B address, the network portion is reduced to a width of 14 bits. Thus, up to 16 384 class B networks can be assigned. Due to the manner by which Class B network addresses are subdivided into network and host portions, such addresses are normally assigned to relatively large organizations with tens of thousands of employees.

### Class C

In a Class C address three octets are used to identify the network, leaving one octet to identify hosts and/or subnets. The use of 21 bits for a network address enables approximately 2 million distinct networks to be supported by the Class C address class. As one octet only permits 256 hosts or subnets to be identified, many small organizations with a requirement to provide more than 256 hosts with access to the Internet must obtain multiple Class C addresses.

### Host restrictions

In actuality the host portion of an IP address has two restrictions which reduce the number of hosts that can be assigned to a network. First, the host portion cannot be set to all zero bits as an all-0 host number is used to identify a base

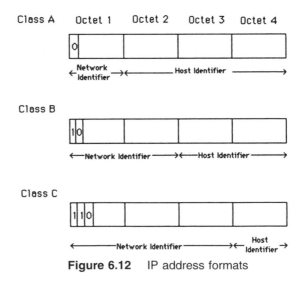

**Figure 6.12**  IP address formats

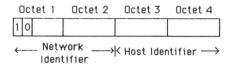

Class B Address Format

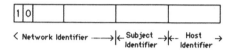

Class B Subnet Address Format

**Figure 6.13**   Class B subnetting

network or subsequent number. Secondly, an all-1 host number represents the broadcast address for a network or subnetwork. Thus, the maximum number of hosts on a network must be reduced by two. For a Class C network a maximum of 254 hosts can then be configured for operation.

*Subnetting*

Through the use of subnetting you can use a single IP address as a mechanism for connecting multiple physical networks. To accomplish subnetting you logically divide the host portion of an IP address into a network address and a host address.

Figure 6.13 illustrates an example of the IP subnet addressing format for a Class B address. In this example all traffic routed to the address XY, where X and Y represent the values of the first two Class B address octets, flow to a common location connected to the Internet, typically a router. The router in turn connects two or more Class B subnets, each with a distinct address formed by the third decimal digit which represents the subnet identifier. Figure 6.14 illustrates a Class B network address location with two physical networks using subnet addressing.

**Subnet masks**

The implementation of a subnet addressing scheme is accomplished by the partitioning of the host identifier portion of an IP address. To accomplish this a 32 bit subnet mask must be created for each network, with bits set to '1' in the subnet mask

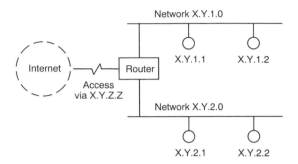

IP datagrams with the destination address X.Y.Z.Z where Z
can be any decimal value represent a Class B network
address that can consist of 254 subnets

**Figure 6.14** A Class B network address location with two physical networks
using subnet addressing

to indicate the network portion of the IP address, while bits are
set to '0' to indicate the host identifier portion. Thus, the Class B
subnet address format illustrated in the lower portion of Figure
6.13 would require the following 32 bit subnet mask:

11111111 11111111 00000000 00000000

The prior mask would then be entered as 255.255.0.0 in
dotted decimal representation into a router configuration screen
as well as in software configuration screens on TCP/IP program
stacks operating on each subnet. Concerning the latter, you
must then configure each station to indicate its subnet and host
identifier so that each station obtains a full four digit dotted
decimal address.

Although the prior example used octet boundaries for creating
the subnet mask this is not an addressing requirement. For
example, you could assign the following mask to a network:

11111111 11111111 00001110 00001100

The only submask restriction is to assign '1' to at least all the
network identifier positions, resulting in the ability to extend
masking into the host identifier field if you desire to arrange the
specific assignment of addresses to computers. However, doing
so can make it more difficult to verify the correct assignment of
addresses in routers and workstations. Due to this, it is highly
recommended that you should implement subnet masking on
integral octet boundaries.

*Domain Name Service*

Addressing on a TCP/IP network occurs through the use of four decimal numbers ranging from 0 to 255, which are separated from one another by a dot. This dotted decimal notation represents a 32 bit address which consists of an assigned network number and a host number as previously described during our examination of IP addressing. As numeric addresses are difficult to work with, TCP/IP also supports a naming convention based upon English words or mnemonics that are both easier to work with and remember. The translation of English words or mnemonics to 32 bit IP addresses is performed by a Domain Name Server. Each network normally has at least one Domain Name Server and the communications established between such servers on TCP/IP networks connected to the Internet are referred to as a Domain Name Service (DNS).

The Domain Name Service (DNS) is the naming protocol used in the TCP/IP protocol suite which enables IP routing to occur indirectly through the use of names instead of IP addresses. To accomplish this, DNS provides a domain name to IP address translation service.

A domain is a subdivision of a wide area network. When applied to the Internet, where the capital I refers to the collection of networks interconnected with one another, there are six top-level and server pending domain names which were specified by the Internet Network Information Center (InterNIC) at the time that this book was prepared. Those top level domains are listed in Table 6.7.

Under each top level domain the InterNIC will register subdomains which are assigned an IP network address. An organization receiving an IP network address can further subdivide their domain into two or more subdomains. In addition, instead of using dotted decimal notation to describe the location of each host, they can assign names to hosts so long as they follow certain rules and install a name server which provides IP address translation between named hosts and their IP addresses.

To illustrate the operation of a name server consider the network domain illustrated in Figure 6.15. In this example we will assume that a well-known government agency has a local area network with several computers that will be connected to the Internet. Each host address will contain the specific name of the host plus the names of all of the subdomains and domains to which it belongs. Thus, the computer 'warrants' would have the official address:

**Table 6.7** Internet top-level domain names

| Domain name | Assignment |
|---|---|
| *Existing* | |
| .COM | Commercial Organization |
| .EDU | Educational Organization |
| .GOV | Government Agency |
| .MIL | Department of Defense |
| .NET | Networking Organization |
| .ORG | Not for Profit Organization |
| *Pending* | |
| .firm | Business/Commercial Firms |
| .store | Goods for Purchase |
| .web | World Wide Web related activities |
| .arts | Culture/Entertainment Organizations |
| .rec | Recreation/Entertainment Organization |
| .info | Information/Services |
| .nom | Individual/Personal Nomenclature |

warrants.telnet.fbi.gov

Similarly, the computer 'cops' would have the address

cops.ftp.fbi.gov

In examining the domain naming structure illustrated in Figure 6.15 note that computers were placed in subdomains using common Internet application names, such as telnet and ftp. This is a common technique that organizations use to make it easier for network users within and outside the organization to remember mnemonics that represent specific hosts on their network.

Although domain names provide a mechanism for identifying objects connected to wide area networks, hosts in a domain require network addresses to transfer information. Thus another host functioning as a name server is required to provide a name to address translation service.

### Name server

The name server plays an important role in TCP/IP networks. In addition to providing a name-to-IP address translation service it must recognize that an address is outside its administrative

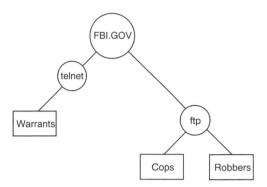

**Figure 6.15** A domain-naming hierarchy

zone of authority. For example, assume that a host located on the domain illustrated in Figure 6.15 will use the address fred.microwear.com to transmit a message. The name server must recognize that that address does not reside in the domain and must forward the address to another name server for translation into an appropriate IP address. As most domains are connected to the Internet via an Internet service provider, the name server on the domain illustrated in Figure 6.15 would have a pointer to the name server of the Internet Service Provider and forward the query to that name server. The Internet Service Provider's name server will either have an entry in its table in cache memory or forward the query to another higher level name server. Eventually a name server will be reached that has administrative authority over the domain containing the host name to resolve and will return an IP address through a reversed hierarchy to provide the originating name server with a response to its query. Most name servers cache the results of previous name queries, which can considerably reduce off-domain or Internet DNS queries. In the event that a response is not received, possibly due to an incorrect name or the entry of a name no longer used, the local name server will generate a 'failure to resolve' message after a period of time that will be displayed on the requesting host's display.

### 6.2.8 TCP/IP configuration

The configuration of a station on a TCP/IP network normally requires the specification of four IP addresses as well as the station's host and domain names. To illustrate the configuration of a TCP/IP station Figures 6.16 through 6.18 show the screen settings on a Microsoft Windows NT workstation used to configure the station as a participant on a TCP/IP network.

Figure 6.16 illustrates the Windows NT Network Settings dialog box with the TCP/IP protocol selected in the installed network software box. Note that at the top of that box the entry NWLink IPX/SPX Compatible Transport is shown. Windows NT has the ability to operate multiple protocol stacks to include NWLink which is Microsoft's implementation of the Novell IPX and SPX protocols. In fact, as we will shortly note, you can use a Windows NT computer to access a Novell network.

Clicking on the button labeled Configure in Figure 6.16 results in the display of another dialog box, this one labeled TCP/IP Configuration. Figure 6.17 illustrates the TCP/IP Configuration dialog box with three address entries shown. Those address entries indicate the IP address of the interface assigned to the selected adapter card, the subnet mask and the IP address of the default gateway. Note that a computer can have multiple adapter cards, thus IP addresses are actually assigned to network interfaces. Also note that the term gateway dates from when such devices routed packets to other networks if their address was not on the local network. Thus, a more modern term for gateway is router.

After configuring the entries shown in Figure 6.17, you will require a few more entries. Those entries include the address of the name server used to translate near English mnemonics into IP addresses as well as the name of your computer and domain. To configure the address of the name server you would first click on the button labeled DNS in Figure 6.17. This action will result

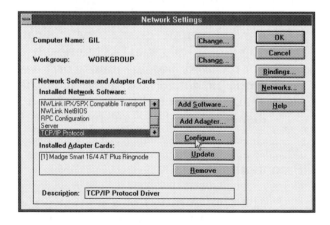

**Figure 6.16**   Using the Windows NT Network Settings dialog box to configure the use of the TCP/IP protocol

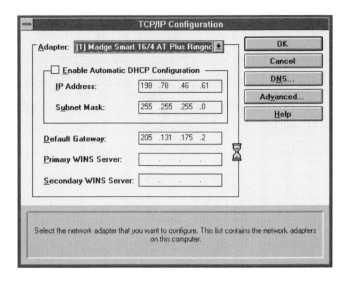

**Figure 6.17**  The Windows NT TCP/IP configuration dialog box with entries for the IP address of the network inferface, subnet mask, and default gateway

in the display of a dialog box labeled DNS Configuration which is shown in Figure 6.18.

The Windows NT DNS Configuration dialog box enables you to specify your host computer name and your domain name. Those entries are optional; however, if you do not include those entries and your local DNS uses this configuration information, other

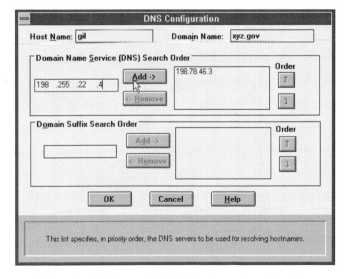

**Figure 6.18**  Using the Windows NT DNS Configuration dialog box to specify the stations name and domain name as well as two name server addresses

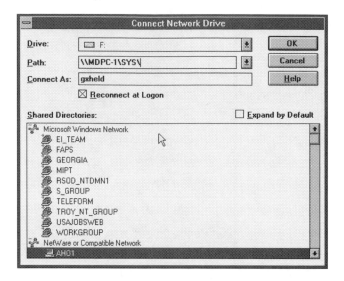

**Figure 6.19**  Using the Windows NT Connect Network Drive dialog box to view Windows and NetWare network devices

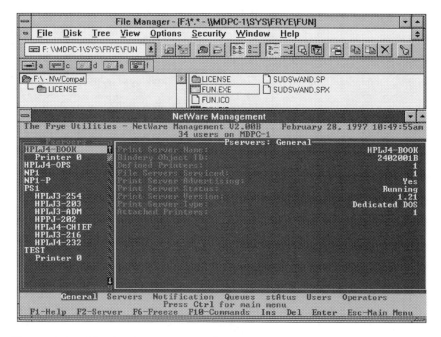

**Figure 6.20**  Viewing the execution of a NetWare server program on a Windows NT workstation

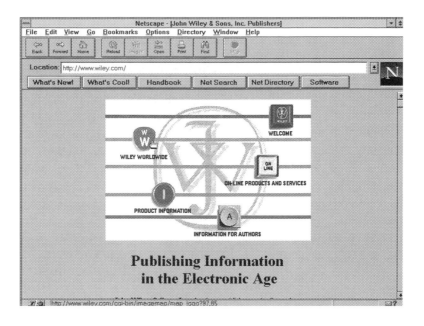

**Figure 6.21** Using the Netscape browser to access the home page of the author's publisher

TCP/IP users either on your network or a distant network will not be able to access your computer by entering your computer's near-English address name which in Figure 6.18 would be gil.xyz.gov. Instead, users would have to know your numeric IP address.

The DNS entry area in Figure 6.18 allows you to specify up to three name servers in the order they should be searched. Many organizations operate two name servers, so the ability to enter three should suffice for most organizations.

## 6.2.9 Operating multiple stacks

In concluding this chapter we will use three Windows NT screens to illustrate the flexibility that you can obtain from operating multiple protocol stacks. In the example that we will shortly view we will use Microsoft's Windows NT to show how we can access both Windows NT and NetWare networks and operate a Netscape browser to run a TCP/IP application.

Figure 6.19 illustrates the use of the Windows NT Connect Network Drive dialog box to view both Microsoft Windows and Novell NetWare network devices that can operate on a common network or network infrastructure. By moving a highlight bar over a particular entry and clicking on the entry, you obtain the ability to log into NT or NetWare servers or access shared directories on NT devices. For those readers from Missouri, Figure 6.20 illustrates the execution of a NetWare server program viewed on a Windows NT workstation. In this example, the NT workstation is running Microsoft's NWLink IPX/SPX compatible protocol which enables it to communicate in a client server environment as a participant on a NetWare LAN.

For our last stack example, since we previously configured TCP/IP we should be able to operate a TCP/IP application. Figure 6.21 illustrates the use of the Netscape browser to access the home page of this author's publisher. Thus, this short section illustrates the worth of operating multiple protocol stacks to access NT and NetWare servers as well as a Web server.

# BRIDGING METHODS

In Chapter 3 an overview of bridge operations was presented along with information concerning the functionality of other local area network hardware and software components. That chapter deferred until now a detailed examination of bridging methods, to include their network utilization and performance issues. In this chapter we will focus our attention upon those issues, examining different methods bridges use for routing frames, performance issues that govern their ability to examine and forward frames without introducing network bottlenecks, and their typical employment to interconnect LANs.

## 7.1 BRIDGING METHODS

Two primary methods are used by bridges to connect local area networks, transparent or self-learning and source routing. Transparent bridges were originally developed to support the connection of Ethernet networks and they were briefly described in Chapter 3.

### 7.1.1 Transparent bridging

A transparent bridge examines media access control (MAC) frames to learn the addresses of stations on the network, storing information in internal memory in the form of an address table. To understand the operation of a transparent bridge in more detail and some of the limitations associated with the use of this device, consider the simple bridged based network illustrated in Figure 7.1. This network consists of three Ethernet local area

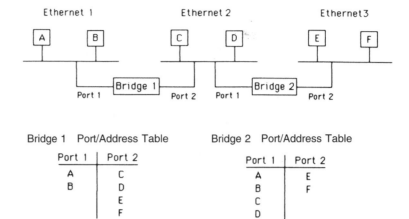

**Figure 7.1** Transparent bridge operation. A transparent or self-learning bridge examines the source and destination addresses to form a port/address bridging table in memory

network segments connected through the use of two self-learning bridges. For simplicity of illustration only two workstations are shown and labeled on each local area network. Those labels represent the 48 bit MAC address of each station.

## Port/address table construction

As frames flow on the first Ethernet, bridge 1 examines the source address of each frame. Eventually, after both workstations A and B have become active the bridge associates their address as being on port 1 of that device. Any frame with a destination address other than workstations A or B is considered to be on another network. Thus, bridge 1 would eventually associate addresses C, D, E and F with port 2 once it receives frames with those addresses in their destination address fields. Similarly, bridge 2 constructs its port/address table. As frames from Ethernet 1 and Ethernet 2 can have source addresses of A, B, C or D, eventually the port/address table of bridge 2 associates those addresses with port 1 of that device. As frames from Ethernet 1 or Ethernet 2 with a destination address of E or F are not on those local area networks, bridge 2 then associates those addresses with port 2 of that device.

The port/address tables shown in Figure 7.1 are normally stored in the bridge memory sorted by MAC address. In addition, the time that the entry occurred is also added to the table, resulting in a three column table. The time of occurrence is used by the bridge to periodically purge old entries. Entry purging is important because inactive entries both use finite memory and extend the search time associated with the reading of each frame received on a bridge port and its comparison to entries in the port/address table. This searching is required to determine if the frame is to be forwarded along with the port onto which the frame should be placed.

To illustrate the necessity for time stamping, bridge port/ address table entries assume the interconnected Ethernet segments shown in Figure 7.1 are expanded by the addition of two additional segments to the right of segment 3, with each new segment containing 50 workstations. Without the use of time stamping and the purging of aged table entries, the port/ address table of bridge 2 would eventually grow to 102 entries, even if each station powered on at 8:00 a.m., connected to their local server, and thereafter did not use the network for the rest of the day. Then, each time a frame arrived at port 2 of bridge 2 the destination address of the frame would need to be compared against a table with 100 inactive entries, consuming valuable work time.

### Advantages

One of the key advantages of a transparent bridge is that it operates independently of the contents of the information field and is protocol independent. As this type of bridge is self-learning, it requires no manual configuration and is essentially a 'plug and work' device. Thus, this type of bridge is attractive for connecting a few local area networks together and is commonly sufficient for most small and medium-sized businesses. Unfortunately, its use limits the development of certain interconnection topologies as we will soon see.

### Disadvantages

To illustrate the disadvantages associated with transparent bridges consider Figure 7.2 in which the three Ethernet local area networks previously connected by the use of two bridges are expanded to where they are interconnected through the use of three bridges. In this example the interconnected networks form a circular or loop topology. Since a transparent bridge views workstations as being connected to either port 1 or port 2, a

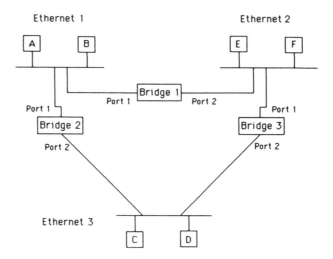

**Figure 7.2** Transparent bridges do not support network loops. The construction of a circular or loop topology through the use of transparent bridges can result in an unnecessary duplication of frames as well as confuse end stations. To avoid those problems the Spanning Tree Protocol (STP) will open a loop by placing one bridge in a standby mode of operation

circular or loop topology will create problems. Those problems can result in an unnecessary duplication of frames which will not only degrade the overall level of performance of the intercon-nected network but quite possibly confuse end-stations. For example, consider a frame whose source address is A and whose destination address is F. Both bridge 1 and bridge 2 will forward the frame. Although bridge 1 will forward the frame to its appropriate network using the most direct route, the frame will also be forwarded by bridge 3 to Ethernet 2, resulting in a duplicate frame arriving at workstation F. At workstation F a mechanism would be required to reject duplicate frames. Even if such a mechanism is available, the additional traffic flowing across multiple internet paths would result in an increase in network utilization approaching 100%. This in turn would saturate some networks, while significantly reducing the level of performance of other networks. For those reasons transparent bridging is prohibited from creating a loop or circular topology.

### Spanning tree protocol

The problem of active loops was addressed by the IEEE Committee 802 in the 802.1D standard with an intelligent algorithm known as the Spanning Tree Protocol (STP). The STP is based upon graph theory and converts a loop into a tree topology by disabling a link. This action ensures that there is a unique path from any node in an internet to every other node. Disabled nodes are then kept in a standby mode of operation until a network failure occurs. At that time, the spanning tree protocol will attempt to construct a new tree using any of the previously disabled links.

*Operation*

To illustrate the operation of the spanning tree protocol, we must first become familiar with the difference between the physical and active topology of bridged networks. In addition, there are a number of terms associated with the spanning tree algorithm defined by the protocol that we should become familiar with. Thus, we will also review those terms prior to discussing the operation of the algorithm.

### Physical versus active topology

In transparent bridging, a distinction is made between the physical and active topology resulting from bridged local area networks. This distinction enables the construction of a network topology in which inactive but physically constructed routes can be put into operation if a primary route should fail and in which the inactive and active routes would form an illegal circular path violating the spanning tree algorithm if both routes were active at the same time.

The top of Figure 7.3 illustrates one possible physical topology of bridged networks. The cost (C) assigned to each bridge will be discussed later in this chapter. The lower portion of Figure 7.3 illustrates a possible active topology for the physical configuration shown at the top of that illustration.

When a bridge is used to construct an active path, it will forward frames through those ports used to form active paths. The ports through which frames are forwarded are said to be in a forwarding state of operation. Ports that cannot forward frames due to their operation forming a loop are said to be in a blocking state of operation.

Under the spanning tree algorithm, a port in a blocking state can be placed into a forwarding state and it provides a path that becomes part of the active network topology. This new path must not form a closed loop, and it usually occurs due to the

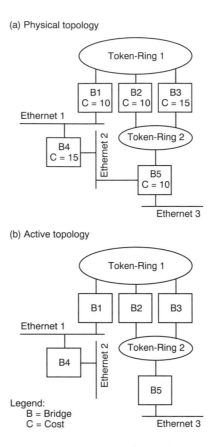

**Figure 7.3** Physical versus active topology. When transparent bridges are used, the active topology cannot form a closed loop in the Internet

failure of another path, bridge component, or the reconfiguration of interconnected networks.

### Spanning tree algorithm

The basis for the spanning tree algorithm is a tree structure because a tree forms a pattern of connections that has no loops. The term spanning is used because the branches of a tree structure span or connect subnetworks.

As a review for readers unfamiliar with graph theory, let us examine the concept behind spanning trees. To appropriately do so we need a point of reference, so let us begin with the graph structure shown at the top of Figure 7.4. A spanning tree of a graph is a subgraph that connects all nodes and represents a

A. Network graph

B. Possible spanning trees

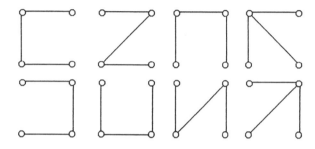

**Figure 7.4** Forming spanning trees from a network graph

tree. The graph shown at the top of Figure 7.4 has eight distinct spanning trees. The lower portion of Figure 7.4 illustrates the spanning trees associated with the graph structure illustrated above.

*Minimum spanning tree*

Suppose that the links connecting each node are assigned a length or weight. Then the weight of a tree represents the sum of its links or edges. If the weights or lengths of the links or tree edges differ, then different tree structures will have different weights. Thus, the identification of the minimum spanning tree requires us to examine each of the spanning trees supported by a graph and identify the structure that has the minimum length or weight.

The identification of the minimum spanning tree can be accomplished by listing all spanning trees and finding the minimum weight or length associated with the list. This is a brute-force method that always works but is not exactly efficient, especially when a graph becomes complex and can contain a significant number of trees. A far better method is obtained by the use of an appropriate algorithm.

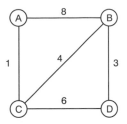

**Figure 7.5** A weighted network graph

*Kruskal's algorithm*

There are several popular algorithms that have been developed for solving the minimum spanning tree of a graph. One of those algorithms is the Kruskal algorithm which is relatively easy to understand and will be used to illustrate the computation of a minimum spanning tree. As we need weights or lengths assigned to each edge or link in a graph, let us revise the network graph previously shown in Figure 7.3 and add some weights. Figure 7.5 illustrates the weighted graph.

Kruskal's algorithm can be expressed as follows:

1. Sort the edges of the graph (G) in their increasing order by weight or length.

2. Construct a subgraph (S) of G and initially set it to the empty state.

3. For each edge (e) in sorted order:
   If the endpoints of the edges (e) are disconnected in S, add them to S.

Using the graph shown in Figure 7.5, let us apply Kruskal's algorithm as follows:

1. The sorted edges of the graph in increasing order by weight or length produce the following table:

| Edge | Weight/Length |
|------|---------------|
| A-C | 1 |
| B-D | 3 |
| C-B | 4 |
| C-D | 6 |
| A-B | 8 |

2.  Set the subgraph of G to the empty state. Thus, S = null.

3.  For each edge add to S as long as the endpoints are disconnected. Thus, the first operation produces:

S = A,C or

The next operation produces:

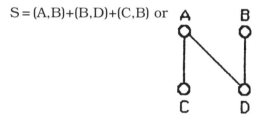

S = (A,C)+(B,D) or

The third operation produces:

S = (A,B)+(B,D)+(C,B) or

Note that we cannot continue as the endpoints in S are now all connected. Thus, the minimum spanning tree consists of the edges or links (A,B)+(B,D)+(C,B) and has the weight 1+4+3, or 7. Now that we have an appreciation for the method by which a minimum spanning tree is formed, let us turn our attention to its applicability in transparent bridge based networks.

*Root bridge and bridge identifiers*

Similarly to the root of a tree, one bridge in a spanning tree network will be assigned to a unique position in the network.

Known as the root bridge, this bridge is assigned as the top of the spanning tree and it has the potential to carry the largest amount of internet traffic due to its position.

As bridges and bridge ports can be active or inactive a mechanism is required to identify bridges and bridge ports. Each bridge in a spanning tree network is assigned a unique bridge identifier. This identifier is the MAC address on the bridge's lowest port number and a two-byte bridge priority level. The priority level is defined when a bridge is installed and functions as a bridge number. Similarly to the bridge priority level, each adapter on a bridge which functions as a port has a two-byte port identifier. Thus, the unique bridge identifier and port identifier enable each port on a bridge to be uniquely identified.

*Path cost* Under the spanning tree algorithm, the difference in physical routes between bridges is recognized and a mechanism is provided to indicate the preference for one route over another. That mechanism is accomplished by the ability to assign a path cost to each path. Thus, you could assign a low cost to a preferred route and a high cost to a route that you only want to be used in a backup situation.

Once path costs have been assigned to each path in an internet, each bridge will have one or more costs associated with different paths to the root bridge. One of those costs is lower than all the other path costs. That cost is known as the bridge's root path cost and the port used to provide the least path cost towards the root bridge is known as the root port.

*Designated bridge* As previously discussed, the spanning tree algorithm does not permit active loops in an interconnected network. To prevent this situation from occurring, only one bridge linking two networks can be in a forwarding state at any particular time. That bridge is known as the designated bridge, while all other bridges linking two networks will not forward frames and will be in a blocking state of operation.

### Constructing the spanning tree

The spanning tree algorithm employs a three-step process to develop an active topology. First, the root bridge is identified. In Figure 7.3B we will assume that bridge 1 was selected as the root bridge. Next, the path cost from each bridge to the root bridge is determined and the minimum cost from each bridge becomes the root path cost. The port in the direction of the least path cost to the root bridge, known as the root port, is then determined for each bridge. If the root path cost is the same for two or more bridges linking LANs, then the bridge with the highest priority will be selected to furnish the minimum path cost. Once the paths have been selected, the designated ports are activated.

In examining Figure 7.3A, let us now use the cost entries assigned to each bridge. Let us assume that bridge 1 was selected as the root bridge, as we expect a large amount of traffic to flow between Token-Ring 1 and Ethernet 1 networks. Therefore, bridge 1 will become the designated bridge between Token-Ring 1 and Ethernet 1 networks.

In examining the path costs to the root bridge, note that the path through bridge 2 was assigned a cost of 10, and the path through bridge 3 was assigned a cost of 15. Thus, the path from Token-Ring 2 via bridge 2 to Token-Ring 1 becomes the designated bridge between those two networks. Hence, Figure 7.3B shows bridge 3 inactive by the omission of a connection to the Token-Ring 2 network. Similarly, the path cost for connecting the Ethernet 3 network to the root bridge is lower by routing through the Token-Ring 2 and Token-Ring 1 networks. Thus, bridge 5 becomes the designated bridge for the Ethernet 3 and Token-Ring 2 networks.

**Bridge Protocol Data Unit**

One question that is probably in readers' minds by now is: how does each bridge know whether or not to participate in a spanned tree topology? Bridges obtain topology information by the use of Bridge Protocol Data Unit (BPDU) frames.

The root bridge is responsible for periodically transmitting a HELLO BPDU frame to all networks to which it is connected. According to the spanning tree protocol, HELLO frames must be transmitted every 1 to 10 seconds. The BPDU has the group MAC address 800143000000 which is recognized by each bridge. A designated bridge will then update the path cost and timing information and forward the frame. A standby bridge will monitor the BPDUs but does not update nor forward them.

When a standby bridge is required to assume the role of the root or designated bridge as the operational states of other bridges change, the HELLO BPDU will indicate that a standby bridge should become a designated bridge. The process by which bridges determine their role in a spanning tree network is an iterative process. As new bridges enter a network they assume a listening state to determine their role in the network. Similarly, when a bridge is removed, another iterative process occurs to reconfigure the remaining bridges.

Although the STP algorithm procedure eliminates duplicate frame and degraded internet performance, it can be a hindrance for situations where multiple paths between networks are desired. Another disadvantage of the spanning tree protocol occurs when it is used in remote bridges connecting geographically dispersed networks. For example, suppose that Ethernet 1 was located in Los Angeles, Ethernet 2 in New York and Ethernet 3 in Atlanta. If the link between Los Angeles and New York were to be put in a standby mode of operation, all frames from Ethernet 2 routed to Ethernet 1 would be routed through Atlanta. Depending upon the traffic between networks, this situation may require an upgrade in the bandwidth of the links connecting each network to accommodate the extra traffic flowing through Atlanta. As the yearly cost of upgrading a 56 or 64 Kbps circuit to a 128 Kbps fractional T1 link can easily exceed the cost of a bridge or router, you may wish to consider the use of routers to accommodate this networking situation. In comparison, when using local bridges, their higher operating rate in interconnecting local area networks will normally allow an acceptable level of performance to occur when LAN traffic is routed through an intermediate bridge.

*Protocol dependency*

Another problem associated with the use of transparent bridges concerns the differences between Ethernet and IEEE 802.3 frame field compositions. As previously noted in Chapter 3, the Ethernet frame contains a type field which indicates the higher layer protocol in use. Under the IEEE 802.3 frame format the type field is replaced by a length field and the data field is subdivided to include logical link control (LLC) information in the form of destination (DSAP) and source (SSAP) service access points. Here the DSAP and SSAP are similar to the type field in an Ethernet frame as they also point to a higher level process. Unfortunately, this small difference can create problems when using a transparent bridge to interconnect Ethernet and IEEE 802.3 networks.

The top portion of Figure 7.6 illustrates the use of a bridge to connect an AppleTalk network supporting several Macintosh

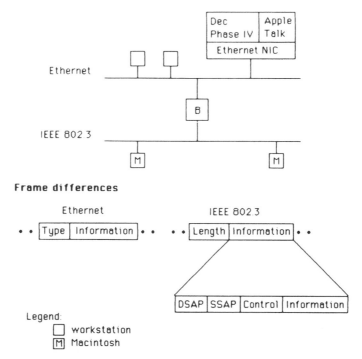

**Figure 7.6** Protocol differences preclude linking IEEE 802.3 and Ethernet networks using transparent bridges. A Macintosh computer connected on an IEEE 802.3 network using AppleTalk will not have its frame pointed to the right process on a VAX on an Ethernet. Thus, the differences between Ethernet and IEEE 802.3 networks require transparent bridges to interconnect similar networks

computers to an Ethernet network on which a Digital Equipment Corporation VAX computer is located. Although the VAX may be capable of supporting DecNet Phase IV which is true Ethernet and AppleTalk if both modules are resident, a pointer is required to direct the IEEE 802.3 frames generated by the Macintosh to the right protocol on the VAX. Unfortunately, the Ethernet connection used by the VAX will not provide the required pointer, and this explains why you should avoid connecting Ethernet and IEEE 802.3 networks via transparent bridges. Fortunately, almost all 'Ethernet' network interface cards (NICs) manufactured today are IEEE 802.3 compatible which alleviates this problem; however, older NICs may operate as true Ethernets and result in the previously mentioned problem.

### 7.1.2 Source routing

Source routing is a bridging technique developed by IBM for connecting Token-Ring networks. The key to the implementa-

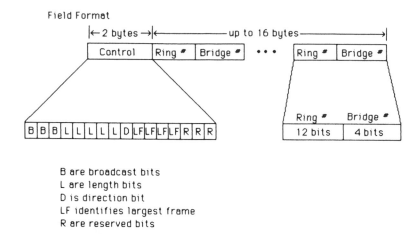

B are broadcast bits
L are length bits
D is direction bit
LF identifies largest frame
R are reserved bits

**Figure 7.7**  Token-Ring route information field. The Token-Ring route information field is variable in length

tion of source routing is the use of a portion of the information field in the Token-Ring frame to carry routing information and the transmission of 'discovery' packets to determine the best route between two networks.

The presence of source routing is indicated by the setting of the first bit position in the source address field to a binary one. When set, this indicates that the information field is preceded by a route information field (RIF) which contains both control and routing information.

Figure 7.7 illustrates the composition of a Token-Ring route information field (RIF). This field is variable in length and is developed during a discovery process which is described later in this section.

The control field contains information which defines how information will be transferred and interpreted as well as the size of the remainder of the RIF. The length bits identify the length of the RIF in bytes, while the D bit indicates how the field is scanned, left to right or right to left. As vendors have incorporated different memory in bridges which may limit frame sizes, the LF bits enable different devices to negotiate the size of the frame. Normally a default setting indicates a frame size of 512 bytes. Each bridge can select a number, and if supported by other bridges, that number is then used to represent the negotiated frame size. Otherwise, a smaller number used to represent a smaller frame size is selected and the negotiation process is repeated.

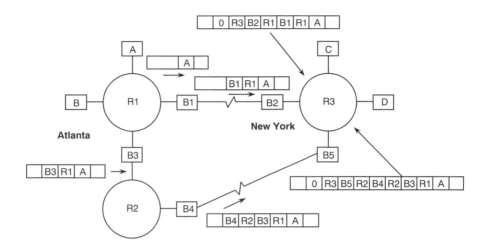

**Figure 7.8** Source routing discovery operation. The route discovery process results in each bridge entering the originating ring number and its bridge number into the route information field

Up to eight route number sub-fields, each consisting of a 12 bit ring number and a four-bit bridge number, can be contained in the routing information field. Both ring numbers and bridge numbers are expressed as hexadecimal characters, with three hex characters used to denote the ring number and one hex character used to identify the bridge number.

*Operation*

To illustrate the concept behind source routing consider the internet illustrated in Figure 7.8. In this example let us assume that two Token-Ring networks are located in Atlanta and one network is located in New York.

Each Token-Ring and bridge is assigned ring and bridge numbers. For simplicity, ring numbers R1, R2 and R3 were used, although as previously explained, those numbers are actually represented in hexadecimal. Similarly, for simplicity, bridge numbers are shown as B1, B2, B3, B4 and B5 instead of a hexadecimal character.

When a workstation wants to originate communications it is responsible for finding the destination by transmitting a discovery packet to network bridges and other network workstations whenever it has a message to transmit to a new destination address. Assuming that workstation A wishes to transmit to station C, it sends a route discovery packet which contains an empty route information field and its source address as indicated in the upper left portion of Figure 7.8. This packet is recognized by each source routing bridge in the network. When received by a source routing bridge, the bridge enters the ring number from which the packet was received and its own bridge identifier in the packet's routing information field. The bridge then transmits the packet to all its connections, with the exception of the connection on which the packet was received, a process known as flooding. Depending upon the topology of the interconnected networks, multiple copies of the discovery packet will reach the recipient. This is illustrated in the upper right corner of Figure 7.8 in which two discovery packets reach station C. Here one packet contains the sequence R1B1R1B2R30 where the zero indicates there is no bridging in the last ring. The second packet contains the route sequence R1B3R2B4R2B5R30. Station C then picks the best route based upon either the most direct path or the earliest arriving packet and transmits a response to the discovery packet originator. The response indicates the specific route to use and workstation A then enters that route into memory for the duration of the transmission session.

## Advantages

There are several advantages associated with the use of source routing. One advantage is the ability to construct mesh networks with loops for a fault-tolerant design which cannot be accomplished with the use of transparent bridges. Another advantage is the inclusion of routing information in the information frames. Several vendors have developed network management software products which use that information to provide statistical information concerning internet activity. Those products may assist you in determining wide area network link utilization, the need to modify the capacity of those links, or whether one or more workstations are hogging communications between networks.

## Disadvantages

Although the preceding advantages are considerable, they are not without a price. That price includes a requirement to specifically identify bridges and links, higher bursts of network activity, and an incompatibility between Token-Ring and Ethernet networks. In addition, due to the structure of the Route Information Field which supports a maximum of seven entries, routing of frames is restricted to crossing a maximum of seven bridges.

When using source routing bridges to connect Token-Ring networks you must configure each bridge with a unique bridge/ ring number. In addition, unless you wish to accept the default method by which workstations select a packet during the route discovery process, you will have to reconfigure your LAN software. Thus, source routing creates an administrative burden not present when using transparent bridges.

Due to the route discovery process the flooding of packets occurs in bursts when stations are powered on or after a power outage. Depending upon the complexity of an internetwork, the discovery process can degrade network performance. Perhaps the biggest problem is for organizations that require the interconnection of Ethernet and Token-Ring networks.

A source routing bridge can only be used to interconnect Token-Ring networks since it operates on Route Information Field data which is not included in an Ethernet frame. Although transparent bridges can operate in Ethernet, Token-Ring and mixed environments, their use precludes the ability to construct loop or mesh topologies and inhibits the ability to establish operationally redundant paths for load sharing. Another problem associated with bridging Ethernet and Token-Ring networks also involves the Route Information Field in a Token-Ring frame. Unfortunately, different LAN operating systems use the RIF data in different ways. Thus, the use of a transparent bridge to interconnect Ethernet and Token-Ring networks may require the same local area network operating system on each network. To alleviate these problems several vendors introduced source routing transparent (SRT) bridges.

## 7.1.3 Source routing transparent bridges

A source routing transparent bridge supports both IBM source routing and IEEE 802.1D transparent spanning tree protocol operations. This type of bridge can be considered as two bridges in one and has been standardized by the IEEE 802.1 committee.

*Operation*

Under source routing the media access control packets contain a status bit in the source field which identifies whether or not source routing is to be used for a message. If source routing is indicated, the bridge forwards the frame as a source routing frame. If source routing is not indicated, the bridge determines the destination address and processes the packet using a transparent mode of operation, using bridging tables generated by a spanning tree algorithm.

*Advantages*

There are several advantages associated with the use of source routing transparent bridges. First and perhaps foremost, its use enables different networks to use different local area network operating systems and protocols. This capability enables you to interconnect networks developed independently of one another and allows an organization's departments and branches to use LAN operating systems without restriction. Secondly and also very importantly, source routing transparent bridges can connect Ethernet and Token-Ring networks while preserving the ability to mesh or loop Token-Ring networks. Thus, its use provides an additional level of flexibility for network construction.

## 7.2 NETWORK UTILIZATION

In this section we will examine the use of bridges to interconnect separate local area networks as well as to subdivide networks to improve performance. In addition, we will also focus our attention on how we can increase network availability by employing bridges to provide alternate communications paths between networks.

### 7.2.1 Serial and sequential bridging

The top of Figure 7.9 illustrates the basic use of a bridge to interconnect two networks serially. Suppose that monitoring of each network indicates a high level of intra-network utilization.

One possible configuration to reduce intra-LAN traffic on each network can be obtained by moving some stations off each of the two existing networks to form a third network. The three networks would then be interconnected through the use of an additional bridge as illustrated in the middle portion of Figure 7.9. This extension results in sequential bridging and is appropriate when intra-LAN traffic is necessary but minimal. Both serial and sequential bridging are applicable to transparent, source routing and source routing transparent bridges which do not provide redundancy nor the ability to balance traffic flowing between networks. Each of these deficiencies can be alleviated through the use of parallel bridging. However, this bridging technique creates a loop and is only applicable to source routing transparent bridges.

### 7.2.2 Parallel bridging

The lower portion of Figure 7.9 illustrates the use of parallel bridges to interconnect two Token-Ring networks. This bridging

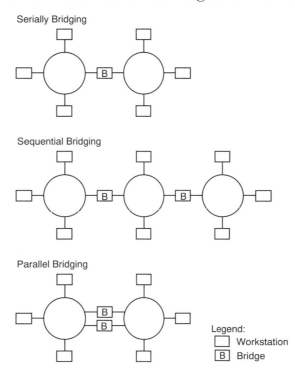

**Figure 7.9**   Serial, sequential, and parallel bridging

configuration permits one bridge to back up the other, providing a level of redundancy for linking the two networks as well as a significant increase in the availability of one network to communicate with another. For example, assume that the availability of each bridge shown in the top part of Figure 7.9 (serial bridging) and in the bottom part of Figure 7.9 (parallel bridging) is 90%. The availability through two serially connected bridges would be $0.9 \times 0.9$ or 81%. In comparison, the availability through parallel bridges would be $1 - ($unavailability of bridge $1 \times$ unavailability of bridge 2) or $1 - (0.1 \times 0.1)$, which is 99%.

The dual paths between networks also improve inter-LAN communications performance as communications between stations on each network can be load balanced. Thus, the use of parallel bridges can be expected to provide a higher level of inter-LAN communications than the use of serial or sequential bridges.

One of the more common uses of parallel bridging is to construct redundant backbone rings within a building. Typically, organizations will establish independent networks on each floor in a building and require a method to both interconnect those networks and obtain a load sharing and redundancy capability. Figure 7.10 illustrates how those goals

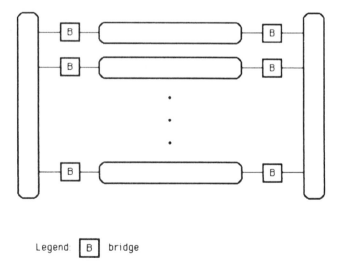

Legend: [B] bridge

**Figure 7.10** Constructing redundant backbone rings. Parallel bridging is often used in building to construct redundant backbone rings. Backbone rings are normally routed vertically within a building and connected via parallel bridges to 'floor' networks

can be accomplished through the use of parallel bridging to connect each 'floor' network to two backbone networks routed up the vertical shafts common in most buildings. Depending upon internetwork communications requirements, the backbone networks could be a different type of network than the floor networks. For example, each floor network might be a 4 Mbps Token-Ring, while the backbone networks could be 16 Mbps Token-Ring or even 100 Mbps FDDI networks.

From a performance perspective, a workstation on one network only requires at most the crossing of two bridges to reach any other workstation in the building. This provides a much lower bridging delay than connecting networks sequentially. In addition, the use of one or more backbone networks simplifies the addition of more floor networks to the building internetwork at a later date. For example, if the organization expands and leases a new floor it can connect a floor network to the building internetwork by the use of one or two bridges.

## 7.3 PERFORMANCE ISSUES

The key to obtaining an appropriate level of performance when interconnecting networks is planning. The actual planning process will depend upon several factors, such as whether or not separate networks are in operation, the type of networks to be connected and the type of bridges to be used, local or remote.

### 7.3.1 Traffic flow

If separate networks are in operation and you have appropriate monitoring equipment you can determine the traffic flow on each of the networks to be interconnected. Once this has been accomplished you can expect an approximate 10–20% increase in network traffic. This additional traffic represents the flow of information between networks after an interconnection links previously separated local area networks. Although this traffic increase represents an average encountered by the author, your network traffic may not represent the typical average. To explore further, you can examine the potential for internet communications in the form of electronic messages that may be transmitted to users on other networks, potential file transfers of word processing files and other types of data that would flow between networks.

### 7.3.2 Network types

The types of network to be connected will govern the rate at which frames are presented to bridges. This in turn will govern the filtering rate at which bridges should operate prior to their use becoming a bottleneck on a network. For example, the maximum number of frames per second will vary between different types of Ethernet and Token-Ring networks as well as between different types of the same network. Thus the operating rate of a bridge may be appropriate for connecting some networks, and inappropriate for connecting other types of networks.

### 7.3.3 Type of bridge

Last but not least, the type of bridge, local or remote, will have a considerable bearing upon performance issues. Local bridges pass data between networks at their operating rates. In comparison, remote bridges pass data between networks using wide area network transmission facilities which typically provide a transmission rate which is a fraction of a local area network operating rate. Now that we have discussed some of the aspects governing bridge and internet performance using bridges, let us probe deeper by estimating network traffic.

### 7.3.4 Estimating network traffic

If we do not have access to monitoring equipment to analyze an existing network or are planning to install a new network, we can spend some time and develop a reasonable estimate of network traffic. To do so we should attempt to classify workstations into groups based upon the type of general activity performed and then estimate the network activity for one workstation per group. Doing so will enable us to multiply the number of workstations in the group by the workstation activity to determine the group network traffic. Summing up the activity of all groups will then provide us with an estimate of the traffic activity for the network.

As an example of local area network traffic estimation let us assume that our network will support 20 engineers, five managers and three secretaries. Table 7.1 shows how we

**Table 7.1** Estimating network traffic

| Activity | Message size (bytes) | Frequency | Bit rate[a] |
|---|---|---|---|
| *Engineering workstations* | | | |
| Request program | 1500 | 1/hour | 4 |
| Load program | 480 000 | 1/hour | 1067 |
| Save files | 120 000 | 2/hour | 533 |
| Send/receive e-mail | 2000 | 2/hour | 9 |
| | | | 1613 |
| Total engineering activity=1613 × 20=32 260 bps | | | |
| *Managerial workstations* | | | |
| Request program | 1500 | 2/hour | 7 |
| Load program | 320 000 | 2/hour | 1422 |
| Save files | 30 000 | 2/hour | 134 |
| Send/receive e-mail | 3000 | 4/hour | 27 |
| | | | 1590 |
| Total managerial activity=1590 × 5=7950 bps | | | |
| Secretarial workstations | | | |
| Request program | 1500 | 4/hour | 14 |
| Load program | 640 000 | 2/hour | 2844 |
| Save files | 12 000 | 8/hour | 214 |
| Send/receive e-mail | 3000 | 6/hour | 40 |
| | | | 3112 |
| Total secretarial activity=3112 × 3=9336 bps | | | |
| Total estimated network activity=49 546 bps | | | |

[a]Bit rate computed by multiplying message rate by frequency by 8 bits/byte and dividing by 3600 seconds/hour.

would estimate the network traffic in terms of the bit rate for each workstation group, and the total activity per group, and then sum up the network traffic for the three groups that will use the network. In this example, which for simplicity did not include the transmission of data to a workstation printer, the total network traffic was estimated to be slightly below 50 000 bps.

To plan for the interconnection of two or more networks through the use of bridges our next step should be to perform a similar traffic analysis for each of the remaining networks. After this has been accomplished we can use the network traffic to estimate inter-LAN traffic, using 10–20% of total intra-network traffic as an estimate of the internet traffic that will result from the connection of separate networks.

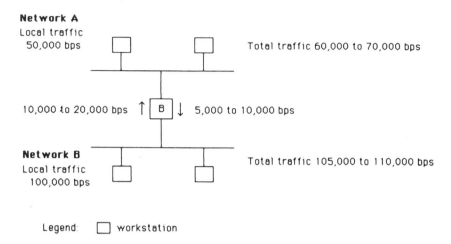

Legend: ☐ workstation

**Figure 7.11** Considering internet data flow. To determine the traffic flow on separate networks after they are interconnected you must consider the flow of data onto each network from the other network

## Internet traffic

To illustrate the traffic estimation process for the interconnection of separate LANs let us assume that network A traffic was determined to be 50 000 bps while the network B traffic was estimated to be approximately 100 000 bps. Figure 7.11 illustrates the flow of data between networks connected via a local bridge. Note that the data flow in each direction is expressed as a range based upon the use of an industry average of 10–20% of network traffic routed between interconnected networks.

## Network types

Our next area of concern is to examine the types of network to be interconnected. In doing so we should focus our attention upon the operating rate of each LAN. If the network A traffic was estimated to be approximately 50 000 bps, then the addition of 10 000 to 20 000 bps from network B onto network A will raise the network A traffic level to between 60 000 and 70 000 bps. Similarly, the addition of traffic from network A onto network B will raise the network B traffic level to between 105 000 and 110 000 bps. In this example the resulting traffic on each network is well below the operating rate of all types of local area networks and will not present a capacity problem for either network to be interconnected.

*Bridge type*

As previously mentioned, local bridges transmit data between networks at the data rate of the destination network. This means that a local bridge will have a lower probability of being an internet bottleneck than a remote bridge, since the latter provides a connection between networks using a wide area transmission facility which typically operates at a fraction of the operating rate of a LAN.

In examining the bridge operating rate required to connect networks we will use a bottom-up and a top-down approach. That is, we will first determine the operating rate in frames per second for the specific example previously discussed. This will be followed by computing the maximum frame rate supported by Ethernet and Token-Ring networks.

For the bridge illustrated in Figure 7.11, we previously computed that its maximum transfer rate would be 20 000 bps from network B onto network A. This is equivalent to 2500 bytes per second. If we assume that data is transported in 512 byte frames, this would be equivalent to 6 frames per second, a minimal transfer rate supported by every bridge manufacturer. However, when remote bridges are used the frame forwarding rate of the bridge will more than likely be constrained by the operating rate of the wide area network transmission facility.

## 7.3.5 Bridge operational considerations

A remote bridge wraps a LAN frame into a higher level protocol packet for transmission over a wide area network communications facility. This operation requires the addition of a header, protocol control, error detection and trailer fields and results in a degree of overhead. Thus, a 20 000 bps data flow from network B to network A could not be accommodated by a transmission facility operating at that data rate.

In converting LAN traffic onto a wide area network transmission facility you can expect a protocol overhead of approximately 20%. Thus, your actual operating rate must be at least 24 000 bps prior to the wide area network communications link becoming a bottleneck that would degrade internet communication. Now that we have examined the bridging performance requirements for two relatively small networks, let us focus our attention upon determining the maximum frame rates of Ethernet and Token-Ring networks.

Doing so will provide us with the ability to determine the rate at which the frame processing rate of a bridge becomes irrelevant, since any processing rate above the maximum network rate will not be useful. In addition, we can use the maximum network frame rate when estimating traffic, since if we approach that rate network performance will begin to significantly degrade when utilization exceeds between 40 and 50% of that rate for Ethernet LANs and between 80 and 90% for Token-Ring networks.

*Ethernet traffic*

In Chapter 3 we noted that an Ethernet frame can vary between a minimum of 72 bytes and a maximum of 1526 bytes. Thus, the maximum frame rate on an Ethernet will vary based upon the frame size.

Ethernet operations require a 'dead' time between frames of 9.6 ms. The bit time for a 10 Mbps Ethernet is $1/10^7$ or 100 ns. Based upon the preceding we can compute the maximum number of frames per second for 1526 byte frames. Here the time per frame becomes:

$$9.6\,\mu s + 1526 \text{ bytes} \times 8 \text{ bits/byte}$$
$$\text{or } 9.6\,\mu s + 12\,208 \text{ bits} \times 100 \text{ ns/bit}$$
$$\text{or } 1.23\,\text{ms}.$$

Thus, in one second there can be a maximum of $1/1.23$ ms or 812 maximum-size frames. For a minimum frame size of 72 bytes the time per frame is:

$$9.6\,\mu s + 72 \text{ bytes} \times 8 \text{ bits/byte} \times 100 \text{ ns/bit}$$
$$\text{or } 67.2 \times 10^{-6}\,\text{s}.$$

Thus, in one second there can be a maximum of $1/67.2 \times 10^{-6}$ or 14 880 minimum-size 72 byte frames. As 100BASE-T Fast Ethernet uses the same frame composition as Ethernet, the maximum frame rate for maximum and minimum length frames are ten times that of Ethernet. That is, Fast Ethernet supports a maximum of 8120 maximum size 1526 byte frames per second

**Table** 7.2 Ethernet frame processing requirements (frames per second)

| Average frame size (bytes) | Frame processing requirements | |
|---|---|---|
| | 50% load | 100% load |
| Ethernet | | |
| 1526 | 405 | 812 |
| 72 | 7440 | 14 880 |
| Fast Ethernet | | |
| 1526 | 4050 | 8120 |
| 72 | 74 400 | 148 800 |

and a maximum of 148 800 minimum size 72 byte frames per second. Table 7.2 summarizes the frame processing requirements for a 10 and a 100 Mbps Ethernet under 50% and 100% load conditions based upon minimum and maximum frame sizes. Note that those frame processing requirements define the frame examination (filtering) operating rate of a bridge connected to an Ethernet or Fast Ethernet Network. For example, that rate indicates the number of frames per second a bridge connected to a 10 Mbps Ethernet local area network must be capable of examining under heavy (50% load) and full (100% load) traffic conditions.

We can extend our analysis of Ethernet frames by considering the frame rate supported by different link speeds. For example, let us consider a pair of remote bridges connected by a 9.6 Kbps line. The time per frame for a 72 byte frame at 9.6 Kbps is:

$$9.6 \times 10^{-6} + 72 \times 8 \times 0.000\,104\,1 \text{ s/bit}$$
$$\text{or } 0.059\,971\,2 \text{ s/frame.}$$

Thus, in 1 s the number of frames is 1/0.059 971 2 or 16.67 frames per second. Table 7.3 compares the frame per second rate supported by different link speeds for minimum and maximum size Ethernet frames. As expected, the frame transmission rate supported by 10 and 100 Mbps links for minimum and maximum size frames are exactly the same as the frame processing requirements under 100% loading as previously indicated in Table 7.2.

In examining Table 7.3 readers should note that the entries in this table do not consider the effect of the overhead of a protocol used to transport frames between two networks. Thus, readers should decrease the frame per second rate by approximately

**Table 7.3**  Link speed versus frame rate

| Link speed | Frames per second | |
| --- | --- | --- |
| | Minimum frame size | Maximum frame size |
| 9.6 Kbps | 16.67 | 0.79 |
| 19.2 Kbps | 33.38 | 1.58 |
| 56.0 Kbps | 97.44 | 4.60 |
| 64.0 Kbps | 111.17 | 5.25 |
| 1.536 Mbps | 2815.31 | 136.34 |
| 10 Mbps | 14 880 | 812 |
| 100 Mbps | 148 800 | 8120 |

20% for all link speeds through 1.536 Mbps. The reason the 10 and 100 Mbps rates should not be adjusted is because they represent local bridge connections that do not require the use of a wide area network protocol to transport frames. Readers should also note that the link speed of 1.536 Mbps represents a T1 transmission facility that operates at 1.544 Mbps. However, since the framing bits on a T1 circuit use 8 Kbps, the effective line speed available for the transmission of data is 1.536 Mbps.

## Token-Ring traffic

In comparison to Ethernet the modeling of a Token-Ring network can be much more complex. This is because the frame rate depends upon the number of nodes in a network, the token holding time per node, the type of wire used for cabling and ring length, and the type of adapter used as a ring interface unit.

The number of nodes and their cabling govern both token propagation time and holding time as a token flows around the ring. The type of adapter used governs the maximum frame rate supported. This rate can vary between vendors as well as within a vendor's product line. For example, Texas Instruments' original MAC code permitted a maximum transmission of 2200 64 Kbyte frames per second. New software from that vendor raised the frame rate to 3300, and a more recent release known as Turbo MAC 2.1 increased it to 4000 frames per second.

The type of cabling and ring length governs the propagation delay associated with the flow of tokens and frames around the ring. Although the data rate around a ring is consistent at either 4 Mbps or 16 Mbps, tokens and frames do not flow instantaneously around the ring and are delayed, based upon the distance they must traverse and the type of cabling used. In addition, a slight delay is encountered at each node since the token must be examined to determine its status.

In developing a model to determine Token-Ring frame rates, let us assume that there are $N$ stations on the network. Then on the average a token will travel $N/2$ stations until it is grabbed and converted into a frame. Similarly, a frame can be expected to travel $N/2$ stations until it reaches its destination and another $N/2$ stations until it returns to the origination station and is reconverted back into a token. In free space the velocity of light is 186 000 miles per second. In a twisted-pair cable the speed of electrons is approximately 62% of the velocity of light in free space. Thus, electrons will travel at approximately $186\,000 \times 0.62$ or 115 320 miles per second. This rate is equivalent to 608 889 600 feet per second or approximately 609 feet per microsecond. To traverse 1000 feet of cable would then require $1.6 \times 10^{-6}$ seconds. At a Token-Ring operating rate of 4 Mbps this is equivalent to a 6.4 $(=1.6 \times 10^{-6}/2.5 \times 10^{-7})$ bit time delay per 1000 feet of twisted-pair cable.

For the development of our Token-Ring performance model let us start with the flow of a token as indicated by the following steps in the model development process.

1. A free token travels on the average $N/2$ stations until it is grabbed and converted into a frame.

2. Each station adds a 2.5 bit time delay to examine the token. At a 4 Mbps ring operating rate a bit time equals $2.5 \times 10^{-7}$ seconds. Thus, each station induces a delay of $6.25 \times 10^{-7}$ seconds.

3. The token consists of three bytes or 24 bits. The time required for the token to be placed onto the ring is:

$$24 \times 2.5 \times 10^{-7} = 60 \times 10^{-7} \text{ seconds.}$$

4. The time for the token to be placed onto the ring and flow around half the ring until it is grabbed then becomes:

$$N/2 \times 6.25 \times 10^{-7} + 60 \times 10^{-7} \text{ seconds.}$$

5. Once a token is grabbed it is converted into a frame. On the average the frame will travel $N/2$ stations to its destination. A frame containing 64 bytes of information consists of 85 bytes since starting and ending delimiters, source and destination addresses and other control information must be included in the frame. Thus, the time required to place the frame on the ring becomes:

$$85 \times 8 \times 2.5 \times 10^{-7} = 1.7 \times 10^{-4} \text{ seconds.}$$

6. The frame must traverse $N/2$ stations on the average to reach its destination. Thus, the time required for the frame to be placed on the ring and traverse half the ring becomes:

$$N/2 \times 6.25 \times 10^{-7} + 1.7 \times 10^{-4} \text{ seconds.}$$

7. The total token and frame time from paragraphs 4 and 6 above is:

$$N/2 \times 6.25 \times 10^{-7} + 60 \times 10^{-7}$$
$$+ N/2 \times 6.25 \times 10^{-7} + 1.7 \times 10^{-4} \text{ seconds}$$

or

$$N \times 6.25 \times 10^{-7} + 60 \times 10^{-7} + 1.7 \times 10^{-4} \text{ seconds.}$$

8. To consider the effect of propagation delay time as tokens and frames flow in the cable we must consider the sum of the ring length and twice the sum of all lobe distances. Here we must double the lobe distances since the token will flow to and from each workstation on the lobe. If we let $C$ equal the number of thousands of feet of cable, we obtain the time in seconds to traverse the ring as:

$$N \times 6.25 \times 10^{-17} + 60 \times 10^{-7} + 1.7 \times 10^{-4} + 1.6 \times 10^{-6} \times C$$

which equals:

$$N \times 6.25 \times 10^{-7} + 1.76 \times 10^{-4} + 1.6 \times 10^{-6} \times C$$

where:

$N$=number of stations
$C$=thousands of feet of cable.

To illustrate the use of the previously developed equation let us assume that a Token-Ring network of 50 stations has 8000 feet of cable. Then, the time for a token and frame to circulate the ring becomes:

$$50 \times 6.25 \times 10^{-7} + 1.76 \times 10^{-4} + 1.6 \times 10^{-6} \times 8$$
$$= 312.5 \times 10^{-7} + 1.76 \times 10^{-4} + 12.8 \times 10^{-6}$$
$$= 0.3125 \times 10^{-4} + 1.76 \times 10^{-4} + 0.128 \times 10^{-4}$$
$$= 2.2005 \times 10^{-4} \text{ seconds.}$$

Then, in 1 second there will be on the average $1/2.2005 \times 10^{-4}$ or 4544 64 byte information frames that can flow on a Token-Ring network containing 50 stations and a total of 8000 feet of cable. To illustrate the use of the previously developed formula let us now consider what happens when the network is reduced in size. Suppose that the number of workstations is halved to 25 and the total cable distance reduced to 4000 feet. Then, the time for a token and frame to flow around the ring becomes:

$$25 \times 6.25 \times 10^{-7} + 1.76 \times 10^{-4} + 1.6 \times 10^{-6} \times 4$$
$$= 0.15625 \times 10^{-4} + 1.76 \times 10^{-4} + 0.064 \times 10^{-4}$$
$$= 1.98025 \times 10^{-4} \text{ seconds.}$$

Thus, in 1 second there will be on the average $1/1.98025 \times 10^{-4}$ or 5049 64 byte information frames. As we would intuitively expect, as the number of stations and cable distance decrease the transmission capacity of the ring increases.

Tables 7.4 and 7.5 indicate the frame rates achievable on Token-Ring networks containing 8000 and 10000 feet of cable. Each table indicates the frame rate based upon the number of stations on the network.

Now let us examine the effect of transmitting larger information frames. Suppose we transmit 4000 byte information frames. Here a total of 4021 bytes are required. Thus, the time required for the frame to be placed on the ring becomes:

$$4021 \times 8 \times 2.5 \times 10^{-7} \text{ or } 80.42 \times 10^{-4} \text{ seconds.}$$

Then, the total token and frame time becomes:

**Table 7.4** Stations versus frame rate: 64 byte information frame, 8000 feet of cable

| Stations | Frames/second |
| --- | --- |
| 10 | 5126 |
| 20 | 4967 |
| 30 | 4818 |
| 40 | 4677 |
| 50 | 4544 |
| 60 | 4418 |
| 70 | 4300 |
| 80 | 4187 |
| 90 | 4080 |
| 100 | 3979 |
| 110 | 3882 |
| 120 | 3790 |
| 130 | 3703 |
| 140 | 3619 |
| 150 | 3539 |
| 160 | 3462 |
| 170 | 3389 |
| 180 | 3318 |
| 190 | 3251 |
| 200 | 3186 |

**Table 7.5** Stations versus frame rate: 64 byte information frame, 10 000 feet of cable

| Stations | Frames/second |
| --- | --- |
| 10 | 5044 |
| 20 | 4889 |
| 30 | 4744 |
| 40 | 4608 |
| 50 | 4479 |
| 60 | 4357 |
| 70 | 4241 |
| 80 | 4132 |
| 90 | 4028 |
| 100 | 3929 |
| 110 | 3835 |
| 120 | 3745 |
| 130 | 3659 |
| 140 | 3577 |
| 150 | 3499 |
| 160 | 3424 |
| 170 | 3352 |
| 180 | 3284 |
| 190 | 3218 |
| 200 | 3154 |

$$N \times 6.25 \times 10^{-7} + 60 \times 10^{-7}$$
$$+ 80.42 \times 10^{-4} + 1.6 \times 10^{-6} \times C \text{ seconds.}$$

Again, let us assume that the number of stations, $N$, is 50, while the cabling distance is 8000 feet. Thus, we obtain the token and frame revolution time as follows:

$$50 \times 6.25 \times 10^{-7} + 60 \times 10^{-7} + 80.42 \times 10^{-4} + 1.6 \times 10^{-6} \times 8$$
$$= 0.3125 \times 10^{-4} + 0.06 \times 10^{-4} + 80.42 \times 10^{-4} + 0.128 \times 10^{-4}$$
$$= 80.9205 \times 10^{-4} \text{ seconds.}$$

Then, in 1 second there will be $1/80.9205 \times 10^{-4}$ or 123.6 frames. As each frame contains 4000 bytes of information, the effective operating rate becomes $123.6 \times 4000 \times 8$ or 3.955 Mbps for a 50-station Token-Ring network with 8000 feet of cable using 4000 character frames. In comparison, a similar Token-Ring network using 64 byte information frames would have a frame rate of 4544 frames per second. However, this rate would be equivalent to an information transfer rate of 2.326 Mbps. Thus, whenever possible larger frame sizes should be used on a Token-Ring network.

The preceding computations which represent simplified models of a 4 Mbps Token-Ring network indicate an important concept. That is, both the cabling distance and number of network stations govern the maximum frame rate that can flow on a Token-Ring network. This tells us that we should consider breaking larger networks into subnetworks interconnected by bridges to improve network performance.

One of the more interesting aspects of Token-Ring frame rates is that the majority of adapter cards from different vendors which use the Texas Instrument chip set support a maximum frame rate of 4000 frames per second. This indicates that a further constraint to the number of nodes and cable length is the adapter cards used in a network. In 1991 Madge Systems introduced an adapter card which was capable of transmitting approximately 12 000 64 byte frames per second. Thus, using that firm's adapter cards or other higher performance adapter cards can significantly improve the performance of a Token-Ring network. However, the use of such 'high performance' adapter cards is irrelevant when a network grows in size in terms of the number of network stations and cable distance. In such situations the capability of high performance network adapter cards will not be effectively used.

Another situation concerning the performance of an adapter card that requires a degree of elaboration is when a vendor specifies a frame processing capability without indicating the frame length being processed. For example, IBM's Direct Networking Winter 1996/1997 Catalog lists a Token-Ring adapter capable of processing over 48 000 frames per second. As a Token-Ring frame has a minimum of 21 bytes of overhead without considering the inclusion of a Routing Information Field, we can perform a few computations to obtain some interesting results. If each frame only contains one character in its Information field, then the frame processing rate results in a data rate of 22 bytes/frame × 8 bits/byte × 48 000 frames/s, or 8.448 Mbps. If each frame carries an average of 64 bytes of information, the frame processing rate would provide a transmission rate of 540.67 Mbps, clearly well above the capability of a Token-Ring network to transport data.

# 8

---

# ROUTERS

---

In Chapter 3 we examined the basic operation and utilization of a variety of local area networking components to include routers. Information presented in that chapter will serve as a foundation for a more detailed discussion of the operation and utilization of routers which is presented in this chapter.

## 8.1 ROUTER OPERATION

By operating at the ISO Reference Model network layer a router becomes capable of making intelligent decisions concerning the flow of information in a network. This enables a router to support the transmission of data on multiple paths between local area networks. Although a multiport bridge with a filtering capability can be considered to perform intelligent routing decisions, the result of a bridge operation is normally valid for only one point-to-point link within a wide area network. In comparison, a router may be able to acquire information about the status of a large number of paths and select an end-to-end path consisting of a series of point-to-point links. In addition, most routers can fragment and reassemble data. This permits packets to flow over different paths and to be reassembled at their final destination. With this capability a router can route each packet to its destination over the best possible path at a particular instant in time and dynamically change paths to correspond to changes in network link status on traffic activity.

Two additional differences between bridges and routers concern their ability to localize broadcast storms and hardware configuration. Bridges will pass broadcast MAC layer frames from one network to another. In comparison, routers can be used to limit broadcasts to individual networks.

Concerning their hardware configuration, most bridges are PC-based, resulting in their configuration flexibility being constrained by the number of system expansion slots in the system unit of the computer. In comparison, many routers are designed based upon the use of a base chassis that can be significantly expanded to accommodate the addition of a large number of LAN and WAN modules. Thus, many routers can support a much wider range of LAN and WAN interfaces. For example, both Bay Networks and Cisco Systems market routers that can be configured to support 10BASE-T, 100BASE-T, Token-Ring, and FDDI LAN connections as well as T1, E1, ISDN, and the High Speed Serial Interface (HSSI) for WAN connections.

Based upon the preceding we can generalize the use of bridges for linking relatively homogeneous protocol networks where interconnected segments form one larger network. In comparison, the use of routers should be considered when we need to establish a hierarchical network structure, limit broadcast traffic between networks, and obtain an alternate routing capability that requires multiple WAN connectors.

## IP support overview

The most popular network layer protocol supported by routers is the Internet Protocol (IP) whose packet format was described in Chapter 6. Each IP network has a distinct network address and each interface on the network has a unique host address that represents the host portion of a 32 bit address. As the IP address occurs at the network layer while frames that move data on a LAN use MAC addresses associated with the data link layer, a translation process is required to enable IP compatible devices to use the transport services of a local area network. Thus, any discussion of how routers support IP requires an overview of the manner by which hosts use the services of a router.

When a host has a packet to transmit, it will first determine if the destination IP address is on the local network or a distant network, with the latter requiring the services of a router. To accomplish this, the host will use the subnet mask bits set in its configuration to determine if the destination is on the local network. For example, assume that the subnet mask is 255.255.255.128. This means that the mask extends the network portion of an IP address to 11111111.11111111.11111111.1, or 25 bit positions, resulting in 7 (32−25) bit positions being available for the host address. This also means that you can have two subnets, with subnet 0 containing host addresses 0 to 127 and subnet 1 having host addresses 128 to 255, with the subnet defined by the value of the 25th bit position in the IP address.

If we assume that the base network IP address is 193.56.45.0, then the base network, two subnets, and the subnet mask are as follows:

Base network 11000001.00111000.00101101.00000000 = 193.56.45.0

Subnet 0:      11000001.00111000.00101101.00000000 = 193.56.45.0

Subnet 1:      11000001.00111000.00101101.10000000 = 193.56.45.128

Subnetmask: 11111111.11111111.11111111.10000000 = 193.56.45.128

Now suppose that a host with the IP address 193.56.45.21 needs to send a packet to the host whose address is 193.56.45.131. By using the subnet mask, the transmitting host notes that the destination, while on the same network, is on a different subnet. Thus, the transmitting host will require the use of a router in the same manner as if the destination host was on a completely separate network.

Figure 8.1 illustrates the internal and external network view of the subnetted network. Note that from locations exterior to the network, routers forward packets to the router connecting the two subnets as if no subnetting existed. The corporate router is configured via the use of subnet masks to differentiate hosts on one subnet from those on the other subnet. From an interior view, packets originating on one subnet must use the resources of the router to reach hosts on the other subnet as well as hosts on other networks.

Once the transmitting host notes that the destination IP address is either on a different network or different subnet, it must use the services of a router. Although each host will be configured with the IP address of the router, the host will transport packets via the data link layer, which requires knowledge of the 48 bit MAC address of the router port connected to the segment the transmitting host resides on.

The translation between IP and MAC addresses is accomplished by the use of the Address Resolution Protocol (ARP). To

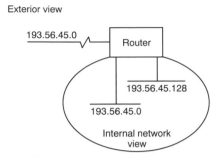

**Figure 8.1**  Using subnet masks to subdivide a common IP network address

obtain the MAC address of the router's LAN interface the host will broadcast an ARP request. This request will be received by all stations on the segment, with the router recognizing its IP address and responding by transmitting an ARP response.

As a continuous use of ARP would rapidly consume network bandwidth, hosts normally maintain the results of ARP requests in cache memory. Thus, once the relationship between an IP address and MAC address has been learned, subsequent requests to transmit additional packets to the same destination can be accomplished by the host checking its cache memory.

When packets arrive at the router destined for a host on one of the subnets, a similar process occurs. That is, the router must obtain the MAC addresses associated with the IP address to enable the packet to be transported by data link layer frames to its appropriate destination. Thus, in addition to being able to correctly support the transmission of packets from one interface to another, an IP compatible router must also support the ARP protocol. Later in this chapter we will discuss and describe additional protocols that routers can support.

### 8.1.1 Networking capability

To illustrate the networking capability of routers consider Figure 8.2 which shows three geographically dispersed locations that have a total of four Ethernet and three Token-Ring networks interconnected through the use of four routers and four wide area network transmission circuits or links. For simplicity, the use of modems or DSUs on the wide area network is not shown. This illustration will be referred to several times in this chapter to denote different types of router operations.

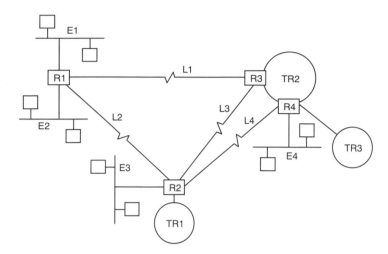

**Figure 8.2** Router operation. The use of routers enables the transmission of data over multiple paths, alternate path routing, and the use of a mesh topology which transparent bridges cannot support

In addition to supporting a mesh structure that is not obtainable from the use of transparent bridges, the use of routers offers other advantages in the form of addressing, message processing, link utilization, and priority of service. Routers are known to workstations that use their service. Hence packets can be directly addressed to a router. This eliminates the necessity for the device to examine in detail every packet flowing on a network, and results in the router only having to process messages that are addressed to it by other devices. Concerning link utilization, assume that a station on E1 transmits to a station on TR3. Depending upon the status and traffic on network links, packets could be routed via L1 and use TR2 to provide a transport mechanism to R4, from which the packets are delivered to TR3. Alternatively, links L2 and L4 could be used to provide a path from R1 to R4. Although link availability and link traffic usually determine routing, routers can support prioritized traffic and may store low priority traffic for a small period of time to allow higher priority traffic to gain access to the wide area transmission facility. Due to these features which are essentially unavailable from the use of bridges the router is a more complex and costlier device.

## 8.2 COMMUNICATIONS AND ROUTING PROTOCOLS

For routers to be able to operate in a network they must normally be able to speak the same language at both the data link and network layers. This means that the routers must communicate with one another using the same route protocol as well as the same routing control protocol.

*Routing protocols*

Examples of route protocols include Transmission Control Protocol and the Internet Protocol (TCP/IP), Xerox Network Services Internet Transport Protocol (XNS), Digital Equipment Corporation's DECnet, Novell's IPX and Apple Computer's AppleTalk. Examples of routing protocols include the Routing Information Protocol (RIP), Open Shortest Path First (OSPF), Intermediate System to Intermediate System (IS–IS), and the Routing Table Maintenance Protocol (RTMP).

### 8.2.1 Handling non-routable protocols

Although many mainframe users consider IBM's System Network Architecture (SNA) as a router protocol, in actuality it is non-routable in the traditional sense of having network addresses. This means that for a router to support SNA or another non-routable protocol, such as NetBIOS, the router cannot compare a destination network address against the current network address as there are no network addresses to work with. Instead, the router must be capable of performing one or more special operations to handle non-routable protocols. For example, some routers may be configurable such that SNA addresses in terms of Physical Units (PUs) and Logical Units (LUs) can be associated with pseudo-network numbers, enabling the router to route an unroutable protocol. Another common method employed by some routers is to incorporate a non-routable protocol within a routable protocol, a technique referred to as tunneling. A third method, and one considered by many to be the 'old reliable' mechanism, is to use bridging. Later in this chapter when we cover protocol-independent routers and in Chapter 10 when we discuss SNA in detail, we will describe methods that can be used to route non-routable protocols, including SNA traffic.

## 8.2.2 Communications protocols

There is a wide variety of communications protocols in use today. Some of these protocols were designed specifically to operate on local area networks, such as Apple Computer's AppleTalk. Other protocols, such as X.25 and frame relay, were developed as wide area network protocols.

Table 8.1 lists 16 popular communications protocols. Readers are cautioned that many routers support only a subset of the protocols listed in Table 8.1.

Depending upon their support of communications protocols, routers can be classified into two classes, protocol-dependent and protocol-independent.

## 8.2.3 Protocol-dependent routers

To understand the characteristic of a protocol-dependent router consider the internet previously illustrated in Figure 8.2. If a workstation on network E1 wishes to transmit data to a second workstation on network E3, router R1 must know that the second workstation resides on network E3 and the best path to reach that network. The method used to determine the network where the destination workstation resides determines the protocol dependency of the router.

**Table 8.1**  Popular communications protocols

| |
|---|
| AppleTalk |
| Applo Domain VINES |
| Banyan |
| CHAOSnet |
| DECnet Phase IV |
| DECnet Phase V |
| DDN X.25 |
| Frame Relay |
| ISO CLNS |
| HDLC |
| NOVELL IPX |
| SDLC |
| TCP/IP |
| Xerox XNS |
| X.25 |
| Ungermann-Bass Net/One |

If the workstation on network E1 tells router R1 the destination location it must supply a network address in every LAN packet it transmits. This means that all routers in the internet must support the protocol used on network E1. Otherwise, workstations on network E1 could not communicate with workstations residing on other networks and vice versa.

## NetWare IPX example

To illustrate the operation of a protocol dependent router let us assume that networks E1 and E3 use Novell's NetWare as their LAN operating system. The routing protocol used at the network layer between a workstation and a server is known as IPX. This protocol can also be used between servers as well as other protocols.

In Chapter 6 we noted the composition of the IPX header which commences with a Checksum field. In comparison to IP where network addresses are assigned by a centralized administrative group (InterNIC), IPX network addresses are administrator-assigned. A four byte destination network and a six byte destination node which represents the MAC address of the destination host function in a manner similar to an IP network and host address. However, since an IPX header includes the physical address of the destination network adapter card, there is no need to perform an ARP operation when a packet reaches the destination network. Instead, the router can use the transported destination MAC address to form an appropriate frame at the data link layer that will transport the IPX packet to its destination.

Figure 8.32a illustrates in simplified format the IPX packet composition for workstation A on network E1 transmitting data to workstation B on network E3 under Novell's NetWare IPX protocol.

After router R1 receives and examines the packet it notes that the destination address E3 requires the routing of the packet to router R2. Thus, it converts the first packet into a router (R1) to router (R2) packet as illustrated in Figure 8.2b. At router R2 the packet is again examined. Router R2 notes that the destination network address (E3) is connected to that router. Thus, router R2 reconverts the packet for delivery onto network E3 by converting the destination router address to a source router

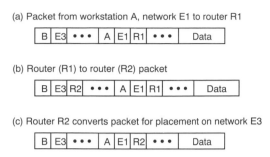

**Figure 8.3** NetWare IPX routing

address and transmitting the packet onto network E3. This is illustrated in Figure 8.2c.

### Addressing differences

In the preceding example note that each router uses the destination workstation and network addresses to transfer packets. If all protocols used the same format and addressing structure, routers would be protocol-insensitive at the network layer. Unfortunately this is not true. For example, under TCP/IP addressing conventions are very different from that used by NetWare. This means that networks using different operating systems require the use of multiprotocol routers that are configured to maintain multiple routing tables, examine each packet received to determine the network layer protocol, and use that information in conjunction with the destination address contained in the packet and its appropriate routing table to correctly forward the packet.

### Other problems

Two additional problems associated with protocol-dependent routers are the time required for packet examination and the fact that not all LAN protocols are routable. Concerning packet examination, if a packet must traverse a large network the time required by a series of routers to both modify the packet and assure its delivery to the next router can significantly degrade

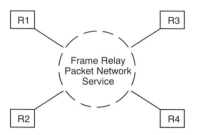

**Figure 8.4** Using a frame relay service. If a frame relay service is used, the packet network provides the capability for interconnecting each network access port to other network access ports. Thus, only one router port is required to obtain an interconnection capability to numerous routers connected to the network

router performance. To overcome this problem organizations should consider the use of a frame relay service.

In addition to providing an enhanced data delivery service by eliminating error detection and correction occurring within the network, the use of a frame relay service can significantly reduce the cost of routers. To illustrate this consider the network previously illustrated in Figure 8.2 in which four routers are interconnected through the use of five links. To support transmission on five links the routers require 10 ports. Normally, each router port is obtained as an adapter card installed in a high performance computer. If a frame relay service is used the packet network providing that service also provides the routing paths to interconnect routers as illustrated in Figure 8.4. This reduces the number of required router ports to four, which can result in a considerable saving.

A second problem associated with protocol-dependent routers is the fact that some LAN protocols cannot be routed using that type of device. This is because some LAN protocols, such as NetBIOS and IBM's LAN Server, unlike NetWare, DECnet and TCP/IP, do not include routing information within a packet. Such protocols are restricted to using the physical addresses of adapter cards, such as Token-Ring source and destination addresses. As a protocol-dependent router must know the network on which a destination address is located, it cannot in a conventional sense route such protocols. Thus, a logical question is: how does a router interconnect networks using an IBM LAN protocol or a similar non-routable protocol? The answer to this question will depend upon the method used by the router manufacturer to support non-routable protocols. As previously discussed, such methods can include bridging, tunneling, or the configuration of a router that enables pseudo-network addresses to be assigned to each device.

### 8.2.4 Protocol-independent router

A protocol-independent router can be considered to function as a sophisticated transparent bridge. That is, it addresses the problem of network protocols that do not have network addresses, by examining the source addresses on connected networks to automatically learn what devices are on each network. The protocol-independent router assigns network identifiers to each network whose operating system does not include network addresses in its network protocol. This activity enables both routable and non-routable protocols to be serviced by a protocol-dependent router.

In addition to automatically building address tables like a transparent bridge, a protocol-independent router exchanges information concerning its routing directions with other internet routers. This enables each router to build a map of the interconnected networks. The method used to build the network map falls under the category of a link state routing protocol which is described later in this chapter.

*Advantages*

There are two key advantages associated with the use of protocol-independent routers. Those advantages are the ability of routers to automatically learn network topology and to service non-routable protocols. The ability to automatically learn network topology can considerably simplify the administration of an internet. For example, in a TCP/IP network each work-station has an IP address and must know the IP addresses of other LAN devices that it desires to communicate with.

IP addresses are commonly assigned by a network adminis-trator and must be changed if a workstation is moved to a different network or a network is segmented due to a high level of traffic or another reason. In such situations all LAN users must be notified about the new IP address or they will not be able to locate the moved workstation. Obviously, the movement of workstations within a building between different LANs could become a considerable administrative burden. In comparison, the ability of a protocol-dependent router to automatically learn addresses removes the administrative burden of notifying users of changes in network addresses.

An exception to the preceding occurs through the use of the Dynamic Host Configuration Protocol (DHCP). Through the use of a DHCP server and appropriate client software, stations are dynamically assigned IP addresses for a relatively short period of time. Once they complete an application the server can reassign the address to a new station. Although the use of the DHCP can ease the administrative burden of configuring and reconfiguring IP workstations, it requires the use of a server and client software. Thus, there continues to be no free lunch in networking.

The ability to route non-routable protocols can be of considerable assistance in integrating IBM System Network Architecture (SNA) networks into an enterprise network. Otherwise, without the use of protocol-independent routers organizations may have to maintain separate transmission facilities for SNA and LAN traffic.

## Supporting SNA traffic

Figure 8.5 illustrates an example of the use of protocol-independent routers to support both interLAN and SNA traffic. This example shows an IBM SNA network in which a 3174 control unit with a Token-Ring adapter (TRA) at a remote site provides communications connectivity to an IBM 3745 front-end processor at a central site. Thus, routers must be capable of routing both SNA and LAN traffic to enable the use of a common transmission facility between the central and remote sites.

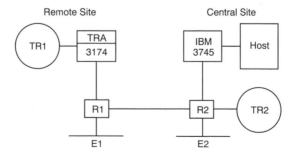

**Figure 8.5** Supporting SNA traffic. A protocol-independent router can support SNA traffic as well as other LAN traffic over a common transmission facility

### Methods to consider

There are essentially three methods by which SNA and LAN traffic can be combined for routing over a common network: encapsulation, conversion or through protocol-independent routing. Under the encapsulation method, SNA packets are modified so that another protocol's header, addressing and trailer fields surround each SNA packet. For example, a TCP/IP protocol-dependent router would encapsulate SNA into TCP/IP packets for routing through a TCP/IP network. As a TCP/IP packet has over 60 bytes of overhead while the average SNA packet is 30 bytes in length, encapsulation can considerably reduce performance when transmission occurs over low speed links. A second disadvantage of encapsulation is that it requires the existence of a corporate network using the encapsulation protocol. Otherwise, you would have to build this network to obtain an encapsulation capability.

The second method used for integrating SNA traffic with LAN traffic occurs through the use of protocol conversion. This technique eliminates the need for adding network headers and enhances the efficiency of the protocol integration efforts.

The third method by which an SNA network can be integrated with LAN traffic is through protocol-independent routing. Protocol-independent routers would assign a LAN device address to each SNA control unit and front-end processor. Then, SNA packets would be prefixed with source and destination addresses to permit their routing through the internet. At the destination router the addressing information is removed and the SNA packets are delivered to their destination in their original form. As the addition of source and destination addresses adds significantly fewer bytes than an encapsulation process, overhead is reduced in comparison to encapsulation. This in turn enables lower speed links to be used to interconnect locations. Readers are referred to Chapter 9 for additional information concerning the use of gateways to integrate SNA and other protocols into a common network infrastructure.

## 8.2.5 Routing protocols

The routing protocol is the key element which enables the transfer of information across an internet in an orderly manner. The protocol is responsible for developing paths between routers

a. Router R1

| Destination | Distance |
|:-----------:|:--------:|
| E1 | 0 |
| E2 | 0 |

b. Router R2

| Destination | Distance |
|:-----------:|:--------:|
| E3 | 0 |
| TR1 | 0 |

**Figure 8.6**  Initial distance vector routing tables

which is accomplished by a predefined mechanism by which routers exchange routing information.

### Vector distance protocol

There are two basic types of routing protocols, vector distance and link state. A vector distance protocol constructs a routing table in each router and periodically broadcasts the contents of the routing table across the internetwork. When the routing table is received at another router, that device examines the set of reported network destinations and the distance to each destination. The receiving router then determines if it knows a shorter route to a network destination, finds a destination it does not have in its routing table, or finds a route to a destination through the sending router where the distance to the destination changed. If any one of these situations occurs the receiving router will change its routing tables.

The term 'vector distance' relates to the information transmitted by routers. Each router message contains a list of pairs known as vector and distance. The vector identifies a network destination, while the distance is the distance in hops from the router to that destination.

Figure 8.6 illustrates the initial distance vector routing table for routers R1 and R2 previously illustrated in Figure 8.2. Each table contains an entry for each directly connected network and is broadcast periodically throughout the internet. Here the distance column indicates the distance to each network from the router in hops.

a. Router R1

| Destination | Distance | Route |
|:-----------:|:--------:|:------:|
| E1 | 0 | direct |
| E2 | 0 | direct |
| E3 | 1 | R2 |
| TR1 | 1 | R2 |

b. Router R2

| Destination | Distance | Route |
|:-----------:|:--------:|:------:|
| E1 | 1 | R2 |
| E2 | 1 | R2 |
| E3 | 0 | direct |
| TR1 | 0 | direct |

**Figure 8.7**   Initial routing table update

At the same time that router R1 is constructing its initial distance vector table other routers are performing a similar operation. The lower portion of Figure 8.2 illustrates the composition of the initial distance vector table for router R2.

As previously mentioned, under a distance vector protocol the contents of each router's routing table are periodically broadcast. Assuming that routers R1 and R2 broadcast their initial distance vector routing tables, each router uses the received routing table to update its initial routing table. Figure 8.7 illustrates the result of this initial routing table update process for routers R1 and R2.

As additional routing tables are exchanged the routing table in each router will converge with respect to the internetwork topology. However, to ensure that each router knows the state of all links, routing tables are periodically broadcast by each router. Although this process has a minimal effect upon small networks, its use with large networks can significantly reduce available bandwidth for actual data transfer. This is because the transmission of lengthy router tables will require additional transmission time in which data cannot flow between routers.

### Examples

Two popular vector distance routing protocols are the TCP/IP Routing Information Protocol (RIP) and the AppleTalk Routing Table Management Protocol (RTMP).

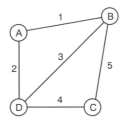

**Figure 8.8** Redrawing the network in Figure 8.2 in terms of its links and nodes

*Routing Information Protocol*

Under RIP participants are either active or passive. Active participants are normally routers which transmit their routing tables, while passive machines listen and update their routing tables based upon information supplied by other devices. Normally host computers operate as passive participants, while routers operate as active participants.

Under RIP an active router broadcasts its routing table every 30 seconds. Each routing table entry contains a network address and the hop count to the network. To illustrate an example of the operation of RIP, let us redraw the network previously shown in Figure 8.2 in terms of its links and nodes, replacing the four routers by the letters A, B, C and D for simplicity of illustration. Figure 8.8 contains the revised network consisting of four nodes and five links.

When the routers are powered up they only have knowledge of their local conditions. Thus, each routing table would contain a single entry. For example, the table of router n would have the following value:

| From n to | Link | Hop Count |
|---|---|---|
| n | local | 0 |

For the router represented by node A, its table would then become:

| From A to | Link | Hop Count |
|---|---|---|
| A | local | 0 |

Thirty seconds after being turned on, node A will broadcast its distance vector (A=0) to all its neighbors, which, in Figure 8.8 are nodes B and C. Node B receives on link 1 the distance vector A=0. Upon receipt of this message, it updates its routing table as follows, adding one to the hop count associated with the distance vector supplied by node 1:

| From B to | Link | Hop Count |
|-----------|-------|-----------|
| B | Local | 0 |
| A | 1 | 1 |

Node B can now prepare its own distance vector (B=0, A=1) and transmit that information on its connections (links 1, 3 and 5).

During the preceding period node C would have received the initial distance vector transmission from node A. Thus, node C would have updated its routing table as follows:

| From C to | Link | Hop Count |
|-----------|-------|-----------|
| C | Local | 0 |
| A | 2 | 1 |

Once it updates its routing table, node C will then transmit its distance vector (C=0, A=1) on links 2, 3 and 4.

Assuming that the distance vector from node B is now received at nodes A and C, each will update their routing tables. Thus, their routing tables would appear as follows:

| From A to | Link | Hop Count |
|-----------|-------|-----------|
| A | Local | 0 |
| B | 1 | 1 |

| From C to | Link | Hop Count |
|-----------|-------|-----------|
| C | Local | 0 |
| A | 2 | 1 |
| B | 3 | 1 |

At node D, its initial state is first modified when it receives the distance vector (B=0, A=1) from node B. As D received that information on link 5, it updates its routing table as follows, adding one to each received hop count:

| From D to | Link | Hop Count |
|---|---|---|
| D | Local | 0 |
| B | 5 | 1 |
| A | 5 | 2 |

Now, let us assume node D receives the update of node C's recent update (C=0, A=1, B=1) on link 4. As it does not have an entry for node C, it will add it to its routing table by entering C=1 for link 4. When it adds 1 to the hop count for A received on link 4, it notes that the value is equal to the current hop count for A in its routing table. Thus, it discards the information about node A received from node C. The exception to this would be if the router maintained alternate routing entries to use in the event of a link failure. Next, node D would operate upon the vector B=1 received on link 4, adding one to the hop count to obtain B=2. As that is more hops than the current entry, it would discard the received distance vector. Thus, D's routing table would appear as follows:

| From D to | Link | Hop Count |
|---|---|---|
| D | Local | 0 |
| C | 4 | 1 |
| B | 5 | 1 |
| A | 5 | 2 |

The preceding example provides a general indication of how RIP enables nodes to learn the topology of a network. In addition, if a link should fail, the condition can be easily compensated for as similar to bridge table entries, those of routers are also time stamped and the periodic transmission of distance vector information would result in a new route replacing the previously computed one.

One key limitation of RIP is the maximum hop distance it supports. This distance is 16 hops, which means an alternative protocol must be used for large networks.

*Routing Table Maintenance Protocol*

The Routing Table Maintenance Protocol (RTMP) was developed by Apple Computer for use with that vendor's AppleTalk network. Under RTMP, each router transmits messages to establish and periodically update routing tables. The update process in which information on an internet is exchanged between routers also serves as a mechanism for implementing alternate routing. This is because the absence of update information for a greater than expected period of time converts the status of an entry in other router routing tables from 'good' to 'suspect' and then to 'bad'.

RTMP is delivered by AppleTalk's Data Delivery Protocol (DDP), which is a network layer connectionless service operating between two upper layer processes referred to as sockets. Four types of packets are specified by RTMP: data, request, route data request, and response. Routing updates are transmitted as data packets. Request packets are transmitted by end nodes to acquire information concerning the identity of internet routers (IRs) to which they can transmit non-local packets. IRs respond to route request packets with response packets, while end nodes that want to receive an RTMP data packet indicate this by sending a route data request packet. The latter packet type is also used by nodes which require routing information from IRs that are not directly connected to their network.

*Routing process*  In the AppleTalk routing process the source node first examines the destination network number. If the packet has a local network address it is passed to the data link layer for delivery. Otherwise, the packet is passed to any of the IRs that may reside on a network segment. The IR will examine the destination address of the packet and then check its routing tables to determine the next hop, routing the packet on a specific port which enables it to flow towards the next hop. Thus, a packet will travel through the internet on a hop-by-hop basis. When the packet reaches an IR connected to the destination network the data link layer is used to deliver the packet to its local destination.

Figure 8.9 illustrates a sample AppleTalk network and the routing table for one router. Each AppleTalk routing table has five entries as indicated. The network range defines the range of network numbers assigned to a particular network segment. The 'distance' entry specifies the number of routers that must be

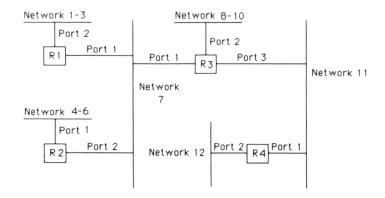

**Routing table for router R1**

| Network Range | Distance | Port | Next IR | Entry State |
|---------------|----------|------|---------|-------------|
| 1-3 | 0 | 2 | 0 | Good |
| 7-7 | 0 | 1 | 0 | Good |
| 4-6 | 1 | 1 | R2 | Good |
| 8-10 | 1 | 1 | R3 | Good |
| 11-11 | 1 | 1 | R3 | Good |
| 12-12 | 2 | 1 | R3 | Good |

**Figure 8.9** AppleTalk routing table example

traversed prior to the destination being reached, while 'port' defines the router port used to provide access to a destination location. The 'next IR' entry indicates the identifier of the next IR on the internet, while 'entry state' defines the status of receiving routing updates. Here an entry state can go from 'good' to 'suspect' to 'bad' if routing updates have not been received within predefined time intervals.

*Link state protocol*

A link state routing protocol addresses the traffic problem associated with large networks that use a vector distance routing protocol. It does this by transmitting routing information only when there is a change in one of its links. A second difference between vector distance and link state protocols concerns the manner in which a route is selected when multiple routes are available between destinations. For a vector distance protocol the best path is the one that has the fewest number of intermediate routers on hops between destinations. In comparison, a link state protocol can use multiple paths to provide traffic balancing between locations. In addition, a link state protocol permits routing to occur based upon link delay, capacity and reliability. This provides the network manager with the ability to specify a variety of route development situations.

### SPF algorithms

Link state routing protocols are implemented through the use of a class of algorithms known as Shortest Path First (SPF). Unfortunately, the name associated with this class of algorithms is a misnomer as routing is not based upon the shortest path.

The use of SPF algorithms requires each participating router to have complete knowledge of the internetwork topology. Each router participating in an SPF algorithm then performs two tasks: status testing of neighboring routers and periodically transmitting link status information to other routers.

To test neighboring routers a short message is periodically transmitted. If the neighbor replies the link is considered to be up. Otherwise, the absence of a reply after a predefined period of time indicates that the link is down.

To provide link status information each router will periodically broadcast a message which indicates the status of each of its links. Unlike the vector distance protocol in which routes are specified, an SPF link status message simply indicates whether or not communications are possible between pairs of routers. Using information in the link status message routers are able to update their network map.

In comparison to vector distance protocols in which tables are required to be exchanged, link state protocols such as SPF algorithms exchange a much lower volume of information in the form of link status queries and replies. Then, SPF participating routers simply broadcast a status of each of their links that other routers use to update their internet map. This routing technique permits each router to compute routes independently of other routers and eliminates the potential for table flooding that can occur when a vector state protocol is used to interconnect a large number of networks.

### Operation example

To illustrate the operation of a link state routing protocol let us return to the internetwork configuration previously illustrated in Figure 8.2. Figure 8.10 indicates the initial network map for

| Destination | Distance | Route | Status |
|---|---|---|---|
| E1 | 0 | direct | up |
| E2 | 0 | direct | up |
| E3 | 1 | R2 | up |
| E3 | 2 | R3,R2 | up |
| E3 | 3 | R3,R4,R2 | up |
| E4 | 2 | R2,R4 | up |
| E4 | 2 | R3,R4 | up |
| E4 | 3 | R3,R2,R4 | up |
| TR1 | 1 | R2 | up |
| TR1 | 2 | R3,R2 | up |
| TR1 | 3 | R3,R4,R2 | up |
| TR2 | 1 | R3 | up |
| TR2 | 2 | R2,R3 | up |
| TR2 | 2 | R2,R4 | up |
| TR3 | 2 | R3,R4 | up |
| TR3 | 2 | R2,R4 | up |
| TR3 | 3 | R3,R2,R4 | up |

**Figure 8.10**  Router R1 initial network map

router R1. This map lists the destination of all networks on the internet from router R1, their distance and route. Note that if multiple routes exist to a destination each route is listed, as doing so defines a complete network topology as well as allows alternate routes to be selected if link status information indicates that one or more routes cannot be used.

Let us assume that at a particular point in time the link status messages generated by the routers in the internet are as indicated in Figure 8.11. Note that both routers R2 and R3 determined that link L3 is down. Using this information router R1 would then update the status column for its network map. As link L3 is down, all routes that require a data flow between R2 and R3 would have their status changed to down. For example, destination E3 via route R3–R2 would have its status changed to down. As the minimum distance to E3 is 1 hop via router R2, the failure of link L3 would not affect data flow from router R1 to network E3. Now consider the effect of link L2 becoming inoperative. That would affect route R2 which has the minimum distance to network E3. This would still leave route R3–R4–R2, although this route would have a distance of three hops. Of course, when a new link status message indicates that a previously declared down link is up, each router's network map would be updated accordingly.

## 8.3 PERFORMANCE CONSIDERATIONS

Regardless of the type of router, its protocol support and routing algorithm used, the processing required for its operation is

R1 link status

| Link | Status |
|------|--------|
| L1 | Up |
| L2 | Up |

R2 link status

| Link | Status |
|------|--------|
| L2 | Up |
| L3 | Down |
| L4 | Up |

R3 link status

| Link | Status |
|------|--------|
| L1 | Up |
| L3 | Down |

R4 link status

| Link | Status |
|------|--------|
| L4 | Up |
| L5 | Up |

**Figure 8.11**  Link status messages

considerably above that required for a bridge. This means that you can expect the packet processing capability of routers to be considerably less than the processing rate of bridges.

High capacity bridges marketed during 1997 could be expected to provide a forwarding rate between 100 000 and 200 000 packets per second. In comparison, most routers have a forwarding capacity rated under 50 000 packets per second. Although this may appear to indicate a poor level of performance in comparison to bridges, readers should note that only when functioning as a local bridge will a high capacity bridge actually use its full capacity. Otherwise, when used to interconnect remote networks via a wide area transmission facility a remote bridge will only be able to use a fraction of its packet processing capability for the forwarding of packets over a relatively slow speed WAN transmission facility. In comparison, when routers are connected to a T1 or E1 line or to a frame relay service they may be able to use their full packet forwarding capability.

# 9

# GATEWAY FUNCTIONS, METHODS AND APPLICATIONS

In Chapter 2 we discussed the basic operation of gateways and how they enable networks with different protocols to communicate. In that chapter we discussed how a gateway operates through the highest layer of the OSI Reference Model, the application layer, and how gateways essentially perform protocol conversion. In Chapter 5 in our discussion of IBM Token-Ring hardware components we described several methods by which a Token-Ring could be connected to an IBM mainframe computer system. Although those methods involved different types of gateway our primary focus of attention until now was to simply discuss concepts and the use of different types of hardware without considering the relationship of network architecture to gateway operations.

As the protocol conversion performed by a gateway is directly related to such architectures as IBM's SNA and Digital Equipment's DECnet, we must obtain a basic understanding of the architecture developed to support access to conventional mainframe computers. This will enable us to obtain an appreciation for the different access methods supported by gateways as well as their functions and applications, which are the focus of this chapter. To accomplish this we will first discuss SNA and IBM's 3270 Information Display System to obtain an understanding of the basic functions of hardware and software used to provide a wide area networking capability that provides local and remote terminal users with access to IBM mainframe computers in an SNA environment. In doing so we will cover both SNA and the more modern Advanced Peer-to-Peer Networking (APPN) evolution of IBM's networking strategy. Using this information as a base will then provide the foundation for discussing gateways from the perspective of their use to exchange information between local area networks and mainframes connected to the dominant computer company network architectures which, with plug compatible computers, represents approximately 70% of all large computer installations. Although the preceding information is primarily focused upon gateways that provide end stations on LANs with the ability to access SNA and APPN based information, there are other types of gateway that warrant discussion. Thus, in the remainder of this chapter, we will turn our attention to several other types of gateway, including SNA to TCP/IP gateways, electronic mail gateways, and application gateways.

## 9.1 SNA AND APPN ARCHITECTURE

To satisfy the requirements of customers for remote computing capability, mainframe computer manufacturers developed a variety of network architectures. Such architectures define the interrelationship of a particular vendor's hardware and software products necessary to permit communications to flow through a network to the manufacturers' mainframe computer.

IBM's System Network Architecture (SNA) is a very complex and sophisticated network architecture which defines the rules, procedures and structure of communications from the input/ output statements of an application program to the screen display on a user's personal computer or terminal. SNA consists of protocols, formats and operational sequences which govern the flow of information within a data-communications network linking IBM mainframe computers, minicomputers, terminal controllers, communications controllers, personal computers and terminals.

As approximately 70% of the mainframe computer market belongs to IBM and plug-compatible systems manufactured by Amdahl and other vendors, SNA can be expected to remain as a connectivity platform for the foreseeable future. This means that a large majority of the connections of local area networks to mainframe computers will require the use of gateways that support SNA operations.

As we will shortly note when examining SNA, it is a mainframe-centric, hierarchical structured networking architecture. While appropriate for most computer communications requirements of the 1980s, the growth in distributed processing and peer-to-peer communications represented a significant problem for network managers and LAN administrators that required access to mainframes in an SNA environment as well as the ability to support peer-to-peer communications. Recognizing this problem, IBM significantly revised SNA in the form of developing a new network architecture known as Advanced Peer-to-Peer Networking (APPN). After becoming familiar with SNA, we will then turn our attention to APPN in this section.

### 9.1.1 SNA concepts

An SNA network consists of one or more domains, where a domain refers to all of the logical and physical components that are connected to and controlled by one common point in the network. This common point of control is called the system services control point, which is commonly known by its abbreviation as the SSCP. There are three types of network-addressable units in an SNA network: SSCPs, physical units and logical units.

*The SSCP*

The SSCP resides in the communications access method operating in an IBM mainframe computer, such as virtual telecommunications access method (VTAM), operating in a System/360, System/370, System/390, 4300 series or 308X, 309X or an Enterprise series computer, or in the system control program of an IBM minicomputer, such as a System/3X or AS/400. The SSCP contains the network's address tables, routing tables and translation tables which it uses to establish connections between nodes in the network as well as to control the flow of information in an SNA network. Figure 9.1 illustrates single and multiple domain SNA networks.

Each network domain includes one or more nodes, with an SNA network node consisting of a grouping of networking components which provides it with a unique characteristic. Examples of SNA nodes include cluster controllers, communications controllers and terminal devices, with the address of

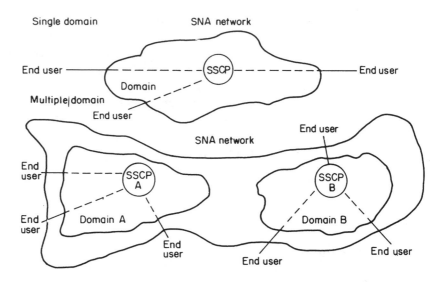

**Figure 9.1**    Single and multiple domain SNA networks

each device in the network providing its unique characteristic in comparison to a similar device contained in the network.

## The PU

Each node in an SNA network contains a physical unit (PU) which controls the other resources contained in the node. The PU is not a physical device, as its name appears to suggest, but rather a set of SNA components which provide services used to control terminals, controllers, processors and data links in the network. In the programmable devices, such as mainframe computers and communications controllers, the PU is normally implemented in software. In less intelligent devices, such as cluster controllers and terminals, the PU is typically implemented in read-only memory. In an SNA network each PU operates under the control of an SSCP. The PU can be considered to function as an entry point between the network and one or more logical units.

## The LU

The third type of network-addressable unit in an SNA network is the logical unit, known by its abbreviation as the LU. The LU is the interface or point of access between the end-user and an SNA network. Through the LU an end-user gains access to network resources and transmits and receives data over the network. Each PU can have one or more LUs, with each LU having a distinct address.

## 9.1.2 SNA network structure

The structure of an SNA network can be considered to represent a hierarchy in which each device controls a specific part of the network and operates under the control of a device at the next higher level. The highest level in an SNA network is represented by a host or mainframe computer which executes a software module known as a communications access method. At the next lower level are one or more communications controllers, IBM's term for a front-end processor. Each communications controller executes a Network Control Program (NCP) which defines the operation of devices connected to the controllers, their PUs and LUs, operating rate, data code and other communications-related functions such as the maximum packet size that can be transmitted. Connected to communications controllers are cluster controllers, IBM's term for a control unit. Thus, the third level in an SNA network can be considered to be represented by cluster controllers.

The cluster controllers support the attachment of terminals and printers which represent the lowest hierarchy of an SNA network. Figure 9.2 illustrates the SNA hierarchy and the Network Addressable Units (NAUs) associated with each hardware component used to construct an SNA network. Readers should note that NAUs include lines connecting mainframes to communications controllers to cluster controllers, and cluster controllers to terminals and printers. In addition, NAUs also define application programs that reside in the mainframe. Thus, NAUs provide the mechanism for terminals to access specific programs via a routing through hardware and transmission facilities that are explicitly identified.

As an example of the communications capability of SNA, consider an end-user with an IBM PC and an SDLC communications adapter who establishes a connection to an IBM mainframe computer. The IBM PC is a PU, with its display and printer considered to be LUs. After communication is established, the PC user could direct a file to his or her printer by establishing an LU-to-LU session between the mainframe and

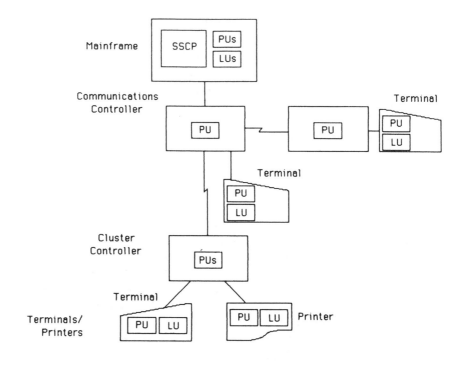

Legend:
  SSCP = system service control port
  PU    = physical unit
  LU    = logical unit

**Figure 9.2** SNA hierarchical network structure. The structure of an SNA network is built upon a hierarchy of equipment, with mainframes connected to communications controllers and communications controllers connected to cluster controllers

printer while using the PC as an interactive terminal running an application program as a second LU-to-LU session. Thus, the transfer of data between PUs can represent a series of multiplexed LU-to-LU sessions, enabling multiple activities to occur concurrently.

## Types of PUs

Table 9.1 lists the five types of physical units in an SNA network and their corresponding SNA node type. In addition, this table contains representative examples of hardware devices that can

**Table 9.1**  SNA PU summary

| PU type | Node type | Representative hardware |
|---------|-----------|-------------------------|
| PU Type 5 | Mainframe | S/370, 43XX, 308X |
| PU Type 4 | Communications controller | 3705, 3725, 3745 |
| PU Type 3 | Not currently defined | N/A |
| PU Type 2 | Cluster controller | 3174, 3274, 3276 |
| PU Type 1 | Terminal | 3180, PC with SNA adapter |

operate as a specific type of PU. As indicated in Table 9.1, the different types of PUs form a hierarchy of hardware classifications. At the lowest level, PU Type 1 is a single terminal. PU Type 2 is a cluster controller which is used to connect many SNA devices into a common communications circuit. PU Type 4 is a communications controller. This device provides communications support for up to several hundred line terminations, where individual lines in turn can be connected to cluster controllers. At the top of the hardware hierarchy, PU Type 5 is a mainframe computer.

### Multiple domains

Figure 9.3 illustrates a two-domain SNA network. By establishing a physical connection between the communications controller in each domain and coding appropriate software for operation on each controller, cross-domain data flow becomes possible. When cross-domain data flow is established, terminal devices connected to one mainframe gain the capability to access applications operating on the other mainframe.

SNA was originally implemented as a networking architecture in which users establish sessions with application programs that operate on a mainframe computer within the network. Once a session is established, a Network Control Program (NCP) operating on an IBM communications controller, which in turn is connected to the IBM mainframe, controls the information flow between the user and the applications program. With the growth in personal computing, many users no longer required access to a mainframe to obtain connectivity to another personal computer connected to the network. Thus IBM modified SNA to permit peer-to-peer communications capability in which two devices on the network with appropriate hardware

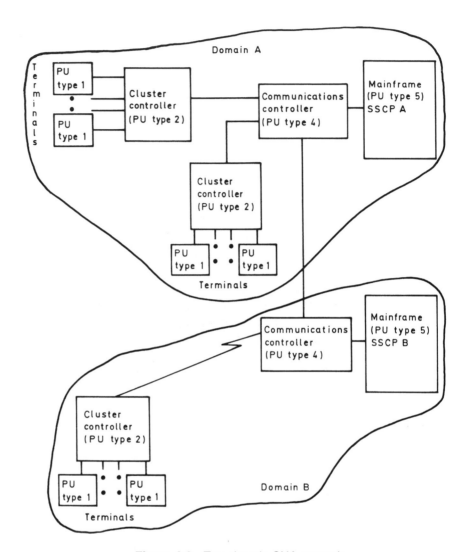

**Figure 9.3** Two-domain SNA network

and software could communicate with one another without requiring access through a mainframe computer. In doing so, IBM introduced a PU2.1 node in 1987 in recognition of the growing requirement of its customers for a peer-to-peer networking capability. Unfortunately, it was not until the early 1990s that APPN became available and provided this networking capability, enabling communications between PU2.1 nodes without mainframe intervention through the use of LU6.2 sessions described later in this chapter.

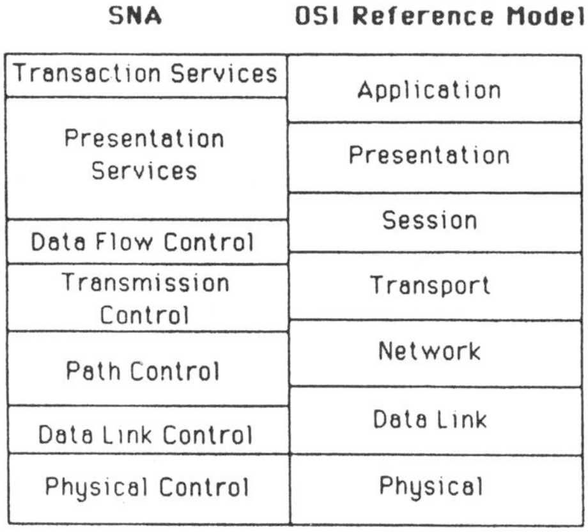

SNA                    OSI Reference Model

| | |
|---|---|
| Transaction Services | Application |
| Presentation Services | Presentation |
| Data Flow Control | Session |
| Transmission Control | Transport |
| Path Control | Network |
| Data Link Control | Data Link |
| Physical Control | Physical |

**Figure 9.4**   SNA and the OSI Reference Model

*SNA layers*

IBM's SNA is a layered protocol which provides seven layers of control for every message that flows through the network. Figure 9.4 illustrates the SNA layers and provides a comparison to the seven-layer OSI Reference Model.

Similarly to the OSI physical layer, SNA's physical control layer is concerned with the electrical, mechanical and procedural characteristics of the physical media and interfaces to the physical media. SNA's data link control layer is also quite similar to OSI's data link layer. Protocols defined by SNA include SDLC, System/370 channel, Token-Ring and X.25; however, only SDLC is used on a communications link in which master or primary stations communicate with secondary or slave stations. Some implementations of SNA using special software modules can also support Bisynchronous Communications (BSC), an IBM pre-SNA protocol still used, as well as asynchronous communications.

Two of the major functions of the path control layer are routing and flow control. Concerning routing, since there can be many data links connected to a node, path control is responsible for ensuring that data is correctly passed through intermediate nodes as it flows from source to destination. At the beginning of an SNA session, both sending and receiving nodes as well as all nodes between those nodes cooperate to select the most efficient route for the session. As this route is established only for the duration of the session, it is known as a virtual route. To increase the efficiency of transmission in an SNA network, the path control layer at each node through which the virtual route is established has the ability to divide long messages into shorter segments for transmission by the data link layer. Similarly, path control may block short messages into larger data blocks for transmission by the data link layer. This enables the efficiency of SNA's transmission facility to be independent of the length of messages flowing on the network.

The SNA transmission control layer provides a reliable end-to-end connection service, similar to the OSI Reference Model transport layer. Other transmission control layer functions include session level pacing as well as encryption and decryption of data when so requested by a session. Here, pacing ensures that a transmitting device does not send more data than a receiving device can accept during a given period of time. Pacing can be viewed as similar to the flow control of data in a network; however, unlike flow control which is essentially uncontrolled, NAUs negotiate and control pacing. To accomplish this the two NAUs at session end-points negotiate the largest number of messages, known as a pacing group, that a sending NAU can transmit prior to receiving a pacing response from a receiving NAU. Here the pacing response enables the transmitting NAU to resume transmission. Session level pacing occurs in two stages along a session's route in an SNA network. One stage of pacing is between the mainframe NAU and the communications controller, while the second stage occurs between the communications controller and an attached terminal NAU.

The data flow control services layer handles the order of communications within a session for error control and flow control. Here, the order of communications is set by the layer controlling the transmission mode. Transmission modes available include full-duplex, which permits each device to transmit at any time, half-duplex flip-flop, in which devices can only transmit alternately, and half-duplex contention, in which one device is considered a master device and the slave cannot transmit until the master completes its transmission.

The SNA presentation services layer is responsible for the translation of data from one format to another. This layer also performs the connection and disconnection of sessions as well as updating the network configuration and performing network management functions. At this layer, the network addressable unit (NAU) services manager is responsible for formatting of data from an application to match the display or printer that is communicating with the application. Other functions performed at this layer include the compression and decompression of data to increase the efficiency of transmission on an SNA network.

The highest layer in SNA is the transaction services layer. This layer is responsible for application programs that implement distributed processing and management services, such as distributed databases and document interchange as well as the control of LU-to-LU session limits.

## SNA developments

The most significant development to SNA prior to the formal introduction of APPN can be considered to be the addition of new LU and PU subtypes to support what is known as advanced peer-to-peer communications (APPC) which represents the communications protocol of an APPN network. Previously, LU types used to define an LU-to-LU session were restricted to application-to-device and program-to-program sessions. LU1– LU4 and LU7 are application-to-device sessions as indicated in Table 9.2, whereas LU4 and LU6 are program-to-program sessions.

The addition of LU6.2, which operates in conjunction with PU2.1 to support LU6.2 connections, permits devices support-ing this new LU to transfer data to any other device also supporting this LU without first sending the data through a mainframe computer. The introduction of new software pro-ducts to support LU6.2 permits a more dynamic flow of data through SNA networks, with many data links to mainframes that were previously heavily utilized or saturated gaining capacity as sessions between devices permit data flow to bypass the mainframe.

## 9.1.3 SNA sessions

All communications in SNA occur within sessions between NAUs. Here a session can be defined and a logical connection established between two NAUs over a specific route for a specific period of time, with the connection and disconnection of a session controlled by the SSCP. SNA defines four types of session: SSCP-to-PU, SSCP-to-LU, SSCP-to-SSCP and LU-to-LU. The first two types of sessions are used to request or exchange diagnostic and status information. The third type of

**Table 9.2** SNA LU session types

| LU type | Session type |
| --- | --- |
| LU1 | Host application and a remote batch terminal |
| LU2 | Host application and a 3270 display terminal |
| LU3 | Host application and a 3270 printer |
| LU4 | Host application and SNA word processor or between two terminals via mainframe |
| LU5 | Currently undefined |
| LU6 | Between applications programs typically residing on different mainframe computers |
| LU6.2 | Peer-to-peer |
| LU7 | Host application and a 5250 terminal |

session enables SSCPs in the same or different domains to exchange information. The LU-to-LU session can be considered as the core type of SNA session since all end-user communications take place over LU-to-LU sessions.

## LU-to-LU sessions

In an LU-to-LU session one logical unit known as the Primary LU (PLU) becomes responsible for error recovery. The other LU which normally has less processing power becomes the secondary LU (SLU).

An LU-to-LU session is initiated by the transmission of a message from the PLU to the SLU. That message is known as a bind and contains information stored in the communications access method (known as VTAM) tables on the mainframe which identifies the type of hardware devices with respect to screen size, printer type, etc., configured in the VTAM table. This information enables a session to occur with supported hardware. Otherwise, the SLU will reject the bind and the session will not start.

## Addressing

Previously we discussed the concept of a domain which consists of an SSCP and the network resources it controls. Within a domain there exists a set of smaller network units that are known as subareas. In SNA terminology each host is a subarea

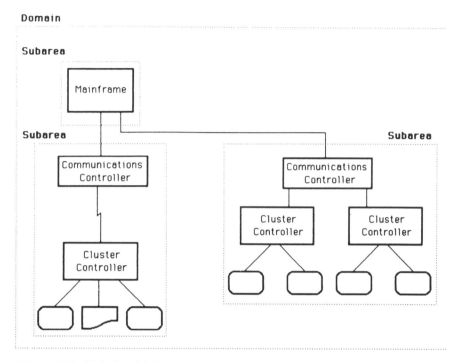

**Figure 9.5** Relationship between a domain and its subareas. A subarea is a host or a communications controller and its peripheral nodes

as well as each communications controller and its peripheral nodes. The identification of an NAU in an SNA network consists of a subarea address and an element address within the subarea having the format subarea:element. Here the subarea can be considered as being similar to an area code, as it identifies a portion of the network. Figure 9.5 illustrates the relationship between a domain and three subareas residing in that particular domain.

In SNA a subarea address is eight bits in length, while the element address within a subarea is also 8 bits in length. This limits the number of subareas within a domain to 255 and also restricts the number of PUs and LUs within a subarea to 255.

Each subarea address is shared by an SSCP and all of its LUs and PUs, and it represents a unique address within a domain. In comparison, element addresses are only unique within a subarea and can be duplicated. A third component of SNA addressing is a character-coded network name that is assigned to each component. Each name must be unique within a domain and SSCPs maintain tables which map names to addresses.

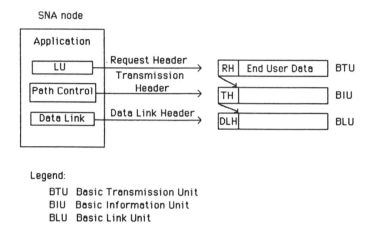

**Figure 9.6** SNA routing based upon the headers in different message units

The routing of packets between SNA subarea nodes occurs through the use of a sequence of message units created at different layers in the protocol stack. An application on an SNA node generates a Request Header (RH) which prefixes user data to form a Basic Transmission Unit (BTU) as shown at the top of Figure 9.6. At the path control layer, a Transmission Header (TH) is added as a prefix to the BTU to form a Basic Information Unit (BIU). The TH contains source and destination addresses that represent the sender and receiver of the packet, with subarea nodes examining the destination address within the TH of the BIU to make forwarding decisions.

Once a packet arrives at its destination subarea, routing must occur between the subarea and peripheral nodes in the destination subarea. That routing is based upon the Data Link Header (DLC) added to the BIU to form a Basic Link Unit (BLU), shown at the bottom of Figure 9.6. Now that we have a basic understanding of SNA, let us turn our attention to APPN.

### 9.1.4 Advanced peer-to-peer networking

Although SNA represents one of the most successful networking strategies developed by a vendor, its centralized structure based upon mainframe centric computing became dated in an evolving era of client-server distributive computing. Recognizing the requirements of organizations to obtain peer-to-peer transmission capability instead of routing data through mainframes, IBM

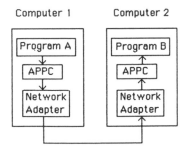

**Figure 9.7** APPC software provides an interface between application programs and the network used

developed its Advanced Peer-to-Peer Networking (APPN) archi-tecture during 1992 as a mechanism for computers ranging from PCS to mainframes to communicate as peers across local and wide area networks. The actual ability of programs on different computers to communicate with one another is obtained from special software known as Advanced Program-to-Program Communication (APPC) which represents a more marketable name for LU6.2 software. As APPC enables the operation of APPN, we will first focus our attention upon APPC prior to examining the architecture associated with APPN.

## APPC concepts

APPC represents a software interface between programs requiring communications with other programs and the net-work computers running those programs. APPC represents an open communications protocol that is available on a range of platforms, including PCs, mainframes, Macintosh, and UNIX based systems as well as IBM 3174 control units and its 6611 Nways router series.

In its most basic structure, APPC can be considered to represent a stack existing above a network adapter but below the application using the adapter. Figure 9.7 illustrates the general relationship of APPC to the software stack on two computers communicating with one another on a peer-to-peer basis. In this example, program A on computer 1 is shown communicating with program B on computer 2.

Under APPC terminology communication between two pro-grams is referred to as a conversation which occurs according to a set of rules defined by the APPC protocol. Those rules specify how a conversation is established, how data is transmitted, and how the conversation is broken or deallocated.

Similarly to most modern programming concepts, APPC supports a series of verbs that provide an application programming interface (API) between transaction programs and APPC software residing on a host. For example, the APPC verb ALLOCATE is used to initiate a conversation with another transaction program; the verb SEND_DATA enables the program to initiate the data transfer to its partner program, and the verb DEALLOCATE would be used to inform APPC to terminate the conversation previously established. Now that we have a general appreciation for the software that enables program-to-program communications, let us turn our attention to the architecture of APPN.

## APPN architecture

APPN is a platform-independent network architecture which consists of three types of computer: low-entry networking (LEN) nodes, end nodes (ENs), and network nodes (NNs). Similarly to SNA, APPN applications use network resources via logical unit (LU) software. LUs reside on each type of APPN node and application-to-application sessions occur between LUs, which in the case of APPN are LU6.2 LUs. APPN nodes can support a nearly unlimited number of LUs in comparison to the 255 SNA supports. In addition, APPN LUs can support multiple users, significantly increasing its flexibility over SNA.

When an application program on one host requires communications with an application on another host, the first host tells its local LU to find a partner LU. The location of the partner LU is accomplished by a process in which several types of searches occur through an APPN network. As those searches depend upon knowledge of the characteristics of the three types of APPN nodes, let us first turn our attention to the features and functions of those nodes.

### LEN nodes

Low-entry networking (LEN) nodes date from the early 1980s when they were introduced as SNA Type 2.1 nodes. LEN nodes can be considered to represent the most basic subset of APPN functionality and have the ability to communicate with applications on other LEN nodes, end nodes, or network nodes.

APPN includes a distributed directory mechanism which enables routes to be dynamically established through an APPN network. However, unlike IP networks that use 32 bit addresses, APPN uses alphanumeric names.

LEN nodes are manually configured with a limited set of LUs. Thus, to use APPN directory services a LEN node requires the assistance of an adjacent APPN node, where adjacency is obtained through a LAN connection or a direct point-to-point link.

### End nodes

End nodes (ENs) can be viewed as a more sophisticated type of LEN. In addition to supporting all of the functions of LEN nodes, end nodes know how to use APPN services, such as its directory services. To learn how to use such services, an end node identifies itself to the network when it is initially brought up. This identification process is accomplished by the end node registering its LUs with a network node server. Here the NN represents the third type of APPN node and is discussed in the next section. In comparison, LEN nodes do not perform this activity.

### Network nodes

Network nodes (NNs) are the third component of an APPN network. NNs provide all of the functions associated with end nodes as well as routing and partner LU location services. Concerning routing, NNs work together to route information between such nodes, in effect providing a backbone transmission capability.

The partner LU location service depends upon network node searches when the partner is not registered by the NN serving the requestor. In such situations, the NN server will broadcast a search request to adjacent network nodes, requesting the location of the partner LU. This broadcasting will continue until the partner LU is located and a path or route is returned. As broadcast searches are bandwidth-intensive, NNs place directory entries that they locate into cache memory, which serves to limit broadcasts being propagated through an APPN network.

*Operation*

To illustrate the operation of an APPN network, let us examine a small network in which two end nodes are connected by a

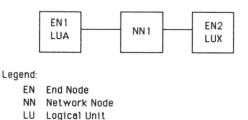

Legend:

    EN  End Node
    NN  Network Node
    LU  Logical Unit

**Figure 9.8**  An APPN network consisting of two end nodes and a network node

network node. Figure 9.8 illustrates an example of this network structure.

When the links between EN1 and NN1 and EN2 and NN1 are activated, the computers on each link automatically inform each other of their capabilities, including whether they are end nodes or network nodes, and ENs will register their capabilities with NNs. Thus, the NN will know the location and capability of both EN1 and EN2. When an application on EN1 needs to locate an LU in the network, such as LUX, it sends a request to its network node server, in this case NN1. As NN1 is the server for EN1, both nodes establish a pair of control-point sessions to exchange APPN control information and EN1 registers its APPC LUs with NN1. Similarly, EN2 and NN1 establish a pair of control-point sessions when the link between those two nodes are brought up. Thus, NN1 knows how to get to EN1 and EN2 and which LUs are located at each node.

When EN1 asks NN1 to find LUX and determine a path through the network, NN1 checks its cache memory and notes that the only path available is 'EN1 to NN1 to EN2'. NN1 passes this path information back to EN1 which enables the application operating on EN1 to establish an APPN session to LUX and initiate the exchange of information.

Now that we have an appreciation for basic APPN routing, let us examine a more complex example in which originating and destination LUs reside on end nodes separated from one another by multiple NNs. Figure 9.9 illustrates this more complex APPN network consisting of four end nodes and three network nodes grouped together in a topology which allows multiple path routing between certain nodes.

Let us assume that an APPN application on EN1 wants to initiate a conversation with an application on EN4. EN1 first requests NN1 to locate EN4 and determine which path through the network should be used. As NN1 is not EN4's network node

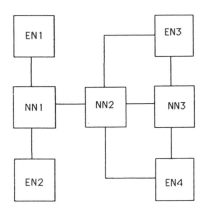

Legend:
    EN   End Node
    NN   Network Node

**Figure 9.9**  A more complex PPN network with multiple paths to some nodes

server, it will initially have no knowledge of EN4's location. Thus, NN1 will transmit a request to each adjacent network node in its quest to locate EN4. As NN2 is the only network node adjacent to NN1, it passes the request to its adjacent nodes. Based upon the configuration shown in Figure 9.9, there is only one adjacent network node, NN3. Although EN4 is connected to both NN2 and NN3, an end node can only have one network node server. Thus, if we assume that NN3 is the server for EN4, then NN2 has no knowledge of EN4 and does not respond on its behalf.

Next, upon locating EN4, NN3 queries EN4 to determine its existing communications links. Upon receipt of information from EN4 that has links to both NN2 and NN3, NN2 passes the information about EN4 to NN2 which passes the information back to NN1. NN1 uses the information received to determine which route to EN4 is best, selects an appropriate route, and passes the selected route back to EN1, allowing that end node to establish an APPC session to EN4.

*Route selection*

Under APPN, routing is based upon network nodes maintaining a 'route addition resistance' value set up by network

| Application | Application Program | | |
| --- | --- | --- | --- |
| | LU Services | | |
| Network Layer | APPC Path Control | | |
| Data Link Layer | LLC2 SNAP Ethernet 2 | LLC2 SNAP | Frame Relay, SDLC |
| Physical Layer | Ethernet/ 802.5 | Token-Ring | FDDI | V.24, V.35, RS232, T1, E1, HSSI |

**Figure 9.10** The general structure of APPN

administrators and a 'class of service' of data to be routed. Class-of-service routing enables different types of data to be routed via paths optimized for batch, interactive, batch-secure, and interactive-secure. APPN uses eight values that are defined for each network link that are used in conjunction with the class of service to select an appropriate route. Values defined for each link include propagation delay, cost per byte, cost for connect time, effective capacity, and security. Using values defined for the links, a batch session might be routed on a path with high capacity and low cost, while an interactive session would probably be placed on a terrestrial link instead of a satellite link to minimize propagation delay.

APPN can be considered to represent a considerable enhancement to SNA as it provides efficient routing services that bypass the requirement of SNA data to flow in a hierarchical manner. However, APPN is similar to SNA in the fact that such networks do not have true network addresses, making pure routing between different networks difficult. In addition, the structure of APPN is similar to SNA with respect to its basic network layer operations which are illustrated in Figure 9.10. In examining Figure 9.10 note that APPN's network layer can be considered to represent APPC which converts LU service requests into frames for transport at the data link layer. Although SNA was originally limited to LLC Type 2 (LLC2) and SDLC transmission via a variety of physical layer interfaces, a number of conversion devices have been developed which extend both SNA and APPN transmission to frame relay.

In addition, other products enable SNA and APPN data to be transported under a different network layer, a technique referred to as encapsulation or tunneling. Once we have reviewed the composition of the IBM 3270 Information Display

System to obtain an appreciation for conventional gateway methods used to connect to SNA and APPN networks, we will then turn our attention to more modern gateway solutions, such as techniques to encapsulate SNA and APPN such that they can be routed over an IP network, a technique referred to as Data Link Switching (DLSw).

## 9.2 THE 3270 INFORMATION DISPLAY SYSTEM

The IBM 3270 Information Display System describes a collection of products ranging from display stations with keyboards and printers that communicate with mainframe computers through several types of cluster controllers.

First introduced in 1971, the IBM 3270 Information Display System was designed to extend the processing power of the mainframe computer to locations remote from the computer room. Controllers, which are more commonly known as control units, were made available to economize on the number of lines required to link display stations to mainframe computers. Typically, a number of display stations are connected to a control unit on individual cables and the control unit, in turn, is connected to the mainframe via a single cable. Both local and remote control units are offered, with the key differences between the two pertaining to the method of attachment to the mainframe computer and the use of intermediate devices between the control unit and the mainframe.

Local control units are usually attached to a channel on the mainframe, whereas remote control units are connected to the mainframe's communications controller. As a local control unit is within a limited distance of the mainframe, no intermediate communications devices, such as modems, are required to connect a local control unit to the mainframe. In comparison, a remote control unit can be located in another building or in a different city and normally requires the utilization of intermediate communications devices, such as a pair of modems, for communications to occur between the control unit and the communications controller. The relationship of local and control units to display stations, mainframes and a communications controller is illustrated in Figure 9.11. Note that this hardware relationship represents the hierarchy of equipment supported by SNA and explains the original hierarchical data flow associated with SNA networks.

## 9.2.1 Data flow

The control unit polls each connected display station to ascertain if the station has data stored in its transmit buffer. If the station has data in its buffer, it will transmit it to the control unit when it is polled. The control unit then formats the data with the display station's address, adds the control unit's address and other pertinent information and transmits it in a synchronous data format to the communications controller or to the I/O channel on the mainframe, depending upon the method used to connect the control unit to the mainframe.

Addressing information flowing to the mainframe initially begins with a terminal address. The control unit formats each data block received from a terminal device and adds its control unit identifier. If the control unit is connected to a communications controller the latter device adds a line identifier address to the data block, indicating the port on the controller where the information was received. After operating upon the data block the mainframe responds by generating a screen of data that will be routed to a specific terminal. To ensure that the response is routed correctly the mainframe includes the line, control unit and terminal address. The communications controller strips off the line identifier and forwards the data onto the appropriate line. As an SNA network supports multidrop circuits in which two or more control units can share the use of a common transmission line, the control unit address defines the control unit which will recognize the data block. That control unit removes the control unit address. Next, it examines the terminal identifier and removes it from the data block once it knows the line to transmit the block so it is received at its appropriate destination.

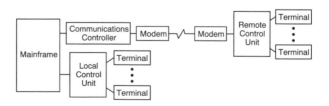

**Figure 9.11** Relationship of 3270 Information Display System hardware products

## 9.2.2 3270 protocols

Two different protocols are supported by IBM to connect 3270 devices to a mainframe. The original protocol used with 3270 devices and which is still periodically used today is the byte-oriented bisynchronous protocol, often referred to as 3270 bisync or BSC. In the late 1970s, when IBM introduced its Systems Network Architecture, it also introduced a bit-oriented protocol for data transmission known as Synchronous Data Link Control, or SDLC. Thus, communications between an IBM mainframe and the control units attached to the communications controller are either BSC or SDLC, depending upon the type of control units obtained and the configuration of the communications controller which is controlled by software. Today almost all BSC control units have been replaced by the use of more modern SDLC devices.

## 9.2.3 Types of control unit

Control units marketed support up to eight, 16, 32 or 64 attached devices, depending upon the model. The IBM 3276 control unit which is essentially an obsolete device supports up to eight devices while the IBM 3274 control unit can support 16 or 32 attached devices. Other older control units, such as the 3271, 3272, and 3275 were replaced by the 3274 and operate only bisynchronously, whereas certain models of the 3274 are 'soft' devices that can be programmed with a diskette to operate with the originally developed bisynchronous protocol or with the newer synchronous data link control (SDLC) protocol.

Devices to include display stations and printers are normally attached to each control unit via coaxial cable. Thus, under this design philosophy every display station must first be connected to a control unit prior to being able to access a mainframe application written for a 3270 type terminal. This method of connection excluded the utilization of dial-up terminals from accessing 3270 type applications and resulted in numerous third- party vendors marketing devices to permit lower-cost ASCII terminals to be attached to 3270 networks. In late 1986, IBM introduced a new controller known as the 3174 Subsystem Control Unit. This controller, which replaced older models, can be used to connect terminals via standard coaxial cable, shielded twisted-pair wire and telephone-type or unshielded twisted-pair wire. Other key features of the controller include an optional protocol converter which can support up to 24 asynchronous ports and the ability of the controller to be attached to IBM's Token-Ring local area network. The latter is accomplished through the use of a Token-Ring adapter card installed in a 3174 slot, converting the 3174 into an active participant on a Token-Ring network.

The 3174 can be obtained to support eight, 16, 32 or 64 ports. A 64 port 3174 supports a maximum of 254 LUs while a 32 port control unit supports a maximum of 128 LUs. All other 3174 control units provide an LU support capability equal to four times the number of ports on the device. Only the 64 port model slightly varies from this scheme, due to LU0 and LU1 being reserved on that device and unavailable for general use.

When used with a Token-Ring adapter (TRA) the TRA in a 3174 is limited to supporting up to 140 downstream PUs. Here the term PU in actuality can be considered as a gateway PC, with the software on each gateway determining the number of LUs supported on the Token-Ring. For example, Novell NetWare gateway software can be obtained to provide support for 16, 32 or 97 LUs. In this type of networking configuration which is illustrated in Figure 9.12, the communications controller polls the control unit, the control unit polls individual PU gateways and each gateway is responsible for polling the LUs serviced by the gateway. In this example the gateway PC is known as a downstream PU, which polls downstream LUs.

As SNA's architecture can be considered as a polling structure it is wise to limit the number of LUs on a gateway. Otherwise the polling time from the gateway PC to the LUs representing different sessions on each workstation or the screen and printer of a workstation can result in excess delays. Thus, a good rule of thumb is to add another downstream PU in the form of an additional gateway for every 32 workstations on a local area network.

## 9.2.4 Terminal displays

IBM 3270 terminals fall into three display classes: mono-chrome, color and gas plasma. Members of the monochrome display class include the 3278, 3178, 3180, 3191 and 3193 type terminals. The 3278 is a large, bulky terminal that covers a significant portion of one's desk and was replaced by the 3178, 3180, 3191 and 3193 display stations which are lighter, more

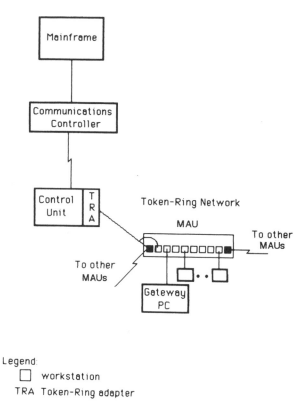

Legend:
☐ workstation
TRA Token-Ring adapter

**Figure 9.12**  Using a control unit TRA to interconnect a Token-Ring network. Through the installation of a TRA, both local and remote control units provide a connection capability to a Token-Ring network

compact and less expensive versions of the 3278. The 3279 color display station was similarly replaced by the 3179 and the 3194 which are lower-cost and more compact color display terminals. The last class of display stations is the gas plasma display, consisting of the 3270 flat panel display.

The physical dimensions of a 3270 type screen may vary by class and model within the class. As an example, the 3178 and 3278 Model 2 display stations have a screen size of 24 rows by 80 columns, while the 3278 Model 3 has a screen size of 32 rows by 80 columns and the 3278 Model 4 has a screen size of 43 rows by 80 columns.

Table 9.3 lists a portion of the family of terminals marketed for use with the IBM 3270 information display system. The reader should note that the 3170 and 3180 display stations can also be used with IBM System/3X minicomputers. In addition, the

**Table 9.3**  IBM display stations

| Model number | Display type | Screen (inches) |
| --- | --- | --- |
| 3178 | Monochrome | 12 |
| 3179 | Color | 14 |
| 3180 | Monochrome | 15 |
| 3191 | Monochrome | 12 |
| 3193 | Monochrome | 15 |
| 3194 | Color | 14 |

**Table 9.4**  3270 terminal field characteristics

| | |
| --- | --- |
| Highlighted | Field displayed at a brighter intensity than normal intensity field |
| Nondisplay | Field does not display any data typed into it |
| Protected | Field does not accept any input |
| Unprotected | Field accepts any data typed into it |
| Numeric-only | Field accepts only numbers as input Autoskip Field sends the cursor to the next unprotected field after it is filled with data |
| Underscoring | Causes characters to be underlined |
| Blinking | Causes characters in field to blink |

3193 and 3194 terminals can support the display of up to four host sessions when connected to the 3174 controller.

Each 3270 screen consists of fields that are defined by the application program connected to the display station. Attributes sent by the application program further define the characteristics of each field as indicated in Table 9.4. As a minimum, any technique used to enable a personal computer to function as a 3270 display station requires the PC to obtain the field attributes listed in Table 9.4.

## 9.2.5  3270 keyboard functions

In comparison to the keyboard of most personal computers, a 3270 display station contains approximately 40 additional keys, which, when pressed, perform functions unique to the 3270 terminal environment. A list of the more common 3270 keys which differ from the keys on most personal computer keyboards is contained in Table 9.5.

**Table 9.5**  Common 3270 keys differing from most personal computer keyboards

| Key(s) | Function |
|---|---|
| CLEAR | Erases screen except for characters in message area, repositioning cursor to row 1, column 1. |
| PA1 | Transmits a code to the application program which is interpreted as a break signal. Thus, in TSO or CMS the PA1 key would terminate the current command. |
| PA2 | Transmits a code to the application program that is often interpreted as a request to redisplay the screen or to clear the screen and display additional information. |
| PFnn | Twenty-four program function keys on a 3270 terminal are defined by the application program in use. |
| TAB | Moves the cursor to the next unprotected field. |
| BACKTAB | Moves the cursor to the previous unprotected field. |
| RESET | Disables the insert mode. |
| ERASEEOF | Deletes everything from the cursor to the end of the input field. |
| NEWLINE | Advances the cursor to the first unprotected field on the new line. |
| FASTRIGHT | Moves the cursor to the right two characters at a time. |
| FASTLEFT | Moves the cursor to the left two characters at a time. |
| ERASE INPUT | Clears all the input fields on the screen. |
| HOME | Moves the cursor to the first unprotected field on the screen. |

As most, if not all, of the 3270 keyboard functions may be required to successfully use a 3270 application program, the codes generated from pressing keys on a personal computer keyboard must be converted into appropriate codes that represent 3270 keyboard functions to enable a PC to be used as a 3270 terminal. Due to the lesser number of keys on a personal computer keyboard, a common approach to most emulation techniques is to use a two- or a three-key sequence on the PC keyboard to represent many of the keys unique to a 3270 keyboard.

*Emulation considerations*

In addition to converting keys on a personal computer keyboard to 3270 keyboard functions, 3270 emulation requires the PC's screen to function as a 3270 display screen. The 3270 display terminal operates by displaying an entire screen of data in one operation and then waits for the operator to signal that he or she is ready to proceed with the next screen of information. This operation mode is known as 'full-screen' operation and is exactly the opposite of TTY emulation where a terminal operates on a line-by-line basis. A key advantage of full-screen editing is the ability of the operator to move the cursor to any position on the screen to edit or change data. Thus, to use a personal computer workstation located on a local area network as a 3270 display station, the transmission codes used to position the 3270 screen and effect field attributes must be converted to equivalent codes recognizable by the PC. This means that individual workstations on the local area network must operate a terminal emulation program. This program works in tandem with the application program and communications controller through the 3174 control unit and gateway to enable the workstation to be recognized as a supported 3270 type terminal. Thus, in addition to gateway software each workstation on the local area network that requires access to the mainframe must operate a terminal emulation program.

## 9.3 SNA AND APPN GATEWAY OPTIONS

Now that we have a basic understanding of the architecture of SNA and APPN and the components and operations of the 3270 Information Display System, let us turn our attention to linking local area networks to IBM and IBM-compatible host computers. In doing so let us first expand upon our knowledge of the use of a control unit's TRA to provide a connection between an Ethernet LAN and an SNA network. Then, let us expand our discussion of gateway methods by examining different methods that can be used to connect LANs to SNA and APPN networks.

### 9.3.1 Ethernet connectivity

In Figure 9.12 we illustrated how a Token-Ring network could be connected to an SNA network through a 3174 control unit Token-Ring adapter. A similar mixture of hardware and software can be used to connect an Ethernet/IEEE 802.3 network to an SNA network. By examining how this is accomplished we can note some of the numerous vendor gateway construction options available for connecting different types of LANs into an SNA or APPN network.

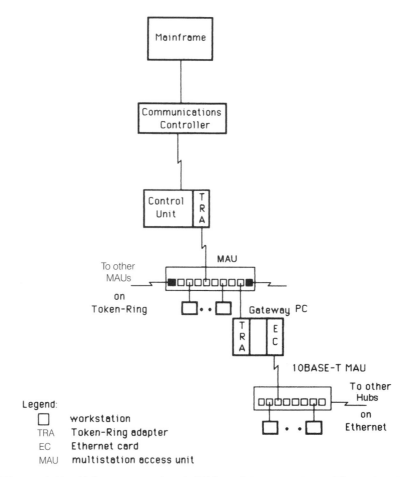

**Figure 9.13** Using a control unit TRA to interconnect an Ethernet network. Through the installation of a Token-Ring adapter and an Ethernet card and appropriate software, the gateway PC provides a connection from a 10BASE-T network to the mainframe via a Token-Ring network

Figure 9.13 illustrates the use of a gateway PC to connect an Ethernet 10BASE-T network to an SNA network. In this example the gateway PC contains a Token-Ring adapter card for connection to a MAU and an Ethernet card for connection to a 10BASE-T wire hub. Although it may appear that the gateway functions as a bridge, it operates at a much higher level, although it does transfer information between the Token-Ring and the Ethernet network. If the Ethernet is operating Novell NetWare, the gateway PC translates LUs into IPX addresses and vice versa. This address conversion is based upon configuring the gateway PC software when the gateway is installed. As LU assignments are defined in the NCP in the communications controller, this means that the gateway installation process must occur in close coordination with NCP programmers that encode the NCP to recognize the gateway as a downstream PU with LUs assigned to that PU. In addition, to enable workstations on the Ethernet to gain full screen access to mainframe applications, each workstation desiring such access must execute an appropriate terminal emulation program similar to that described for the previous Token-Ring network.

In the example illustrated in Figure 9.13 one vendor markets a gateway that can be configured to operate as one to eight separate PUs, with each PU capable of supporting up to 32 LUs. As two LUs on one PU are reserved, that vendor's product provides the ability to support up to 254 LUs. This provides the servicing of up to 127 workstations that use separate LUs for screen and printer or a lesser number of workstations that require the ability to execute multiple SNA sessions in the form of additional LUs.

### 9.3.2 Alternative gateway methods

The previous Token-Ring and Ethernet gateways used the services of a TRA on a control unit, requiring the physical presence of a control unit to interconnect to an SNA network. Recognizing the additional hardware cost of a control unit can limit the effectiveness of that gateway method, several vendors, including IBM and third-party vendors such as Eicon Technology of Montreal, Canada, market alternative solutions which enable different types of local area networks to access SNA networks over wide area network facilities. Thus, let us look at a few of those alternative solutions.

*SDLC connectivity*

An SDLC gateway consists of a pair of adapter cards installed in a personal computer and appropriate software that performs the required conversion from the packet format used on the local area network to an SNA data stream. One card is an SDLC adapter which provides the framing for the bit-oriented protocol used by SNA. In actuality, most vendor SDLC gateways include SNA functions in Read Only Memory (ROM) on the adapter card, which makes the card function as if it was a series of 3274

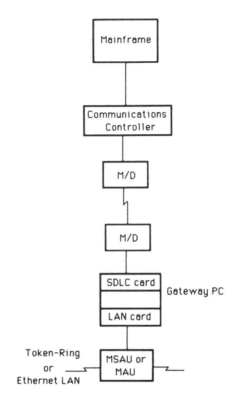

Legend:
M/D    modem or data service unit
MSAU multistation access unit
MAU    media access unit

**Figure 9.14** Using a SDLC gateway. An SDLC gateway provides access to an SNA network by providing communications between a LAN and a communications controller

control units (multiple PUs) with each PU associated with a group of LUs. This second adapter is typically a Token-Ring or Ethernet adapter, used to connect the gateway to either a Token-Ring or Ethernet local area network.

Figure 9.14 illustrates the use of an SDLC gateway to obtain access to a communications controller via a wide area network or an extended distance cable. Concerning the latter, the use of an SDLC gateway may permit the connection of a LAN to a communications controller via a lengthy cable within a building. This may be more attractive than the use of the gateway via a control unit TRA whose cable distance is limited to LAN cabling restrictions.

Both RS-232 and V.35 connectors can be obtained with most SDLC adapters. The use of an RS-232 connector limits the SDLC transmission rate to 19.2 Kbps while the use of a V.35 connector enables digital transmission facilities at 56 Kbps to be used to connect the gateway to the communications controller.

Some SDLC gateways are limited to supporting one PU and 32 LUs. Other SDLC gateways considerably expand upon that basic level of support. For example, an Eicon SNA gateway product which uses SDLC connectivity to a communications controller supports 32 PUs and up to 254 sessions. In addition, an Eicon gateway can be configured using up to four cards which results in a total of 128 PUs and 1016 sessions that can be supported by one gateway PC. Of course, limiting the transmission to either 19.2 Kbps or 56 Kbps per card may severely restrict LAN performance when accessing the mainframe.

## X.25 connectivity

As previously mentioned in this chapter, SNA networks support the CCITT X.25 protocol. This support is not a standard part of an SNA network, requiring an IBM software program known as NCP Packet Switching Interface (NPSI) to be obtained and loaded as an NCP module in a communications controller. Through the use of NPSI an IBM communications controller, such as the 3745, can be directly connected to a packet switching network. This in turn enables any terminal device capable of supporting the X.25 protocol to communicate with the communications controller via the use of a packet network's transmission facilities.

To take advantage of NPSI and the use of a packet switching network as a data transport mechanism several vendors introduced X.25 gateways. This type of gateway is also constructed through the use of adapter cards installed in the system unit of a personal computer. Typically, two or three adapter cards may be required, with the actual number dependent upon a vendor's use of ROM versus loadable software. One adapter card provides the connection to the local area network while a second adapter card packetizes data for transmission on the packet network. Either a third card or perhaps loadable software makes the gateway PC function as a downstream PU with LUs, in effect functioning as a control unit. Data from the local area network is converted into a 3270 format

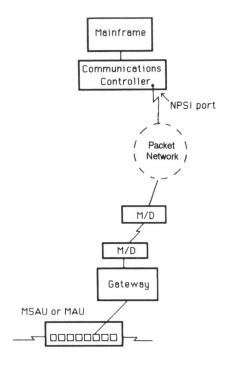

Legend:

    M/D   modem or data service unit
    MSAU multistation access unit
    MAU  media access unit

**Figure 9.15** X.25 gateway operation. An X.25 gateway converts LAN packets into a 3270 data stream and encapsulates the data into X.25 packets for transmission through a packet network

and encapsulated into an X.25 data stream by the gateway personal computer. That data is routed through the packet network to the IBM communications controller, where the NPSI port converts the datastream back into the 3270 format created by the gateway PC. Figure 9.15 illustrates the operation of an X.25 gateway.

Similar to an SDLC gateway, the major constraint of an X.25 gateway concerns its operating rate, throughput, and PU and LU support. The operating rate of an X.25 card is limited to 64 Kbps; however, its throughput may be considerably less than that of an SDLC gateway operating at the same data rate. This is because the X.25 gateway not only packetizes data, adding additional overhead, but in addition has its data checked as it flows through the packet network. The additional delays due to the error checking performed at packet switches can add between 0.25 and 0.5 seconds to the response time of network users in comparison to the use of an SDLC gateway. However, one NPSI port can provide support for more than one X.25 gateway connected via a packet network to the mainframe location. In comparison, each SDLC gateway requires the use of a separate SDLC port on the communications controller, making the decision between the use of SDLC and X.25 gateways consider the cost of public network usage charges versus building a network, as well as a trade-off between performance and hardware cost in the form of additional communications controller ports. As an X.25 gateway can be considered to encapsulate the functions of an SDLC gateway into X.25 packets, it should come as no surprise that their PU and LU support should be the same. This appears to be true for all vendor products examined by the author.

## The TIC connection

The use of a Token Interface Coupler (TIC) installed in a communications controller provides a gateway access method very similar to a control unit with a TRA. That is, the TIC is cabled to an MAU port and one or more gateway PCs are also cabled to an MAU port.

The primary differences between the use of a communications controller TIC and a control unit TRA are in the areas of cost, network interconnection distance, operating rate and PU and LU support.

A TIC can cost well over $10 000. In comparison a TRA costs under $200. Concerning the network interconnection distance, the use of a TIC restricts access to the LAN cabling distance since the communications controller must be cabled to an MAU under lobe length distance restrictions. In comparison, a local control unit can be connected via coaxial cable to a communications controller which enables the gateway distance to be extended. If a remote control unit is used that device functions similar to a remote communications controller since both the TRA and the TIC cabling distances to an MAU are governed by lobe distance restrictions.

In a local environment the communications controller and control unit are both channel attached to a host computer, plus their data transfer capabilities are similar. In a remote environment the transmission rate of a control unit is restricted to a maximum of 56 Kbps. In comparison, a remote communications controller can operate at T1/E1 data rates, providing over 20 times the data transfer capability of a control unit. Thus, the TIC can provide a higher level of throughput when used at a remote location.

The biggest difference between the use of a TRA and a TIC is in the area of PU and LU support. The NCP on a communications controller can support up to 9999 PUs per TIC. Then, each gateway PC functioning as a PU will support a grouping of LUs based upon the gateway software used. Another key difference between the use of a TRA and a TIC concerns the method of gateway communications.

When a control unit TRA provides a connection to the Token-Ring network the communications controller polls the control unit and the control unit polls each downstream PU, with each gateway polling its LUs. When a TIC is used each downstream PU requests service from the TIC by using a 'dial-up' service when it requires service. Thus, this can considerably reduce the polls flowing on an attached local area network and results in the TIC being able to theoretically support up to 9999 PUs.

*3278/9 coaxial connection*

A rather outdated and limited function gateway is based upon the use of a 3278/9 coaxial adapter card. Instead of emulating a 3X74 control unit like SDLC and X.25 gateways, the coaxial adapter permits a gateway PC to be connected to a port on a 3X74 control unit. That port can be configured as a distributed function terminal (DFT) port. When used in this manner the DFT port provides access to five sessions as it represents five LUs. Gateway software then divides the five SNA mainframe sessions among contending workstations on the local area network. This means that a coaxial adapter-based gateway is limited to providing a maximum of five simultaneous host sessions. Similar to the other gateways described in this section, a Token-Ring or Ethernet adapter card would be installed in the gateway to provide a connection to the local area network. Figure 9.16 illustrates the hardware used to provide a 3278/9 coaxial cable gateway.

Although a coaxially connected gateway is limited in its session support, it operates at coaxial cable data transfer rates to the control unit. If a local control unit is used the operating rate of a coaxially connected gateway can approach

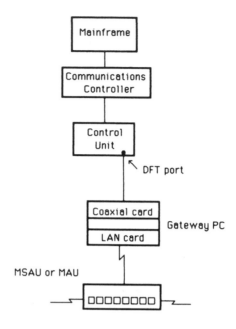

Legend:

DFT    distributed function terminal
MSAU   multistation access unit
MAU    media access unit

**Figure 9.16**  3278/9 coaxial connectivity. Through the use of a 3278/9 coaxial adapter card, LAN card, and a DFT port on a control unit, up to five LAN workstations can simultaneously access an SNA network

2 Mbps. In comparison, SDLC and X.25 type gateways are limited to a 56 Kbps data transfer rate. Thus, coaxially connected gateways can provide a high level of SNA access performance for small local area networks when such networks are at the mainframe location. In addition, this method eliminates the necessity to obtain a TIC or TRA and can be used with older 3274 control units that cannot support the installation of a Token-Ring adapter. Thus, the coaxially connected gateway also represents the lowest cost gateway.

### 9.3.3 Using the 3172 Interconnect Controller

The IBM 3172 Interconnect Controller can be considered to represent the Swiss Army knife equivalent of gateway computers. The 3172 can be directly channel attached to S/370 and

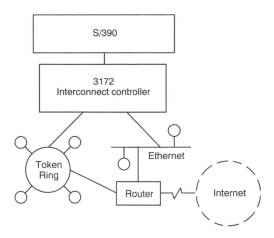

**Figure 9.17**  Using the 3172 Interconnect Controller

S/390 computers either via a parallel or ESCON channel, and supports the connection of a variety of LAN and WAN connections as well as a mixture of protocols that can run over those connections.

Although we previously examined the general networking capability of the 3172 Interconnect Controller in Chapter 3, we will now look at a specific example of its flexibility. Figure 9.17 illustrates how a 3172 Interconnect Controller can be used as a gateway between an IBM host and the Internet. In this example, the 3172 Interconnect Controller enables TCP/IP communications to flow on the Token-Ring and Ethernet networks shown connected to the 3172. This in turn enables the router-based connections to the Internet to reach the mainframe via the 3172. As a word of caution, this schematic relies upon the filtering capability of the router for security. Many organizations will prefer an additional level of protection in the form of a firewall, whose operation is discussed in Chapter 10.

*Software considerations*

Although the 3172 and other gateway products provide users with the ability to route data between devices that communicate using different protocols, you must also consider the software on the end station accessing the host to obtain a full gateway capability. As previously noted in section 2, IBM's 3270 Information Display system uses special codes to enable and

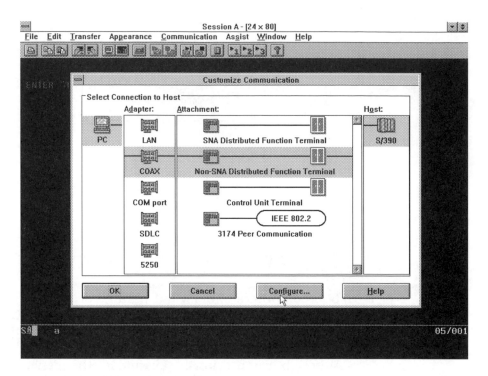

**Figure 9.18** Using PCOM/3270 to select an appropriate attachment method when using a coaxial cable adapter for host communicatons

disable a variety of terminal features associated with that vendor's original series of fixed logic terminal devices. As PCs began to replace dumb terminals, emulation programs were required to enable PC-based LAN workstations to obtain keyboard and screen operation compatibility with IBM hosts. One of the most popular IBM 3270 display station emulation programs is the PCOM/3270, an acronym for IBM's Personal Communications/3270 series of emulation programs.

If the 3172 can be considered as the Swiss Army knife of gateways, the PCOM/3270 might represent the Swiss Army knife of emulation programs. PCOM/3270 supports a variety of mainframe attachment methods, ranging from LAN adapters and coaxial cable to asynchronous and synchronous serial communications. Figure 9.18 illustrates the PCOM/3270 customize communications display screen which shows four options for communicating from a coaxial based PC to a S/390 host. In examining Figure 9.18, note that the entry Coax in the column labeled Adapter is shown selected, which results in the

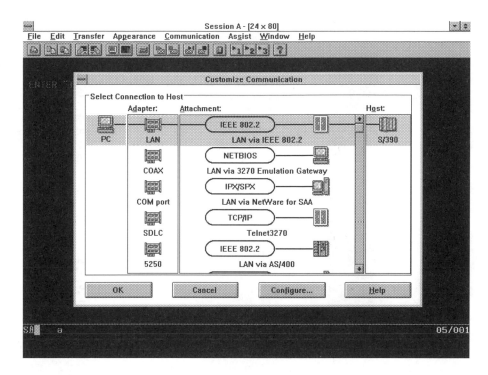

**Figure 9.19** Using PCOM/3270 to select a LAN attachment via an IEEE 802.2 network

display of four attachment methods shown in the middle of the illustration. In comparison, the use of a LAN adapter card provides a terminal emulation capability for a larger number of attachment options. Figure 9.19 illustrates the PCOM/3270 configuration display after the LAN option was selected for the adapter card. In this example, the highlighted bar is shown placed over the IEEE 802.2 attachment method. Thus, if we were configuring a LAN station or an Ethernet or Token-Ring network connected to a S/390 via a TIC or a similar gateway method, we would select that attachment method.

Once you have selected your attachment method, you can customize your workstation's session parameters. Figure 9.20 illustrates the customization screen for an SDLC connection from a PC to a S/390 host. Although the default screen display of 24 lines by 80 columns is shown, PCOM/370 supports a number of screen size options that work relatively well with SVGA based workstations. For example, if your requirements include a 132 column display you can easily adjust the screen size by a simple point and click operation.

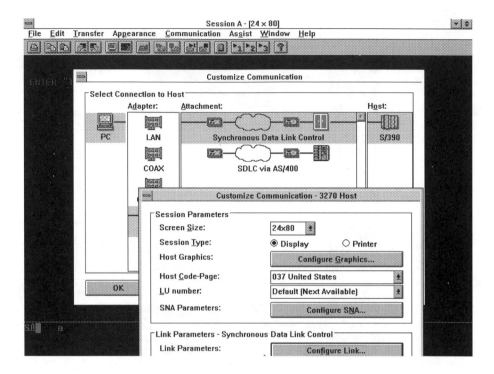

**Figure 9.20** Using PCOM/3270 to adjust session parameters

*TN3270 operations*

One of the more interesting methods for accessing S/390 hosts is via a special version of Telnet known as TN3270. Through the use of a TN3270 program you can access IBM mainframes connected to the Internet via the Internet. This capability results from the fact that TN3270 represents a TCP/IP program that operates on top of a TCP/IP protocol stack.

Figure 9.21 illustrates the connection configuration of the NetManage Chameleon TN3270 terminal emulation program to initiate a session with a mainframe whose IP address is 192.76.46.1. Note that the session request will occur on TCP port 23 and the PC running TN3270 will operate as a 3270 model 2 display which uses a 24 by 80 character display. Figure 9.22 illustrates a TCP/IP connection to a S/390 using TN3270 via an Internet connection to a 3172 which in turn is connected to a S/390 mainframe. Although the TN3270 program used by the author uses a GUI interface, the actual display generated by

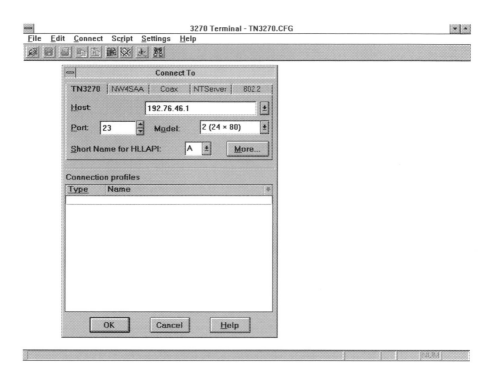

**Figure 9.21** Using the NetManage Chameleon TN3270 terminal emulation program to obtain TCP/IP access to an IBM SNA host

the S/390 host is text-based. This is illustrated in Figure 9.22 which illustrates the use of TN3270 to access the author's calendar stored on a mainframe calendar system. Now that we have an appreciation for APPN and SNA gateways and the use of emulation software, we can turn our attention to the integration of APPN and SNA traffic into a TCP/IP network. As this capability can be considered to represent an SNA to TCP/IP gateway performed by Data Link Switching, we will next focus our attention upon this gateway technique.

## 9.4 DATA LINK SWITCHING

One of the major problems associated with SNA and APPN based networks is the fact that both are essentially proprietary. As the use of TCP/IP expanded for interconnecting LANs on private intranets as well as for communications with the Internet, many organizations were forced to maintain two separate networks,

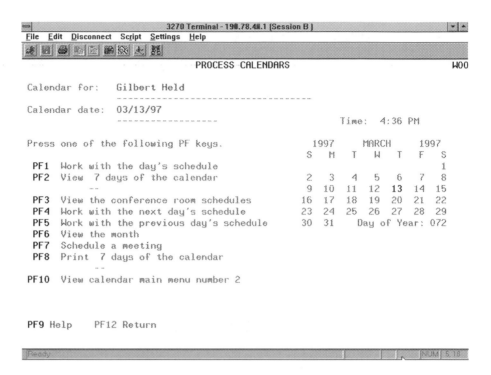

**Figure 9.22**  Using a TN3270 session to access a mainframe-based calendar system

one for SNA and one for a second network protocol which is commonly TCP/IP.

In an effort to better support customer requirements for improving connectivity and lowering the cost associated with multiprotocol networking, IBM developed a tunneling mechanism referred to as Data Link Switching (DLSw). DLSw was first introduced by IBM in 1992 as a feature of its 6611 bridge-router series of products referred to as the Nways 6611 Network Processor. IBM submitted its effort to the Internet Engineering Task Force (IETF) which resulted in DLSw being standardized as RFC 1434. It was also standardized by an IBM-sponsored multivendor forum known as the APPN Implementors' Workshop.

### 9.4.1 Overview

Data Link Switching was developed as a mechanism to support SNA and NetBIOS data traffic via both bridged and router-based networks in a multiprotocol environment. Although DLSw is primarily used to tunnel SNA and NetBIOS under IP, it can also be used to tunnel other protocols. As DLSw enables organizations to merge their SNA and APPN networks with their IP-based networks, many redundant communications links become candidates for removal, enabling organizations to operate a more efficient and less costly network infrastructure.

### 9.4.2 Operation

Under DLSw the connection-oriented protocols of SNA and NetBIOS in the form of Logical Link Control Type 2 (LLC2) and Synchronous Data Link Control (SDLC) packets are encapsulated into IP packets. Figure 9.23 illustrates an example of the manner by which point-to-point SDLC traffic and LAN based LLC2 traffic are integrated into an IP router-based network. In examining Figure 9.23, note that the tunneling effort involves wrapping the IP header around SDLC or LLC2 data. As such data then becomes encapsulated, as you might expect, another term used to refer to the transport of SDLC and LLC2 data in IP packets is encapsulation.

Although the actual tunneling or encapsulation process appears to be relatively simple to accomplish, in actuality it is a complicated process. The complication results from the fact that SNA uses connection-oriented protocols, LLC2 and SDLC, which are based upon positive acknowledgment with retransmission (PAR). As such, if an ACK is not received within a period of time after a sequence of frames have been transmitted, a timer will expire, resulting in the sending station retransmitting the data. If, due to network congestion a circuit failure or other impairments repeat, after a predefined number of repeats the connection will be terminated, resulting in the loss of any in progress SNA and NetBIOS sessions. As IP is a connectionless protocol, the transport of SDLC and LLC2 data within IP would very likely result in periodic session timeouts as traffic density varies during the day. To prevent this situation from occurring, DLSw relies on spoofing, with the sending router acknowledging frames as they are received. The routers then use a reliable transport protocol, such as TCP, to ensure that data arrives at its intended destination. A slightly different procedure is used for SDLC which relies on the constant polling between primary and secondary SDLC stations. DLSw capable routers perform proxy polling. That is, the sending router intercepts polls from

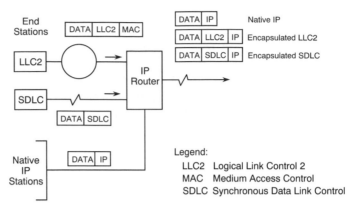

**Figure 9.23** The DLSw tunneling process

the SDLC primary station while another router polls the SDLC secondary station as if it was the SDLC primary station. Since polls are not passed onto the IP network, transmission efficiency is enhanced.

Although any encapsulation or tunneling method adds overhead in the form of an additional header, the use of spoofing and proxy polling can be considered as a significant counterbalance. Thus, in most cases the overhead associated with the use of additional headers will have a negligible effect upon the overall performance of DLSw.

## 9.5 COMMUNICATIONS SERVERS

A communications server is a relatively new term being used for a multifunction protocol gateway. The idea behind the communications server is to provide network managers and LAN administrators with protocol independence, enabling network design and restructuring decisions to be made independent of existing network topology constraints associated with network protocols currently being used.

Although Data Link Switching can be considered to represent a mechanism that provides a multiprotocol gateway capability, it is based upon the use of tunneling of LLC2 and SDLC in IP. Thus, it is restricted to enabling specific protocols to be transported under IP which, while an acceptable solution for the networking requirements of many organizations, may not be sufficient for use by other organizations. Another problem associated with the use of tunneling or encapsulation is the fact that application data must first be structured through one protocol stack prior to being encapsulated and processed through a second protocol stack. This means that in addition to an additional load being placed on the network in the form of dual headers, there is also an additional processing time at each device that performs the encapsulation function.

## 9.5.1 MPTN

Recognizing the above problems, IBM developed a protocol conversion facility which works on several types of hardware platform operating its AIX and OS/2 operating systems as well as under Microsoft's Windows NT. This protocol conversion facility is called Multiprotocol Transport Networking (MPTN) and it employs protocol conversion instead of encapsulation whenever possible.

MPTN operates at the Application Programming Interface (API) layer. Operating at the lower portion of the Application Layer in the protocol stack, MPTN would, for example, convert the sockets interface to use SNA protocols instead of TCP/IP or the APPC interface to use TCP/IP protocols instead of SNA. Through the use of MPTN, an application invokes its preferred API without knowledge of the actual network protocol that will be used. MPTN then converts the API calls to use the protocol of the desired transport network. Figure 9.24 provides a comparison between protocol encapsulation and MPTN's protocol conversion.

Through the use of protocol conversion the transport of information is not tied to a specific protocol. This means that from a theoretical basis a communications server could be developed to provide a large number of protocol conversions that could provide organizations with a protocol-independent capability. However, from a practical standpoint the development of conversion software is a time-consuming effort and most communications servers are limited to providing a gateway between SNA and TCP/IP networks, although certain IBM products also provide a conversion capability for Novell IPX as well as IBM's LAN Manager's NetBIOS.

Figure 9.25 illustrates the use of two communications servers to integrate IPX and TCP/IP based LANs with an SNA network. In this example one communications server provides conversion from the TCP/IP based networks to SNA while the second server performs a similar function for an IPX network.

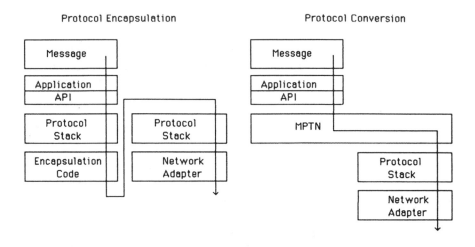

Legend:
    API    Application Program Interface
    MPTN   Multiprotocol Transport Networking

**Figure 9.24**   Comparing protocol encapsulation and converion

## 9.5.2 Other gateways

As any conversion device can be considered to represent a gateway there are numerous gateway products network managers and administrators can consider when linking LANs

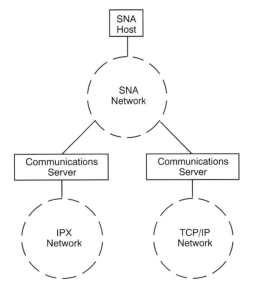

**Figure 9.25**   Using communications servers

and WANs. Some of those products include electronic mail gateways which provide you with the ability to interconnect different email systems, application gateways, and trusted gateways. An application gateway is another name for a proxy server and represents a more secure type of firewall. The proxy, which functions at one layer of the protocol stack, services all requests from clients, and, if allowed, forwards them to the other side of the network to their intended destination. In comparison, a trusted gateway represents a firewall whose software operates on a very secure operating system. Readers are referred to Chapter 10 for detailed information concerning the operation and utilization of firewalls as well as the different features supported by this class of communications equipment.

# 10

# NETWORK SECURITY

One of the major goals of any organization that connects an internal private network to a public network is to do so in a manner that minimizes the possibility of security threats to the internal network. Although we would obviously prefer to eliminate all risk, the complexity of hardware and software may result in loopholes that hackers may be able to exploit. Thus, we should assume that there will always be some risk associated with the connection of a private internal network to a public network and consider the use of hardware and software to minimize that risk.

In this chapter we will examine the operation and utilization of two networking devices that can be used to minimize the threat associated with connecting a private network to a public network, such as the Internet. The first device we will examine is the router, which provides the ability to block data transfers based upon network and transport layer information. Although this level of protection may be sufficient for many networks, it precludes the ability to stop a variety of network attacks, as well as ignoring such key security items as authentication and encryption. Thus, in the second portion of this chapter, we will turn our attention to the use of firewalls and their operational capability in the form of proxy services that can be used to plug the holes associated with a reliance upon routers for network security.

## 10.1 ROUTERS

Routers operate at layer 3 of the ISO Reference Model. This means that they can read network layer information. Recognizing that routers provide the basic mechanism by which private and public networks are interconnected, and also recognizing the need of organizations to control access to their internal network, router manufacturers added a packet filtering capability to their products. This capability, frequently implemented in the form of a list of access permissions, is also commonly referred to as a router's access list and is the focus of this section.

## 10.1.1 Access lists

An access list represents a sequential collection of permit and deny conditions that are applied to network addresses based upon a particular protocol. As the most common internetworking protocol is TCP/IP, we will focus our attention upon router access lists designed to predefine the data flow between networks connected by routers transferring TCP/IP packets. Thus, the use of router access lists can be used to govern the data flow between segments on an internal corporate private network as well as between a private and public network. Readers should note that although our examination of access lists will be focused upon the TCP/IP protocol, it is also applicable, if supported by the router manufacturer, to other network layer protocols to include NetWare IPX, AppleTalk, and DecNET.

As previously indicated in Chapter 3, the IP header contains both a source address and a destination address field. Under IPv4 those fields are 32 bits in length, whereas under the evolving IPv6 they are 128 bits in length. For both versions of IP the source address identifies the originator and the destination address identifies the recipient. Although IP represents the routable network layer of the TCP/IP protocol stack, end-to-end transmission is a layer 4 responsibility. At layer 4 the TCP/IP protocol suite supports two transport protocols, the Transport Control Protocol (TCP) and the User Datagram Protocol (UDP). Although TCP and UDP headers differ, both contain 16 bit Source and Destination ports that identify the port number of the sending and receiving process, respectively. As each IP header is followed by either a TCP or a UDP header, a router can control the data flow of TCP/IP packets by operating upon up to four distinct fields that define the sender, recipient, and process. This method of control is commonly referred to as packet filtering and is controlled by the creation of an appropriate access list. Thus, let us turn our attention to the configuration of several access lists to meet different organizational requirements.

## Configuring an access list

Although there are considerable differences between routers with respect to their use of access lists, most devices operate very similarly with respect to two key operations. First, they commonly compare packet fields sequentially against the contents of the access list. This means that the first match determines if a router will accept or reject a packet. Secondly, routers either have a default of permit or deny. This means that unless an access list has entries to override the default, the default condition will be applied to all non-listed situations. As the best way to become familiar with access lists is by example, let us do so. In doing so we will use a generic command format for illustrative purposes that may or may not be applicable to specific routers.

For our first example we will assume that a router's access list is applicable to incoming packets received on a WAN connection and that the router using the list has only one LAN port. Thus, the access list does not include a port specification. Figure 10.1 illustrates an example of the network configuration associated with the router. In this example we will use an access list to control access to computers on the internal Ethernet LAN shown connected to the Internet.

Based upon the preceding, let us assume the format of the access list is as follows:

Access-list {permit | deny} source address, port

In the preceding access list format, the port represents the numeric associated with the TCP or UDP process and is also referred to as the well-known port. Table 10.1 lists ten examples of well-known TCP/UDP ports.

If we assume that the asterisk is used as a wildcard in IP address and port process value fields, two examples of access list entries follow:

access-list permit 198.*.*.*, *
access-list deny *.*.*.*, 80

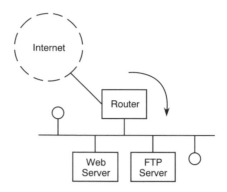

By programming access lists based upon source and
destination address and well-known port, you can control
access to computers on your internal private network

**Figure 10.1** Using a router access list to control packet flow from the Internet onto a private Ethernet LAN

**Table 10.1** Well-known TCP/UDP ports

| Port number | Use |
| --- | --- |
| 20 | FTP (data) |
| 21 | FTP (control) |
| 23 | Telnet |
| 25 | SMTP |
| 43 | Whois |
| 53 | DNS |
| 69 | TFTP |
| 70 | Gopher |
| 79 | finger |
| 80 | HTTP |

In the first example any packet with a source address on a 198 network regardless of port value is permitted. In the second example, incoming HTTP (port 80) from any address is denied. Readers should note that the two access list entries placed together in an access list would have the unintended effect of allowing all packets from network 198 including HTTP packets to be permitted to flow through the router. Thus, if you wish to deny HTTP from network 198 you could either move the second access list entry to the top of the access list, or prefix the two access list entries with the following entry:

Access-list deny 198.*.*.*, 80

Reversing access list entries would result in the following access list:

access-list deny *.*.*.*, 80
access-list permit 198.*.*.*, *

Now the first entry would deny all HTTP inbound traffic while the second entry would allow all traffic from network 198; however, since HTTP was previously barred, the second entry would only enable non-HTTP traffic from network 198.

The use of three entries in the access list would result in the following list:

access-list deny 198.*.*.*, 80
access-list permit 198.*.*.*, *
access-list deny *.*.*.*, 80

Now the first entry specifically denies HTTP access from network 198 and the second entry allows all traffic from network 198 other than HTTP that was previously barred. The third entry denies HTTP from all other network locations.

It should be noted that depending upon whether the general access default is permit or deny, you may at worst be required to modify your access list or at best have extraneous statements in your access list. For example, if your router's default is to deny all packets unless specifically permitted and you want to allow all packets from network 198 to include HTTP, you would only need one access list entry. That entry would be:

access-list permit 198.*.*.*, *

### Extended access lists

Recognizing that routers can have multiple LAN interfaces, a logical extension of an access list is to apply list entries to specific ports. Thus, a second generic access list format is shown below:

access-list {permit|deny} port-out, source address, port

Here the port-out entry is a numeral which identifies a LAN interface.

To illustrate the application of this extended access list, let us assume that a router is used to interconnect two LANs to the Internet as illustrated in Figure 10.2. Further assume that the Token-Ring network provides connectivity to an internal corporate network while the Ethernet LAN contains a public access Web server. Thus, one possible extended access list might be as follows:

access-list permit 1, *.*.*.*, 80
access-list permit 2, *.*.*.*, 25

The first entry in the access list permits packets from any address containing HTTP (port 80) to be routed through the router and placed onto the Ethernet LAN. The second entry permits packets from any address containing SMTP (port 25) email to be routed through the router onto port 2 which is the Token-Ring network. If we presume a default of denial of service unless explicitly permitted, all other packets are sent to the great bit bucket in the sky. Thus, this short access list only permits email to flow onto the Token-Ring network and Web access to the Ethernet public access network.

### Additional extensions

Some routers permit packet filtering based upon source and destination addresses as well as well-known ports for both inbound and outbound traffic. Thus, such routers may have an access list format similar to the following:

access-list {permit | deny} port-in, port-out, source, destination

When you obtain the ability to filter packets based upon inbound or outbound direction, you must usually include the direction of packet flow in the form of port-in to port-out port numbers. Other routers only require one physical port number to be specified; however, they then require a direction field in the access list to indicate if filtering should occur on inbound or outbound packets. Regardless of the method used, the ability to perform filtering based upon inbound and outbound packets provides additional security in the form of limiting access of organizational employees. For example, if your organization is using the Internet to connect several geographically dispersed corporate locations, you can use outbound filtering to limit

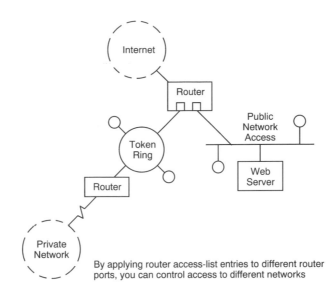

By applying router access-list entries to different router
ports, you can control access to different networks

**Figure 10.2**   Connecting two LANs to the Internet

employees to accessing only other corporate locations, prevent-
ing inadvertent downloading of viruses from an anonymous FTP
site. Thus, the ability to perform filtering on both inbound and
outbound traffic can enhance the ability of network managers to
control communications.

### 10.1.2 Router access

As access to the configuration capability of a router controls its
filtering capability, it is important to control such access. All too
often persons forget to change the default login password, which
can result in a hacker easily taking control of your router. Most
routers provide access control not only via a console port, but, in
addition, via Telnet and SNMP. This means that if a person
knows or stumbles upon the IP address of an interface of the
router via Telnet or SNMP, they can first try some common
default passwords to gain access to the router's console
capability. To prevent this situation from occurring, you should
consider disabling such access. If you need the ability to
remotely configure a router, you should change the default
password. In doing so, you should use an alphanumeric string
instead of a common name to prevent a dictionary attack. Many

hackers purchase or otherwise acquire an electronic dictionary and write a program to try each entry in an attempt to break into routers and servers. Although such passwords as heather, administration, bozo, and georgia might be easy to remember, they would all fail upon a dictionary attack. Thus, adding numerals to a name precludes the ability of a dictionary attack to be successful.

Now that we have an appreciation for the level of security afforded by the packet filtering capabilities of routers, let us discuss why you may wish to consider additional security in the form of a firewall by examining some common threats that routers cannot prevent.

### 10.1.3 Threats not handled

There are numerous security threats that the packet filtering capability of routers cannot control. Table 10.2 lists six common threats presented in alphabetical order that can result in security-related problems that a router cannot detect. Although you could use a router's filtering capability to bar access to an FTP server, you cannot selectively control different FTP commands. Thus, the use of unauthorized commands would represent an all or nothing issue when working with router filters. To provide an additional level of security beyond packet level filtering, organizations commonly turn to the use of a firewall.

## 10.2 FIREWALL

Unlike a router, which simply passes packets from one interface to another, firewalls include a proxy service capability which results in IP packets being barred from directly passing from input to output destinations. Instead, the firewall obtains the capability to examine the contents of each packet at each layer in the ISO Reference Model up through the application layer. Depending upon the capabilities programmed into the firewall, the use of proxy services makes the device able to detect suspicious activity on a given connection, generate alerts in response to suspicious activity, differentiate between different file transfer modes, and make authentication and authorization decisions. Thus, a firewall can be considered to represent a

**Table 10.2**  Common security threats not controllable by routers

| Threat | Description |
| --- | --- |
| Communications monitoring | A tap of your organization's Internet connection provides passwords and user account information as well as the ability to read data transferred. |
| Dictionary attack | Hacker tries each entry in electronic dictionary to gain access to device. |
| Password guessing | Hacker uses default installation password or common passwords such as 'cisco' for accounts. |
| Terminal session monitoring | Hacker monitors active user, capturing keystrokes in an attempt to learn login to another system. |
| Virus upload | A program containing a virus is placed onto a corporate FTP server or as an attachment to an email. |

much more sophisticated security device than that obtainable through the use of the packet filtering capability of a router.

### 10.2.1 Placement

When connecting an internal private network to the Internet or to a similar public network, a firewall is placed between the two, protecting inside users from outside users. Although you can place a firewall on an internal network and have all incoming access first directed to that device, if a person learns your internal network addressing scheme, it becomes possible to bypass the firewall and direct packets to recipients that may be better served by a packet examination process performed by the proxy service capability of most firewalls. Thus, the most common method used to install a firewall is to locate it on a separate network, a network commonly referred to as a demilitarized zone, or DMZ. The term DMZ or DMZ LAN obtains its name from the fact that that LAN contains no directly connected organizational computers. Instead, a DMZ LAN only has two connections, a router connection and a firewall connection. Thus, all incoming packets must be first processed by the firewall prior to being transferred to the private network.

Figure 10.3 illustrates the placement of a firewall on a DMZ Token-Ring LAN which would consist of a MAU with two

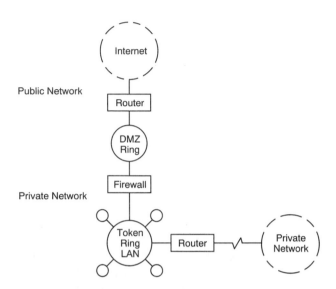

**Figure 10.3**   A firewall is normally connected to a DMZ LAN

connections, one for the router and a second for the firewall. Note that the second firewall connection is to another Token-Ring; however, this ring represents part of the corporate network that is protected by the firewall.

### 10.2.2  Features

With over 50 vendors actively marketing firewalls, you would be quite correct in assuming that their features and operational capability can considerably differ between vendor products. Table 10.3 lists six basic firewall features that you should, as a minimum, consider when acquiring this communications device. Due to the importance of these features, let us review each.

*Proxy services*

A proxy represents a code that performs handshaking for a specific application, such as FTP, Telnet, or HTTP. Through the proxy services capability of a firewall, specific users or groups of users can be allowed or denied access to a server or to a subset of a server's functionality. For example, through the use of FTP proxy services, you may be able to enable or disable the use of

**Table 10.3** Basic firewall features to consider

| |
| --- |
| Proxy services |
| Address translation |
| Stateful inspection |
| Alerts |
| Authentication |
| Packet filtering |

GET, MGET, PUT, MPUT, and other FTP commands for all addresses or selected IP addresses. Thus, it is important to examine both the type of proxy services supported by a firewall as well as the commands supported for each service supported.

Readers should note that proxy services can vary considerably between different firewall products. However, this functionality does not exist in routers nor firewalls that simply provide an expanded packet filtering capability. Thus, proxy services represent a feature that can be used to differentiate a more capable firewall from less capable products.

To illustrate the configuration of proxy services and some additional firewall features, this author captured several configuration screens generated by the Technologic Interceptor firewall. Figure 10.4 illustrates the Interceptor's Advanced Policy Options screen in which the cursor is shown pointed to the toggled check associated with the FTP Put command to block FTP uploads. In examining Figure 10.4 and subsequent Interceptor screen displays, you will note that they represent HTML screens displayed using a Netscape browser. The Technologic Interceptor firewall generates HTML forms to enable network managers to view, add, and modify firewall configuration data. To secure such operations the firewall uses encryption and authentication by supporting Netscape's Secure Sockets Layer (SSL) protocol for encrypting all traffic between the firewall and a Web browser used to configure the firewall, while passwords are used for authentication. This means that network managers can safely configure the firewall via the World Wide Web.

### Using classes

The Technologic Interceptor firewall includes a class definition facility which provides users with a mechanism to replace address patterns, times of day, or URLs by symbolic names. Classes are initiated by selecting the Classes button on the left portion of the configuration screen. By using an equals

**Figure 10.4**   Using the Technologic Interceptor firewall configuration screen to block all FTP Put commands

sign (=) as a prefix, they are distinguished from literal patterns.

Through the use of classes you can considerably facilitate the configuration of the firewall. For example, suppose that you want to control access from users behind the firewall to Internet services. To do so you would first enter the IP addresses of computers that will be given permission to access common services that you wish them to use. Then you would define a class name that would be associated with the group of IP addresses and create a policy that defines the services that the members of the class are authorized to use.

Figure 10.5 illustrates the use of the Technologic Interceptor Edit Policy configuration screen to enable outbound traffic for FTP, HTTP, Telnet, and SMTP. Note that this policy uses the class name =ALL-Interval-Hosts in the box labeled From. Although not shown, you would have first used the class configuration to enter that class name and the IP addresses you want associated with that class. Then this new edit policy would allow those IP addresses in the predefined class =ALL-Internal-Hosts to use FTP, HTTP, Telnet, and SMTP applications.

*Address translation*

One method commonly used to protect internal networks from unauthorized access attempts is obtained through address translation. When address translation is employed by a firewall, it hides IP addresses of the private network from outside users, functioning similar to the process used to obtain an unlisted telephone number. IP address translation can be accomplished in one of two ways: IP hiding or one-to-one mapping. Under IP hiding clients behind the firewall are restricted to initiating sessions and incoming packets are barred. When one-to-one mapping is employed, the firewall permits a bi-directional packet flow; however, addresses behind the firewall are hidden and substituted by the use of a different set of IP addresses.

As IP addresses are becoming a scarce commodity until IPv6 arrives, network managers and administrators can consider using IP addresses specified in RFC 1918 which allocated three blocks of IP address space for private internets. Those address blocks allocated for private internets include:

10.0.0.0 to 10.255.255.255
172.16.0.0 to 172.31.255.255
192.168.0.0 to 192.168.255.255

Any of the addresses in the preceding IP address blocks can be used behind a firewall, enabling the use of existing Class A, B, or C addresses to serve as translation addresses for use on the public side of the firewall.

*Stateful inspection*

The term stateful inspection was originally coined by Checkpoint Systems to refer to the examination of packets at the network layer. Although this feature is similar to filtering, there are several key differences. First, the analysis is performed on each packet based upon the context of previous transmission. This is similar to tracking a series of telephone calls and it permits a firewall to become aware of suspicious trends for which it may be configured to either bar further access attempts or to generate an alert to a designated person. Secondly, by tracking data from higher layers which are analyzed based upon the context of previous transmissions, the firewall becomes capable of providing a detailed audit trail of events. Thus, a stateful inspection capability can provide a higher level of protection than packet filtering as well as utilization information that may be useful in determining what services internal and external users have trouble accessing.

**Figure 10.5** Using the Technologic Interceptor firewall to create a policy allowing outbound FTP, HTTP, Telnet, and SMTP traffic from all users in the previously defined class All=Internal-Hosts

*Alerts*

Stateful inspection by itself may provide a limited protection capability unless a firewall automatically terminates suspicious activity or alerts a network manager or administrator to a possible attack on their network. Figure 10.6 illustrates the Technologic Interceptor Add Alert screen display with the IP-Spoof pattern shown selected. Note that the interceptor's patterns can be considered as equivalent to stateful inspection events.

In the example shown in Figure 10.6 the IP Spoof alert is used as a mechanism to denote a connection request occurring from a host claiming to have an IP address which does not belong to it. In actuality, it can be very difficult to note the occurrence of IP spoofing. This is because unless the firewall previously obtained information about IP addresses, such as their locations on segments whose access is obtained via different firewall ports, or notes restrictions on service by IP address, it will assume that an IP address is valid. In comparison, other patterns such as refused connections or failed authentication are much easier to note. For each alert you would first specify a name for the alert definition, such as IP-Spoof for that pattern. After selecting the pattern, you can specify the days and times of day and the frequency of occurrence that, when matched, should generate an alert. The Interceptor supports two methods of alert

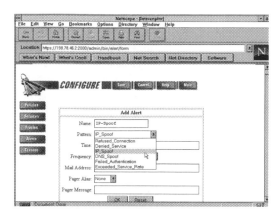

**Figure 10.6** Using the Technologic Interceptor Add Alert configuration screen

generation: either via email or a pager. If you select the use of a pager to transmit an alert, you can include a message, such as a numerical alert code, to inform the recipient of the type of alert.

## *Authentication*

Authentication is a mechanism used to verify the identity of a user requesting access to a specific service. A firewall can either directly perform authentication or operate in conjunction with one or more authentication servers located on the private side of the device.

There is a variety of methods used by firewalls or authentication servers to perform authentication. Those methods include static passwords, tokens, and one-time passwords.

### Static passwords

Static passwords represent the least secure method of authentication, as over a period of time the possibility of the password being compromised increases. In comparison, the use of tokens that change every minute or so, as well as one time passwords, do a hacker no good if captured. Thus, most firewalls that perform authentication either do not support the use of static passwords or their documentation recommends other methods.

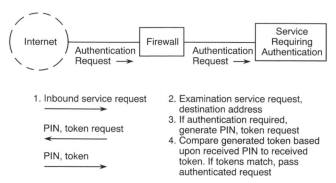

**Figure 10.7**   The firewall authentication process

### Token-based passwords

The most common form of token-based authentication involves the use of a credit card token generator by personnel requiring authenticated access to a service. The token generator issues a new password every 60 seconds or so, based upon a predefined algorithm and seed burnt into the card. If the firewall directly performs authentication, it prompts the user to enter a PIN and the token generated by the user's token generator card, usually a 6 or 8 digit random number. The firewall generates its own token based upon the user's PIN and compares the token it generated to the one transmitted by the user. If the two match, the requested service is allowed, otherwise access to the requested service is denied. If the actual authentication process runs on a separate server, such as FTP, Telnet, or a World Wide Web server, the firewall functions as a proxy, relaying authentication requests to the server providing the service that requires authentication.

Figure 10.7 illustrates the firewall authentication process. In this example, the firewall can be considered as a front end to the service, as it either enables or disables access based upon whether or not the token generated by the firewall matches the transmitted token.

### One-time passwords

Although one-time passwords can be considered similar to token-based authentication due to the fact that they generate passwords that are only valid for use one time, there are two major differences between the two authentication methods. First, the token-based authentication method involves the use of hardware by the client in the form of a credit card sized device that generates tokens. In comparison, one-time passwords are generated through the use of software. A second difference between the two is the fact that token-based authentication methods are commercial products, whereas some one-time password generators are in the public domain and available for use without incurring additional expense.

### Bellcore S/KEY

One example of a popular one-time password system is the Bellcore S/Key. Currently there are two versions of S/KEY. An early version, referred to as the S/KEY reference implementation, is available from Bellcore via anonymous FTP; however, it has not been upgraded nor has the code been maintained over the past five years. A second version of the product, simply referred to as S/KEY, is a commercial product from Bellcore that operates on a number of client and server platforms.

_Operation_   The S/KEY one-time password authentication system is based on the use of two software programs. One program, referred to as the key login program, operates on a server at the host site. The second program, which is called the S/KEY One-Time Password Generator, resides on the client computer. At the time this book was written, server software platforms supported included SunOS, IBM AIX, HP-UX, and Solaris. Client platforms supported include MS-Windows 3.1, Windows 95, Windows NT, SunOS, IBM AIX, HP-UX, Solaris, and Apple Macintosh.

The authentication process begins when a client attempts to access a protected network. The network server running S/KEY server software, which can be a firewall or a separate computer behind the firewall, issues a challenge to the client. The challenge consists of a number and a string of characters which forms a seed. The operator at the client workstation will enter the seed as well as a secret phrase into the S/KEY program running on the client workstation, resulting in the calculation of a response to the server's challenge. Thus, this method of one-time password entry is also commonly referred to as a challenge-response system.

In responding to the server's challenge, the client uses the challenge number and seed originally transmitted by the S/KEY server as well as the user's secret phrase to generate a secure hash function. This hash function is generated in the form of a one-time password consisting of six English words. This password is then transmitted to the S/KEY server. That server generates its own hash function and compares the result with the stored one-time password used for the most recent login. If they match, the user is allowed access and the server decrements the challenge number and stores the newly used one-time password for use with the next login attempt.

As each access attempt commences with the generation and validation of a one-time password, this technique is similar to the use of a token generator in that it eliminates vulnerability from a 'sniffing' attack where a hacker learns and later uses the ID and password of legitimate network user. As unscrupulous persons can also reside on an internal private network, many organizations use token generators or one time passwords either in conjunction with firewalls or with separate servers to protect their internal network from internal threats.

### Packet filtering

Although the packet filtering capability of firewalls functions similarly to that router feature, the firewall is usually easier to configure and provides more flexibility in enabling or disabling access based upon the set of rules that can be developed. As we examined the use of a router's basic access-list to enable or disable network services based upon IP addresses in the first section of this chapter, let us return to the use of the Technologic Interceptor firewall's configuration screen to examine how packet filtering is expanded upon by firewalls. Figure 10.8 illustrates the Technologic Interceptor Network Services display which lists the protocols for which this firewall accepts connections. Note that the HTTP protocol is shown selected as we will edit that service. Also note the columns labeled Max and Rate. The column labeled Max indicates the maximum number of simultaneous connections allowed for each service, while the column labeled Rate indicates the maximum rate of new connections for each service on a per minute basis. By specifying entries for one or both columns you can significantly control access to the network services you provide as well as balance the loads on heavily used services.

Figure 10.9 illustrates the Interceptor Edit Service display configuration screen. In this example, HTTP service is enabled for up to 256 connections, and a queue size of 64 was entered, limiting TCP HTTP pending connections to that value. The Max Rate entry of 300 represents the maximum rate of new connections that will be allowed to an HTTP service. Once this

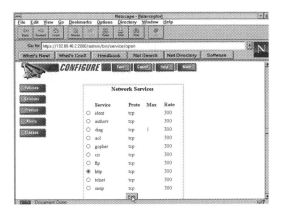

**Figure 10.8** Using the Technologic Interceptor firewall configuration screen to edit HTTP network services

rate has been exceeded, the firewall will temporarily disable access to that service for a period of one minute. If you allow both internal and external access to an internal Web server, the ability to control the maximum rate of incoming connections to a particular service can be an important weapon in the war against so-called denial of service attacks. Under this technique, a malicious person (or persons) programs a computer to issue bogus service initiation requests using random IP addresses that more than likely do not exist. As each access request results in a server initiating a handshake response, the response is directed to a bogus IP address that does not respond. The server will typically keep the connection open for 60 to 120 seconds which represents a connection a valid user may not be able to use. Thus, if a hacker can issue 256 or more bogus connections and your Web server is configured to support that number of simultaneous connections, legitimate users could be barred from accessing the server. Although there is no one uniform solution to this problem, you could use the Max Connects to limit inbound HTTP connections so you will always be able to let internal users access your Web server. In addition, if you specify a low Max Connects rate, you can negate some of the flooding of bogus connection attempts that will allow some legitimate users to reach your organization's Web server.

As the firewall must examine each packet to determine whether or not to allow a connection, it is performing packet filtering. However, this is a much more sophisticated type of packet filtering than that provided by most router manufacturers which is typically restricted to decisions being

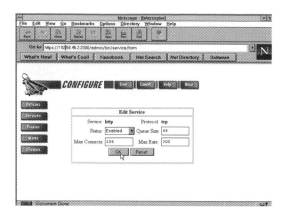

**Figure 10.9**   Using the Technologic Interceptor firewall Edit service configuration display to set a series of rules to govern access to HTTP

implemented based upon IP address and well-known port number. Thus, a firewall's packet filtering capability should also be carefully examined as it may provide you with the ability to control events that are beyond the capability of most routers.

### 10.2.3 The gap to consider

Although routers and firewalls can be used to prevent unauthorized access to your network hosts, they do not guarantee the security of the communications connection between client and server nor the security of the data being transferred. To obtain this security, you must use some type of encryption-based product. For example, when using Web browsers, you should consider the use of two related Internet protocols, Secure Sockets Layer (SSL) which was developed by Netscape, or the Secure Hypertext Transfer Protocol (S-HTTP) which was developed by Enterprise Integration Technologies. Both protocols support several cryptographic algorithms that use public key encryption methods. This allows a server to transmit upon request its public key to a client. The client uses that key to encrypt all communications for the session, enabling secure communications between client and server.

# 11

# vLANs AND VIRTUAL NETWORKING

There are two evolving technologies that have the potential to provide a significant impact upon the use of LANs and how geographically separated networks are connected. Those technologies, which are the focus of this chapter, are virtual LANs (vLANs) and virtual networking.

## 11.1 vLANs

A virtual LAN, or vLAN, can be considered to represent a broadcast domain. This means that transmission generated by one station on a vLAN is only received by those stations defined by some criteria to be in the broadcast domain.

The use of vLANs may provide you with the ability to make more efficient use of network bandwidth as broadcasts can be limited to the domains you create through the assignment of different virtual LANs. In addition, through the construction and use of different types of vLANs you may be able to simplify LAN administration and enhance LAN security. As an understanding of the rationale for the use of different types of vLANs depends upon an appreciation of the operating characteristics of each type of vLAN, let us turn our attention to the methods used to construct virtual LANs. In doing so we will examine port grouping, MAC-based, Layer-3 based, and rule-based vLAN creation methods.

### 11.1.1 Port-grouping vLANs

As its name implies, a port-grouping vLAN represents a virtual LAN created by defining a group of ports on a switch or router to form a broadcast domain. Thus, another common name for this type of vLAN is a port-based virtual LAN.

The most common method used to implement a port-based vLAN creation capability is through the use of a LAN switch. That switch includes hardware which enables frames arriving on any port to be output to any other port. Although most switches were originally designed to operate on MAC addresses contained in frames, it was a relatively easy process for switch manufacturers to add vLAN creation based upon ports grouped into a domain.

## Operation

Figure 11.1 illustrates the use of an intelligent LAN switch to create two vLANs based upon port groupings. In this example the switch was configured to create one virtual LAN consisting of ports 0, 1, 5 and 6, and a second virtual LAN was created based upon the grouping of ports 2, 3, 4 and 7 to form a second broadcast domain.

## Port versus segment switching

In examining the vLANs created by grouping ports through the use of a LAN switch, note that although a segment-based switch is shown in Figure 11.1, this method of vLAN creation is also applicable to a port-based switch. When a port-based switch is used, only one station per port can be linked into a vLAN broadcast domain. In comparison, when a segment-based switch is used, multiple stations connected to a port will be grouped into a virtual LAN.

## Advantages

Advantages associated with the use of LAN switches for creating port-based vLANs include the ability to use the switching capability of the switch, the ability to support multiple stations per port, and internetworking capability.

## Disadvantages

Although the use of a LAN switch provides a number of advantages over the use of a wiring hub with respect to the

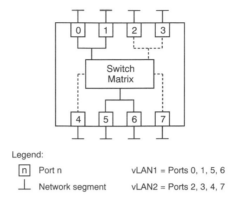

Legend:

| n | Port n | vLAN1 = Ports 0, 1, 5, 6 |
| ⊥ | Network segment | vLAN2 = Ports 2, 3, 4, 7 |

**Figure 11.1**  Creating port grouping vLANs using a LAN switch

creation of vLANs, they also have certain disadvantages associated with their use. Those disadvantages include the cost of LAN switches and the inability to associate multiple vLANs to a network segment connected to a switch port. Concerning the latter, this means that moves from one vLAN to another affect all stations connected to a particular port. This also means that a station requiring access to more than one vLAN must do so using multiple network interface cards if the station can support the use of multiple cards.

*Supporting inter-vLAN communications*

The use of multiple network interface cards provides an easy-to-implement solution to obtaining an inter-vLAN communications capability when only a few vLANs must be linked. This method of inter-vLAN communications is applicable to all methods of vLAN creation; however, when a built-in routing capability is included in a LAN switch, you would probably prefer to use the routing capability rather than obtain an install additional hardware.

Figure 11.2 illustrates the use of a server with multiple network interface cards to provide support to two port-based vLANs. Not only does this method of multiple vLAN support require additional hardware and the use of multiple ports on a switch, but, in addition, the number of NICs that can be installed in a station is typically limited to two or three. Thus, the use of a large switch with hundreds of ports configured for

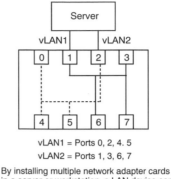

vLAN1 = Ports 0, 2, 4. 5
vLAN2 = Ports 1, 3, 6, 7

By installing multiple network adapter cards
in a server or workstation, a LAN device can
become a member of multiple vLANs

**Figure 11.2**   Overcoming the port-based constraint where stations can only join a
single vLAN

supporting three or more vLANs may not be capable of enabling
a common server to support all stations connected to the switch.

### 11.1.2 MAC-based switching

A second type of vLAN creation is based upon the burnt-in
universally administered or software configured logically administered address of each device connected to a switch. Known as
MAC-based switching in recognition of the use of Media Access
Control addresses, this method of vLAN creation is also referred
to as a layer 2 vLAN because the vLAN creation occurs at the
Data Link Layer. MAC-based switching requires a true switching hub or router as the hardware platform. That platform uses
software to associate MAC addresses with a broadcast domain
which in turn forms a virtual LAN.

When MAC addresses are associated with the creation of
virtual LANs, a vLAN capable switch can provide a high degree of
versatility. For example, selective users on a segment connected
to a port, as well as individual workstations connected to other
ports on a switch, can be configured into a broadcast domain
representing a virtual LAN. To illustrate the advantages and
disadvantages associated with layer-2 vLANs, let us first focus
our attention upon the use of a LAN switch which supports
layer-2 vLAN creation.

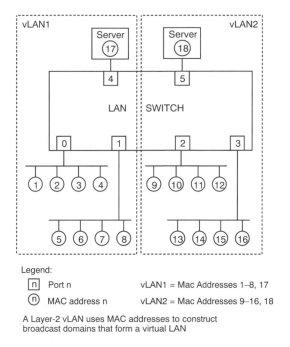

Legend:

$\boxed{n}$  Port n                               vLAN1 = Mac Addresses 1–8, 17

$\textcircled{n}$  MAC address n                vLAN2 = Mac Addresses 9–16, 18

A Layer-2 vLAN uses MAC addresses to construct
broadcast domains that form a virtual LAN

**Figure 11.3**   Layer-2 vLAN

*Operational example*

Figure 11.3 illustrates the use of an 18-port switch to create two virtual LANs. In this example, eighteen devices are shown connected to the switch via six ports, with four ports serving individual network segments. Thus, the LAN switch in this example is more accurately refered to as a segment switch with a MAC or layer-2 vLAN capability. This type of switch can range in capacity from small 8 or 16 port devices capable of supporting segments with up to 512 or 1024 total addresses to large switches with hundreds of ports capable of supporting thousands of MAC addresses. For simplicity of illustration we will use the six port segment switch to denote the operation of layer-2 vLANs as well as their advantages and disadvantages.

In turning our attention to the vLANs shown in Figure 11.3, note that we will use the numeric or node addresses shown contained in circles as MAC addresses for simplicity of illustration. Thus, addresses 1 through 8 and 17 would be grouped into a broadcast domain representing vLAN1, while addresses 9 through 16 and 18 would be grouped into a second broadcast domain to represent vLAN2. At this point in time you would be tempted to say 'so what', as the use of MAC addresses in creating layer-2 vLANs resembles precisely the same effect as if you used a port-grouping method of vLAN creation. For example, using a vLAN creation method based upon port grouping would result in the same vLANs as those shown in Figure 11.3 when ports 0, 1 and 4 are assigned to one virtual LAN and ports 2, 3 and 5 to the second.

To indicate the greater flexibility associated with the use of equipment that supports layer-2 vLAN creation, let us assume that users with network node addresses 7 and 8 were just transferred from the project associated with vLAN1 to the project associated with vLAN2. If you were using a port-grouping method of vLAN creation, you would have to physically recable nodes 7 and 8 to either the segment connected to port 2 or the segment connected to port 3. In comparison, when using a segment switch with a layer-2 vLAN creation capability, you would use the management port to delete addresses 7 and 8 from vLAN1 and add them to vLAN2. The actual effort required to do so might be as simple as dragging MAC addresses from one vLAN to the other when using a GUI interface to entering one or more commands when using a command line management system. The top of Figure 11.4 illustrates the result of the previously mentioned node transfer. The lower portion of Figure 11.4 shows the two vLAN layer-2 tables, indicating the movement of MAC addresses 7 and 8 to vLAN2.

Although the reassignment of stations 7 and 8 to vLAN2 is easily accomplished at the MAC layer, it should be noted that the partitioning of a segment into two vLANs can result in upper layer problems. This is because upper layer protocols, such as IP, require all stations on a segment to have the same network address. Some switches overcome this problem by dynamically altering the network address to correspond to the vLAN on which the station resides. Other switches without this capability restrict the creation of MAC-based vLANs to one device per port, in effect limiting the creation of vLANs to port-based switches.

## Advantages

The use of MAC-based vLAN creation provides several advantages over the use of a port-grouping vLAN creation method. Those advantages include additional flexibility with respect to the reassignment of stations from one vLAN to another, greater bandwidth, and additional expendability.

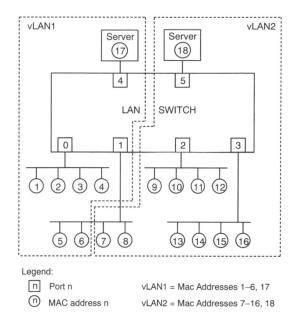

**Figure 11.4** Moving stations when using a layer 2 vLAN

### Flexibility

As indicated by the movement of network nodes illustrated in Figure 11.4, a key advantage associated with the use of a layer-2 vLAN creation is flexibility. That is, unlike a port-grouping method of vLAN creation which requires the recabling of workstations when workstation users are reassigned to a different vLAN, a layer-2 vLAN enables such reassignments via a command line entry or drag and move operation when using a GUI. In addition, if you simply wish to move a workstation to a different location, but wish to maintain the station's membership in the assigned vLAN, a switch performing layer-2 vLAN creation will automatically retain the station's membership. This is because membership is by MAC address, which enables the switch to retain the workstation's vLAN membership.

### Bandwidth and expendability

Other advantages of layer-2 vLAN switches concerns bandwidth and expendability. As membership in a workgroup grows and its bandwidth requirements increase, the use of a layer-2 LAN switch enables workgroup members to be placed on multiple network segments while maintaining vLAN broadcast domains. In doing so the addition of extra servers to the switch which are configured into the same vLAN domain results in the ability of multiple client-server operations to occur which provides additional bandwidth. An example of this situation is illustrated in Figure 11.5. In this example a new server with the MAC address of 18 was added to vLAN1. Two in-progress client-server communications are shown occurring on vLAN1, in effect doubling the bandwidth available for users associated with that virtual LAN. In comparison, perhaps because of an absence of a requirement for additional performance, only one server is connected to vLAN2 which restricts the bandwidth available for users associated with virtual LAN.

*Disadvantages*

Although the use of MAC-based vLAN creation provides more flexibility and greater expendability than the use of a port-based vLAN creation method, there are certain limitations associated with the MAC-based vLAN creation process. Those limitations include the use of MAC addresses, which are not very intuitive, interswitch communications, the configuration of switches, and the difficulty associated with attempting to support mobile users attaching to fixed docking stations.

**MAC address lists**

The creation of a MAC address list can represent a time-consuming effort. This is because a MAC address is a sequence of hexadecimal numbers burnt onto the network interface card and used as such when universally administered addressing is employed or obtained from a configuration file when locally administrated addressing is employed. For either situation, obtaining MAC addresses may require a visit to each work-station. The entry of those addresses into switch tables can be a long and tedious task.

**Interswitch communications**

Similarly to the port-grouping method of vLAN creation, a layer-2 vLAN is normally restricted to a single switch; however, some vendors include a management platform which enables multiple switches to support MAC addresses between closely located

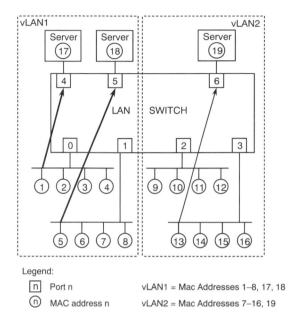

**Figure 11.5** The use of a switch to form layer 2 vLANs can provide additional bandwidth by supporting multiple client-server operations

switches. Unfortunately, neither individual or closely located switches permits an expansion of vLANs outside of the immediate area, resulting in the isolation of the virtual LANs from the rest of the network. This deficiency can be alleviated in two ways. First, for inter-vLAN communications you could install a second adapter card in a server and associate one MAC address with one vLAN; while the second address is associated with the second virtual LAN. Although this method is appropriate for a switch with two vLANs, you would require a different method to obtain interoperability when communications are required between a large number of virtual LANs. Similarly to correcting the interoperability problem with the port-grouping method of vLAN creation, you would have to use routers to provide connectivity between layer-2 vLANs and the rest of your network.

### Router restrictions

When using a router to provide connectivity between vLANs, there are several restrictions you must consider. Those restrictions typically include a requirement to use a separate switch port connection to the router for each virtual LAN and the inability to assign portions of segments to different vLANs. Concerning the former, unless the LAN switch either internally supports layer 3 routing or provides a trunking or aggregation capability that enables transmission from multiple vLANs to occur on a common port to the router, one port linking the switch to the router will be required for each vLAN. As router and switch ports are relatively costly, internetworking of a large number of virtual LANs can become expensive. Concerning the latter, this requirement results from the fact that in a TCP/IP environment routing occurs between segments. An example of inter-vLAN communications using a router is illustrated in Figure 11.6.

When inter-vLAN communications are required the layer-2 switch transmits packets to the router via a port associated with the virtual LAN workstation requiring such communications. The router is responsible for determining the routed path to provide inter-vLAN communications, forwarding the packet back to the switch via an appropriate router to switch interface. Upon receipt of the packet the switch uses bridging to forward the packet to its destination port.

Returning to Figure 11.6, a workstation located in vLAN1 requiring communications with a workstation in vLAN2 would have its data transmitted by the switch on port 5 to the router. After processing the packet the router would return the packet to the switch, with the packet entering the switch on port 6. Thereafter, the switch would use bridging to either broadcast the packet to ports 2, 3 and 7 if the destination MAC address is unknown or transfer the layer 2 frame to a specific port if the MAC address was previously learned. The frame would then be recognized by a destination node in vLAN2 and copied into an appropriate network interface card.

Although routing enables inter-vLAN communications, there are several disadvantages associated with the configuration shown in Figure 11.6. First, routers on a per port cost basis are considerably more expensive than switches. Thus, the support of a large number of virtual LANs can become a budget-buster. Secondly, from a performance perspective, the switch must forward each inter-vLAN packet twice. First the packet is forwarded from the originating node to the switch port cabled to the router that represents the originating vLAN switch to router connection. Next, the packet received from the router must be forwarded to its appropriate destination node. A third

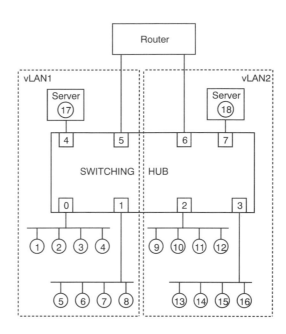

**Figure 11.6** Inter-vLAN communications requires the use of a router

problem is the addition of the router which adds another device to configure and manage.

*Configuration and support*

Two additional disadvantages associated with using MAC addresses to form vLANs include the configuration of switches and the inability to support the random use of docking stations. Concerning the configuration of switches, although this may not be a labor-intensive operation for a small switch, a very large network containing hundreds or thousands of users can require a considerable amount of setup time. To overcome this problem, some switches include an auto-setup feature which first initializes each subnet to a default vLAN and provides graphical tools to facilitate modifying those settings.

In today's mobile environment, many organizations use docking stations with built-in LAN adapters to provide network connectivity while employees move about the office, perform sales calls, and work at home using notebooks that mate into the docking stations upon their return to the office. As the MAC address is burnt into the LAN adapter, this means that a user who utilizes a different docking station than the one associated with the virtual LAN they belong to may not be able to join the intended vLAN. Although this problem could be alleviated by reconfiguring the switch, rather than perform this operation each time you could override universally administrated addressing and use a configuration file in the notebook computer to establish a locally administrated address. Then each time the notebook moves to a different docking station it would retain a fixed MAC address.

### 11.1.3 Layer-3 based vLANs

A layer-3 based vLAN is constructed using information contained in the Network Layer header of packets. As such, this precludes the use of LAN switches that operate at the Data Link Layer from being capable of forming layer-3 vLANs. Thus, layer-3 vLAN creation is restricted to routers and LAN switches that provide a layer 3 routing capability.

Through the use of Layer 3 operating switches and routers there are a variety of methods that can be used to create layer-3 vLANs. Some of the more common methods supported resemble the criteria by which routers operate, such as IPX network numbers and IP subnets, AppleTalk domains and layer-3 protocols.

The actual creation options associated with a layer-3 vLAN can vary considerably based upon the capability of the LAN switch or router used to form the virtual LAN. For example, some hardware products permit a subnet to be formed across a number of ports and may even provide the capability to allow more than one subnet to be associated with a network segment connected to the port of a LAN switch. In comparison, other LAN switches may be limited to creating vLANs based upon different layer-3 protocols.

#### Subnet-based vLANs

Figure 11.7 illustrates the use of a layer-3 LAN switch to create two virtual LANs based upon IP network addresses. In examining the vLANs created through the use of the LAN switch, note that the first virtual LAN is associated with the subnet 198.78.55 which represents a Class C IP address, and the second vLAN is associated with the subnet 198.78.42 which represents a second Class C IP address. Also, note that since it is assumed that the LAN switch supports the assignment of more than one subnet per port, port 1 on the switch consists of

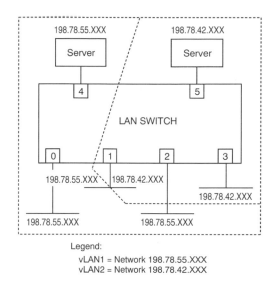

Legend:
vLAN1 = Network 198.78.55.XXX
vLAN2 = Network 198.78.42.XXX

**Figure 11.7**   vLAN creation based upon IP subnets

stations assigned to either subnet. Although some LAN switches support this subnetting capability, it is also important to note that other switches do not. Thus, a LAN switch that does not support multiple subnets per port would require stations to be recabled to other ports if it was desired to associated them to a different virtual LAN.

### Advantages

Three of the major advantages associated with layer-3 vLANs using subnetting include their flexibility, configuration, and inter-vLAN communications capability. Concerning the flexibility of layer-3 vLANs, as a user moves to another segment but retains their subnet number, many switches will 'follow' the relocation, permitting moves to be accomplished without requiring the reconfiguration of a LAN switch.

The configuration of vLANs can be automatically formed, unlike port and MAC-based virtual networks whose setup can be tedious and time-consuming. Thus, the cost of support of a layer-3 vLAN may be less than other types of virtual networks, and by itself can represent an important acquisition consideration.

The third advantage of a layer-3 vLAN is the fact that it supports routing. This means that it implicitly supports inter-vLAN communications, eliminating the necessity to obtain a separate router to support this capability.

### Disadvantages

Although layer-3 vLANs using subnetting as a virtual LAN creation criteria address the flexibility problems of port-based vLANs and the configuration problems of MAC-based vLANs, they are not problem-free. Two limitations associated with vLANs using subnetting include the configuration required to ensure network stations are using the correct protocol and network address, and the inability of some switches to support multiple subnets on a port. Although the second limitation can be overcome through the selection of a more capable LAN switch, the first limitation is associated with all types of layer-3 vLANs.

## Protocol-based vLANs

In addition to forming virtual LANs based upon a network address, the use of the layer-3 transmission protocol as a method for vLAN creation provides a mechanism which enables vLAN formation to be based upon the layer-3 protocol. Through the use of this method of vLAN creation, it becomes relatively easy for stations to belong to multiple vLANs. To illustrate this concept, consider Figure 11.8, which illustrates the creation of two vLANs based upon their layer 3 transmission protocol. In examining the stations shown in Figure 11.8, note that the circles with the upper case I represent those stations configured for membership in the vLAN based upon the use of the IP protocol, while those stations represented by circles containing the upper case X represent stations configured for membership in the vLAN which uses the IPX protocol as its membership criteria. Similarly, stations represented by circles containing the characters I/X represent stations operating dual protocol stacks which enable such stations to become members of both vLANs.

Two servers are shown at the top of the LAN switch illustrated in Figure 11.8. One server is shown operating dual IPX/IP stacks which results in the server belonging to both vLANs. In comparison, the server on the upper right of the switch is configured to support IPX and could represent a NetWare file server restricted to membership in the vLAN associated with the IPX protocol.

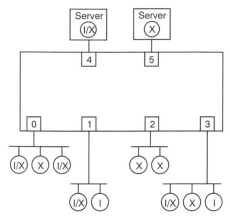

I = vLAN1 membership   X = vLAN2 membership

I/X = membership in both LANs

Legend:

⬜n⬜  Port n

Ⓘ  IP Protocol used by station

Ⓧ  IPX Protocol used by station

Ⓘ/ⓧ  IPX and IP Protocols used by station

**Figure 11.8**   vLAN creation based upon protocol

### Advantages

Similar to layer-3 vLANs that use subnetting, a major benefit associated with vLAN creation based upon protocol is networking flexibility. This flexibility enables stations to be moved from one network segment to another without losing its vLAN membership. Another aspect associated with networking flexibility is the ability to obtain the bandwidth advantages associated with the use of LAN switches while tailoring traffic to support different services. For example, assume a requirement to connect stations on vLAN1 to the Internet develops. To support this new requirement you could add a port to the LAN switch and connect a router to that port. Figure 11.9 illustrates the expanded LAN switch with a router connected to port 6 of the switch. Note that although you might be tempted to anticipate bandwidth problems resulting from the connection of the Internet to vLAN1, only inbound traffic directed to the network address associated with the IP-based vLAN is broadcast to the vLAN domain. In addition, as with most router-based Internet connections, you can use the filtering capability of the router to limit inbound traffic to the vLAN. In the outbound direction, only IP

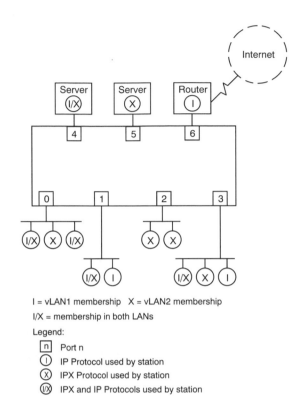

**Figure 11.9**  Expanding a vLAN to support Internet access

traffic with a network address differing from the address associated with vLAN1 will be forwarded by the router to the Internet. Thus, the basic operational capability of the router can be used to limit both inbound and outbound traffic to and from the virtual LAN connected to the Internet via the router.

Other advantages associated with the use of layer-3 protocols for vLAN creation are similar to the advantages described for subnet based vLANs. That is, those advantages include the automatic configuration of the switch and an implicit inter-vLAN communications capability.

### Disadvantages

Layer-3 vLANs that use protocols for their creation method have similar disadvantages as subnet-based vLANs. That is, you must obtain equipment that supports the use of protocols for vLAN creation as well as verifies that stations are configured correctly.

### 11.1.4 Rule-based vLANs

A recent addition to vLAN creation methods is based upon the ability of LAN switches to look inside packets and use predefined fields, portions of fields, and even individual bit settings as a mechanism for the creation of a virtual LAN.

*Capabilities*

The ability to create virtual LANs via a rule-based methodology provides, no pun intended, a virtually unlimited virtual LAN creation capability. To illustrate a small number of the almost unlimited methods of vLAN creation, consider Table 11.1 which lists eight examples of rule-based vLAN creation methods. In examining the entries in Table 11.1, note that in addition to creating vLANs via the inclusion of specific field values within a packet, such as all IPX users with a specific network address, it is also possible to create vLANs using the exclusion of certain packet field values. The latter capability is illustrated by the next to last example in Table 11.1, which forms a vLAN consisting of all IPX traffic with a specific network address but excludes a specific node address.

*Multicast support*

One rule-based vLAN creation example that deserves a degree of explanation to understand its capability is the last entry in Table 11.1. Although you might be tempted to think that the assignment of a single IP address to a vLAN represents a typographical mistake, in actuality it represents the ability to enable network stations to dynamically join an IP multicast group without adversely effecting the bandwidth available to other network users assigned to the same subnet, but located on different segments attached to a LAN switch. To understand why this occurs, let me digress and discuss the concept associated with IP multicast operations.

IP multicast references a set of specifications that allows an IP host to transmit one packet to multiple destinations. This one to many transmission method is accomplished by the use of Class D IP addresses (224.0.0.0 to 239.255.255.255), which are mapped directly to Data Link Layer 2 multicast addresses. Through the use of IP multicasting, a term used to reference the use of Class D addresses, the need for an IP host to transmit multiple packets to multiple destinations is eliminated. This in

**Table 11.1** Rule-based vLAN creation examples

---

*     All IP users with a specific IP subnet address.
*     All IPX users with a specific network address.
*     All network users whose adapter cards were manufactured by the XYZ
      Corporation.
*     All traffic with a specific Ethernet Type field value.
*     All traffic with a specific SNAP field value.
*     All traffic with a specific SAP field value.
*     All IPX traffic with a specific network address but not a specific node
      address.
*     A specific IP address.

---

turn permits more efficient use of backbone network bandwidth; however, the arrival of IP Class D addressed packets at a network destination, such as a router connected to an internal corporate network, can result in a bandwidth problem. This is because multicast transmission is commonly used for audio and/or video distribution of educational information, videoconferencing, news feeds, and financial reports, such as delivering stock prices. Due to the amount of traffic associated with multicast transmission, it could adversely effect multiple subnets linked together by a LAN switch that uses subnets for vLAN creation. By providing a registration capability that allows an individual LAN user to become a single user vLAN associated with a Class D address, Class D packets can be routed to a specific segment even when several segments have the same subnet. Thus, this limits the effect of multicast transmission to a single segment.

*Advantages*

The major advantages associated with a rule-based method of vLAN creation include its easy use of configuration and its operational flexibility. A rule-based creation method is similar to the manner by which filters are created when bridges and routers are used. Thus, the ability to configure one or more vLANs is relatively easy. Concerning flexibility, the ability to create vLANs based upon the value of a portion of a packet or the value of several fields or portions of packet fields makes vLAN creation able to satisfy just about any networking requirement a LAN manager or administrator may have. Thus, a rule-based vLAN creation capability should provide the most flexible method for creating virtual LANs.

## Disadvantages

The major disadvantages associated with the use of a rule-based vLAN creation method include the configuration of vLANs and the efficiency of the switch. Due to the potential for creating vLANs based upon the value of a bit within a field of a packet, it can become a laborious task to correctly configure a complex vLAN association. Concerning switch efficiency, as the number of rules associated with the creation of a vLAN increase, the examination effort required for packets flowing through the switch increases. This in turn can result in an increase in packet latency through the LAN switch performing the rule-based comparisons.

## 11.1.5 Comparing vLAN creation features

Prior to examining how we can communicate with distant LANs via virtual networking, let us turn our attention to comparing the features and operational capabilities associated with the four major methods used to create vLANs. Table 11.2 provides a summary comparison of the features and operational capability of port-grouping, MAC-based, layer-3 based, and rule-based vLAN creation methods.

## Connectivity beyond the workgroup

As indicated by the footnote in Table 11.2, both port-grouping and MAC-based methods of vLAN creation can provide for station connectivity beyond a workgroup by the installation of multiple adapters in the station. In comparison, the use of a layer-3 vLAN creation method implies a built-in routing capability which allows connectivity beyond a station's workgroup.

## Ease of station assignment

Port-grouping is a relatively simple method of assigning stations to vLANs. Thus, this technique is easy to administer. In comparison, locating and entering MAC addresses can be a time consuming and tedious task, resulting in the 'difficult' entry in the table. Both layer-3 and rule-based vLAN creation methods can range from easy to difficult with respect to the ease of station assignments, with the level of difficulty based upon the actual assignment method used.

## Flexibility

If we define flexibility as the ability to vary the composition of a vLAN to organizational changes, we can say that port-grouping represents an inflexible method of vLAN creation. In comparison, MAC-based and layer-3 based vLAN creation methods permit stations to physically move without requiring the reconfiguration of hardware. Thus, those methods of vLAN creation can be considered to provide a moderate level of flexibility. As a rule-based vLAN creation method permits a high degree of tailoring of the composition of packets to an organization's vLAN creation requirements, it provides higher degree of flexibility.

## Improved workgroup bandwidth

All vLAN assignment methods listed in Table 11.2 permit the use of a LAN switch. As a LAN switch enables multiple client-server sessions to occur simultaneously, its use can result in improved workgroup bandwidth.

## Multicast support

To effectively support the association of Class D addresses to the Data Link Layer address requires the use of a routing capability. Thus, both layer-3 and rule-based vLAN creation methods provide an efficient method of multicast support. In addition, since a rule-based vLAN creation method also provides the ability to associate a single segment to a Class D address even when multiple segments have the same subnet, this method of vLAN creation becomes very efficient with respect to multicast support.

## Multiple vLANs per port

Although the ability to have multiple vLANs on a port is common to MAC, layer-3, and rule-based vLAN creation methods, a word

**Table 11.2**  vLAN assignment method comparison

|  | Port-grouping | Switch | MAC based | Layer-3 based |
|---|---|---|---|---|
| Connectivity beyond the workgroup | No* | No* | Yes | Yes |
| Ease of station assignment | Easy | Difficult | Easy–Difficult | Easy–Difficult |
| Flexibility | None | Moderate | Moderate | High |
| Improved workgroup bandwidth | Yes | Yes | Yes | Yes |
| Multicast support | Inefficient | Inefficient | Inefficient | Inefficient |
| Multiple vLANs per port | No | Possible | Possible | Possible |
| Security | High | Low–High | Low–High | Selectable |
| vLAN spanning switches | Possible | Possible | Yes | Yes |

*Installation of multiple adapters permits connectivity to other workgroups.

of caution is warranted. As previously noted in this chapter, not all LAN switches have this capability. Thus, it is important to verify the capability of the switch to support this feature if this feature is required to satisfy your organization's operational requirements.

*Security*

The use of a port-grouping vLAN creation method provides the highest level of security since all stations on a segment must reside on the same vLAN. In comparison, MAC and Layer-3 based vLAN creation methods that permit multiple vLANs per switch port would have a low level of security, and those vLAN creation methods that do not support multiple vLANs per port would have a high level of security. The reason multiple vLANs on a segment connected to a switch port results in a low level of security is due to the fact that users associated with one vLAN could use a protocol analyzer to read frames associated with another vLAN. Thus, the ability to associate multiple vLANs to a switch port can result in a security loophole. Due to the ability of a rule-based vLAN creation method to allow the manager to create their membership criteria, security is selectable under that vLAN creation method.

*vLAN spanning*

The use of a LAN switch for creating a vLAN based upon port-grouping, as well as the creation of a vLAN using a MAC-based creation method, may allow the expansion of the vLAN beyond a single switch. To do so, switches will commonly use a management port connection to interconnect switches, which allows table entries to be transferred between switches as well as allows for the transmission of frames between switches. As Layer 3 and rule-based vLAN creation methods employ routing, they enable multiple switches to be linked together.

## 11.2 VIRTUAL NETWORKING

When we refer to virtual networking we are actually referring to several concepts. First, virtual networking can be considered to represent the process by which virtual LANs are interconnected to one another. This process can occur locally with two or more vLANs on one LAN switch, or vLANs located on two or more switches directly or indirectly interconnected to one another or remotely, with routers employed to link switches geographically separated from one another. Secondly, the connection of both conventional and virtual LANs does not have to occur on the fixed paths predominantly used by corporations and government agencies to interconnect geographically separated locations. Instead, a more flexible network structure can be used whereby transmission occurs using the facilities of another organization. Through the use of those facilities, different transmission sessions between the same connection points can occur on different transmission paths, with the actual path used based upon a variety of factors. This second method of virtual networking has its roots in packet-switched services. Due to the growth in the Internet, that network of interconnected networks now represents a viable virtual networking facility that many organizations may wish to consider using to replace conventional point-to-point transmission facilities that currently constitute the bulk of private networks. Thus, in this section we will focus our attention upon two types of virtual networking, interconnecting virtual LANs locally and using the Internet as a virtual network.

## 11.2.1 Rationale

The rationale for virtual networking varies based upon the type of virtual networking you wish to perform. For example, assume that you are attempting to interconnect two or more vLANs on a common switch or located on local switches or routers to provide a virtual LAN that spans a wide area within a building or campus. Then the rationale is simply to extend your virtual LANs beyond a single physical location. If you are considering the use of the Internet as a virtual network to interconnect geographically separated locations, the rationale to do so involves considering reliability, economics, and the ability to integrate voice and data applications.

*Reliability*

From a reliability perspective, the Internet resembles a mesh network structure. This means that there is normally more than one path between locations linking Internet Service Providers to the backbone networks used for the main transmission path between the networks linked to and from the Internet. In comparison, due to cost constraints, most corporate, government and private networks are constructed using point to point transmission facilities. Thus, once traffic reaches an Internet Service Provider it is more than likely that communications will obtain a higher level of reliability than if traffic flowed on a private network where the flow of data primarily occurred on point-to-point transmission facilities that do not have redundant paths for alternate routing.

To understand how the Internet can provide a more reliable method of communications, consider the two networks shown in Figure 11.10. Those network diagrams provide a general comparison between the network infrastructure of a private three node network and the backbone of the Internet used to connect three corporate locations via the Internet. In examining the private network structure at the top of Figure 11.10, note that any line failure automatically disables communications between two of the three corporate locations. In comparison, when each corporate location is connected to the Internet through a circuit routed from that location to an Internet Service Provider's Internet access point of presence, the failure of a circuit is far more limited. For example, the failure of the circuit linking corporate location A to an Internet Service Provider only affects transmission to and from that location. If a circuit failure occurs within the Internet 'cloud' alternate routing may allow all sites to continue communicating, since routers within the Internet may automatically switch transmission to alternate paths. Thus, the use of the Internet can be expected to provide a more reliable transmission service than obtainable from the installation of point-to-point circuits commonly used to construct a private network.

## Economics

Conventional point-to-point analog leased lines are tariffed based upon mileage. Digital leased lines are tariffed based upon the operating rate of the circuit and the mileage between interconnected locations. In comparison, most Internet Service Providers charge users a monthly fee based upon the operating rate of the connection. Although the preceding comparison may not at first appear to be significant, let us consider a few examples to illustrate how using the Internet as a virtual network can result in significant economic savings.

First, let us assume a 500 mile distance between locations A and B and A and C, and that each pair of locations will be connected via a digital T1 line operating at 1.544 Mbps. As the monthly cost of a T1 line is approximately $3.00 per circuit mile, the monthly cost for the private network shown at the top of Figure 11.10 would be approximately $3000. Assuming that each corporate location is within a major metropolitan area, the connection of each location to the Internet via an Internet Service Provider can be expected to cost between $750 and $1000 per month. At a monthly cost of $750, the use of the Internet could save the organization $750 per month, while a monthly connection cost of $1000 would not produce any economic benefits.

Now, let us assume that locations A, B and C represent New York City, Miami, and Los Angeles, resulting in the distance for the two circuits expanding to approximately 3500 miles. At a monthly cost of $3.00 per mile for a T1 circuit, the communications cost of the private network will increase to $10 500. In comparison, since access to the Internet within major metropolitan areas is distance-insensitive, the cost for using the Internet would remain the same as previously discussed, somewhere between $2260 and $3000 per month.

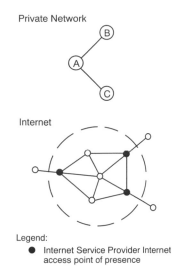

**Figure 11.10**  Comparing network structures

Based upon the two previous examples, we can make a general statement concerning the economics associated with replacing point to point private network communications circuits with the use of the Internet as a virtual network. That is, the greater the distance between locations to be connected, the greater the probability that the use of the Internet will result in economic savings in comparison to the construction of a private network.

## 11.2.2 Applications

In addition to traditional data communications, the Internet provides a potential mechanism for integrating voice, data, and fax. Although throughput delays and a lack of predictability upon occasion limits the transmission of voice over the Internet to having users speak CB-style, the ability to use one common Internet connection, as well as the distance-insensitive tariff associated with using the Internet, makes it an attractive vehicle for integrating corporate communications. If backbone bandwidth continues to be enhanced, it is a distinct possibility that in the near future a variety of voice, data, and fax applications will be integrated for use on the Internet. As there is a reasonable probability that the transmission of voice and fax via the Internet will reach a level acceptable to the corporate environment, let us examine how this can be accomplished.

*Voice and fax*

In a traditional LAN internetworking environment routers are used to link corporate sites via the Internet. As digitized voice and fax can be transported as data via a router, the key requirement for adding a voice and fax capability to LAN internetworking is to obtain appropriate hardware and software that digitizes voice and data for transport by a router. One product that was released in late 1996 that provides this capability and which warrants a description is Micom Communications Corporation's voice-over-IP (V/IP) equipment.

*Micom's V/IP*

Micom Communications Corporation's V/IP capability is based upon the use of the firm's V/IP cards installed in a server. Those cards enable a server to obtain a connection to a corporate PBX via a local wire pair that supports the simultaneous transmission of up to 24 voice conversations at a T1 line operating rate. The V/IP cards compress voice based upon the ITU-T G.729 voice compression standard, resulting in an 8 Kbps data stream instead of the conventional 64 Kbps data stream associated with Pulse Code Modulation (PCM) voice digitization. Although the conversion of digitized voice into IP packets would require a higher data rate of approximately 10 Kbps due to frame overhead, Micom's V/IP cards obtain a further reduction in the voice digitization rate by suppressing gaps in speech, resulting from silences inherent in voice conversations. As human speech typically has 50% or more periods of silence, the actual bandwidth required to transport one voice conversation is reduced to an average of approximately 4 Kbps. Thus, a full complement of 24 voice conversations from a PBX would require an average bandwidth under 100 Kbps.

Figure 11.11 illustrates how a Micom server with V/IP cards could be used to add a voice and fax transport capability between corporate locations via the Internet. Fax transmission, which is analog and would normally require a 64 Kbps PCM signal to digitize, is handled differently by the Micom V/IP cards. Those cards, to include the ability to automatically detect a fax signal on a voice channel as well as its modulation scheme, enables the signal to be converted back into its digital format, resulting in a digitized fax signal that requires 9.6 Kbps or less bandwidth. When received at the destination, the signal is then re-modulated for delivery to the receiving fax machine.

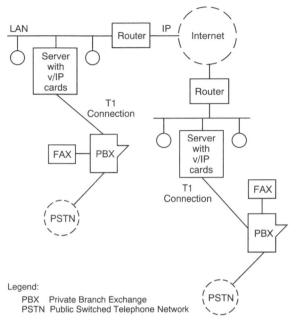

**Figure 11.11**  Adding a voice and fax transport capability via the Internet

As bandwidth bottlenecks associated with the Internet are alleviated, the integration of corporate voice and fax as well as data for transport via the Internet offers the opportunity for significant cost savings. Even if not totally practical today, the use of the Internet should be considered as a backup facility for expensive private networks, especially those that include international circuits.

### 11.2.3 Remote server access

One of the most talked about methods of virtual networking is the use of the Internet to provide both individual and local area network based users with the ability to access servers on a distant LAN. Several protocols were developed during 1996 and 1997 to facilitate the creation of tunnels through the Internet. Three of those protocols which we will discuss in this section include PPTP, L2TP, and L2F.

*PPTP*

The Point-to-Point Tunneling Protocol (PPTP) was jointly developed by Ascend Communications, 3Com, Telematics, Microsoft, and US Robotics as a mechanism to enable remote users to access corporate networks via the Internet. PPTP is a Layer 2 tunneling method by which Point-to-Point Protocol (PPP) frames are encased in IP packets for transmission over the Internet. In doing so, PPTP supports two basic types of packets: data which are variable in length and encapsulated in IP, and control which are fixed in length and set via TCP connections.

PPTP supports the transmission of IP, IPX, and NetBEUI datagrams in IP packets. The actual encapsulation occurs using the Internet Generic Routing Encapsulation Protocol version 2 (GREv2) which is an enhancement to RFCs 1701 and 1702. GREv2 adds octets for PPTP functions such as the protocol carried and Call ID, and allows acknowledgments to be carried with data.

**Utilization**

Support for PPTP was included in Microsoft's Windows NT Server 40 and Windows NT Workstation and was scheduled to be added to Windows 95. Although PPTP operates as a client-server method of communications you can use PPTP via the services of an Internet Service Provider (ISP) or directly from a client.

Figure 11.12a illustrates the use of PPTP via the facilities of an ISP. In this example, the client requests a connection to a Windows NT Remote Access Service (RAS) facility and the ISP responds by establishing a virtual private network via initiating a PPTP session. Information from the client in the form of a conventional Point-to-Point Protocol (PPP) is encapsulated by the ISP router and transmitted via a PPTP session that represents a tunnel formed by the ISP to the NT Server. This method of connection permits any client with a PPP capability to include UNIX, Macintosh and even PCs running OS/2 to connect to a distant server.

The second method of PPTP tunneling is through the use of a PPTP-enabled client. Figure 11.12b illustrates this technique. In this tunneling method a client dials an ISP and establishes a PPP session. Next, the client dials a second time concurrent to the PPP session to set up a PPTP channel and contact RAS on a Windows NT server. Once a connection has been made, the

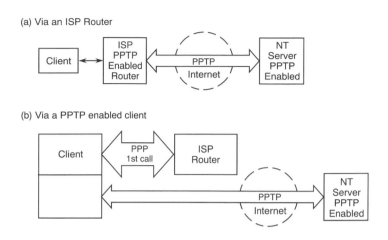

(a) Via an ISP Router

(b) Via a PPTP enabled client

**Figure 11.12**   Methods to create a PPTP tunnel

client connects as a virtual node on the corporate LAN. Although this method does not depend upon the ability of the ISP router to support PPTP, when this book was written only PPTP-enabled clients who were Microsoft products could use this method.

## L2F

At the same time PPTP was in its initial development Cisco Systems developed a similar tunneling method called Layer 2 Forwarding (L2F). L2F functions in both a dial-up to LAN as well as a LAN-to-LAN transmission method. In comparison, PPTP's initial release was restricted to remote dial-up although a LAN to LAN extension was planned.

## L2TP

Recognizing the need to have tunneling supported by a large base of vendors, many features of L2F and PPTP were combined into the Layer 2 Tunneling Protocol (L2TP). In mid-1996 Microsoft and Cisco Systems proposed L2TP to the Internet Engineering Task Force (IETF) although Microsoft intends to support L2TP in addition to PPTP.

Under L2TP, an ISP will provide support for the creation of a PPP tunnel as illustrated in Figure 11.13. The actual tunnel will be created using a frame relay connection, and a router or

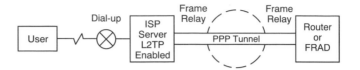

**Figure 11.13**   Using layer 2 tunneling protocol

Frame Relay Access Device (FRAD) at the distant location will strip off L2TP headers and forward the PPP packet to its destination. Thus, L2TP creates a tunnel that does not depend upon the use of a particular type of vendor server since PPP is a standard. In addition, any PPP client can connect to the ISP.

### 11.2.4  Local virtual networking

Earlier in this chapter we noted that the interconnection of vLANs, either residing on the same switch or on different switches within close proximity of one another, can be considered to represent local virtual networking. In this section we will focus our attention upon this topic, noting how vLANs can be interconnected.

#### *Inter-vLAN, intra-switch communications*

The first category of communications between vLANs represents those domains established on the same LAN switch, a method I will refer to as inter-vLAN, intra-switch communications. As noted in section 1, there are two basic methods that you can consider to obtain an inter-vLAN, intra-switch communications capability. First, you can use multiple LAN adapter cards or multiple protocol stacks and a single adapter card. I will refer to this method as creative communications, while the second method employs the use of a router.

#### Creative communications

The left portion of Figure 11.14 illustrates the use of multiple LAN adapter cards to obtain an inter-vLAN communications capability. Note that this method requires the attachment of the station to two or more LAN switch ports, with each port associated with a different vLAN. As each adapter card has a distinct MAC address this method of vLAN interconnection can be accomplished using either a Layer 1 (port-grouping) or Layer 2 (MAC-based) vLAN creation method. In comparison, the top right portion of Figure 11.14 illustrates how a dual protocol stack on a workstation or server can be used with a single connection to a LAN switch to obtain an inter-vLAN communications capability on the switch. In this example, multiple protocols are transmitted via a common switch port and each protocol stack provides a connection to a vLAN based upon a Layer 3 protocol. Thus, this method of inter-vLAN communications is restricted to a Layer 3 vLAN creation method based upon protocol. Although either method shown at the top of Figure 11.14 provides an inter-vLAN communications capability, both require the setup to occur at each station, which can result in a time consuming process. In addition, connecting more than two vLANs together is usually difficult, if not impossible, due to hardware and software limitations associated with workstations. That is, many workstations may not have a sufficient number of expansion slots for additional adapter cards nor have sufficient memory to support additional protocol stacks.

### Using a router

The second major method used to provide an inter-vLAN, intra-switch communications capability is through the use of a router. When using a router to connect vLANs on the same switch, the method of connection will be based upon the functionality of the switch and the router. When a Layer-2 vLAN creation method is used by a switch, each router port contains a MAC address that is associated with a Layer-2 broadcast domain. Thus, one port to router connection will be required for each vLAN requiring an inter-vLAN communications capability on the switch, resulting in traffic from one vLAN to another being routed by the router. This method of inter-vLAN communications is illustrated in Figure 11.14c.

If a Layer 3 vLAN creation method is supported by the LAN switch, vLANs can be created based upon different IP subnets on IPX network addresses. Then, if the switch does not support a trunking capability, different switch ports can be grouped together by subnet or network address, resulting in predefined router ports being associated with a specific vLAN at Layer 3.

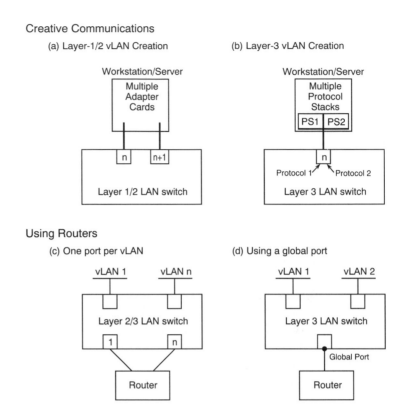

**Figure 11.14**  Inter-vLAN communications method

The router would then forward traffic from one vLAN to another based upon destination subnet or network address.

If a LAN switch has a trunking capability it becomes possible to use a single global port to connect the switch to the router to obtain an inter-vLAN, intra-switch communications capability. Figure 11.14d illustrates the hardware connection between a router and a global port on a switch. Here the term global port refers to a switch port that belongs to all vLANs configured on the switch, in effect resulting in the switch obtaining a trunking capability.

The configuration illustrated in Figure 11.14d is only applicable to certain switches and routers. When a router is used with a Layer 3 switch, the router must be modified to perform, in effect, a routing trick to enable it to provide an inter-

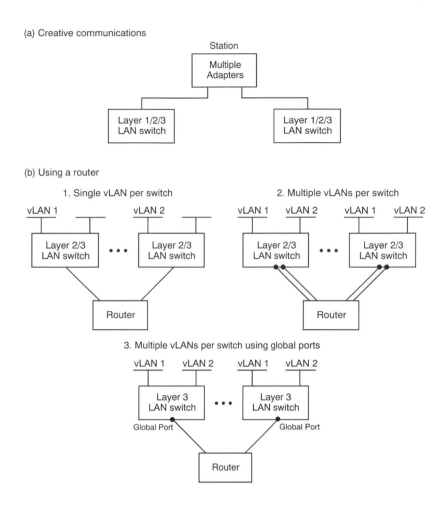

**Figure 11.15** Inter-vLAN, inter-switch communications

vLAN, intra-switch communications capability. For example, a RAD Network Devices router, referred to as Vgate, uses a different MAC address for each vLAN it provides connectivity for. One port on the Vgate uses a unique MAC source address for each IP and IPX defined vLAN. This action enables traffic generated by the Vgate to the switch to have a different source MAC address based upon the subnet that the address is associated with, resulting in it being forwarded through the switch to other switch ports that belong to the virtual LAN. This technique enables a single connection between RAD's Vgate and a LAN switch to appear to the switch as multiple router connections. In comparison, a conventional router cannot support multiple IP subnets or IPX network addresses on a single port, making it incapable of providing routing via a trunk or global port connection.

### Inter-vLAN, inter-switch communications

A second type of communications between virtual LANs involves the situation where stations reside on different switches. I will refer to this type of communications as inter-vLAN, inter-switch communications. Similar to our discussion of inter-vLAN, intra-switch communications, there are two basic methods that can be considered to obtain an inter-vLAN, inter-switch communications capability: creative communications and the use of routers. In addition, a third method via the use of backbone switches may be possible if vendor equipment provides this capability.

#### Creative communications

The top portion of Figure 11.15 illustrates the use of multiple adapter cards in a LAN station to link vLANs on two switches together. As discussed earlier in this chapter, this method of linkage is only applicable for connecting a station to two or three vLANs due to hardware constraints. In addition, if the necessity arises to provide an interconnection capability to a large number of workstations and/or servers, the cabling and use of switch ports can result in a considerable expenditure of funds. For such reasons this method of providing an inter-vLAN, inter-switch communications capability should probably be limited to being considered when very few network stations need this capability. For example, if two or three servers needed to become members of two vLANs on separate switches, you might consider this method for providing inter-vLAN, inter-switch communications.

#### Using a router

There are three basic methods by which routers can be used to provide inter-vLAN, inter-switch communications. Two methods assume the lack of LAN switch support for trunking or global ports, while one method assumes LAN switches support this capability.

### Single vLAN per switch

Figure 11.15b1 illustrates the use of a router to link switches that are configured to support a single vLAN. In this example either Layer 2 or Layer 3 vLAN creation methods can be used by the LAN switches. When a Layer 2 vLAN creation method is used, the MAC address of one router port is associated with the vLAN on one switch while the MAC address of the other router port is associated with the vLAN on the second switch. When a Layer 3 vLAN creation method is used there are two methods by which vLANs can be created. First, vLANs can be created based upon IP subnet or IPX network address. When this method of vLAN creation is used, the router simply examines the destination subnet or network address and routes data based upon the address. If a vLAN creation method based upon protocol is used, one port on the router could be configured to support a protocol used by one switch while the second router port could be configured to provide support for the protocol used on the second switch. This method of inter-vLAN, inter-switch communications is much less common as it requires the router to perform protocol conversion and operate as a gateway. As an alternative, some routers can be configured to provide a translation bridging operation which allows operations to occur at the Layer 2 level of the OSI Reference Model.

### Multiple vLANs per switch

When multiple vLANs are configured on LAN switches there are two methods you can consider to provide an inter-vLAN, inter-switch communications capability. First, if the LAN switches do not support a trunking or global port capability, you can use multiple switch to router connections, with each connection joining one vLAN on a switch to the router. This method of connectivity is illustrated in Figure 11.15b2. Secondly, if the LAN switches support a trunking or global port capability, you can use a single connection between each LAN switch and a router. The topology associated with providing an inter-vLAN, inter-switch communications capability when multiple vLANs are configured on LAN switches and the switches support a trunking or global port capability is illustrated in Figure 11.15b3.

### Backbone switching

A third method that can be considered to provide an inter-vLAN, inter-switch communications capability can be obtained through the use of backbone switches. The topology associated with the use of a backbone switch would be similar to that shown in Figure 11.15b1 and 11.15b2, with the router replaced by a backbone switch. The backbone switch commonly represents a high speed switch with a limited number of ports, such as a 100BASE-T, FDDI, or an ATM switch. A legacy switch, such as a 100BASE-T or FDDI switch, would use bridging to provide communications between vLANs on different switches or multiple vLANs on the same switch. As most high speed backbone switches operate at the MAC layer, the use of backbone switching to provide an inter-vLAN, inter-switch communications capability is normally limited to the use of Layer 2 LAN switches.

### ATM considerations

The use of ATM backbone switches to interconnect Ethernet or Token-Ring switches adds a layer of complexity that should be considered as it affects both vLAN creation and inter-switch performance. So-called legacy LANs, such as Ethernet, Token-Ring and FDDI, primarily operate using a connectionless technology where traffic is transmitted on a path and can be viewed by many stations prior to the destination recognizing its address in a frame and copying the frame 'off the wire'. In comparison, ATM is a connection-oriented transmission method in which a direct path or circuit is established between the source and the destination station. For connectionless traffic to flow through a connection-oriented network, the ATM network must emulate the broadcast nature of legacy LANs, as well as providing a mapping or resolution process that converts MAC addresses to ATM addresses. Those functions are performed by an ATM Forum standard known as LAN Emulation (LANE).

In Chapter 3 we examined the operation of LAN Emulation, including the role of different ATM server components, such as the LAN Emulation Server (LES), the Broadcast and Unknown Server (BUS), and the LAN Emulation configuration Server (LECS). In examining the use of ATM LAN emulation to interconnect legacy switches, note that the emulation process occurs from the LEC in the ATM interface of the LAN switch through the LES in the ATM switch to the LEC in the ATM interface in the destination LAN switch. That process is transparent to vLAN creation methods using MAC addresses, and allows LAN switches to control whether or not frames from one switch should be destined via the ATM backbone to another LAN switch. If vLANs are defined by a port grouping method, each ATM interface on a LAN switch would be considered as just another LAN switch port. Thus, if ATM ports on each LAN switch are defined for inclusion in a LAN switch port-based vLAN, the vLAN can also span multiple switches via an ATM backbone. Another method of associating legacy LAN stations to vLANs via an ATM backbone involves the use of the LECS. As the LECs assigns individual LAN Emulation clients to emulated LANs by directing them to an appropriate LES you can establish multiple LES and configure the LECS to create, in effect, multiple vLANs by the assignment of clients to different LAN Emulation Servers.

*Performance issues*

Although most persons consider the use of ATM backbone switches as a mechanism to enhance performance, in some situations the LAN emulation process may result in the throughput of a 155 Mbps ATM switch becoming less than that obtainable from the use of a 100 Mbps Fast Ethernet switch. This is because the LAN emulation process, as previously indicated, requires a considerable amount of LEC to LES interaction to obtain the MAC to ATM address resolution prior to a switched virtual call being able to be set up to actually transport the frame between switches.

Now that we have an appreciation for the concepts behind local virtual networking, let us extend the distance between switches so that we can consider the use of the Internet as a mechanism for obtaining a virtual networking capability.

## 11.2.5 Using the Internet

It was previously noted in this chapter that there are compelling economic and reliability reasons for considering the use of the Internet as a virtual network. Unfortunately, there are also a few compelling reasons why some organizations may wish to bypass using the Internet as a mechanism to replace leased lines. Two of the more compelling reasons to bypass the Internet include security and performance issues. As we will shortly note, with the addition of appropriate hardware it becomes possible to overcome security problems associated with the use of the Internet.

*Security considerations*

The connection of a corporate network to the Internet exposes that network to attacks from hackers, crackers, and other unscrupulous persons beyond the direct control of the manager of a private network. This situation is true regardless of whether your Internet connection is established to enable corporate employees to access the World Wide Web or to use the Internet as a virtual network. For either or both situations, there are several security mechanisms that can be used to obtain a significant barrier between the public Internet and corporate private networks to enhance corporate security. Those security mechanisms include the use of a firewall, encryption, a proxy server, and an authentication server. As we covered network security including the use of firewalls in Chapter 10, we will primarily focus our attention upon encryption and authentication in this section, as those two firewall features are essential for obtaining what is known as a secure tunnel through the Internet.

*Encryption*

As the flow of corporate data via the Internet makes such information vulnerable to being read by other organizations and individuals, many organizations will require firewalls to provide an encryption capability. Through encryption the information content of packets becomes unrecognizable, providing protection of information routed through the Internet. When packets are encrypted for transmission via the Internet, the term encrypted tunnel is often used to refer to the transportation of such data. Here the term tunnel refers to the process of tunneling whereby information transported from one point to another is encapsulated in wrapper packets. In actuality, the term tunnel can be misleading as there are several methods by which firewalls can encrypt data. One method, in which the contents of entire packets originating on a public network are first encrypted and then encapsulated in new packets using the destination address of another firewall, is indeed tunneling. Another method in which only the information field of a packet originating on a private network is encrypted does not alter any control information in the packet header. Thus, this technique does not require the packet to be encapsulated for transmission and does not actually represent tunneling. Regardless of the

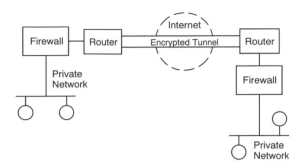

**Figure 11.16**   Using firewalls to create an encrypted tunnel

method of encryption, both methods hide the contents of information carried through the Internet, providing a level of protection to the contents of packets.

Figure 11.16 illustrates the use of a pair of firewalls to provide an encrypted group tunnel through the Internet to link two geographically separated private networks. Although encryption safeguards the contents of packets from observation, by itself it does not verify the data originator nor provide a mechanism to limit the ability to restrict users on the Internet to subsets of services for which you want to provide access. Recognizing this limitation, many firewall vendors now incorporate authentication services within their products.

*Authentication*

Although passwords represent a form of authentication, they are only periodically changed and they represent a vulnerability as their flow over the Internet can be monitored. Recognizing this problem, many firewalls now include an advanced authentication service which integrates one-time passwords in the form of tokens generated by a pseudo-random number generator with access to specific services behind the firewall. For example, a firewall may support the use of credit card size numeric password generators which generate a new five or six digit code every minute. When a user attempts to access a specific service, he or she is prompted by the firewall's authentication program for their PIN number and numeric code displayed on their security card. The firewall uses the PIN to execute an algorithm associated with the PIN, producing a numeric code that is compared to the received code. As codes change on a short time basis, typically every 30 or 60 seconds, some authentication programs will compare the received code to a series of codes that could have been generated a minute before or after the code was received. Assuming that the received code matches one of those generated codes, the remote user is authenticated and allowed access to the requested service. However, once passed through the firewall, a second level of security in the form of a Telnet or FTP server password request is commonly required to actually access the requested service.

Although it is possible to place individual authentication programs on separate servers, the use of a firewall simplifies administration as well as reducing the cost of authentication. For example, if your organization wanted to provide authenticated access to several Telnet and FTP hosts, you would require the installation of authentication software on each host as well as the distribution of separate token-generating cards to authorized users of each system. Users requiring access to two or more hosts might then require multiple security cards unless authentication software on each host could be coordinated with the software on other hosts. In comparison, centralizing authentication at the firewall enables management of token generation cards to be simplified. Figure 11.17 illustrates the general operational steps performed by a firewall performing authentication for predefined host services.

In planning for firewall authentication you should examine the methods of authentication supported. Although most firewalls support several methods, selecting different methods for different users can considerably add to your administrative burden without enhancing the security of your private network. If you select a time-based token system where passwords or numeric codes change every 30 or 60 seconds, you should consider the fact that remote access to your firewall can result in transmission delays that can easily result in a mismatch between the entry of a valid token and its rejection upon arrival at the firewall. Thus, it is important to be able to set a comparison time variance that enables the firewall to compute valid tokens preceding and succeeding the token that it generates at the time an incoming token arrives.

## 11.2.6 Testing considerations

The variance between the capabilities of different vendor products, as well as the differences associated with implementing

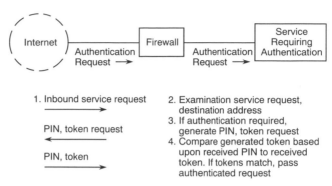

**Figure 11.17** Firewall authentication process

rules on different products, can result in your best intentions going astray. To avoid potential embarrassments as well as security gaps, it is highly recommended that you consider installing a firewall on a network segment established to enable the testing of the firewall's configuration prior to it being placed into a production environment. Although doing so will usually result in the necessity to change a few IP addresses on the external side of the firewall from their intended addresses, the ability to significantly test the firewall can provide indications of configuration problems that can be corrected without seriously affecting the operational capability of your organization.

## 11.2.7 Performance issues

As previously noted, there are considerable advantages in terms of reliability, economics, and application integration associated with the use of the Internet as a replacement or supplement for private analog and digital leased lines. Unfortunately, in addition to security you must also cope with performance issues that can place the proverbial 'fly in the ointment' with respect to the use of the Internet as a replacement for private leased lines.

During 1996 and 1997 the tremendous growth in World Wide Web traffic threatened to turn portions of the Internet into the Long Island Expressway at the rush hour, in effect resulting in substantial bottlenecks that significantly degraded transmission performance. In fact, many pundits were predicting a catastrophic collapse of portions of the Internet due to the success of its unrestricted growth. What started as a mechanism for the exchange of text-based electronic mail messages has evolved into a transport mechanism for downloading weather maps and pictures of Madonna, accessing on-line magazines and even placing individual telephone calls. The 500 character email long ago was commonly replaced by the hundred thousand byte message including a 95 Kbyte picture of the author or an attached binary encoded document, whereas short interactive Telnet sessions with 2000 bytes screens have been, to a significant degree, replaced by Web surfing where downloading a page with imbedded graphics can result in the transmission of 200 000 bytes. At the same time transmission requirements were growing by several orders of magnitude, the number of Internet users was experiencing an exponential growth rate. Although the growth in content transmission and user population resulted in significant delays in many applications during 1997, from a personal perspective this author believes that evolving and planned Internet backbone communications modifications can provide significant relief for performance bottlenecks. For example, some Internet backbone carriers during mid-1997 upgraded their facilities from a T3 operating rate of approximately 45 Mbps to an ATM operating rate of 155 Mbps, with a further upgrade to 622 Mbps planned for implementation in the near future. This increase in Internet backbone capacity should alleviate many existing bottlenecks. In addition, the commitment of seven companies to continue to enhance the Internet backbone may enable capacity to eventually surpass demand. For example, through the use of wavelength division multiplexing the transport capacity of fiber can be significantly increased, in some situations providing a 10 Gbps transmission capacity. Thus, as new capacity and new techniques are added to circuits used for Internet transmission, the Internet can be expected to evolve into a network capable of transporting corporate time-sensitive information in the form of voice, fax, and data. Thus, corporations may wish to periodically test the use of the Internet to ascertain its capability to serve as a replacement or supplement for the computer network. In the interim, time-insensitive information in the form of such diverse applications as electronic mail and fax should be considered for placement on the Internet if doing so can provide sufficient economic gains.

# 12

---

# PERFORMANCE ISSUES

---

In concluding this book we will examine a frequently discussed but very rarely explained area of internetworking: the wide area network operating rate required to provide an acceptable level of performance. From reading trade articles readers cannot help but obtain the impression that T1/E1 data links are almost an absolute requirement to interconnect LANs or to provide the transport facility to connect a local area network to a wide area network.

Although the transport capability of the wide area network is certainly an important criterion with respect to the ability to transfer data in a reasonable period of time, it is not the only criterion for selecting a wide area network transmission facility. Of far more importance is the necessity to determine the activity of traffic that will flow on the transmission facility and then use that information to determine the type of transmission facility that will provide a reasonable level of service within your organization's budgetary constraints. As different organizations by their very nature have different transmission requirements, for the most part we will avoid defining what is a reasonable level of service. Instead, we will focus our attention upon interactive and file transfer activities and the time required to perform each operation at different data rates. Doing so will provide us with the ability to select a reasonable level of performance which lies within the budgetary constraints of our organization.

## 12.1 INTERACTIVE SESSIONS

In an interactive environment a workstation user on one local area network interacts with a mainframe application on a host computer which generates responses to queries or a similar application on a file server on the same or a different local area network. Although the portion of a screen being updated has a major bearing on the time required to transmit a new image we can focus our efforts upon examining a few worst case scenarios. That is, we can examine the transfer time required to transmit the contents of a full screen of information. Doing so provides a frame of reference we can use for scaling to our actual environment in which partial screens of information are transferred.

As there are significant differences between the number of bits required to represent text and graphic display images we will examine each type of display as a separate entity. First we will examine the transfer time required for reproducing a full screen of text on a monochrome display. Next we will turn our attention to the popular Video Graphics Array (VGA) color screen to investigate the effect of color graphics.

### 12.1.1 Text display

A full screen of text is represented by 80 columns of 25 characters per column. In an IBM environment two bytes are used to define each screen position. One byte defines the character as one of $2^8$ or 256 types of ASCII characters. The second byte is known as the character's attribute. That byte defines the color of the character as well as other information, such as whether it is to be displayed in normal or high intensity, blinking or non-blinking, underlined, and so on. Thus, the number of bits required to be transferred to faithfully reconstruct a full text screen image becomes $80 \times 25 \times 16$ or 32 000 bits.

Table 12.1 indicates the relationship between the data transmission rate and screen transfer time in seconds to transport a full text screen to include attributes. Note that the screen transfer time is an optimum time which does not consider the effect of the overhead associated with a wide area network protocol nor the delay associated with the bridging or routing of data.

Also note that the screen transfer time is for one screen and does not consider the effect of multiple local area network users simultaneously or near simultaneously requesting screen transfers.

**Table 12.1** Data rate versus full text screen transfer time

| Data rate (bps) | Screen transfer time (s) |
| --- | --- |
| 2400 | 13.333 33 |
| 4800 | 6.666 67 |
| 9600 | 3.333 33 |
| 19 200 | 1.666 67 |
| 56 000 | 0.571 43 |
| 64 000 | 0.500 00 |
| 128 000 | 0.250 00 |
| 384 000 | 0.083 33 |
| 1 544 000 | 0.020 73 |
| 2 048 000 | 0.015 63 |
| 4 000 000 | 0.008 00 |
| 10 000 000 | 0.003 20 |
| 16 000 000 | 0.002 00 |

In examining the entries in Table 12.1 it is clear that data rates below 9600 bps result in relatively lengthy transfer times. However, what can be inferred from that table concerning data transfer rates at or above 9600 bps?

The use of a wide area transmission facility at 9600 bps results in $3\frac{1}{3}$ seconds to transfer a text screen image, excluding the overhead of the protocol and processing delays associated with computers performing the screen transfer operations. By itself $3\frac{1}{2}$ seconds is not an excessive amount of time, since most screen transfers involve only a portion of a screen actually being transferred. What we must consider is the potential for multiple transfer requests by other local area network workstations that can result in the operating rate of the transmission facility becoming a bottleneck.

## Considering multiple transfer requests

Let us assume that our local area network has 100 workstations. Through monitoring let us assume that we measured average intraLAN traffic as 12 frames per second and peak traffic at 20 frames per second, with an average frame length of 500 data characters. From experience the use of interLAN or a LAN-to-mainframe wide area network transmission facility can be expected to add 20% to the traffic flow on a local area network. Stated another way, we can estimate interLAN or LAN-to-mainframe traffic by multiplying existing average and peak LAN traffic by 20%. Based upon our previous assumed monitoring, this would result in an average of 2.4 and a peak of 4.0 500 byte frames requiring transfer each second. An average of 2.4 500 byte frames per second is equivalent to 9600 bits. Thus, projected average interLAN or LAN-to-mainframe transmission would use all of the available bandwidth of a 9600 bps circuit; when the WAN protocol overhead is considered, the average traffic on the local area network destined for transmission over the wide area network's 9600 bps transmission facility would experience cumulative delays. Thus, a 9600 bps transmission facility would be clearly unacceptable for this situation without even considering peak utilization.

When peak utilization is considered four 500 byte frames can be expected to flow across the wide area network transmission facility each second. This means that a peak servicing rate of $4 \times 500 \times 8$ or 16 000 bps would be required to ensure that cumulative delays do not occur.

Suppose that we consider the use of a 19 200 bps transmission facility. Assuming a protocol overhead of 20%, that line speed becomes capable of transferring 15 360 bits per second. Although this data rate is capable of supporting the average transfer requirements of LAN users, it will result in slight delays when peak traffic conditions occur. In this situation each succeeding peak second of transfer adds an additional 0.0416 seconds $((16\,000 - 15\,360)/15\,360)$ to the 1.667 second transfer time indicated in Table 12.1. Thus, you would have to estimate the average length of peak traffic to determine if the use of a 19 200 bps transmission facility would result in excessive delays. As a 56 000 Kbps data rate supports both average and peak loads without the possibility of queuing, all transfer times in Table 12.1 at 56 000 Kbps and higher data rates would not have to be adjusted for peak traffic activity. Thus, as explained, screen transfer times must be viewed from both the operating rate of the transmission facility as well as from the perspective of the traffic activity that it will be required to support.

### 12.1.2 Graphics display

When using a graphics operating environment, such as Microsoft's Windows, each screen pixel is treated and addressed

**Table 12.2** Data rate versus VGA mode 12 screen transfer time

| Data rate (bps) | Screen transfer time (s) |
|---|---|
| 2400 | 1024.000 00 |
| 4800 | 512.000 00 |
| 9600 | 256.000 00 |
| 19 200 | 128.000 00 |
| 56 000 | 43.885 71 |
| 64 000 | 38.400 00 |
| 128 000 | 19.200 00 |
| 384 000 | 6.400 00 |
| 1 544 000 | 1.591 71 |
| 2 048 000 | 1.200 00 |
| 4 000 000 | 0.614 40 |
| 10 000 000 | 0.245 76 |
| 16 000 000 | 0.153 60 |

as a separate entity. As there are 13 screen formats are presently defined under the Video Graphics Array (VGA) standard, we will examine the screen with the most intensive pixel requirements to obtain an understanding of how a graphics environment can considerably increase the necessity for obtaining higher speed wide area network transmission facilities.

VGA screen mode displays graphics using a 640 by 480 pixel resolution. The color of each pixel is defined by an eight-bit byte. This results in a full VGA screen requiring the transmission of $640 \times 480 \times 8$ or $2\,457\,600$ bits to be faithfully reproduced. Table 12.2 illustrates the relationship between the data rate and the screen transfer time for a VGA 640 by 480 pixel screen. In comparing the times listed in Tables 12.1 and 12.2 it is apparent that the transmission of graphic images can in many instances slow a network to a snail's pace of operation. Fortunately, even when a workstation uses a graphics environment most information is transferred in the form of text characters. However, if your local area network resides in a radiology laboratory, real estate office, or similar organization where a high probability exists for the transfer of graphic images, you may wish to explicitly examine the type of data to be transferred. Doing so may enable you to avoid an unknown surprise and ensure that the wide area transmission facility does not become a LAN bottleneck.

## 12.2 FILE TRANSFERS

Similarly to the calculations presented in the preceding section, you can compute the time required to transfer files at different data rates. However, since file transfers can considerably vary in size we should probably focus our efforts upon the most common type of file transfer that occurs on a local area network. That type of file transfer is represented by the loading of a program from a server on the network or from a linked network.

### 12.2.1 Transfer time

Table 12.3 lists the file transfer times required to transmit a 640 Kbyte (1024 bytes per Kbyte) file at different data rates. Although most DOS and Macintosh application programs are under 640 Kbytes in size, the entries in Table 12.3 provide a 'reasonable' worst case expectation for the effect of loading a large file. Readers should again note that the data transfer times presented in each table in this chapter do not consider the effect of a wide area network protocol's overhead to encapsulate information. Depending on the wide area network protocol used, the transfer times listed in each table may have to be adjusted upward by as much as 20% to account for the overhead associated with the use of the protocol.

**Table 12.3**   Data rate versus 640 kbyte file transfer time

| Data rate (bps) | File transfer time (s) |
| ---: | ---: |
| 2400 | 2184.533 33 |
| 4800 | 1092.266 67 |
| 9600 | 546.133 33 |
| 19 200 | 273.066 67 |
| 56 000 | 93.622 86 |
| 64 000 | 81.920 00 |
| 128 000 | 40.960 00 |
| 384 000 | 13.653 33 |
| 1 544 000 | 3.395 65 |
| 2 048 000 | 2.560 00 |
| 4 000 000 | 1.310 72 |
| 10 000 000 | 0.524 29 |
| 16 000 000 | 0.327 68 |

## 12.2.2 Issues

From an examination of the entries in Table 12.3 two issues become readily apparent. First, large file transfers are similar to the transmission of graphic screen images in that a relatively high data transmission facility is required to provide a reasonable level of performance. This means that whenever possible files should be located on local servers. Doing so provides LAN users with access to the files at the local area network operating rate, at a transmission rate which is usually significantly greater than the data rate of a wide area network transmission facility. If this is not possible, the placement of files for interLAN usages should be attempted first by the use of servers located on network connected by the use of a local bridge. Here the use of a local bridge enables interLAN communications to occur at a very high data rate in comparison to the data rates supported by most wide area network communications facilities. Only as a last resort should wide area network transmission facilities be used for significant interLAN file transfers as doing so can result in electronic mail, mainframe access and other activities relying upon the use of WAN transmission facilities being adversely affected. Thus, readers may wish to move applications to 'more' local servers to reduce or eliminate program loadings via wide area network transmission facilities.

When examining different possible WAN connections to interconnect geographically separated LANs, the best advice this author can provide is to think about available options and then think again. This is because we have the luxury of using a variety of transmission facilities and methods to satisfy organizational networking requirements. By carefully examining all available networking options against current and potential organizational requirements, we can select a mechanism that provides an efficient and cost effective method to interconnect LANs. This author simply considers this process as smart networking and hopes that the information presented in this book provides you with the ability to consider the variety of options to achieve your own smart networking capability.

# INDEX

Access lists
  and security 434–40
  configuring 435–7
  extended 437–9
Adapter cards 6
Adapter Support Interface (ASI), IBM 179
Address Resolution Protocol (ARP) 304, 363–4
Address translation, security 445
Adjusted Ring Length (ARL) 217–19
Advanced Peer-to-Peer Networking (APPN) 398–405
  and Systems Network Architecture (SNA) 387
  architecture 400–3
  End Nodes (ENs) 401, 402–3
  gateway options 412–25
  Low-entry Networking (LEN) nodes 400–1
  Network Nodes (NNs) 401, 402–3
  rout selection 403–5
Advanced Program-to-Program Communication (APPC) 399–400
Advanced Research Projects Agency Network (ARPANET) 297
AIX operating system, IBM 429
Amplitude Modulation Phase Shift Keying (AM PSK) 38
Analog leased lines 251–2
Analogue circuit switched telephone network 237–9
AppleTalk routing 367, 379, 434
Application Programming Interface (API) 178
Application software 189–90
APPN see Advanced Peer-to-Peer Networking (APPN)

Asymmetric Digital Subscriber Line (ADSL) 240–2, 243
Asynchronous Transfer Mode (ATM) 10, 12, 100–16
  and LANs 57–8
  and virtual networking 488
  ATM Adaptation Layer (AAL) protocol 102, 104, 115
  ATM cell 100–1
  ATM Forum 29–30
  ATM Layer 104–5
  ATM Physical Layer 105
  ATM protocol stack 103–5
  ATM router 107
  ATM service processor 108
  ATM switches 107–8
  Available Bit Rate (ABR) traffic 103
  backbone switches 489
  cell headers 109–13
  Cell Loss Priority (CLP) field 112
  cell switching 114
  connection identifiers 114–15
  connections 113
  Continuous Bit Rate (CBR) traffic 103
  data transmission rates 12–13
  error rates 12–13
  Generic Flow Control (GFC) field 109–10
  Header Error Check (HEC) field 112–13
  LAN switches 106–7, 166, 167
  Network Interface Cards (NIC) 106
  operation 106–8
  Payload Type Identifier (PTI) field 112
  Permanent Virtual Circuit (PVC) 113
  scalability 101
  Switched Virtual Circuit (SVC) 113
  traffic classification 102–3
  transparency 101–2

Asynchronous Transfer Mode (ATM) (*Contd.*)
  Unspecified Bit Rate (UBR) traffic  103
  Variable Bit Rate—Non-Real Time (VBR/NRT) traffic  103
  Variable Bit Rate—Real Time (VBR/RT) traffic  103
  Virtual Channel Identifier (VCI) field  111–12
  Virtual Channel (VC) switch  114
  Virtual Path Identifier (VPI) field  110–11, 115, 166
  Virtual Path (VP) switch  114
Asynchronous transmission, FDDI  91–2
AT&T
  divestiture  8
  fast packet switching  272–3
ATM *see* Asynchronous Transfer Mode (ATM)
ATM Forum  29–30
Attachment Unit Interface (AUI)  195–7
Authentication
  firewalls  447–52
  Internet  491–2
Available Bit Rate (ABR) traffic  103


Backbone cabling standards  50
Backbone operation, LANs  164–8, 230–1
  performance  230–1
Backbone switching, and virtual networking  487–9
Backbones, creating a collapsed  231
Baseband signalling, LANs  36–7, 38–9, 44
Basic Rate Interface (BRI), for ISDN  245–7
Batch terminals  2
Bay Networks routers  362
Bellcore S/Key one-time passwords  449–50
Binary Synchronous Communications (BSC)  23
Bridge Protocol Data Unit (BPDU) frames  337–9
Bridges/bridging  121–32, 327–60
  Ethernet traffic performance  352–4
  fabrication  131
  features  127–32
  filtering/forwarding  125, 127–9
  flooding  123–4
  frame encapsulation  131
  frame translation  130
  local and wide area interface support  129–30
  methods  327–44
  multiple port support  129
  multiport bridge  123
  operation  121–3
  parallel  345–7
  routing method  132
  serial and sequential  344–5
  token ring performance  354–60
  translating  126–7
  *see also* Source routing; Traffic flow, bridges; Transparent bridges
Broadband coaxial cable, for LANs  47–8, 59
Broadband signalling, LANs  36–8
Broadcast and Unknown Server (BUS)  167, 488
Brouters
  operation  137–8
  utilization  138–9
Burst Tolerance (BT)  102
Bus Interface Unit (BIU)  54


Cable television (CATV) cable  46
Cabling standards
  LANs backbone cabling  50
  LANs horizontal cabling  50–1
  LANs UTP categories  51–2
  *see also* IBM cabling system
Carrier-Sense Multiple Access with Collision Avoidance (CSMA/CA)  55–6

Carrier-Sense Multiple Access with Collision Detection (CSMA/CD)  53–5, 144
Carrierless Amplitude/Phase (CAP) modulation  241, 242–3
Carterphone decision  8
CD-ROM systems  16
Cell Delay Variation Tolerance (CDVT)  102
Cell headers, ATM  109–13
Cell Loss Priority (CLP) field, ATM  112
Channel banks  254–5
Channel Service Unit (CSU)  256
Circuit switched networks  235–48
  analogue  237–9
  Digital Subscriber Line (DSL)  239–43
  Integrated Services Digital Network (ISDN)  245–8
  switched digital  243–5
Cisco Systems routers  362
Clarkson Packet Drivers  179
Client/server processing  142
Client/server relationship  173
Coax adapter  200–1
Coaxial cable  45–6, 59, 64–5

10BASE-5 backbone network 196
  compared with twisted pair wire 44–55
  hardware interface 46–7
Coding methods *see* Encoding techniques
Collision avoidance 55–6
Collision detection 54–5
Committed Information Rate (CIR) 275, 277–80
Communications controllers 4–5, 6
Communications monitoring security threat 441
Communications servers 428–31
Compression *see Data compression*
Computer Aided Design (CAD) 48
Computer-communications evolution 1–5
Concentrators 8, 84
Connection identifiers, ATM 114–15
Consultative Committee for International Telephone and Telegraph (CCITT) 17
Continuous Bit Rate (CBR) traffic 102
Control units 4–5
Controlled Access Unit (CAU) (IBM model 8230) 221–2
Copper Distributed Data Interface (CDDI) 40
Cyclic Redundancy Check (CRC) 62, 80, 155–6, 232

Data compression 238–9
Data Delivery Protocol (DDP), Apple 379
Data Link Connection Identifier (DLCI) 273
Data Link Switching (DLSw) 425–8
Data service unit (DSU) 6, 243–5, 256
Data Terminal equipment (DTE) 258
Data Transfer Unit (DTU) 232
Data transmission rates *see* Transmission rates
Datagrams
  datagram packet networks 262–3
  versus virtual circuits 300–3
Dataphone Digital Service (DDS) 255–6
DecNET 434
Dedicated Access Facility (DAF) 269
Dedicated Token Ring (DTR) standard 232–3
Demultiplexing 253
Destination Services Access Point (DSAP) 95, 338
Dictionary attack security threat 441
Differential Manchester coding 39–40
Digital channel banks 254–5

Digital Equipment Corporation 134
Digital Subscriber Line (DSL) 239–43
Digital transmission facilities 255–6
Discrete Multitone (DMT) modulation 241, 242
Distributed Function Terminal (DFT) port 419
Domain Name Service (DNS) 283, 319–20
DOS, and networking 170–2
Dual Attached Station (DAS) 83
Dynamic Host Configuration Protocol (DHCP) 372

E1 circuits 8, 10, 12
Early token release 81
Electronic Industries
  Association/Telecommunications Industry Association (EIA/TIA cabling standards) 45, 51
Electronic mail (e-mail) 15, 16
Encoding techniques
  4B5B encoding 42–3, 72, 73, 85, 86
  8B6T block 70–1
  high speed 39–43
  Manchester coding 39–40
  MLT-3 encoding 40–1
  popular schemes 42
Encryption 452
  Internet 490–1
End Nodes (ENs), APPN 401, 402–3
Error checking
  Cyclic Redundancy Check (CRC) 155–6, 232
  Header Error Check (HEC) field 112–13
Error correction, forward, Reed-Solomon 242
Error rates 12–13, 15
Ethernet 5–6, 53, 59–65
  10BASE-T network 191–205, 413
  10BASE-T network expansion 201–5
  802.3 frame 97–8
  and virtual networking 488
  APPN connectivity 412–25
  Attachment Unit Interface (AUI) 195–7
  bottleneck creation 149–50
  bridge segmentation 203–5
  coax adapter 200–1
  concentrators 193–4
  connecting to 10BASE-2 networks 201
  connecting to 10BASE-5 196
  fiber adapters 198–200

Ethernet (*Contd.*)
  fiber hubs  198
  fiber optic technology  197–8
  hub operation  147–50, 192–5
  interconnecting hubs  194–5
  LAN switches with  150–3
  network access units  195
  performance  352–4
  segmentation options  202–3
  SNA connectivity  412–25
  SNAP  97–9
  *see also* Fast Ethernet
Ethernet frame  60–2
Ethernet interframe gap  157


Fast Ethernet  65–72, 205–8
  100BASE-FX  72
  100BASE-T4  69–71
  100BASE-T  67–9, 205, 206–7, 488
    switches  164
  100BASE-TX  71–2, 205, 206
  backbone operation  206–7
  cable span distances  206
  CSMA protocol  27–8
    Medium-Dependent Interface (MDI)  69
    Medium Independent Interface (MII)  69
  performance  352–4
  physical layer  68–9
  Physical Medium Attachment (PMA) sub-
    layer  69
  repeater rules  206
  segmentation methods  206
  stream delimiters  67
  switch segmentation  208
Fast Ethernet frame  66
Fast packet switching  272–3
Fat pipes  161
Fax, virtual networking  478, 479
Fiber adapters  198–200
  distance limits  199–200
Fiber Distributed Data Interface (FDDI)
    82–94
  advantages  82–3
  asynchronous transmission  91–2
  bandwidth allocation  89
  Dual Attached Station (DAS)  84
  encoding and signalling  40, 85–6
  frame format  88–9
  frame formats  86–9
  Single Attached Station (SAS)  84
  status  93

synchronous transmission  91
  timers  90
  token format  88
  traffic classes  89–90
  transmission example  92–3
Fiber hubs  198
Fiber optic cable, for LANs  49–50, 59
Fiber Optic Repeater Link (FOIRL)  197, 200
Fiber optic repeaters  50
Fiber optic technology, with 10BASE-T
    Ethernet  197–8
Fiber optical transceivers  198
File servers
  communications  143
  location considerations  144–5
  modem pooler  143
  remote access  143
  types of  142–3
File Transfer Protocol (FTP)  25, 299
File transfers, performance  500–1
Filtering, bridges  125, 127–9
Firewalls  440–52
  address translation  445
  and IBM model 6611 network processor
    223
  and routers  440–1
  authentication  491–2
  classes, use of  443–4
  encryption  490
  on Internet  490
  packet filtering  450–2
  passwords  447–50
  placement  441–2
  proxy services  442–4
  stateful inspection  445–6
Flooding, bridges  123–4
Flow control  165
Forwarding, bridges  125, 127–9
Fractional T1 (FT1) service  256–7
Fractional T3 (FT3) service  257, 258
Frame Check Sequence (FCS) field  155
Frame encapsulation, LAN bridges  131
Frame Relay
  Access Device (FRAD)  273–4, 280–1, 482
  Committed Information Rate (CIR)  275,
    277–80
  compared to ITU-T X.25  273–5
  compared to X.25 recommendations  275,
    282
  Frame Relay Forum  281
  operation  276–7
  utilization  275–6

voice over  280–2
WAN connections  224
Frame translation, LAN bridges  130
Frames see Ethernet frame; Fast Ethernet frame
Frequency Division Multiplexing (FDM)  241, 249–52
ITU-T FDM recommendations  250–1
Frequency modulation  38
Frequency Shift Keying (FSK)  37
Full Duplex Transmission (FDX)  165

Gateway
definition  140–1
multi-protocol  141
operation  141
Generic Flow Control (GFC) field, ATM  109–10
Generic Routing Encapsulation Protocol (GREv2)  480
Graphics display, performance  498–9

Hacking  441
Header Error Check (HEC) field, ATM  112–13
High-level Data Link Control (HDLC)  22–3
High Speed Serial Interface (HSSI)  258, 362
Horizontal cabling standards  50–1
Hub-centric 10BASE-T networks  147
HyperText Transport Protocol (HTTP)  25, 297
and security  436–8

IBM 3172 Interconnect Controller  420–3
software  421–3
IBM 3174 Subsystem Control Unit  407–8
IBM 3270 Information Display System  3–5, 405–123
control unit types  407–8
data flow  406
emulation considerations  411–12
keyboard functions  410–12
LAN-based workstations with  6
PCOM/3270 emulation program  422, 423
protocols  407
terminal displays  408–10
IBM 3276 control unit  407
IBM 3278/9 coaxial adapter connection  419–20
IBM 6611 network processor  222–4, 223, 426
IBM cabling system
and EIA/TIA cabling standards  211

connectors  214
lobe maximum distances  214–15
Type 1 cable  212
Type 2 cable  212
Type 3 cable  212
Type 5 cable  213
Type 6 cable  213
Type 7 cable  213
Type 8 cable  213
Type 9 cable  214
wiring constraints  217–19
IBM PC  5
IBM PC Network Program  171
IBM poll and select software  4
IBM Reduced Instruction Set Computer (RISC) System/6000  222, 226
IBM Systems Network Architecture (SNA) see Systems Network Architecture (SNA), IBM
IBM Token-Ring networks see Token-Ring networks
IEEE  17, 26–66
IEEE 802 Project/standard  23
802.3 standard  26–7, 55, 59–64, 94, 97, 192–4, 195–6, 200, 201–29
802.4 standard  27, 74, 94
802.5 standard  27, 78, 94
see also Token-Ring networks
802.5r Dedicated Token-Ring (DTR) standard  232–3
committees  26–8
datalink subdivision  28–9
physical layer subdivision  29
Institute of Electrical and Electronic Engineers see IEEE
Integrated Services Digital Network (ISDN)  245–8
Basic Rate Interface (BRI)  245–7
Primary Rate Interface (PRI)  247–8
utilization  248
Intelligent hubs  145–6
International Standards Organization (ISO)  18–19
ISO OSI see Open Systems Interconnection (OSI) Reference Model
International standards organizations  16–30
de facto standards  17
see also ATM Forum; Consultative Committee for International Telephone and Telegraph (CCITT); IEEE; International Standards Organization (ISO); International Telecommunications Union Telecommunications (ITU–T)

International Telecommunications Union Telecommunications (ITU-T)  17, 18
ITU-T FDM recommendations  250–2
ITU-T packet network recommendations
　X.25  260–1, 264–8, 269–71, 273–5, 282
　X.28/X.29/X.75  260–1
Internet
　and remote server access  479
　authentication  491–2
　encryption  490–1
　performance  493
　security considerations  489–90
Internet Control Message Protocol (ICMP)  304
Internet Network Information Center (Inter-NIC)  319
Internet Network Service Providers (NSPs)  257
Internet Protocol (IP)  311–21
　router support by  362–4
　see also Transmission Control Protocol and Internet Protocol (TCP/IP)
Internet protocol suite  see Transmission Control Protocol and Internet Protocol (TCP/IP)
Internet Service Providers (ISPs)  16, 257, 480
Internetwork Packet Exchange (IPX)  23, 134, 172, 174, 182–3, 284–9
Interoffice and intraoffice calls  236
ISO  see International Standards Organization (ISO)
ITU-T  see International Telecommunications Union Telecommunications (ITU–T)

Kruskal algorithm  334–5

LAN  see Local Area Network (LAN)
LAN Emulation Configuration Server (LECS)  488–9
LAN Emulation (LANE)  106, 108
LAN Emulation Server (LES)  108, 488
Large Internet Packet Exchange (LIPX)  285–6
Layer 2 Forwarding (L2F)  481
Layer 2 Tunneling Protocol (L2TP)  481–2
Layered architecture  see Open Systems Interconnection (OSI) Reference Model
LLC  see Logical Link Control (LLC)
Lobe Attachment Models (LAMs)  221–2

Local Area Network (LAN)  10–16, 31–116
　access methods  52–8
　baseband signalling  36–7, 38–9
　benefits  15–16
　broadband coaxial cable for  47–8
　broadband signalling  36–8
　bus topology structure  33, 35–6
　cabling standards  50–2
　coverage area  11–12, 15
　data routing  14, 15
　data transmission rates  12–13, 15, 48
　encoding techniques  39–43
　error rates  12–13, 15
　Ethernet on  60–5
　fibre optic cable for  49–50
　hardware interface to coaxial cable  46–7
　information types  14–15
　LAN Emulation Configuration Server (LECS)  166–7
　LAN Emulation (LANE)  106, 108, 166, 167
　LAN Emulation Server (LES)  108, 166–7
　LAN switch  106–7
　legacy LANs  166, 167–8
　listener device mode  53
　loop topology structure  32–3
　mainframe access  5–7
　mixed topology structures  35
　Network-to-Node/Network-to-Network Interface (NNI)  108–9
　ownership  13, 15
　printing with  48
　regulation  13–14
　ring topology structure  33–4, 35, 56, 57
　signalling methods  36–9
　star topology structure  34, 35
　talker device mode  53
　technological characteristics  31, 59
　token-ring  5–7, 56, 57
　topologies  32–6
　topology  14, 15
　transmission medium  43–50
　tree topology structure  34, 36
　user-to-network interface  108
　WAN comparison  11–15
　see also Ethernet; Fast Ethernet; Fiber distributed data interface; Local Area Network (LAN) software; Local Area Network (LAN) switches; Local Area Networking; Logical Link Control (LLC); Token-Ring networks

Local Area Network (LAN) software  169–90
  Adapter Support Interface (ASI), IBM  179
  Application Programming Interface (API)  179
  application software  189–90
  Clarkson Packet Drivers  179
  DOS  170–2
  IBM PC Network Program  171
  Internetwork Package eXchange (IPX)  172, 174, 182–3, 284–9
  multiple protocol support  177–89
  NetBios Extended User Interface (NET-BEUI)  175–6
  NetWare Core Protocol (Novell)  174, 289, 294–7
  NetWare (Novell)  173–5, 325–6
  Network Basic Input/Output System (Net-BIOS)  171
  network operating system  172–89
  O/S2 operating system, IBM  188
  Open Data-Link Interface (ODI)  181–2
  Sequenced Packet eXchange (SPX), Novell  174
  TCP/IP  179, 181, 182–4
  Windows NT, Microsoft  172, 175–6
  see also Virtual LANs (vLANs)
Local Area Network (LAN) switches  146–68
  advantages  152
  and bridge segmentation  203–5
  ATM switches  166, 168
  backbone operation  164–8
  backpressure  165
  components  151–2
  cross-point switching  154–5
  cut-through switching  154–5
  delay times  153–4
  fat pipes  161
  flow control  165
  hub bottlenecks  147–50
  hybrid switch  157–8
  latency  153, 154–5
  network redistribution  161–2
  port-based switching  158–9
  segment-based switching  159–61
  server segmentation  162–3
  store-and-forward switch  155–7
  switching operations  150–4
  token-ring hub operation  149
Local area networking  117–90
  bridges  121–32, 150–1
  broughters  137–9

file servers  142–5
gateway  139–42
repeaters  118–21
routers  132–7
wire hubs  145–6, 192–55
Logical Channel Number (LCN)  266–7
Logical Link Control (LLC)  23, 78, 87, 179, 338
  classes of service  95–7
  Destination Services Access Point (DSAP)  94, 338
  frame determination  99
  frame format  94–100
  Protocol Data Unit (PDU)  94
  Service Access Points (SAPs)  94
  Type 1 service  96
  Type 2 service  96–7
  Type 3 service  97
Logical Link Control Type 2 (LLC2)  427
Logical Unit (LU)  366, 388–9, 395–6, 413–14, 419
Login passwords  439–40
Low-entry Networking (LEN) nodes  400–1


MadgeSmart Plus token-ring card  185
Mainframes, LAN access  5–7
Manchester coding  39–40
Manufacturing Automation Protocol (MAP)  27
Media Access Control (MAC)  23, 78, 87, 94, 108, 167, 362–33
  Fast Ethernet  67
  see also Virtual LANs (vLANs), MAC-based switching
Media Attachment Unit (MAU)  192, 196
Medium Independent Interface (MII), Fast Ethernet  69
Medium-Dependent Interface (MDI), Fast Ethernet  69
Micom's V/IP  478–9
Microcom Networking Protocol (MNP)  238
Microsoft Networks (MS-NET) program  171
Minimum Cell Rate (MCR)  102
Modem pooler  143
Modems  37–8, 238–9, 251–2
  common switched network types  238
  radio frequency (RF)  47
Modulation methods  37–8
Multiple port support, LAN bridges  129
Multiple transfer requests, performance  497–8

Multiplexers  8
  M13  257
  versus packet switching  259
  see also Frequency Division Multiplexing
    (FDM); Time Division Multiplexing
    (TDM)
Multiprotocol Transport Networking (MPTN)
  429–30
Multistation access units (MAUs)  74–5, 120,
  145, 149, 209–11, 217–19, 225, 418

NCP Packet Switching Interface (NPSI)  416–
  18
NetBios Extended User Interface (NETBEUI)
  175–6
NetWare, Novell  173–5, 325–6
NetWare Core Protocol (NCP), Novell  174,
  289, 294–7
NetWare Ethernet-802.3 frame  98
NetWare Internetwork Packet Exchange (IPX)
  284–9
  routing  368–9, 434
NetWare Sequence Packet Exchange (SPX)
  289–2
Network Access Units (NAUs)  195, 198
Network Addressable Units (NAUs)  389, 394
Network Basic Input/Output System (Net-
  BIOS), for LANs  171, 366, 429
Network construction  7–10
Network Control Program (NCP)  389, 391
Network Driver Interface Specification (NDIS)
  179, 186
Network flow see Traffic flow, bridges
Network interface card (NIC)  62–3, 106, 108,
  195–7, 208, 339
Network Nodes (NNs)  21, 401, 402–3
Network Termination 1 (NT1)  247
Network Termination 2 (NT2)  247
Network-to-Node/Network-to-Network Inter-
  face (NNI), LANs  108–10
  private  110
  public  110
Non-Return to Zero (NRZ) signals  39

O/S2 operating system, IBM  188, 429
Open Data-Link Interface (ODI)  179, 190–6
Open Systems Interconnection (OSI) Reference Model  19–25, 28–9, 265, 298–9
  layer 1 -physical layer  22
  layer 2 -data link layer  22–3
  layer 3 -network layer  23, 265

layer 4 -transport layer  23
layer 5 -session layer  24
layer 6 -presentation layer  24
layer 7 -application layer  24
layered architecture  20–5

Packet Assemblers/disassemblers (PADs)
  260, 264–5
Packet Driver Specification (PDS)  179
Packet filtering, security  434–40, 450–2
Packet switching networks  259–82
  advantages  269
  and value added networks  261–2
  architecture  262–4
  delay problems  271–2
  fast package switching  272–3
  frame relay  273–82
  internetwork utilization  269–70
  ITU-T recommendations  260–1
  network construction  259–60
  packet formation  264–8
  remote access  270–1
  technological advances  271–82
  versus multiplexing  259
Paradyne device  243
Passwords
  and routers  439–40
  firewalls  447–50
  guessing threat  441
  one-time  449–50
  static  447–8
  token-based  448
Payload Type Identifier (PTI) field, ATM  112
Peak Cell Rate (PCR), ATM  102
Performance issues  495–501
Peripheral Component Interconnect (PCI)
  local bus  216
Peripheral sharing  16
Permanent Virtual Circuit (PVC), ATM  57,
  113
Phase Modulation  38
Physical Media Dependent (PMD) sublayers
  67
Physical Medium Attachment (PMA) sub-
  layer  69
  Fast Ethernet  69
Physical Unit (PU)  360, 366, 388, 395–6,
  414, 419
Point of Presence (POP)  280
Point-to-point Tunneling Protocol (PPTP)
  480–1
Primary Rate Interface (PRI), for ISDN  247–8

Printer sharing  16
Printing, with LANs  48
Private Virtual Circuits (PVCs)  276, 277–9
Project Authorization Request (PAR), IEEE
  28
Protocol Data Unit (PDU)  94
Public Data Network (PDN)  261–2
Pulse Code Modulation (PCM)  245, 253
Punched cards  1–2

Quadrature Amplitude Modulation (QAM)
  242
Quality of Service (QoS)  102, 105

RAD Network Devices router (Vgate)  485–6
Radio Frequency (RF) modems  47
Reed-Solomon forward error correction  242
Remote Access Service (RAS), Windows NT
  480
Remote batch terminals  2
Remote batch transmission  2–3
Remote bridging  252
Repeaters
  electrical  118–19
  electrical-optical  118–19
  rules for  119–20, 121
  utilization  119–20
Reverse Address Resolution Protocol (RARP)
  185
Route Information Fields  343
Routers  7, 132–7, 361–83, 432–40
  access  439–40
  addressing differences  369
  advantages  135–7
  bridges, differences from  361–2
  communications protocols  367
  flow control  136–7
  frame fragmentation  137
  inter-vLAN
    inter-switch communications  486–7
    intra-switch communications  483–6
  Internet Protocol (IP) support  362–4
  LAN protocol problems  369–71
  link state protocol  380–2
  link utilization  365
  multiple path transmission and routing
    control  136
  NetWare IPX  368–9
  network address utilization  134–5
  networking capability  364–5
  non-routable protocols  366–7

operation  361–4
packet examination  369–70
performance  382–3
popular communications protocols  367
protocol-dependent  367–71
protocol-independent
  advantages  371–2
  methods  373
  SNA traffic support  372
RAD Network Devices router (Vgate)  485–6
Routing Information Protocol (RIP), TCP/IP
  289, 294, 375–8
routing protocols  366
Routing Table Maintenance Protocol (RTMP),
  Apple  379–80
  security  433–40
  Shortest Path First (SPF) algorithms  381
  table operation  135
  uncontrollable threats  440, 441
  vector distance protocol  374–80
  *see also* Source routing
Routing Information Field (RIF)  79, 232
Routing Information Protocol (RIP), TCP/IP
  289, 294, 375–8
Routing Table Maintenance Protocol (RTMP),
  Apple  379–80

SDLC *see* Synchronous Data Link Control
  (SDLC)
Secure Hypertext Transfer Protocol (S-
  HTTP)  452
Secure Sockets Layer (SSL) firewall, Netscape
  443, 452
Security  433–52
  access lists  434–40
  and routers  433–40
  encryption  452
  Internet  490
  uncontrollable threats with routers  440,
    441
  virtual LANs (vLANs)  473
  *see also* Firewalls
Sequenced Packet eXchange (SPX), Novell
  174, 289–92
Serial communications adapters  2
Server Information Tables (SITs)  293–4
Server software module  166
Servers *see* File servers
Service Access Point (SAP)  94
Service Advertising Protocol (SAP)  289,
  292–4
Shortest Path First (SPF) algorithms  381

Signalling methods, LANs  36–9
Simple Mail Transport Protocol (SMPT)  140
Simple Network Management Protocol (SNMP) services  87
Single Attached Station (SAS)  84
SNA *see* Systems Network Architecture (SNA), IBM
Source routing  339–43
  advantages  342
  disadvantages  342–3
  operation  341–2
  transparent bridges  344
Source Routing Transparent (SRT) bridges  343–4
Source Service Access Point (SSAP)  95, 338
Spanning tree algorithm  332–6
Spanning Tree Protocol (STP)  331–7
Standards organizations *see* IEEE; International standards organizations
Stateful inspection, security  445–6
Station Management (SMT) standard  87
Statistical Time Division Multiplexer (STDM)  9
Sustainable Cell Rate (SCR), ATM  102
Switched digital transmission  243–5
Switched Virtual Call (SVC)  236
Switched Virtual Circuit (SVC), ATM  57, 113, 237
Switches *see* Asynchronous Transfer Mode (ATM); Ethernet; Local Area Network (LAN) switches
Synchronous Data Link Control (SDLC)
  adapter connectivity  227, 414–16
  and DLSw  427–8
  and packet formation  264
Synchronous transmission, FDDI  91
Systems Network Architecture (SNA), IBM  386–98, 412–25
  and APPN  387, 392, 404
  and DLSw  427
  and MPTN  429
  and routers 366–7, 372, 373
  and the 3270 information display system  407
  concepts  387–9
  developments  395
  Ethernet connectivity  412–14
  gateway options  412–25
  IBM 3278/9 connection  419–20
  layers
    data flow control  394
    path control  393–4

  physical control  393
  presentation services  394–5
  transaction services  395
  transmission control  394
  Logical Unit (LU)  388–9, 395–6, 413–14
  multiple domains  391–2
  network structure  389–95
  Physical Units (PUs)  388, 390–1, 395–6
  SDLC connectivity  414–16
  session types  395–6
  subarea addresses  396–8
  Systems Services Control Point (SSCP)  387–8, 395–6
  TIC connection  418–19
  VTAM  228
  with IBM 3172 Interconnect Controller  420–3
  X.25 connectivity  416–18
Systems Services Control Point (SSCP)  387–8, 395–7

T1 circuits  8, 10, 12, 255–6
T3 circuits  10, 256–9
T-carrier evolution/facilities  253–9
  digital channel banks  254–5
Tail circuits  9
Target Token Rotation Time (TTRT)  90
TCP/IP *see* Transmission Control Protocol and Internet Protocol (TCP/IP)
Technologic Interceptor
  Add Alert screen display  446–7
  firewall  443–4
  Network Services display  450–1
Telnet TN3270  424–5
Terminal Adapter (TA)  247
Terminal Equipment (TE) functional grouping  247
Terminal session monitoring security threat  441
Text display, performance  496–7
Time Division Multiplexing (TDM)  58, 253, 254
Token Holding Timer (THT)  90–2
Token Interface Coupler (TIC)  418–19
Token passing  56
  bus operation  72–4
Token pipe support  233–4
Token Rotation Timer (TRT)  90–1
Token-Ring Adapter (TRA)  372, 408, 418–19
Token-Ring Interface Coupler (TIC)  6, 225
Token-Ring networks  74-81, 209–34

adapter cards  226
Adjusted Ring Length (ARL)  217–19
and IEEE 802.5r Dedicated Token-Ring
    (DTR) standard  232–3
and virtual networking  488
backbone ring collapsing  231
backbone ring performance  230
bridge  220–1
connectivity  224–6
Controlled Access Unit (CAU) (model 8228/
    8230)  221–2
gateways  226–8
hub operation  149
Interface Coupler (TIC)  6, 225
Lobe Attachment Models (LAMs)  221–2
model 3172 interconnect controller  228–9
model 3278/9 connectivity  227–8
model 6611 network processor  222–4
Multistation Access Units (MAUs)  209–11,
    217–19, 225, 418
network adapters  215–17
performance  354–60
repeaters, copper  219–20
repeaters, fiber  219–20
ring sizes  217
SDLC adapter connectivity  227
switching  229–34
Token-Ring Adapter (TRA)  372, 408, 418–
    19
token/frame formats  75–81
Traffic flow, bridges
bridge type effects  348, 351
estimating network traffic  348–51
network type effects  348, 350
Translating bridges  126–7
Transmission Control Protocol and Internet
    Protocol (TCP/IP)  179, 180, 183–6,
    304–9
Address Resolution Protocol (ARP)  304,
    363
and MPTN  429–30
and routers  373
configuration  321–5
datagrams versus virtual circuits  300–3
development  297–8
Internet Control Message Protocol (ICMP)
    304
Internet Protocol (IP)  311–21
operating multiple stacks  326
Routing Information Protocol (RIP), TCP/IP
    289, 294, 375–8
security with  434

structure  298–300
User Datagram Protocol (UDP)  301, 310–
    11
Transmission medium, for LANs  43–50
Transmission rates
LANs  12–13, 48
WANs  12–13, 15
Transmit Immediate (TXI) protocol  232–3
Transparent bridges  125–6, 130, 327–39
advantages  329
Bridge Protocol Data Unit (BPDU) frames
    337–9
disadvantages  329–30
operation  328
physical versus active topology  331–2
port/address table construction  328–30
protocol dependency  338–9
Source Routing Transparent (SRT)  343–4
spanning tree algorithm  332–6
Spanning Tree Protocol (STP)  331–7
Transport Control Protocol (TCP)  24
and security  434
Tunneling  131, 490
Twisted-pair wire *see* Unshielded Twisted-
    Pair (UTP) wire

Universal Resource Locator (URL)  243
Unshielded Twisted-Pair (UTP) wire  29, 59,
    192, 194, 215
categories  51–2
compared with coaxial cable  44–55
Unspecified Bit Rate (UBR) traffic  103
User Datagram Protocol (UDP)  24, 297, 301,
    303, 310–11
and security  434
User-to-network interface, LANs  109

Valid Transmission Timer (TVX)  90
Value added networks *see* Packet switching
    networks
Variable Bit Rate—Non-Real Time (VBR/
    NRT) traffic  102
Variable Bit Rate—Real Time (VBR/RT)
    traffic  103
Vector distance protocol  374–80
Very Large Scale Integration (VLSI)  272
Vgate (RAD Network Devices router)  485–6
Video Graphics Display (VGA), screen perfor-
    mance  498–9
Virtual Channel Identifier (VCI) field, ATM
    111–12, 115, 166

Virtual Channel (VC) switch, ATM   114
Virtual circuit packet networks   263–4
Virtual LANs (vLANs)   453–74
  connectivity beyond workgroup   471
  flexibility   472
  layer-3 protocol-based
    advantages   467–8
    disadvantages   468
    principle   466–7
  layer-3 subnet-based
    advantages   465–6
    disadvantages   466
    principle   464–5
  MAC-based switching
    address lists   460
    advantages   458–60
    disadvantages   460–4
    flexibility   459
    interswitch communications   460–1
    operation   456–8
    router restrictions   461–4
  multicast support   472
  multiple vLANs per port   472–3
  port grouping vLANs
    advantages   454
    disadvantages   454–5
    implementation   453–4
    inter-vLAN support   45–65
    operation   454
    port versus segment switching   454
  rule-based
    advantages   470–1
    capabilities   469
    disadvantages   471
    multicast support   469–70
  security   473
  spanning   474
  station assignment, ease of   471–2
  workgroup bandwidth   472
Virtual networking   474–94
  applications   477–9
  concept   474
  economics   476–7
  fax   478
  inter-switch communications
    creative   486
    using router   486–7
    with backbone switching   487–9
    with multiple vLANs per switch   487
  Internet use   489–92

  intra-switch communications
    creative   482–3
    using router   483–6
  Layer 2 Forwarding (L2F)   481
  Layer 2 Tunneling Protocol (L2TP)   481–2
  local   482–9
  Micom's V/IP   478–9
  performance   493–4
  Point-to-point Tunneling Protocol (PPTP)
    480–1
  reliability   475
  testing   492–3
  voice   478
Virtual Path Identifier (VPI) field, ATM   110,
    115, 166
Virtual Path (VP) switch, ATM   114
Virtual Telecommunications Access Method
    (VTAM)   228–9, 387
Virus upload threat   441
Voice, virtual networking   478, 479

Wide Area Networks (WANs)   1–10
  computer-communications evolution   1–5
  coverage area   11–12, 15
  data routing   14, 15
  data transmission rates   12–13, 15
  error rates   12–13, 15
  information types   14–15
  LAN comparison   11–16
  mainframe access   5–7
  network characteristics   10
  network construction   7–10
  ownership   13, 15
  regulation   13–14
  topology   14, 15
  see also Circuit switched networks; Packet
    switching networks
Windows NT (Microsoft)   172, 175–6, 325–6
  DNS configuration   322–5
  workstation   322–5
Wire hubs   145–6, 192–5
Workstation, interactive performance   495–6
World Wide Web   493–4

X.25/28/29/75 ITU-T recommendations
    260-1, 264–8, 269–71, 273–5, 281, 416–
    18
Xerox Corporation, CSMA/CD system   55,
    59–60

# LOCAL AREA NETWORKING

**PROTECTING LAN RESOURCES**
**A Comprehensive Guide to Securing, Protecting and Rebuilding a Network**

With the evolution of distributed computing, security is now a key issue for network users. This comprehensive guide will provide network managers and users with a detailed knowledge of the techniques and tools they can use to secure their data against unauthorised users. Gil Held also provides guidance on how to prevent disasters such as self-corruption of data and computer viruses.
**1995  0  471  95407  1**

**LOCAL AREA NETWORK PERFORMANCE**
**Issues and Answers**
**Second Edition**

The performance of LANs depends upon a large number of variables, including the access method, the media and cable length, the bridging and the gateway methods. This revised text covers all these variables to enable the reader to select and design equipment for reliability and high performance.
**1996  0  471  96926  5**

**LAN TESTING AND TROUBLESHOOTING**
**Reliability Tuning Techniques**

Network testing is becoming a major requirement in corporate, industry and government computing. This book focuses on networking systems and the testing tools on the market today.
**1996  0  471  95880  8**

**HIGH-SPEED NETWORKING WITH LAN SWITCHES**

The demand for switching is on the increase as higher bandwidths are required from LANs, the internet and intranets. This book focuses on different types of LAN switches and how they fit in with current network devices.
**1997  0  471  18444  6**

**VIRTUAL LANs**
**Construction, Implementation and Management**

Virtual LANs allow network administrators to group users in a logical network rather than one based upon physical location. The book examines this new way of setting up networks from an intermediate level.
**1997  0  471  17732  6**